HISTORY OF THE
GREAT CIVIL WAR
Vol IV

Samuel Rawson Gardiner was one of Britain's most distinguished historians. His *History of the Great Civil War* and *History of the Commonwealth and Protectorate* are among the finest achievements of British historiography. Gardiner was born in Ropley, in Hampshire, on 4 March 1829 and educated at Winchester and Christ Church, Oxford. Both his parents belonged to the Irvingite church and Gardiner himself married the youngest daughter of Edward Irving in 1856.

He supported his writing career by teaching and lecturing, first at Bedford College, London (1863–81), then at King's College, London (1872–77, becoming professor of modern history there in 1877), and the Society for the Extension of University Teaching in London (1877–94). Gardiner published numerous influential books and articles on what he termed 'the Puritan Revolution', but was only slowly rewarded with official recognition. His cause was championed by Lord Acton who persuaded Gladstone to grant Gardiner a civil list pension in 1882. He was elected a fellow of All Souls, Oxford in 1884, and was later appointed a fellow of Merton College, but refused the Regius professorship when it was offered by Rosebery in 1894.

Samuel Rawson Gardiner died on 23 February 1902. He had finished only one chapter in what was to be the fourth and final volume of *History of the Commonwealth and Protectorate*, a project completed for him by his friend and disciple C.H. Firth. Firth summed up his friend's achievements after his death: 'He sought to interest his readers by his lucid exposition of facts and the justice of his reflections rather than by giving history the charms of fiction, and was content with the distinction of being the most trustworthy of nineteenth-century historians.'

BOOKS BY S.R. GARDINER

History of the Great Civil War
(four volumes) (Phoenix Press)

History of the Commonwealth and Protectorate
(four volumes) (Phoenix Press, forthcoming)

HISTORY OF THE GREAT CIVIL WAR 1642–1649

Volume IV – 1647–1649

S.R. Gardiner

PHOENIX
PRESS

5 UPPER SAINT MARTIN'S LANE
LONDON
WC2H 9EA

A Windrush Press Book

A PHOENIX PRESS PAPERBACK

First published in Great Britain
by Longmans, Green & Co in 1894
Reprinted by The Windrush Press in 1987
This paperback edition published in 2002 by
The Windrush Press in association with Phoenix Press,
a division of The Orion Publishing Group Ltd,
Orion House, 5 Upper St Martin's Lane,
London WC2H 9EA

Phoenix Press
Sterling Publishing Co Inc
387 Park Avenue South
New York
NY 10016-8810
USA

The Windrush Press
Windrush House
12 Adlestrop
Moreton in Marsh
Glos GL56 0YN

A CIP catalogue record for this book
is available from the British Library.

Printed and bound in Great Britain by
Clays Ltd, St Ives plc

ISBN 1 84212 642 3

CONTENTS

OF

THE FOURTH VOLUME.

———

CHAPTER LVI.

THE FLIGHT TO CARISBROOKE.

CHAPTER LVII.

THE FOUR BILLS.

CHAPTER LVIII.

THE VOTE OF NO ADDRESSES.

CHAPTER LIX.

A ROYALIST REACTION.

CHAPTER LX.

A GATHERING STORM.

CHAPTER LXI.

THE EVE OF THE SECOND CIVIL WAR

CHAPTER LXII.

ST. FAGANS AND MAIDSTONE

CHAPTER LXIII.

COLCHESTER AND ST. NEOTS.

CHAPTER LXIV.

PRESTON.

CHAPTER LXV.

THE SURRENDER OF COLCHESTER.

CHAPTER LXVI.

THE TREATY OF NEWPORT.

CHAPTER LXVII.

THE REMONSTRANCE OF THE ARMY.

CHAPTER LXVIII.

PRIDE'S PURGE.

CHAPTER LXIX.

THE PRELIMINARIES OF THE KING'S TRIAL.

CHAPTER LXX.

THE HIGH COURT OF JUSTICE.

CHAPTER LXXI.

THE LAST DAYS OF CHARLES I.

MAPS.

THE GREAT CIVIL WAR.

———⋄———

CHAPTER LVI.

THE FLIGHT TO CARISBROOKE.

THE ground on which Cromwell had taken his stand had for some time been giving way beneath his feet. On October 22,

1647.
Oct. 22.
The Scottish
commis-
sioners with
the King. the Scottish commissioners, Loudoun, Lauderdale, and Lanark, visited Charles at Hampton Court. They had previously given him a verbal assurance that, if he would in other respects satisfy them about religion, the Covenant would not be pressed against him ;[1] and they now declared in writing that Scotland was prepared

Oct. 23.
They urge
Charles to
escape. to assist him in the recovery of his throne. Not long afterwards they reappeared at Hampton Court with a suite of fifty horsemen, and urged Charles to make his escape under their escort. Charles answered that he had given his word of honour not to escape, and that 'till he had freed himself of that, he would die rather than break his faith.'[2]

Charles's first attempt to free himself from his obligation had that character of indirectness which he dearly loved.

Ashburn-
ham with-
draws his
parole. Some time before, Ashburnham had engaged to Whalley that the King would not escape, giving Whalley to understand that the King's word was pledged with his own. Ashburnham now, by Charles's orders,

[1] The Scottish Commissioners to the King, Oct. 22, *Clar. St. P.* ii. 380 ; Grignon to Brienne, Nov. $\frac{1}{11}$, *R.O. Transcripts.*

[2] *Burnet*, v. 123.

withdrew his parole, on the plea that ' the Court was so much
Scottified that he feared there would be workings to get ' the
King 'away.' Though the words implied that it was merely
Ashburnham's parole which was withdrawn, Charles was
capable of so interpreting them as to claim that he had
recovered his own freedom of action as well.[1]

Though Whalley does not appear to have suspected
Charles's intention, Ashburnham's words had been enough to
render him suspicious, and he now posted his
guards within the palace itself, a precaution which
he had not hitherto taken.   A few days later
Charles complained that the sleep of the Princess Elizabeth,
then on a visit to him, was disturbed by the soldiers, and
asked that the guard might be removed.   Whalley replied by
asking him to renew his parole.   On his refusal to
do so, Whalley communicated the fact to Fairfax.
The news was the more startling, as the story of
the Scottish offer to assist the King to escape had leaked
out, and was being repeated in a most exaggerated form.
Charles, it was said, had actually fled with a thousand horse
provided for him by the Scots.[2]   Accordingly, on
the 31st the guards at Hampton Court were
strongly reinforced.   Amongst the military Levellers exasperation grew to the highest pitch.   Some
talked of carrying the King to Ely, where the Scots
would be unable to reach him.[3]   On the same day, a Sunday,
the prayers of the congregation were asked in several of the

Whalley grows suspicious.

Charles declines to renew his parole.

Oct. 31. The guards reinforced.

Exasperation of the Levellers.

---

[1] Ashburnham indeed declared afterwards (Ashburnham to Lenthall,
Nov. 26, E. 418, 4) that he told Whalley that he withdrew his parole on
the King's behalf.   This, however, was by anticipation denied by Whalley
(*Message by Col. Whalley*, E. 419, 14).   Whalley told the House of
Commons, on Nov. 23, that his conversation with Ashburnham took
place ' about three weeks ago,' *i.e.* about Oct. 23.   If Whalley had really
understood that the King's parole was withdrawn, the more vigorous
measures which were taken some days later would surely have been taken
then.

[2] Newsletter, Nov. $\frac{9}{19}$, *Roman Transcripts, R.O.*

[3] Letter of Intelligence, Nov. 4, *Clarendon MSS.* 2,640.

London churches 'for the good success of the great design.'

Nov. 1.
Charles's
attendants
removed.
On November 1 most of the King's attendants, Berkeley and Ashburnham among the number, were ordered to leave Hampton Court [1]

When the Army Council met again on November 1,[2] the effect of Charles's refusal to renew his parole became at once

Another
meeting of
the Army
Council.
manifest. Cromwell opened the discussion by a motion 'that every one might speak their experiences as the issue of what God had given in answer to their prayers,' that is to say, to the prayers for

Answers to
prayer.
unity in the meeting of October 29. The answers were given glibly enough. Captain Allen[3] said that his experience, and that of 'divers other Godly people,' was 'that the work that was before them was to take away the negative voice of the King and Lords.' Captain Carter's experience was 'that he found not any indication in his heart as formerly to pray for the King that God would make him yet a blessing to the kingdom.' Commissary Cowling held that their liberties could only be recovered by the sword, as their ancestors had recovered theirs from the Danes and Normans, 'when they were under such slavery that an Englishman was as hateful as an Irishman is now.'

Before long Cromwell thought it time to intervene. The King, he said, was King by contract. Let him that was

Cromwell
intervenes.
without sin amongst them cast the first stone at him. If they and the Parliament had been free from

Faults on
both sides.
transgression towards the King, they might justly require that he should be cut off as a transgressor, 'but, considering that we are in our own actions failing in many par-

Parlia-
mentary
authority to
be main-
tained.
ticulars, I think there is much necessity of pardoning of transgressors.' Cromwell then proceeded to ask how discipline was to be maintained if the army was to throw off the authority of the Parliament to which it owed its existence. "Either," he said, "they are a

---

[1] *Clar. St. P.* ii. App. xli.   [2] *Clarke Papers*, i. 367–406.
[3] Francis Allen, not William Allen, the Agitator, who, as Mr. Firth has shown, was probably identical with Ludlow's Adjutant-General Allen. *Clarke Papers*, i. 432.

Parliament or no Parliament. If they be no Parliament, they are nothing, and we are nothing likewise." If they were a Parliament, it was the duty of the army to make its proposals to them. Before he could be of another opinion, he must see 'a visible presence of the people, either by subscriptions or numbers . . . for in the government of nations that which is to be looked after is the affections of the people.' Forms of government were of little account. The people of Israel had been happy under many different governments. If they were going to put to hazard their lives and fortune to obtain what they called freedom, they would bring the State to desolation. It was for Parliament to settle what the government was to be, though they might provide that Parliament should be fairly representative, and should not perpetuate itself.

The affections of the people indispensable.

Forms of government of little account.

The army, it seems, according to Cromwell, might secure the existence of a Parliament which could really speak in the name of the nation ; it must not dictate to Parliament a system which only approved itself to a few enthusiasts, who imagined that their opinions were the opinions of the nation. As to Rainsborough's proposal to call the army to a rendezvous [1] that it might be asked to support the *Agreement of the People*, it was enough that Fairfax had given no orders to that effect. "I must confess," said Cromwell, "that I have a commission from the General, and I understand that I am to do by it. I shall conform to him according to the rules and discipline of war . . . and therefore I conceive it is not in the power of any particular men, or any particular man in the army, to call a rendezvous of a troop, or regiment, or [in the] least to disoblige the army from the commands of the General." Throwing off authority would be their destruction. It was said amongst the Royalists that if rope enough were given to the soldiers they would hang themselves. "Therefore," concluded Cromwell, "I shall move what we shall centre upon. If it

Cromwell's view of the functions of the army.

The authority of the General to be respected,

and authority, even the most doubtful.

[1] See vol. iii. p. 390.

have but the face of authority, if it be but a hare swimming over the Thames, I [1] will take hold of it rather than let it go."

In his strong sense of the danger of anarchy, Cromwell had passed lightly over the immediate difficulty, the abhorrence with which the King regarded any terms likely to be proposed to him. Cromwell, in short, was large minded rather than constructive, and he was forced to listen to language which he deprecated from men who fixed their eyes more intently than he did upon one particular aspect of the

Jubbes asks that the House may be purged;

problem. Lieutenant-Colonel Jubbes put the searching question, whether it would not be necessary to purge Parliament of its peccant members;

a purged Parliament being far more likely than the present

and a declaration of the King's guilt obtained from it.

one to satisfy the just desires of the army, and to 'declare the King guilty of all the bloodshed, vast expense of treasure, and ruin that hath been occasioned by all the wars both of England and Ireland.' Jubbes inconsequently added that when the King had thus been declared guilty, they might 'receive him as King again for avoiding of further wars.' Others were present who were likely to push his reasoning to a more logical conclusion.

The fanatical element was never absent from the Army Council, and this time it was represented by Goffe. Their

Goffe declares that heaven is against Charles.

duty, he said, was to listen to the voice of God to whomsoever revealed, and it was clear to him 'that this hath been a voice from heaven to us, that we

Cromwell's reply.

have sinned against the Lord in tampering with his enemies.' To this Cromwell at once replied that, though it was their duty to give ear to all that was revealed to any one, they must not forget the Scriptural injunction,

He does not follow revelations,

"Let the rest judge !" [2] As for himself, he would never abandon the right of judging whatever was submitted to him as a divine revelation. If mistakes of fact or argument were made, he held himself at liberty

---

[1] 'He' in text.
[2] "Let the other judge," 1 Cor. xiv. 29.

to show that they were mistakes, 'for no man receives anything in the name of the Lord further than the light of his conscience appears.' He had heard, he said later in the debate, 'many contradictions, but certainly God is not the author of contradictions.'

He himself, too, Cromwell declared, was 'one of those whose heart God hath drawn out to wait for some extra-
but dispen- ordinary dispensations, according to those promises
sations. that He hath held forth of things to be accomplished in the latter time.' Here lies the key to the secret of Cromwell's superiority over men like Goffe. He sought wisdom not in personal impressions, but in the totality of events. He believed, as he would himself have said, more in dispensations than in revelations.[1]

Dispensations had in truth carried Cromwell much farther from the King than he was when he made his great speech in
Cromwell the House of Commons on October 20.[2] Charles's
no longer communications with the Scots and the withdrawal
hopes much
from the of his parole had left little room for hope. They
King. were all agreed, he now said, that their aim was 'to deliver this nation from oppression and slavery.' "I think," he added, "we may go thus far farther, that we all apprehend danger from the King and from the Lords." Sexby indeed had said that an attempt was being made to 'set up' the King
His and the House of Lords. Against this description
attitude of the opinions of himself and his supporters,
towards the
King and Cromwell warmly protested. "If it were free before
the Lords. us," he said, "whether we should set up one or other, I do, to my best observation, find a unanimity amongst us all that we would set up neither." "I must," he added, "further tell you, that as we do not make it our business or intention to set up the one or the other, neither is it our intention to preserve the one or the other with a visible danger and destruction to the people and the public interest." What

---

[1] "I pray he," *i.e.* Vane, "make not too little, nor I too much, of outward dispensations." Cromwell to St. John, Sept. 1, 1648, *Carlyle,* Letter lxvii.

[2] See vol. iii. p. 381.

he objected to was to have them lay it down as an ascertained truth that there could be no safety if the King and the Lords retained any interest in public affairs, on the ground that God would 'destroy these persons and their power, for that they may mistake in.' This he said, though he himself concurred with them in thinking it probable that God intended to destroy them.

A disinterested bystander might safely have calculated that Cromwell's hesitating attitude would before long pass into

Cromwell hesitating. active hostility. At the time it was wanting in that definite conviction which alone impresses a doubting

Fiery talk. audience. Captain Bishop said that he found 'after many inquiries in' his 'spirit' that the root of their sufferings was 'a compliance to preserve that man of blood, and those principles of tyranny which God from heaven, by His many successes, hath manifestly declared against.' Cromwell, how-

Question of the negative voice. ever, had his way so far, that the discussion passed from the question of preserving the King's person to preserving to him, and the House of Lords, the negative voice on the determinations of the House of Commons. Ultimately, the whole of the constitutional arrangements were referred to the committee.

On the following day, November 2, the committee adopted a lumbering device, which apparently reflected the passing

Nov. 2. The committee at work. mood of Cromwell and Ireton. Every Commoner was to be subject to the House of Commons alone, as well as every officer of justice or minister of State, whether he was a Commoner or a Peer, implying that neither the King nor any Peer was to be bound by a vote of the Commons, so far as his personal interests were concerned.

Parliament to be asked to postpone its Propositions. Before the sitting was ended, the committee adopted the greater part of the reserves proposed in the *Agreement of the People.*[1] It further resolved that Fairfax should be invited to request Parliament not to present its own Propositions to the King, before the recommendations of the army had been laid before it.

---

[1] *Clarke Papers,* i. 407-409. Compare pp. 394, 395.

November 3 was taken up with discussions in committee on the militia and on delinquents, the recommendations of the committee being adopted by the Army Council on the 4th.[1]   On the 4th, too, the committee came to a decision on the thorny question of the suffrage. All who were not servants or beggars were to be allowed a vote.[2]

Nov. 3, 4.
Militia and delinquents.

At the council which met on the 5th, Fairfax was present, being sufficiently recovered to attend to his military duties. How strongly the tide was running against Cromwell and Ireton is shown by the contents of a letter which was despatched from the council to the House of Commons.   In this letter the council disclaimed on behalf of the army a statement alleged to have been made in the House of Commons, to the effect that the army was favourable to the Propositions on which that House was now engaged. Ireton, from whom the statement had either proceeded or was believed to have proceeded, naturally took offence, and when the council, at its next meeting, on the 6th, refused to withdraw the letter, he walked out of the church, declaring that he would never attend another meeting.[3]   Indirectly the letter now sent revoked the order formerly given by the council for a message to ask Parliament to keep back the Propositions,[4] as it referred to the 'tenderness' with which the army regarded 'the privileges of Parliamentary actings' as a bar to any interference with the proceedings of the Houses.

Nov. 5.
A strange letter.

Ireton is offended,

Nov. 6.
and leaves the council.

The fact was that the Levellers objected to the scheme of the committee, not merely because it did not altogether accord with their ideas, but also because, under the influence of Cromwell and Ireton, it had taken the form of an application to Parliament instead of a constitution emanating directly from the people.

The scheme of the committee finished.

---

[1] They are given in *A Perfect Diurnal,* E. 520, 3.

[2] *A Copy of a Letter,* E. 413, 18 ; *Perfect Occurrences,* E. 520, 2.

[3] The Council to the Speaker, Nov. 5 ; *A Message to Both Houses,* E. 413, 3 ; *A Copy of a Letter,* E. 413, 18.   Compare *Clarke Papers,* i. 440.   [4] See p. 7.

Already on the 5th the predominance of the Levellers in the Council of the Army had been shown in other ways than

in the adoption of the letter which had given offence to Ireton. Rainsborough declared it to be the sense of the army that no further addresses should

be made to the King,[1] and either he or some other of the Levelling party carried a vote that a general rendezvous should be held, doubtless with the object of eliciting the opinion of the soldiers in favour of the *Agreement of*

the People, and against the proposals of the committee. On the 6th Cromwell consented to allow a discussion on the question 'whether it were safe either for the army or the people to suffer any power to be given to the King.'[2]

The growth of the feeling against the King in the army was paralleled with the growth of a similar feeling in the House of

Commons. On the 6th, having completed its Propositions, the House voted 'that the King of England for the time being is bound in justice, and by the duty of his office, to give his assent to all such laws as by the Lords and Commons, assembled in Parliament, shall be adjudged to be for the good of the kingdom, and by them tendered to him for his assent.' In virtue of this declaration they would now, if the assent of the Lords were obtained, present to Charles their Propositions, not for discussion but for acceptance.[3]

It is not improbable that both Parliament and army hardened their hearts against Charles in consequence of a

growing suspicion that a crisis of one kind or another was impending. On or about November 3[4] Charles communicated with Ashburnham through Legge, the former governor of Oxford, who had been allowed to remain at Hampton Court when Ashburnham and Berkeley

---

[1] Newsletter, Nov. 8, *Clar. St. P.* ii. App. xli.

[2] *A Copy of a Letter*, E. 413, 18.   [3] *C.J.* v. 352.

[4] The date is arrived at by arranging the days given in Ashburnham's narrative, taking for a fixed point Nov. 5, the day on which the letter of the Scottish commissioners was written.

were expelled. On this occasion Legge informed Ashburnham

thinks of that the King meant to make his escape and thought
going to
Jersey. of Jersey as his place of refuge. Ashburnham urged
Ashburnham the adoption of a bolder course. Why should not
recommends Charles, having secured the support of the Scottish
him to go to
London. commissioners, make his way to London and rally
the City to his cause? The Scottish commissioners were will-
Nov. 5. ing to do their best for the King, and on the 5th
Assurances they appeared at Hampton Court, with the strongest
of the Scots.
assurances that nothing should be wanting on their
part to smooth his way.[1] It would seem that Charles deprecated violence, and still hoped to gain his ends by diplomacy,
Their letter as on their return from Hampton Court the commis-
to the House sioners wrote a letter to the Speaker of the House of
of Lords.
Lords, asking that the King might be removed to
London with a view to the opening of a personal negotiation
between himself and the Houses.

The reading of this letter in the House of Lords on the 6th
roused the greatest indignation. The very apprentices, said
Nov. 6. one of the Peers, could not have done worse.[2] It
Effect of may fairly be assumed that the demand which the
the letter.
Commons on that day addressed to the King took
its colour from the feeling roused by the same letter. No one
doubted that the entrance of Charles into London would be
the prelude to a reaction, which would culminate in an unconditional restoration.

On the 7th, which happened to be a Sunday, the excitement at Putney was even greater than at Westminster. The
Nov. 7: army indeed was not wholly of one mind. "Let
Excitement my colonel be for the devil an he will," said one
at Putney.
of the soldiers, "and I will be for the King."[3] The
speaker was by no means solitary in his opinion ; whilst, on
the other hand, there were not a few who had for some days

---

[1] Ashburnham's *Narrative*, i. 101–106.

[2] The Scots Commissioners to the Speaker of the House of Lords,
Nov. 5, *L.J.* ix. 512 ; Grignon to Brienne, Nov. 8, *R.O. Transcripts.*

[3] *Clarke Papers*, i. 410.

been crying out for 'an immediate and exemplary justice on the chief delinquent.'[1]

It needed but this to rouse Cromwell to action. As in May he had clung to the principle of subordinating his own Cromwell wishes to the authority of Parliament long after he roused. had become conscious that Parliament was leading the country to destruction, so in October he had clung to the authority of the King long after he had known that no tolerable settlement was to be obtained from Charles. When November came, he turned wistfully from Charles to Parliament, and again from Parliament to Charles. In despair of either, he listened not very hopefully to the scheme of the Levellers, and did his best to fit it in with some shadow of constitutional authority to which he could cling, though, to use his own words, it were but as a hare swimming over the Thames. On one point, however, he was quite clear. The discipline of the army must be maintained. On Saturday, with the knowledge that there was to be a general rendezvous, he had agreed that there should be a discussion in the Army Council on the King's authority. If it be supposed that in the course of Sunday he came to the conclusion that the Levellers intended to appeal from the Army Council to the whole body of the soldiery, there would be no need to seek further for explanation of the course which he took on Monday.[2]

However this may have been, when the Army Council met on Monday, the 8th, Cromwell had made up his mind that the time for hesitation was at an end. Singling out the proposal of the Levellers to adopt manhood suffrage, he declared that it

---

[1] News from London, Nov. 4, *Clarendon MSS.* 2,645.

[2] The following statement about the intentions of the Levellers is probably not far from the truth:—"The design was to have nulled the House of Lords, and made them no House of Parliament ; no competent judges of that great judicature ; to purge the House of Commons of all that sat in the Speaker's absence, and bring in new members in their room, such as should comply with their designs, and then draw up an impeachment against the King's Majesty to take away his life for causing the late wars and bloodshed, and in the meantime to have his Majesty kept at Warwick Castle or some other prison where they might guard his person."—*His Majesty's Declaration*, E. 420, 5.

'did tend very much to anarchy,' and put it to the vote whether both officers and Agitators should be sent to their

Nov. 8.
Cromwell
declares
against the
Levellers. respective regiments, in order that they might compose the minds of the soldiers before the day appointed for the rendezvous. An affirmative vote prevented for the present the revival of that discussion of the very foundations of the constitution which threatened to rend the army in twain.[1]

No one knew better than Cromwell that military discipline could only be maintained if the soldiers were contented, and

Letter from
Fairfax. on November 9, doubtless with the full consent of the Lieutenant-General, Fairfax wrote to the Speaker requesting that the lands of the Deans and Chapters might be sold, in order to provide for the soldiers' pay,[2] a request which shows that even Fairfax at this time despaired of coming to

Nov. 9.
The Army
Council
appoints a
fresh Com-
mittee. terms with Charles. On the 9th, at another meeting of the Army Council—from which the more aggressive members were now absent—it was resolved that a fresh committee, consisting of officers alone, should be appointed to examine how far the acceptance of the *Agreement of the People* was consistent with former engagements of the army.[3]

If Parliament and army were provoked by Charles's manifest intention to reject any terms which they were likely to offer,

Nov. 7.
A confer-
ence at
Thames
Ditton. Charles was equally provoked by the no less manifest intention of Parliament and army to offer him no terms which he was likely to accept. On the 7th, a conference was held at Thames Ditton between Berkeley, Ashburnham, and Legge. All three were ready to aid in the King's escape, but a difference of opinion arose between Berkeley and Ashburnham as to the course to be taken by Charles after he had freed himself from restraint. Berkeley, with his usual common sense, wished Charles to make his way to the Continent, whilst Ashburnham, either from an unfounded confidence in his own diplomatic skill, or

---

[1] *Clarke Papers*, i. 411, 412 ; *The Copy of a Letter*, E. 513, 18.

[2] Fairfax to Lenthall, Nov. 9, *Rushw.* vii. 687.

[3] Resolution of the Army Council, *Clarke Papers*, i. 415.

because he expressed his master's views rather than his own, wished the King to secure himself in some place in England, and to make one more attempt to recover his throne. Berkeley persisted in his own opinion, and asked Ashburnham to make a bargain with the owners of two or three vessels which were to be stationed in various ports, so that whatever direction Charles might take after leaving Hampton Court, he might be able to effect his escape to the Continent. Ashburnham did not indeed return a direct refusal, but he took no steps to carry out a plan which differed from his own.[1]

On the 8th, the Sunday on which Cromwell was brooding over the signs of mutiny in the army, Berkeley and Ashburn-

Nov. 8. Conversation between Berkeley and Ashburnham.

ham rode to Putney to procure passes to enable them to cross the sea. On their return, Ashburnham suddenly informed his companion of the plan for removing the King to London, which had re-

Ashburnham suggests the Isle of Wight as a refuge for the King.

cently been discussed with the Scottish commissioners. Finding Berkeley's objections insuperable, he proposed that Charles should take refuge in the Isle of Wight. A new governor, Robert Hammond,

Robert Hammond.

had recently been appointed, who was a nephew of Henry Hammond, the well-known Royalist divine.

It was true that by his marriage with Hampden's daughter he was also connected with Cromwell, and that he had been personally attached to Cromwell himself, especially at the time when the Lieutenant-General had been striving to conciliate the King. Recently, however, Hammond had stood aloof from Cromwell in proportion as Cromwell had drawn away from the King. Hammond was, in fact, a sensitive and conscientious man, unhappy at having to choose between conflicting duties, and when Fairfax offered him the Governorship of the Isle of Wight he went off to his new post with a feeling of relief, as if he had at last found a quiet nook in which the waves of controversy would trouble him no more.

[1] Berkeley's *Memoirs*, 46; Ashburnham's *Narrative*, ii. 106. Ashburnham is looser about details than Berkeley, and I have therefore given the preference to Berkeley where the two authorities differ. Fortunately the points of difference are of no great historical importance.

Meeting Ashburnham, as he was on the way to his new post, he told him that 'he was going down to his government, because he found the army was resolved to break all promises with the King ; and that he would have nothing to do with such perfidious actions.'[1]

To Ashburnham, or rather to Charles, whose mouthpiece he was, Hammond's impulsive utterance appeared to be a rock *Charles's double project.* on which to build. As usual, Charles had two alternative plans. On the one hand the rendezvous of the army might result in a declaration by the officers in his favour. On the other hand the Scots might make him more explicit promises than they had as yet given. If Hammond would secure him in the Isle of Wight from immediate danger, he might put himself up to auction to the Scots and to the officers at the same time, whilst if neither could bid high enough, he would have the sea close at hand, and the way of escape to France would lie open before him.[2]

On the evening of the 9th, Charles gave orders to make actual preparations for his flight, though even then Berkeley *Nov. 9. Charles prepares for flight.* was unable to draw from him any information about his intended place of retreat.[3] It is true that in the morning he had held a long conversation with the Scottish commissioners, and had, with their warm approval, declared himself ready to betake himself to Berwick, *Proposes to go to Berwick.* where, though still in England, he would have a Scottish army in his immediate neighbourhood. As, however, Lauderdale had warned him that, without full concessions in the matter of religion, the Church-party in

[1] Ashburnham's *Narrative*, ii. 108. Compare Cromwell's Letter to Hammond, Nov. 28, 1648, *Carlyle*, Letter lxxxv.

[2] Berkeley's *Memoirs*, 49. The question of escaping to France is not mentioned by Berkeley, but subsequent events show that it was entertained, and indeed it could hardly be otherwise.

[3] *Ibid.* 48 ; Ashburnham's *Narrative*, ii. 112. Berkeley asserts and Ashburnham denies that Charles named the Isle of Wight. I fancy he did so, but in private conversation with Ashburnham alone. Charles distrusted Berkeley and gave his confidence to the more supple courtier.

Scotland would do nothing for him,[1] it is no wonder that he came to the conclusion that it would be better to be in a place from which he could watch events than in one in which he was exposed to be mastered by them.

Charles, indeed, had come to believe that he could no longer remain at Hampton Court with safety to himself. The cry

Nov. 9.
Charles is
told that his
life is in
danger. of the Levellers for his blood had of late been waxing louder, and whilst he was pondering the words of the Scottish commissioners he received a letter informing him that eight or nine of the Agitators had, on the evening before, decided on putting him to death.[2] It is not unlikely that the writer was Henry Lilburne, who was lieutenant-colonel in his brother Robert's regiment. Whether the tale was true or false, it was too consonant with information which had reached Charles from other sources to be received with hesitation.

On Wednesday, November 10, a relay of horses was sent on to Bishop's Sutton, Thursday, the 11th, being fixed for the

Nov. 10.
Horses
sent on.

The day of
escape
fixed. actual escape, as the King was in the habit of passing some hours in his bedchamber on Thursday evenings in writing letters for the foreign post. A considerable time would therefore elapse before his absence from the public apartments would be noticed.[3]

Cromwell, too, was growing anxious. The designs of the

---

[1] *Burnet*, v. 123. The date of the interview is given in a Letter from London, Nov. 11, *Clarendon MSS.* 2,650; *His Majesty's Declaration*, E. 420, 5.

[2] The letter is signed E. R., but this may be merely to conceal the writer's name (*L.J.* ix. 520). It gives the information as being derived from the writer's brother. *The People's Prerogative*, p. 52, E. 427, 4. On November 28 nine Agitators petitioned Fairfax to do them justice against Henry Lilburne's calumnies in this matter. *Clarke MSS.* In the second part of *England's New Chains Discovered*, p. 6 (E. 548, 16), Henry Lilburne is charged with accusing his brother John. Possibly John told Henry some story, which shocked him, about talk of bringing the King to trial, which Henry treated as equivalent to a design to murder him.

[3] Berkeley's *Memoirs*, 50; Whalley's *More Full Relation*, E. 416, 23.

Levellers were no secret to him, and, on the morning of the 11th, at a meeting of the recently appointed committee of

Nov. 11.
Harrison
calls for the
prosecution
of the King.

officers,[1] Harrison, uncontrollable fanatic as he was, burst out into a cry that the King was a man of blood, and declared that 'they were now to prosecute him.' Cromwell replied by putting cases in which blood-shedding was not to be the subject of judicial inquiry, citing the example of David, who left the murderer of Abner unpunished, lest he should ' hazard the spilling of more blood, in regard the sons of Zeruiah were too hard for him.' [2]

Cromwell had no mind that Charles should fall into the hands of the Levellers. " Dear cousin Whalley," he wrote to

A warning
to Whalley.

his kinsman at Hampton Court, "there are rumours abroad of some intended attempt on his Majesty's person ; therefore, I pray, have a care of your guard ; for if such a thing should be done, it would be accounted a most horrid act." [3] Whalley showed the letter to Charles, assuring him that as long as he was in command there would be no

Intentions
of the
Levellers.

danger. Either in his letter to Whalley or in one specially directed to the King, Cromwell referred to the intention of the Levellers to place the King under a new guard of their own choosing.[4]

[1] See p. 12.

[2] *Clarke Papers*, i. 417.

[3] Cromwell to Whalley, *Carlyle*, Letter 1. The letter is undated, but Whalley said that he received it on the 11th, and it was probably, therefore, written on the morning of that day, perhaps after Harrison's outburst.

[4] Berkeley (*Memoirs*, 54) says that when he was sent to Hammond in the Isle of Wight he carried from Charles copies of two letters, ' one from Cromwell, the other without a name.' " Cromwell's and the other letter contained great apprehension and fears of the ill intentions of the Levelling party in the army and city against his Majesty ; and that from Cromwell added that, in prosecution thereof a new guard was the next day to be put upon his Majesty of that party." Nothing of this kind appears in Cromwell's letter to Whalley as it is printed, but as only a fragment was published, the words may very well have been in the part which has not reached us. Unless Cromwell intended merely to frighten the King he must certainly have added some assurance of his ability to cope with the danger. The Royalists at least believed the danger to be

Charles had no need of such information to drive him to a step which he had already decided on taking. In the evening

Escape of the King. of the 11th he stepped from his bedchamber before the guards were set for the night, and rode off, attended by Berkeley, Ashburnham, and Legge. The King

a real one. One of them, writing on the 11th, expresses a belief that Rainsborough and Pride will be employed to guard the King, and Major Huntington dismissed. "The doubling of guards," he writes, "troubles me not, but the employing of such devils doth." He writes again on the 15th as follows :—"Upon Friday last," *i.e.* the 12th, "the King was certainly designed to be murdered, but God . . . prevented those hellish intentions by his Majesty's escape." It was high time, he adds, for the King to secure his person 'against which certainly the Agitators had very bloody designs.' Letters of Intelligence, Nov. 11, 15, *Clarendon MSS.* 2,650, 2,651.

It has often been asked whether the King's flight was not designed by Cromwell. The form which this took in the lines of Andrew Marvell, when he says of Cromwell that

> " Twining subtle fears with hope,
> He wove a net of such a scope
> That Charles himself might chase
> To Carisbrooke's narrow case,
> That thence the royal actor borne
> The tragic scaffold might adorn!'

is too absurd to need refutation, especially now that the *Clarke Papers* are before us. A more tenable hypothesis is that Cromwell, having learnt the designs of the Levellers, frightened Charles away in order to save his life. The main support of this view is that Charles fled to the Isle of Wight, of which Cromwell's cousin Hammond was governor. We are, however, in a position to know, what contemporaries did not know, that the idea of going to the Isle of Wight arose in the counsels of Charles and Ashburnham, and commended itself to them on the ground that Hammond might be relied on because he was at that time hostile to Cromwell. Another difficulty in the way of accepting this theory is that Cromwell could not be certain that Charles would really go to the Isle of Wight. What if he took shipping at some seaport and made for France? In France, no doubt, he could do little harm ; but if he made his way from France to Scotland—and from the late intercourse between him and the Scots commissioners it was likely enough that he would do so—the danger to Cromwell and his party would be enormous. It is unlikely that Cromwell was otherwise than confident of his own power to cope with the Levellers. If he did want to frighten the King without assuring him on and his companions missed their way in the dark, and did not reach Sutton till after daybreak. There they found the inn occupied by the Hampshire County Committee, and were consequently obliged to push on without taking rest. Eventually they reached Lord Southampton's house at Titchfield, whence

Nov. 12.
He reaches
Titchfield.

Charles, keeping Legge with him, despatched Berkeley and Ashburnham across the Solent to sound Hammond, telling them that, if they did not return on the following day, he would himself take shipping for the Continent.

On the morning of the 13th Berkeley and Ashburnham came up with Hammond on the road between Carisbrooke

Nov. 13.
Berkeley
and Ash-
burnham
in the Isle
of Wight.

and Newport, and, telling him that the King had left Hampton Court to escape assassination, asked him to give his word to protect the Royal fugitive, or, if this proved impossible, to allow him to quit the island in safety. To Hammond the unexpected communication came as a terrible shock. " O gentlemen ! " he cried, " you have undone me by bringing the King into the island ; if at least you have brought him ; and, if you have not, pray let him not come ; for what between my duty to his Majesty, and my gratitude for this fresh obligation of confidence, and my observing my trust to the army, I shall be confounded." At last a promise was dragged from Ham-

Hammond's
vague en-
gagement.

mond, in a form so vague as to bind him to nothing. If the King, he said, 'pleased to put himself into his hands, whatever he could expect from a person of honour or honesty, his Majesty should have it be made good to him.' If ever there was an answer which should have inspired caution it was this. Yet, at Ashburnham's instance, Hammond was invited to accompany the messengers to the presence of the King.

---

this point, his object was probably to induce him to reconsider the overtures of the army which he had recently rejected. It may be added that Charles informed Whalley that his flight was not caused by Cromwell's letter. " I assure you," he wrote, " that it was not the letter you showed me to-day that made me take this resolution, nor any advertisement of that kind." The King to Whalley, Nov. 11, *L.J.* ix. 520.

When in the course of the day the three arrived at Titch-field, Charles was naturally displeased at the disclosure to Hammond of his place of retreat, especially as he had ordered a vessel from Southampton to carry him to France in case of his failing to obtain satisfactory assurances from the governor of the Isle of Wight. Ashburn-ham, with a light heart, offered to murder Hammond, but Charles declined to be served in such a fashion, and con-tented himself with making excuses for lingering at Titch-field, whilst he watched for the appearance of the expected vessel on the not far distant shore of Southampton Water. An embargo had, however, been placed on all shipping in the southern ports as soon as the King's escape was known at Westminster, and the expected vessel never arrived. In the evening Charles, having now no other course open to him, crossed the Solent in the company of Hammond and his own three attendants.

Hammond at Titch-field.

Charles looks in vain for a vessel to take him to France.

He goes to the Isle of Wight,

On the following morning Hammond conducted the King to Carisbrooke Castle. Though the accommodation was rough, Charles felt himself more at home than in Hampton Court. The islanders were well disposed toward him, and were prepared to secure him against any attempt of the Levellers to murder him. Moreover, as the garrison of the castle consisted of no more than a dozen old soldiers, he imagined that it would be easy for him to leave the island at any time, even if Hammond attempted to throw obstacles in his way.[1]

Nov. 14, and is lodged in Carisbrooke Castle.

When the news of Charles's flight reached London the wildest rumours spread from mouth to mouth. The King, said some, was gone to Scotland, to Ireland, or to France. Others said that he had been carried off by the Agitators and shut up in a fortress; others again that he had been concealed by Fairfax and Cromwell

Nov. 12. Rumours in London.

[1] Berkeley's *Memoirs*, 55; Ashburnham's *Narrative*, ii. 113. There is plenty of discrepancy between the two authorities, but not on essential points. See also Hammond's letter to Manchester, Nov. 13, *L.J.* ix. 325; and *The Oglander Memoirs*, 64-69.

to save him from the Agitators.[1] The first real intelligence was derived from a letter directed to the Houses, which Charles had left behind him at Hampton Court. In this he declared that Presbyterians, Independents, Royalists, Scots and soldiers, should all receive equal justice at his hands. Though fear for his personal safety had driven him into seclusion, he had never lost sight of the necessity of securing peace, and with this in view he added a special recommendation of the interests of the army. "To conclude," he ended by saying, "let me be heard with freedom, honour, and safety; and I shall instantly break through this cloud of retirement, and show myself really to be *Pater Patriæ.*"[2]

Charles's letter to the Houses.

Though Charles no longer looked with hope to Cromwell or Ireton, it is evident, from the tone of this letter, that he still expected support from the rank and file, and he was certainly not wrong in believing that there were large numbers in the army to whom a victory of the Levellers would be as unwelcome as to Cromwell himself. On the very day on which Charles left Hampton Court, Major White invited Fairfax's regiment to join the Levellers. The men at once replied with hearty shouts of "A King! A King!" which speedily passed into "This King! This King!" In Parliament the prevailing uncertainty strengthened what Royalist sentiment existed. "Mr. Speaker," asked a member, "are you neither contented with nor without a King?"[3]

He looks to the army for support.

Feeling in the army,

and in Parliament.

---

[1] Newsletter, Nov. $\frac{12}{22}$, $\frac{19}{29}$. *Roman Transcripts, R.O.*

[2] The King to the Houses, Nov. 11, *L.J.* ix. 519.

[3] Letter of Intelligence, Nov. 15, *Clarendon MSS.* 2,651.

CHAPTER LVII.

THE FOUR BILLS.

CROMWELL was now an object of suspicion with both the extreme parties. The Royalists counted him as a hypocritical

1647.
Attacks on
Cromwell.

dissembler because, after long negotiation with Charles, he had not restored him to the throne. The Levellers formed the same opinion of him because he had carried on that negotiation long after its deceptive character had been revealed. Rainsborough and

Talk of
im, each-
ing him.

Marten even talked of impeaching him, and Rainsborough, after expressing himself confidently of his ability to carry the army with him, added that he would have the support of 20,000 citizens as well. It was a matter of speculation at Westminster whether Cromwell would overcome his foes 'or follow his predecessor Hotham.' [1]

According to one story, the truth of which it is impossible to test, still darker proposals were entertained by the wilder

Reported
proposal
to murder
him,

Levellers. Fairfax was to be secured by the soldiers when they arrived at the place of rendezvous on the evening before the appointed review was held, whilst Cromwell was to be shot in his bed at midnight. When the

and to
pros cute
the King.

regiments were drawn up in the morning, the conspirators were to produce a charge against the King 'which they would effectually prosecute, and require the Parliament to join with them, resolving to cut the throats of those that should refuse the same.' [2]

It was indeed a time for prompt action. A third part of the army was to rendezvous on the 15th on Corkbush Field,

---

[1] Grignon to Brienne, Nov. $\frac{15}{25}$, *R.O. Transcripts.*
[2] *Walwyn's Wiles,* p. 18, E. 554, 24.

near Ware. On the 14th, with the intention of satisfying all reasonable aspirations of the soldiers, a manifesto was drawn up, to be issued on the following day in the name of Fairfax and the Army Council. In this manifesto Fairfax declared that, unless discipline were restored, he would lay down his command. On the other hand, if he remained at his post, he would advocate the fixing of a date for the speedy dissolution of Parliament, and the adoption of provisions which would make the future House of Commons 'as near as may be, an equal representative of the people that are to elect.' To this was added a form of adhesion to Fairfax and the Army Council which every soldier was to be asked to sign. The ideas contained in the manifesto accord so thoroughly with those expressed by Cromwell in the Army Council on November 1 [1] that he may be safely credited with its inspiration. Parliament was not to be pressed by the army to make such and such alterations of the law, but it might be pressed to bring itself into closer constitutional relations with the people.[2]

Nov. 14.
A manifesto prepared.

The adhesion of the army to be asked.

When, on the morning of the 15th, Fairfax appeared on Corkbush Field he found little difficulty in maintaining his authority over the four regiments of horse and three of foot who had been ordered to await him there. Rainsborough, who stepped forward to present to him a copy of the *Agreement of the People*, was easily waved aside, whilst Colonel Eyre,[3] Major Foot, and a few other dissatisfied officers, called in vain on the soldiers to stand by the Agreement. The men, shutting their ears to them, readily signed the engagement circulated in the ranks, and the insubordinate officers were placed under arrest, with the exception of Major Scott,[4] who, being a member of Parliament, was sent up to Westminster to be judged by the House of Commons.

The rendezvous on Corkbush Field.

---

[1] See pp. 3–5.   [2] *L.J.* ix. 529.

[3] William Eyre, to be distinguished from the Thomas Eyre who was governor of Hurst Castle.

[4] To be distinguished from Scott the Regicide. Thomas was the Christian name of both.

Very different was the behaviour of two other regiments—
those of Robert Lilburne and Harrison—whose very presence
on the field was an act of mutiny ; that of Lilburne
having been ordered to the North to take part in
watching the movements of the Scots, whilst that of
Harrison had been directed to appear at one of the
other places of rendezvous. Of the two, Lilburne's, which had
driven away most of its officers whilst still on the march, was
the most mutinous, but the soldiers of both regiments appeared on the field with copies of the *Agreement of the People*
stuck in their hats, with the addition of the motto, " England's
freedom ! Soldiers' rights ! " Harrison's regiment was soon
brought to submission by a few words of reproof from Fairfax,
but Lilburne's was not in so compliant a mood. Cromwell,
seeing that persuasion alone would not avail him here, rode
along the ranks, sharply ordering the men to tear
the papers from their hats, and on finding no signs
of obedience, dashed amongst the mutineers with
his sword drawn. There was something in his stern-set face
and resolute action which compelled obedience. The instincts
of military discipline revived, and the soldiers, a moment
before so defiant, tore the papers from their hats and craved
for mercy. The ringleaders were arrested, and three of them
condemned to death by an improvised court-martial. The
three were, however, allowed to throw dice for their lives, and
the loser, whose name was Arnold, was shot in the presence
of his comrades. Thus, at the cost of a single life, discipline
was restored, without which the army would have dissolved
into chaos.[1]

The remainder of the army gave no trouble, and on the
19th Cromwell received the thanks of the House of Commons for the service which he had rendered. Now
that the King had left Hampton Court there was
no longer any reason for keeping the head-quarters
of the army in the immediate neighbourhood of London, and

Mutiny in the regiments of Harrison and Lilburne.

Cromwell compels obedience.

Nov. 19. Cromwell thanked.

[1] *Rushw.* vii. 875 ; *Clar. St. P.* App. xlii. ; Fairfax to Manchester.
Nov. 15, *L.J.* ix. 527 ; *The Moderate Intelligencer,* E. 416, 8 ; *Merc.
Elencticus,* E. 416, 13.

they were consequently removed from Putney to Windsor.[1]
The hostile feeling which prevailed between the army and the
City was, however, by no means allayed, and as the City con-
tinued remiss in the payment of its assessments, Fairfax

Hewson
sent to
London.

ordered Hewson to enter London with his regiment
in order to enforce payment. On the 20th the
House of Commons, taking alarm at this open

Nov 20.
He is
stopped by
the Com-
mons

interference of the military commanders with the
affairs of government, directed Cromwell to stop
Hewson's march. At the same time the House

urged the City to pay the money for want of which the soldiers were compelled to live at free quarter.[2] In spite of all
that could be said, the citizens kept their purses closed, well
pleased if by refusing the army the means of paying its way
they could make its very existence intolerable to the nation.

Whatever might be the future relations between the army
and the City, the restoration of military discipline left no

Nov. 16.
A message
from the
King.

doubt in Charles's mind that if he was to win the
army at all he must deal with the officers, and not
with the Levellers. Accordingly, on November 16,

the day after the rendezvous on Corkbush Field, he sent to t..e
Houses a message evidently intended as a compromise between
his own views and *The Heads of the Proposals.* As far as the

Proposals
rel ting to
the Church,

Church was concerned, he stood upon the maintenance of Episcopacy and the restoration of
Church lands, though he was ready to consent that

bishops should be assisted by their presbyters in conferring
orders and in exercising jurisdiction, whilst their powers were
to 'be so limited that they be not grievous to the tender consciences of others.' Then followed the stipulation, so often
announced, that the Presbyterian system was to be untouched
for three years, during which divines were to be consulted with
a view to an ultimate settlement 'by his Majesty and the two
Houses.' Charles further required that full liberty of worship
should during these three years be accorded to himself and to
'all others of his judgment,' as well as 'to any other who

---

[1] Fairfax to Scawen, Nov. 19, *L.J.* ix. 536.
[2] *C.J.* v. 364.

cannot in conscience submit thereunto,' and also agreed that when the final settlement was reached there should be 'full liberty to all those who shall differ upon conscientious grounds from that settlement,' provided that there should be no toleration for 'those of the Popish profession,' or for 'the public profession of Atheism or blasphemy contrary to the doctrine of' the three creeds.

As a security for his performance of these engagements, Charles offered to surrender the militia for his own life if the *to the militia and other demands.* claims of his successors to full power over it were left untouched. On other points he was conciliatory, especially recommending to the Houses the consideration of the demands of the army relating to 'the succession of Parliaments, and their due election.' Upon the strength of these offers, Charles asked to be admitted to a personal treaty in London.[1]

It may readily be conceded that in making these proposals Charles believed himself to be dealing fairly with all persons *Character of the offer.* and interests; and even that, admitting that he could be trusted to act in the spirit as well as in the letter of his engagements, the acceptance of his overtures would offer a fair prospect of bringing back the country to the orderly struggles of constitutional progress. With their experience of Charles's character, however, the Houses could not do less than scrutinise closely the possibilities left open to him and it could hardly be doubted that the possession of the negative voice, conjoined with the general eagerness for peace, would render him master of the situation when the three years of Presbyterianism had come to an end. What was really needed was security that the King would abandon his ingrained habit of twisting the law in his own favour in order to be able to rule independently of Parliament and the nation. It was the increasing belief that Charles would never allow the will of the nation to prevail over his own which, far more than any difference of opinion as to the nature of the required settlement, made any understanding with him impossible.

[1] The King to the Houses, Nov. 16, *Const. Documents,* 243.

Yet, though Parliament and army, in their different ways, upheld the right of the nation to mould its own destinies, they were unable to conceal from themselves

Position of the army and Parliament towards it ;

that at least for the moment the nation desired a surrender to the King almost at any price. Those who had most to gain by the restoration of order and the disbandment of the army welcomed Charles's message as in every way satisfactory, and though the Scottish commissioners condemned it in private as granting 'a full toleration of heresy and schism for ever,' they openly demanded of the Houses the admission of the King to the personal treaty which he desired.[1]

and of the Scottish commissioners.

For some days after the message arrived the Houses were inclined to take no notice of it, and to content themselves with pushing on their own propositions. The army leaders, on the other hand, were more anxious to test Charles's sincerity than to examine any proposals which he might think fit to make. His friendliness with the Scottish commissioners, and possibly also information received from Hammond, led them to suspect that Charles had motives in escaping from Hampton Court beyond those arising from a sense of personal danger. Was it not possible, for instance, that he intended to escape by sea to Scotland, there to put himself at the head of the invading army with which they had for some time been threatened ? So deeply had this suspicion sunk into their minds, that on the 18th or 19th Ireton, ' standing by the fireside at his quarters at Kingston, and some speaking of an agreement likely to be made between King and Parliament now the person of the King was out of the power of the army, replied, with a discontented countenance, that he hoped it would be such a peace as we might with a safe conscience fight against them both.'[2]

The Houses hesitate.

The army leaders wish to test Charles's sincerity.

Nov. 18. Ireton's language about the King.

[1] The King to Lanark, Nov. 19; Loudoun, Lauderdale, and Lanark to the King, Nov. 22, *Burnet*, v. 125, 126 ; the Scottish Commissioners to Manchester, Nov. 17 ; Paper from the Scottish Commissioners, Nov. 25, *L.J.* ix. 532, 542.

[2] Huntington's *Sundry Reasons*, p. 11, E. 458, 3. Huntington puts

On the 21st, Ireton wrote to Hammond hinting at the sus-
Nov. 21. picions entertained at head-quarters, and encouraging
His letter to Hammond. him to hold the King fast, and to trust rather to a
Cromwell 'on scout.' guard of soldiers than to one composed of inhabi-
tants of the Isle of Wight. "The Lieutenant-
General," he added in a postscript, "is at London or Putney,
and on scout I know not where." [1]

These enigmatical words may fairly be elucidated by a
story which in various forms was current in the end of the
Cromwell and Lord Broghill. seventeenth and the beginning of the eighteenth
century. Lord Broghill, a younger son of the first
Earl of Cork, and after the Restoration created Earl
of Orrery, was during the Commonwealth and Protectorate on
terms of close intimacy with Cromwell. In a life of Orrery [2]
Morrice's story. written by his chaplaiñ, Thomas Morrice, a story is
told as having been related by Orrery himself, of his
asking Cromwell in 1649 why the army had not persisted in
its attempt to come to terms with the King. "The reason,"
Cromwell is alleged to have replied,[3] "why we would once

the date of this conversation 'about six days after it was fully known by
the Parliament and army that the King was in the Isle of Wight,' which
would be on the 21st. On the 21st, however, Ireton was certainly at
Windsor, whereas his regiment was reviewed at Kingston on the 19th,
for which purpose it would arrive at Kingston on the 18th. If we suppose that Huntington meant six days after the King's flight was known,
it would bring the date exactly to the 18th. On the other hand, Huntington may have been merely mistaken about the date.

[1] Ireton to Hammond, Nov. 21, *Letters between Hammond and the
D.H. Committee,* p. 22.

[2] Prefixed to *A Collection of State Letters of . . . Roger Boyle . . .
first Earl of Orrery.*

[3] The story is straightforward, and to my mind in the main probable,
though absolute accuracy in detail is not to be expected in such a case.
Mr. Firth has pointed out to me that it receives an incidental confirmation
from a passage in Sir T. Herbert's *Memoirs* (ed. 1702), p. 63, in which
the writer, speaking of Hamilton's preparations, adds that 'it hath been
suggested by some . . . that the King by a letter from the Queen was
acquainted therewith, which letter was intercepted, the seal violated, and
the letter read by some great officers of the army, members of the
Commons House,' and that Dugdale in his *Short View of the late Troubles*
(ed. 1681), p. 378, mentions that it had been said that Cromwell really

have closed with the King was this: we found the Scots and the Presbyterians began to be more powerful than we; and if they made up matters with the King we should have been left in the lurch, therefore we thought it best to prevent them by offering first to come in upon any reasonable conditions; but while we were busied in these thoughts there came a letter from one of our spies who was of the King's bedchamber,[1] which acquainted us that on that day our final doom was decreed; that he could not possibly tell what it was, but we might find it out if we could intercept a letter sent from the King to the Queen, wherein he declared what he would do.[2]

intended to restore the King, ' but that after he was brought to Hampton Court a certain letter from the Queen was intercepted by them and privately opened; the contents whereof were that she did thereby acquaint him that the Scots were raising or preparing to raise an army in order to his restoration, or expressions to that effect, and that Cromwell having seen this letter and made it up artificially that no violation of the seal could appear, conveyed it to the King, and the next morning sent Ireton on purpose to his Majesty, to enquire of him what he knew of any hostile preparations then in hand by the Scots to the purpose aforesaid. Unto which the King briefly saying that he did neither know nor believe anything thereof, Ireton returned with the answer, and that thereupon both of them concluding that his Majesty was not to be further trusted they did thenceforth resolve to proceed against him.' Both these writers give reasons for disbelieving the story told by themselves; but, what is of more importance, they agree in referring Cromwell's breach with the King to a discovery of his intrigue with the Scots. In this they agree with Morrice, though they refer that discovery to an intercepted letter from the Queen instead of to one from the King.

[1] This seems to mean a gentleman of the bedchamber, which could not be, as neither Ashburnham nor Berkeley was likely to act as a spy. Probably Morrice or his informant Orrery really meant to refer to some person employed by Hammond to attend on the King. The household afterwards appointed by Parliament was not yet named.

[2] Here comes in the only real difficulty about the story. How could any one employed by Hammond know that the King was going to write to the Queen on such a subject? The difficulties would be considerably lessened if we accept in the main the stories referred to by Herbert and Dugdale. If Cromwell had seen a letter from the Queen to the King suggesting his throwing himself on the Scots—and it would be very strange if she did not write to this effect—he would naturally expect that the King's answer would, if he could get hold of it, certify him as to the

The letter, he said, was sewed up in the skirt of a saddle, and the bearer of it would come with the saddle upon his head about ten of the clock that night to the Blue Boar Inn in Holborn,[1] for there he was to take horse and go to Dover with it. This messenger knew nothing of the letter in the saddle, but some persons in Dover did. We were at Windsor when we received this letter, and immediately upon the receipt of it Ireton and I resolved to take one trusty fellow with us, and with troopers' habits to go to the inn in Holborn; which accordingly we did, and set our man at the gate of the inn, when the wicket only was open, to let people in and out. Our man was to give us notice when any person came there with a saddle, whilst we, in the disguise of common troopers, called for cans of beer, and continued drinking till about ten o'clock. The sentinel at the gate then gave notice that the man with the saddle was come in. Upon this we immediately arose, and, as the man was leading out his horse saddled, came up to him with drawn swords and told him we were to search all that went in and out there, but as he looked like an honest man we would only search his saddle and dismiss him. Upon that we ungirt his saddle, and carried it into the stall where we had been drinking, and left the horseman with our sentinel. Then, ripping up one of the skirts of the saddle, we there found the letter of which we had been informed. As soon as we had the letter we opened it; in which we found the King had acquainted the Queen that he was now courted by both the factions, the Scotch Presbyterians and the army, and which bid fairest for him should have him, but he thought he should close with the Scots sooner than the others. Upon this we took horse and went to Windsor, and finding we were not likely to have any tolerable terms from the King, we immediately, from that time forward, resolved his ruin."

King's acceptance or rejection of his wife's advice. I suspect that the spy, knowing this, simply wrote to say that the answer was coming in a particular way, and that either Cromwell, Orrery, or Morrice subsequently imputed to the spy more knowledge than he actually possessed.

[1] The site is now occupied by the Inns of Court Hotel. See Cunningham's *Handbook to London, Past and Present.*

In addition to this story, in which the cause of the breach between Cromwell and the King is assigned to the intrigues of Another story. the latter with the Scots, another and quite different tradition assigned it to the discovery of Charles's intention to shake himself loose from all promises made by him to the army and Ireton after his restoration to power. This second story is first heard of in 1696, when it was told by Roger Coke as a mere rumour.[1] It reappears in an assertion which Wagstaffe made in 1711,[2] to the effect that he had heard that the intercepted letter of Charles, which was alleged to have revealed his intentions, was in the hands of Millington, the auctioneer, but that on making application to Millington he had been refused even a sight of it.[3] The story took a lasting shape in a conversation held about 1743, when Bolingbroke told Pope that Lord Oxford had assured him that he had had in his hands an intercepted letter from Charles to the Queen, and, as it would seem from Bolingbroke's reported language, also the letter of the Queen to which it had been an answer. According to the most probable account of the contents of the letters, Henrietta Maria having desired her husband 'not to yield too much to the traitor,' Charles replied that 'she need not have any concern in her mind on that head, for whatever agreement they might enter into, he should not look upon himself as obliged to keep any promises made so much on compulsion whenever he had power enough to break them.'[4]

[1] Coke's *Detection* (2nd edit. 1699), i. 166.

[2] Wagstaffe's *Vindication* (3rd ed. 1711), p. 13.

[3] Possibly fearing that Wagstaffe might want to destroy evidence against the ' martyr king.'

[4] Spence's *Anecdotes* (ed. 1820), 298; Richardson's *Richardsoniana* (ed. 1776). The statement that Pope derived his information from Bolingbroke is taken from Richardson, but I have inserted the statement of what Bolingbroke said about the contents of the letter as it is given by Spence. Richardson's report is far more rhetorical, as he alleges that Bolingbroke quoted Charles as saying that ' he should know in due time how to deal with the rogues who, instead of a silken garter, should be fitted with a hempen cord.' The language attributed to him in Spence's report, on the other hand, is no more than he is known to have used on other occasions. It is most unlikely that there should have been two sets of intercepted letters, and, though these two stories coming from entirely

On the supposition that these two stories be substantially true, it becomes possible, at least conjecturally, to explain the postscript of Ireton's letter of the 21st.[1] By that time, it is to be supposed, the Queen's letter had come into Cromwell's hands. He would, therefore, be 'on scout,' making arrangements for intercepting the expected reply. Upon his return to Windsor a day or two later, perhaps on the 23rd or 24th, he would have received intelligence from the spy at Carisbrooke, and, in Ireton's company, have waylaid the King's answer at the Blue Boar in Holborn.[2]

Ireton's postscript explained.

If, again, the discovery be assigned to the 23rd or 24th, an explanation is found for the part so suddenly taken on the 25th by the House of Lords, which was at this time in the hands of an Independent majority.

Nov. 25.
Sudden action of the Lords.

However this may have been, the Lords now, after allowing the King's offer [3] to remain unnoticed for no less than nine days, appointed a committee to select some of the propositions formerly presented at Newcastle and Hampton Court to be laid before the King 'for our present security.' After a short delay, the committee reported that four of the propositions were suitable for the purpose. The first gave Parliament authority over the militia directly for twenty years, and indirectly for all time to come, by declaring that the Crown should never exercise it without the consent of the Houses. The second and third revoked Charles's declarations against the Houses, and annulled the honours which he had recently granted; whilst the fourth gave to the existing Parliament the right of adjourning itself to any place which the Houses thought desirable.[4]

Four Propositions to be laid before the King.

different sources do not in any way corroborate one another, yet each of them may have referred to a different part of a real letter. This view of the case receives additional corroboration from the neatness with which the narrative given of their discovery fits in with facts known from other sources.   [1] See p. 27.

[2] The visit to the Blue Boar is said to have taken place when Cromwell and Ireton were at Windsor, and therefore, necessarily, not before Nov. 19.

[3] See p. 24.   [4] *L.J.* ix. 541.

On the 26th, the Lords sent the Four Propositions to the Commons, that they might there be converted into Bills,

Nov. 26.
The Propositions to be turned into Bills.

accompanying them with a recommendation that, when they had passed both Houses, the King should be informed that, as soon as he had given to them the royal assent, he would be at liberty to come to

The King to come to London if he accepts them.

London in order to treat personally with Parliament on all other points at issue. On the following day the Commons accepted the Lords' suggestion by the small majority of nine.[1]

If at first sight this scheme, which proceeded from the Independent House of Lords, seems to have been but an

Nov. 27.
An Independent policy.

ungenerous response to the conciliatory offer recently made by Charles,[2] it should be remembered that those who drew it up had the strongest reason to doubt Charles's sincerity. Though the Independents, knowing all that they knew, were not yet prepared to cast away all hope of a reconciliation with Charles, they con-

A searching test.

sidered that a reconciliation must now be based on a searching test of the King's sincerity. If Charles accepted the fourth proposition, he would practically abandon the intention attributed to him of coercing Parliament with the help of the Londoners, whilst if he accepted the first he would place the military forces of the nation in the hands of Parliament. When once the Crown had been stripped of its control over the militia, the precise nature of the constitutional reforms which were demanded on all sides might be left to free discussion and to the play of natural forces in Parliament or elsewhere. These, as can hardly be doubted, were the ideas which now inspired the action of the Houses in the selection of the Four Propositions.

Cromwell had not to wait for the King's answer till the

---

[1] *C.J.* v. 370. The tellers for the majority were Algernon Sidney and Sir John Evelyn, both Independents ; for the minority, Morley and Henry Marten. Probably the minority was composed both of those who wished to have no treaty with the King and of those who wished to subject him to less stringent terms.

[2] See p. 24.

Propositions were presented. Though Charles was probably serious in his offer to abandon authority for a term of years,

Charles
hostile
to it. or even for his own lifetime, it was always on the understanding that the powers which he had received from his father should ultimately return to his son. He could never comprehend how wide a gulf there was between himself and the most conciliatory of his opponents. Even now, when the news of the Lords' vote on the Four

Nov. 26.
He appeals
to Fairfax. Propositions reached his ears, he fancied that the army chiefs must be on his side, and on the 26th he despatched Berkeley to urge Fairfax to support his request for an unconditional personal treaty.[1]

On November 28, Berkeley appeared before the Council of the Army at Windsor[2] as the bearer of a message, which

Nov. 28.
Berkeley at
Windsor. was virtually a demand, that officers and soldiers should oppose Parliament by placing the King, without conditions, in a commanding position. It

He meets
with a
rebuff. was no matter of wonder that Berkeley met with a rebuff. Fairfax told him briefly 'that they were the Parliament's army, and therefore could not say anything to his Majesty's motion of peace, but must refer those matters to them to whom he would send his Majesty's letters.' Cromwell and Ireton had but cold looks for the disappointed messenger.[3]

Before many hours passed, Berkeley was in possession of what he believed to be the key to the mystery. In the dead

Berkeley
receives
information
that
Cromwell
has aban-
doned the
King. of the night he received a visit from a general officer[4] who continued to sympathise with the King, and who now poured forth a long invective against Cromwell and Ireton. They were now, he affirmed, seeking to make their peace with the army on account of the apprehensions which they entertained for their own

---

[1] The King to Fairfax, Nov. 26, *Propositions from the King's Majesty*, E. 418, 8.　　　　[2] *The Moderate Intelligencer*, E. 418, 9.

[3] *Propositions from the King's Majesty*, E. 418, 8; Berkeley's *Memoirs*, 70.

[4] The term was more loosely employed at that time than it is now, such a person, for instance, as a Scoutmaster General being included in it.

personal safety. It had been proposed, the officer added, 'to send eight hundred of the most disaffected of the army to secure' the King, 'and then to bring him to his trial.' Cromwell, too, had openly declared 'that the glories of this world had so dazzled his eyes that he could not discern clearly the great works the Lord was doing; that he was ˙resolved to humble himself, and desire the prayers of the saints, that God would be pleased to forgive his self-seeking.'

Bitter as was the language of Berkeley's informant, he said no word from which it could be inferred that Cromwell was

Its general accuracy.

personally concerned in the design of bringing the King to trial, whilst all that he had to say about his motives was manifestly founded on conjecture alone. There is, however, no reason to doubt that Cromwell at this time openly announced that he had abandoned his desire to re-establish Charles upon the throne, and that he accompanied the announcement with pious acknowledgment of his own past self-seeking and pride. It was Cromwell's usual way of saying that he had found himself to have been mistaken, and there is no reason to suppose that he had not convinced himself that his mistake was a moral fault as well as an intel-

Nov. 29. Cromwell announces to Berkeley his breach with the King.

lectual blunder. On the following morning, if, at least, he is accurately reported, he sent a message to Berkeley more after the fashion of the world. "He sent me word," wrote Berkeley afterwards, "that he durst not see me, it being very dangerous to both; and bid me be assured that he would serve his Majesty as long as he could do it without his own ruin, but desired that I would not expect that he should perish for his sake."[1] Berkeley's mission had, indeed, revealed to Cromwell that the test which he had sought to impose on Charles

His position towards Charles.

had been rejected. From that time he made up his mind that Charles could never, with advantage to the nation, be readmitted to any real share in its government. He had not yet come to the conclusion that it was either right or prudent to punish him for his past misconduct.

[1] Berkeley's *Memoirs*, 76.

That the same knowledge which cleared away Cromwell's hesitations acted on the far weaker mind of Hammond there

Cromwell and Hammond.

can be little doubt. Hammond had for some days after the King's arrival been passing through what Cromwell, in writing to him, styled his 'temptation';[1] temptation, it may be presumed, to let the King go where he would, and thus to free himself of all responsibility in the matter. Hammond now seems to have made up his mind that he would not suffer the King to escape,[2] though he took care that his change of view should not be known to

Dec.
The King supposes it to be still easy to escape.

Charles. When, early in December, Berkeley returned to the Isle of Wight, he was firmly convinced that nothing but the King's own irresolution stood in the way of his flight, and when, on December 4,

Dec. 4.

the Scottish commissioners proposed to Charles that he should betake himself to Berwick, they did not suggest the existence of any obstacle in his way.[3]

It is not unlikely that Charles was encouraged to hold his ground by a change in the attitude of the Commons. Either

Nov. 27-30.
Change in the attitude of the House of Commons.

because the Presbyterians who had supported the Independent leaders in the division on the Four Propositions began to realise the true meaning of the vote which they had given, or from some other cause now unknown, the last days of November were allowed to slip by without any attempt to convert the Propositions

Dec. 1.
A City petition.

into Bills. On December 1 the Presbyterians resumed the offensive. On that day a petition was presented by the City asking that the army might be

Vane's threat.

removed to a greater distance and the Covenant fully observed,[4] and it was only after Vane had threatened the

---

[1] Cromwell to Hammond, Jan. 3, 1648, Letter lii.

[2] When Berkeley was at Windsor, Cromwell and Ireton, on receiving from him Hammond's recommendatory letter, 'smiled with much disdain upon it.' This looks as if they knew that Hammond had already made up his mind against the King, though it is, of course, no evidence that he had done so.

[3] Berkeley's *Memoirs*, 79; Loudoun, Lauderdale, and Lanark to the King, Dec. 4, *Burnet*, v. 132.

[4] *L.J.* ix. 550; *C.J.* v. 374.

House with a fresh military intervention,[1] and a large number
of Presbyterians had left the House in disgust, that the peti-

The
petition
rejected.

Fears of
the Inde-
pendents.

tion was practically rejected. It was expected that
if the result had been different the Presbyterians
would follow up their victory by a vote restoring
to their seats the ten survivors of the eleven members, and also the impeached lords, and there was
no reasonable doubt that a solid Presbyterian majority thus
formed in both Houses would have welcomed a personal
treaty with Charles without imposing upon him any test whatever. So great was the indignation caused amongst the
Presbyterians by Vane's language that there was even some
talk of surprising the House into a vote for its own dissolution,
and of thus solving all questions in dispute by an appeal to the
electorate.[2]

For the present, however, the fear of the army prevailed.
On the 27th of November the attendance had been 225.

Dec. 1–3.
The Four
Bills pro-
ceeded with.

On the afternoon of the 1st of December the Commons, with sadly diminished numbers, there being
only 138 members present, proceeded to convert
the Propositions into Bills. On the 3rd of December the
Four Bills, as they were now called, were read for the second
time.[3]

A victory obtained by such means served only to strengthen
Charles in his conviction that public opinion was on his side,

Dec. 6.
A fresh
appeal for
a personal
treaty.

Dec. 14.
The Four
Bills passed.

and on December 6, turning a deaf ear to Berkeley's
warning that, if he lingered much longer in the Isle
of Wight escape would cease to be possible, he addressed to Parliament a fresh appeal for a personal
treaty.[4] As Parliament was now composed, it was
not likely to give ear to his request, and on the 14th,
the Four Bills having passed through their final stages, a com-

---

[1] "Young Vane openly threatened the bringing up again of the army."
Letter of Intelligence, Dec. 2, *Clarendon MSS.* 2,672.

[2] Grignon to Brienne, Dec. $\frac{13}{23}$, *R.O. Transcripts*; Letter of Intelligence, Dec. $\frac{2}{12}$, *ibid.* 2,671, 2,672.

[3] *C.J.* v. 373, 375.

[4] The King to the Houses, Dec. 6, *L.J.* ix. 567.

mittee was appointed to carry them to Carisbrooke for the King's acceptance.[1]

As the days passed on Charles turned himself more decidedly in the direction of the Scots. Yet the Scottish com-

Charles applies to the Scottish Commissioners, missioners, men of the world as they were, had certain requirements to insist on, and on December 7 [2] they sent Traquair to Carisbrooke to induce Charles to relax his pretensions in the matter of religion.

Dec. 13. but fails to satisfy them. On December 13, after Traquair's return to London, they had to inform him that if he could not give better satisfaction on that point Scotland would do

He continues to trust Hammond. nothing for him.[3] Of his own power to effect his escape Charles had still no doubt, not having the slightest suspicion that his letter to the Queen had been intercepted, with the result of converting Hammond, who had been half disposed to assist him, into a spy on behalf of his opponents.[4]

A mere escape to a place of safety was, however, not what Charles had in mind, and on the 15th he sent to the Scottish commissioners the draft of a memorandum setting down the terms to which he was now willing to agree.[5] Contrary to his expectation, the commissioners declared that further altera-

---

[1] *L.J.* ix. 574. The Four Bills themselves are in *Const. Documents*, 248.

[2] Traquair was at Carisbrooke on the 8th. The King to Loudoun, Lanark, and Lauderdale, Dec. 8, *Burnet*, v. 136.

[3] Loudoun, Lauderdale, and Lanark to the King, Dec. 13, *ibid.* v. 137.

[4] "Though no time hath been nor shall be lost for my going from hence; yet, contrary to expectation, it will be ten days before the ship can be ready; and I confess that this had been too late if the governor had permitted forces in hither; wherefore I am confident that I shall not be surprised for time." The King to Loudoun, Lauderdale, and Lanark, Dec. 14, *ibid.* v. 138. After Berkeley's visit to Windsor Cromwell had interfered to stop the issue of a warrant for his arrest, and to permit Ashburnham and Legge to remain at large (Letter of Intelligence, Dec. 2, *Clar. St. P.* ii. app. xlii.). Probably Cromwell's object was to make it easier to discover the King's projects.

[5] Postscript, dated Dec. 15, to the King's letter of the 14th, *Burnet*, v. 138.

tions would be necessary. They were, however, encouraged by
the tone of Charles's offer to fulminate at inordinate length a

Dec. 15.
The draft of
an engage-
ment sent to
the Scots.

Dec. 18.
Protest of
the Scots.

fierce protest against the proceedings of the Parliament and army, concluding with demands for a
personal treaty with the King, the maintenance of
the Covenant, the establishment of Presbyterianism
in England, the disbandment of all armies, and the
restitution of the rights of the King, especially his
authority over the militia, and his power of negativing bills
presented to him by Parliament.[1]

On December 24 the joint committee of the Houses, with
Denbigh at its head, presented the Four Bills to Charles,

Dec. 24.
The Four
Bills pre-
sented to
Charles.

The Scottish
commis-
sioners at
Carisbrooke.

informing him that he would be allowed four days
to consider his answer. About the same time the
three Scottish commissioners, Loudoun, Lauderdale
and Lanark, had appeared at Carisbrooke to urge
him to further concessions to themselves. There
could be no doubt in Charles's mind which of the
rival groups of emissaries he would prefer. Whatever the Scots might demand, they were prepared to hold
cheaply the liberties of Englishmen, and to leave to the

Charles
decides to
accept their
terms.

monarchy the supreme military authority and the
negative voice by which the King had been able to
stop all legislation obnoxious to himself; whilst the
English committee, by insisting on divesting the crown of
power over the militia, would have reduced the King to a
position of subordination to the national will expressed in
Parliament. The main political issues of the Revolution were
embodied in this opposition between the Englishmen and the
Scots now in his presence, and it was but natural that Charles,
regarding the matter from his own point of view, should decide
in favour of the Scottish commissioners.

Whether his so doing would win the Scottish nation to his
side was another question. The present commissioners, with
the doubtful exception of Loudoun,[2] represented the Scottish

---

[1] The answer of the Commissioners, *L.J.* ix. 591.

[2] Loudoun was now working with the Hamilton party, but he subsequently reverted to his natural position as a Campbell in Argyle's following.

nobility, not the Scottish Church. Their objects were political rather than religious, and if in questions of religion they in-
Temper of the Scottish Commis- sioners.
sisted on stricter terms than Charles liked to grant, he had at least the knowledge that they were not the men to be very seriously indignant if he after- wards found it impossible or inconvenient to carry out to the letter all the promises that he made.

Accordingly, on December 26, Charles signed an agree- ment—known as the Engagement—between himself and the
Dec. 26. The en- gagement signed.
Scottish commissioners. On the question of the Covenant Charles accepted a compromise. He agreed to confirm it by Act of Parliament, so far
The scheme for a religious settlement.
as to give security to those who had taken it, but he refused to allow any one to be constrained to take it in future. In other respects he stood by his offer made on May 12.[1] The Presbyterian system was to be established for three years, during which time plans for a final settlement of all Church questions were to be discussed in the Assembly of Divines, reinforced by twenty members appointed by himself, though no resolution of this body was to have any binding force till it had received his assent and that of the two Houses. The solution here proposed, as the com- missioners could not fail to perceive, was not likely to make the Church of England permanently Presbyterian.

On another point Charles and the commissioners agreed to have no ambiguity. Charles declared himself ready to do everything in his power ' for suppressing the opinions
Heretics to be sup- pressed,
and practices of Anti-trinitarians, Anabaptists, Anti- nomians, Arminians, Familists, Brownists, Separatists, Independents, Libertines, and Seekers, and generally for sup- pressing all blasphemy, heresy, schism, and all such scandalous doctrines and practices as are contrary to the light of nature or to the known principles of Christianity, whether
and Scottish Acts con- firmed.
concerning faith, worship, or conversation : or to the power of Godliness, or which may be destructive to order and government or to the peace of the Church and

[1] See iii. 252.

kingdom.' Charles likewise expressed his readiness to confirm
all Acts passed in the last Scottish Parliament.

On these terms Charles proposed that the kingdom of
Scotland should engage to support his demand for a personal
treaty in London, and for the disbandment of all
armies with a view to a peaceable discussion. If
this demand was refused, the Scots were to issue a
Declaration 'wherein they shall assert the right which belongs
to the Crown in the power of the militia, the Great Seal,
bestowing of honours and offices of trust, choice of Privy
Councillors, the right of the King's negative voice in Parliament, and that the Queen's Majesty, the Prince, and the rest
of the royal issue, ought to remain where his Majesty shall
think fit, in either of the kingdoms, with safety, honour, and
freedom.' Upon the issue of this Declaration, a Scottish army
was to be sent into England to settle a lasting peace, 'in
pursuance whereof the kingdom of Scotland' was to 'endeavour
that there may be a free and full Parliament in England, and
that his Majesty may be with them in honour, safety, and
freedom, and that a speedy period be set to this present
Parliament, and that the said army shall be upon the march
before the said peaceable message and Declaration be delivered
to the House.'

Suggested Scottish intervention.

All persons in England or Ireland supporting the King in
pursuance of this agreement were to be protected, and might
join in his defence. When peace was settled there
was to be an Act of Oblivion. For the present the
King or Prince was to go to Scotland if invited to do so.
The King was to do everything in his power 'both at home
and abroad' to assist the Scots in carrying on the war, and to
authorise them to possess themselves of 'Berwick, Carlisle,
Newcastle, Tynemouth, and Hartlepool' as long as the war
lasted. Moreover, Charles was to secure to his Scottish subjects the money still owing to them by the votes of the English
Parliament, and if possible to bring about a complete union
between the kingdoms, or, if that could not be effected, to
establish complete freedom of trade between them. Besides
this, his Majesty's ships were to guard the coasts of Scotland.

The King's offer.

By additional articles, Charles promised to employ Scots
equally with Englishmen in foreign negotiations, to admit 'a
considerable and competent number of Scotsmen'
to the English Privy Council, the same number of
Englishmen being admitted to the Scottish Council.
A third part of the persons employed in places of trust about
the King, the Queen, and the royal family were always to be
Scots; and the King and Prince were to reside in Scotland as
often as they were able to do so.

Privileges to be given to Scots.

On the 27th, the three Scottish commissioners declared
under their signatures their personal acceptance of the Engagement, and their confidence that it would be
adopted in Scotland. The King then took them to
witness that he did not bind himself in any way
to forward the Presbyterian government in England,
or to cause any to suffer for rejecting it, excepting
those who were excepted in the clause against toleration.[1]

*Dec. 27.
The com-
missioners
personally
accept the
Engage-
ment.*

The Engagement thus signed was wrapped in lead and
buried in the Castle garden till a convenient opportunity for
carrying it with safety out of the island should arise.
There was no longer room for dallying with the
commissioners of the English Parliament. On the
28th, Charles dismissed them with a written answer addressed
to the two Houses, in which he definitely rejected
the Four Bills, pleading against them with no slight
ability as prejudging the questions at issue, and
giving permanently to the Houses an arbitrary and unconstitutional power over the militia. In reality the most important
question at issue between Charles and the framers of the Four
Bills was the value of his own word. Yet it was precisely this
that Charles, even in the recesses of his own mind, was never
likely to admit, far less in a manifesto addressed to the
Parliament and nation.

*The En-
gagement
buried.*

*Dec. 28.
Charles
rejects the
Four Bills.*

[1] The Engagement and the Additional Articles, Dec. 26, 27, *Const.
Documents,* 259, 264.

CHAPTER LVIII.

THE VOTE OF NO ADDRESSES.

As far as the government of England was concerned, the scheme propounded in the Engagement was substantially the

1647.
The scheme
of the En-
gagement
compared
with that
of the
Restoration.

one adopted at the Restoration. The armies were to be disbanded, a new Parliament called, the authority of the militia restored to the King, and his right of refusing his assent to Bills acknowledged. If a Scottish army was to be introduced to give effect to this plan, it was to come, according to Charles's apprehension at least, not to impose its will on a reluctant nation, but to liberate England from overmastering force.

Nevertheless the difference between the situations in 1647 and in 1660 was in reality enormous. It is to be measured

Charles I.
and
Charles II.

not by comparing documentary stipulations but by comparing the personal characters of Charles I. and his son. Charles II. might be trusted not to push his claims farther than suited his own convenience. His first thought would be to keep on fairly good terms with his Parliament, because in that way only could he avoid exile from the pleasures and amusements of Whitehall. In the hands of such a man, powers verbally fatal to political liberty would be robbed of half their terrors. In the hands of Charles I., even the loosest acknowledgment of the claims of the monarchy would be dangerous. He was at the same time conscientious and untrustworthy. He would insist upon doing that which he honestly believed to be right, and would attempt to gain his ends by deceiving those with whom he had to deal so long as the deception did not involve the utterance of a direct falsehood, though even this latter rule he did not consider binding upon him in every case.

How hopeless it was to expect straightforward dealing from Charles I. might easily have been made clear if only those who were his accusers had had access to the Engagement. In his message to the Houses, sent on November 16, he had declared for toleration.[1] In the Engagement, on December 26 he declared against it.[2] The conclusion is obvious that in one or other case, if not in both, he was insincere, and that he regarded his promises merely as stepping-stones to the restoration of an authority which he intended to exercise in accordance with his own ideas.

Charles's contradictory promises about toleration.

It was thus in reality against entrusting the government of the nation to a man in whom no confidence could be placed that the army had raised its protest; and its dissatisfaction with Charles's conduct was greatly heightened by a well-founded belief that Charles intended to call in a Scottish army to redress the balance of the constitution in his own favour. An army, like all other minorities, even when placed in conditions favourable to action, cannot hope for more than temporary success unless it can bring the majority round to its own way of thinking, and it was not likely that the political principles which had prevailed in the Army Council at Putney would commend themselves to the nation for many a year to come. On the temporary question of barring the way against Charles's personal restoration to power, the army had every chance of success if only its own discipline could be maintained. Charles's partisans were indeed numerous, but they had little clear insight into the problem which they hoped to solve, and many of them were from time to time driven by some fresh revelation of Charles's insincerity to regard with alarm the attainment of that very object which they had in view.

Position of the army.

Whatever else Charles might succeed in accomplishing, he had at least restored unity of action to the army. There were some, no doubt, who continued to wish for the King's trial and execution. There were others who wished for his trial and

[1] See p. 25.   [2] See p. 39.

deposition, whilst others, again, would have been content to set him aside without any sort of trial.[1]   On the practical question

Cromwell and Rainsborough.

of the day, however, all, including men who in other respects differed from one another as widely as Cromwell and Rainsborough, were in complete accord. If the King and his Scottish allies were to be opposed, it was only in the name of the existing Parliament, whatever might be its demerits, that the battle could be fought, and to gain that end, subsidiary questions must for the present be waived.

Accordingly, the causes of difference at head-quarters were quietly dropped. Rainsborough and his friends abandoned all

Dec. 21. An agreement in the army.

pretence of winning their objects by encouraging mutiny, and Cromwell, now assured that discipline would be maintained, raised no obstacle to the liberation of such officers and soldiers as had been imprisoned for the part which they had taken in the late disturbances. On

Dec. 22. A prayer meeting.

December 22 there was held at Windsor a great prayer meeting, at which many of the officers and soldiers, including Cromwell and Ireton, prayed fervently from nine in the morning to seven at night. In the

Rainsborough to be Vice-Admiral.

evening, the Council of the Army adopted a resolution that Fairfax should be asked to forgive Rainsborough's offence and to request Parliament to confer on him the office of Vice-Admiral.[2]   On the following

Dec. 23. The mutineers pardoned.

morning, a number of soldiers and officers, brought up for trial as mutineers before the Council of the Army, were pardoned on promises of submission.

In asking for Rainsborough's appointment, the Council of

Dec. 24. The Commons vote for Rainsborough's appointment, but the Lords refuse their consent.

the Army was probably to some extent influenced by a desire to place a trustworthy officer in command of the ships about to be sent to guard the sea round the Isle of Wight.   On the 24th the Commons gave their approbation to the request, but the Lords, who held all Levellers in horror, refused their consent.[3]   Both Houses, however, concurred in providing, so

---

[1] Grignon to Brienne, Jan. $\frac{1}{15}$, *R.O. Transcripts.*

[2] *Rushw.* vii. 943.

[3] *C.J.* v. 403 ; *L.J.* ix. 606.

far, at least, as ordinances could provide, for the levying of
money for the soldiers, requiring in return that the
system of free quarter should be abandoned, and all
supernumerary forces enlisted since August disbanded.

The army's arrears and pay to be secured.

There was the greater reason why Cromwell and the
Levellers should come to terms as, even before the rejection
of the Four Bills, there had been signs that if the
King could in any way raise his standard again,
popular support would not be wanting to his cause.

Charles's prospects of popular support.

Though there is nothing to show that the people at large were
hostile to the ecclesiastical changes which passed over their
heads, they were exasperated at the curtailment of
their amusements which had followed in the wake of
Puritanism, especially when on Christmas Day the
authorities perversely enforced the opening of the shops and
forbade the customary merry-makings.

Opposition to the restriction of amusements.

Christmas Day in 1647 was marked by an explosion of
feeling far more general than in any former year. At Canterbury, where the Mayor ordered a market to be
held, a crowd appeared in the street with a football, and, forcibly shutting up the few shops which
had been opened, proceeded to play in the street.
The Mayor, attempting to quell the disturbance, was
knocked down, and the windows of his supporters broken. On
the 27th the rioting was renewed. Shouts were
raised of, "Up with King Charles, and down with
Parliament and Excise!" The Mayor, together
with the other magistrates and some of the clergy, were driven
out of the city and the gates barred against them. The County
Committee brought 3,000 of the trained bands to suppress the
disturbance; and afterwards took the gates off their hinges
and made a breach in the wall. How widely spread was the
dissatisfaction is shown by the fear expressed by the committee,
that unless the sheriff chose a notoriously partial jury, it should
be impossible to procure a conviction of the offenders.[1]

Dec. 25. Christmas Day at Canterbury.

A riot in the streets.

Dec. 27. Renewal of the riot.

---

[1] **The Committee of Kent to Lenthall, Jan. 4, 5, 21,** *Tanner MSS.*

Disturbances of the same kind occurred in many places.
" The counties," wrote a London news-writer, " are full of discontents, many insurrections having been lately
made, even near this city, for the customs of Christmas." [1]   At Ipswich the riot was nearly as difficult
to suppress as at Canterbury.[2]   In London popular discontent
showed itself in a less violent form.   Churches and public
places were adorned with rosemary and bay, and ministers
deprived for malignancy occupied the pulpits and used the
Book of Common Prayer.[3]   In the City itself, the
apprentices decorated a pump in Cornhill with holly
and ivy.   The officers sent to pull down the greenery were
driven back and chased through the street, and the Lord Mayor
Warner had to intervene in person before order was restored.
As his election to office had been forced by Parliament on the
City after the troubles of the summer, resistance to him commended itself to municipal as well as to religious sentiment.[4]

So strong indeed was the current in favour of the King's
restoration that Parliament found it impossible to control the
Royalist press.   For the first time since the beginning of the quarrel with the King, the great majority
of newspapers and pamphlets published in London were
strongly Royalist, while the Parliamentary prints contented
themselves with giving a bald narrative of events, seldom
making any attempt to vindicate the policy of their patrons.
Though the tone of the defenders of the monarchy was always
scurrilous and sometimes blasphemous,[5] no serious attempt
was made to arrest either the authors or the printers.

Marginal notes:
Dec. 25. Disturbances elsewhere.
Christmas in London.
The Royalist press.

lviii. fols. 645, 653, 672 ; *Canterbury Christmas*, E. 421, 22 ; *A Declaration of many thousands of Canterbury*, E. 421, 23 ; *Rushw.* vii. 948.
   [1] Letter of Intelligence, Jan. 6, *Clarendon MSS.* 2,698.
   [2] *The Perf. Weekly Account*, E. 421, 33.
   [3] *A Word in Season*, E. 422, 26.
   [4] *Rushw.* vi. 944 ; *The Kingdom's Weekly Post*, E. 422, 1.
   [5] The most offensive of these is *Ecce the New Testament* (E. 427, 22),
published on February 18.   It is a parody on the first four chapters of
St. Matthew's Gospel, and begins, " The book of the generation of John
Pym, the son of Judas, the son of Beelzebub."   Verses 12 and 13 of
chapter i. run thus : " Now the birth or beginning of this Parliament was

For this combination of dangers Cromwell's mind could suggest no remedy, and in all probability no remedy of any kind was to be found. The one thing which he saw clearly was that it was necessary that Presbyterians and Independents should be united against Charles. On the 29th,[1] when certain Parliamentary commissioners arrived at head-quarters to make financial arrangements in pursuance of the recent vote of the Houses, they were assured by the chief officers that 'the spirit of the army was that since God hath put an opportunity now into their hands of purpose to settle the kingdom, if God should honour the army to be further helping to them, the army would live and die with them and for them willingly.' On the 31st Cromwell, Ireton, and other officers dined with the commissioners before their return to Westminster. "The agreement," wrote one who was present, "was sweet and comfortable, the whole matter of the kingdom being left to Parliament." [2]

Cromwell's view of the situation.

Dec. 31. A friendly dinner.

Thus did Cromwell disguise from himself the undoubted fact that Parliament was in reality acting under pressure. To the extreme Levellers he appeared as a dastardly time-server, changing sides in December from King to Parliament, as he had changed sides in June from Parliament to King, actuated by considerations of the merest self-interest. The press now teemed with pamphlets, in which he was charged with hypocrisy of the lowest kind, one of the ablest and most virulent being *Putney Projects*, written by Wildman under an assumed name and published on

Cromwell and the Levellers.

on this wise: When as their mother the Kingdom of England was allied or espoused to a great desire of reforming abuses; and had therefore nominated their knights, citizens, and burgesses; who (as soon as ever they came together) were found with child of schism, sedition, and rebellion; then King Charles, being a just man and not willing to have him and the people ruinated, was minded to dissolve them," &c.

[1] The meeting ended on the 31st after lasting for three days. The language given above can hardly have been used except at the opening of the discussion.

[2] *A Perfect Diurnal* E. 520, 21.

December 30. Some even of those who were now willing
heartily to co-operate with him, found it difficult to reconcile
Dec. 30.
Putney
Projects. his present action with his former persistent maintenance of the King's authority, and to this feeling
Hazlerigg's
saying. Hazlerigg gave expression in his own blunt fashion :
" If you prove not an honest man," he blurted out
to Cromwell himself, " I will never trust a fellow with a great
nose for your sake." [1]

All that could as yet be done to provide against a Scottish
invasion was done.   Lambert had some time before been sent
Lambert in
the north. down to take the command as major-general of all
the forces in the north of England, and on December
Hazlerigg to
be Governor
of New-
castle. 30, the House of Commons confirmed Fairfax's
appointment of Hazlerigg to the governorship of
the important post of Newcastle.[2]

The greater the danger from Scotland the more necessary
it became to secure Charles in England, lest he should place
himself at the head of the invading army.   The remissness
with which he had hitherto been guarded had indeed made
flight easy for him.   The ship which he had for some time
expected had at last arrived at Southampton, and on the
Dec. 28.
Charles
attempts to
escape. 28th, after delivering to the Parliamentary commissioners his answer to the Four Bills, Charles
resolved to take advantage of their absence to
make his escape, especially as Hammond, who attended
them as far as Newport, had also left the Castle.   A small
vessel was in readiness to carry him to Southampton, and
the wind was fair.   Dressing himself hurriedly for the journey,
he glanced once more at the vane, and discovered to his
horror that the wind had changed and blew steadily from
the north, making the passage down the Medina River and up
Southampton Water impossible.[3]

---

[1] " It's very like him," adds the reporter of this saying ; "he is very
downright usually according to his principles." *A Word to Lieut.-Gen.
Cromwell*, p. 19, E. 341, 30. No date is given to this conversation, but
the pamphlet was published on Dec. 30, and the words were probably
spoken after the prayer meeting on Dec. 22.

[2] *C.J.* v. 439.

[3] The story is told by both Berkeley and Ashburnham. Ashburnham

Before counsel could be taken, Hammond returned from Newport, locked the gates of the castle, and doubled the
Hammond secures him. guards. He then sat down to write to the Houses and to Fairfax, imploring them that either the King might be removed from the island, or he himself be discharged from the thankless office of guarding such a prisoner. Hammond at least had no doubt that Charles's rejection of the Four Bills was tantamount to a declaration in favour of the Scots, and that it would now be his duty to become, in a real sense, the gaoler of the King. On the
Dec. 29. Dismissal of Ashburnham, Berkeley, and Legge. following morning he ordered Ashburnham, Berkeley, and Legge to leave the castle. Charles, as he well knew how, assumed a tone of injured innocence, and told Hammond that his action was unworthy of a gentleman or a Christian.[1]

As soon as it was known in Newport that Charles was practically a captive, a certain Captain Burley beat a drum to
Burley attempts to rescue the King. summon the islanders to follow him to the rescue of the King. A crowd of women and boys gathered round him, but he was secured without difficulty by the Mayor, as scarcely a man had joined him, and his means of resistance was limited to a single musket in the hands of one of his followers.[2]

Charles was now, in a sense in which he had never been before, a prisoner. He was treated with respect, and a staff
Charles a prisoner. of attendants was appointed by the Houses to wait upon him, but his rides about the island with all their possibilities of escape were at an end.[3] It can hardly

places the attempt about six days before the arrival of the commissioners with the bills. This date, however, is improbable, in the first place because Charles, in writing to the Scottish commissioners on the 14th, says that the ship would not arrive for ten days (see p. 37, note 4), and in the second place, because he is not likely to have wanted to fly before the Engagement had been signed. I have therefore accepted Berkeley's date of the 28th.

[1] Berkeley's *Memoirs*, p. 91 ; Hammond to Manchester, *L.J.* ix. 620.

[2] *A Design by Capt. Burley*, E. 421, 24.

[3] "The castle," according to a newswriter, was "not much differing from an old bishop's house : three or four great rooms for hospitality, the

be doubted that Hammond was acting in accordance with

Hammond
probably
acting under
instructions.
instructions from Fairfax,[1] probably confirmed by
the Parliamentary commissioners before their departure.   On the 30th Fairfax despatched three

Dec. 30.
Fairfax
supports
Hammond.
officers to the island to strengthen Hammond in
his resolution.   On the 31st both Houses, reject-

Dec. 31.
Charles to
be secured.
ing Hammond's request to be relieved from his
burden, resolved that the King should be detained

1648.
Jan. 1.
Rains-
borough to
command in
the Solent.
in custody at Carisbrooke, whilst on January 1 the
Commons, no longer heeding the opposition of
the Lords, instructed Rainsborough to take command of the ships which guarded the Solent.[2]

Lords and Commons were, however, now divided on a far
more important question than that of Rainsborough's appoint-

Jan. 3.
Proposal
that no more
addresses
shall be
made to the
King.
ment to a command at sea.   On January 3, when
the King's answer to the Four Bills was taken into
consideration by the Commons, Sir Thomas Wroth
moved that Charles should be impeached and the
kingdom settled without him.   This proposal, it
is said, probably with truth, was warmly supported by Cromwell and Ireton.[3]   If Clarendon is to be trusted, Cromwell

---

rest receptacles for soldiers and sea-gulls."   *The Moderate Intelligencer,*
E. 419, 18.

[1] "Now, blessed be God," wrote Cromwell to Hammond, "I can
write and thou receive freely.   I never in my life saw more deep sense
and less will to show it unchristianly than in that which thou didst write
to us when we were at Windsor, and thou in the midst of thy temptations
—which indeed, by what we understand of it, was a great one and
occasioned the greater by the letter the General sent thee, of which thou
wast not mistaken when thou didst challenge me to be the penner."
Cromwell to Hammond, Jan. 3, *Carlyle*, Letter lii.   If the letter here
referred to had been preserved we should be in a better position to understand Hammond's relations with his superior officers.   The most likely
explanation is that Fairfax in the letter penned by Cromwell instructed
Hammond to watch Charles's intercourses with the Scottish commissioners.
Hammond may have disliked being employed as a spy, and in this way
his temptation to connive at Charles's escape would be increased.

[2] *L.J.* ix. 620 ; *C.J.* v. 413.   See p. 44.

[3] Walker's *Hist. of Independency*, 74.   An impeachment did not
necessarily imply a design to put Charles to death.   Probably what

gave as a reason for refusing his confidence to Charles that, 'whilst he professed with all solemnity that he referred himself wholly to the Parliament and depended wholly on their wisdom and counsel for the composing of the distractions of the kingdom, he had at the same time secret treaties with the Scots' commissioners how he might embroil the nation in a new war and destroy the Parliament.'[1]

The outcome of the debate was a proposal for a Vote of No Addresses, such as Rainsborough had proposed in the Council of the Army two months before.[2] No further addresses were to be made to Charles, and those who ventured to make them without leave from Parliament were to incur the penalties of high treason. The Houses also declared that they would receive no more messages from Charles. This proposal was carried by 141 to 91,[3] showing that the House was again full, and that many Presbyterians concurred with the Independents in thinking it impossible to come to terms with Charles now that he was bargaining with the Scots. Nothing, however, was done towards impeaching the King or deposing him, and there can be no doubt that if either measure had been proposed the majority which supported the vote of No Addresses would have fallen hopelessly to pieces.

If the Independent leaders were compelled to postpone to a more convenient season the difficult problem of finding a substitute for the King,[4] they had no hesitation in putting a

The vote of No Addresses.

Cromwell at this time wanted was that a formal charge should be brought against Charles, with a view to his deposition, and perhaps a sentence of imprisonment either for life or as long as there remained danger to the state from his intrigues with the Scots or others.

[1] *Clarendon*, x. 146. In this part of his history Clarendon writes from hearsay, many years after the events he records. Here, however, the words attributed to Cromwell are just what would be expected from him.

[2] See p. 9.   [3] *C.J.* v. 415.

[4] According to the French ambassador they thought it more prudent to accustom the people to a practical experience of a government without a king before they gave it the name of a republic ; but this may have been merely the guess of a looker-on. Grignon to Brienne, Jan. $\frac{10}{20}$, *R.O. Transcripts.*

summary end to the existing connection of the Scottish commissioners with the government of England.   Without a dissentient voice the House of Commons declared for
the dissolution of the Committee of Both Kingdoms,
and placed the supervision of public affairs in the
hands of the English members of the late committee,
who from thenceforward were known from the place in which
they met as the Committee of Derby House.   A
further vote added to their numbers three decided
Independents in the place of three Presbyterians
who were either dead or disqualified.   Another committee
was also named to draw up a declaration in justification of the
Vote of No Addresses, and it was significant of the temper
aroused in a House of which the majority was almost certainly Presbyterian that the first name on the list was that of
Henry Marten.[1]

The Committee of Both Kingdoms dissolved.

The Committee of Derby House.

Though the House of Lords had been, since the recent
impeachments, in the hands of an Independent majority, its
members, as a body, showed little inclination even
to consider the Vote of No Addresses,[2] knowing
full well that those who were most eager to abolish monarchy
were no less eager to abolish the House of Lords.   On January
11 the Council of the Army came to the help of the
Commons with a declaration, drawn up at Windsor
two days before, in favour of their policy,[3] whilst
some of the Independents talked of reviving the old
scheme of amalgamating the two Houses.[4]   These threats so
far prevailed that on the 13th the Lords went into
committee upon the Vote sent up to them by the
Commons.   The opposition was led by Northumber-
land on the ground that it was unwise to destroy one form of
government before another had been created to take its place.

Hesitation of the Lords.

Jan. 11.
The army comes to the help of the Commons.

Jan. 13.
Opposition in the Lords.

---

[1] *C.J.* v. 416.   [2] *L.J.* ix. 643, 660.

[3] *Rushw.* vii. 962 ; *C.J.* v. 426.

[4] "We are very confident," wrote a furnisher of intelligence, "that
the Lords shall be compelled to come and sit in the House of Commons,
whether they consent to the vote of the House against the King or not."
Letter of Intelligence, Jan. 13, *Clar. St. P.* ii. App. xliv.

On the 14th a special committee was named to prepare a resolution on which a vote might be taken, but it was under-

Jan. 14.
A hostile
committee.

stood that the result would not be such as to give satisfaction to the Commons.[1] Unless the army intervened, the Vote of No Addresses would go forth as the resolution of a single House.

A pretext for military intervention was easily found. Money was needed for paying off the supernumeraries of the

Disturbance
in the City.

army,[2] and an attempt to levy a tax for the purpose met with resistance in the City. A soldier was beaten by the mob, and the sheriffs, when they attempted to allay the disorder, were driven off the ground with shouts 'for

Soldiers to
come to
Whitehall.

the King and no plunder.' On this the Commons asked Fairfax to send 2,000 men to occupy White-hall and the Mews for the protection of Parliament.[3]

Before this hint the opposition in the Lords melted away. The three Peers whose dislike of the Vote was strongest,

Jan. 15.
The opposi-
tion in the
Lords melts
away.

Stamford, North, and Robartes, absented themselves from the House, and the Vote of No Addresses was allowed to pass, with a preamble grounding the refusal to continue negotiations with the King on

The vote of
No Ad-
dresses
accepted by
the Lords.

his rejection of the Four Bills, and on the necessity of using the 'utmost endeavours speedily to settle the present government.'[4] On the 17th the pre-

Jan. 17.

amble, having been accepted by the Commons, was issued together with the Vote itself as the resolution of both Houses. An address, which had been hitherto kept back was then presented to the Lords in the name of the army, assuring them of the intention of the soldiers to support the peerage in its just rights and in the prosecution of the common cause.[5] On the following day, in spite of this conciliatory

---

[1] Grignon to Brienne, Jan. $\frac{17}{27}$, *R.O. Transcripts*.

[2] See p. 45.

[3] Letter of Intelligence, Jan. 13, *Clarendon MSS.* 2,703; *C.J.* v. 432.

[4] *L.J.* ix. 662; *Rushw.* vii. 967; Grignon to Brienne, Jan. $\frac{17}{27}$, *R.O. Transcripts.*

[5] *L.J.* ix. 664.

language, Barkstead's regiment of foot took up its quarters at
Whitehall, and Rich's regiment of horse at the Mews.[1]
The permanent presence of soldiers at Westminster
made the power of the army more directly felt in
London than it had ever been before.

Jan. 18.
Regiments
at Whitehall
and the
Mews.

It had been easy, by barely concealed threats of military
violence, to secure at least the semblance of constitutional
sanction to the breach with the King.   It was far less easy to
provide a substitute for the authority that had been overthrown,
and it is no matter for surprise that the Levellers saw in all
that had taken place a mere attempt to substitute
the rule of King Noll for the rule of King Charles.
Lilburne was now at liberty—the Commons, much to the
annoyance of the Lords, having admitted him to
bail—and, on the 17th, he and Wildman addressed a
meeting of Levellers held in East Smithfield, in a
strain of unmeasured violence against the House of Lords.

"King
Noll."

The Level-
lers in East
Smithfield.

On the 19th the Commons, satisfied with their
victory over the other House, ordered both the
speakers to be committed for trial on a charge of
sedition.   Lilburne, indeed, after his usual fashion,
questioned the validity of this order ; but on the
20th his arrest was effected, and a sacrifice was thus
made to the unreal union between the Houses.[2]

Jan. 19.
Order for the
committal of
Lilburne and
Wildman.

Jan. 20.
Lilburne
arrested.

Whatever might be the ultimate determination of the
Houses and the army on the constitutional question, the
Commons at least proceeded as if their resolution
had settled everything against the King.   On
January 22, Captain Burley[3] was brought to trial at
Winchester as a traitor, his alleged treason consisting simply
of his foolish attempt to deliver Charles from imprisonment.
Burley having been condemned to death on the verdict of a

Jan. 22.
Captain
Burley tried.

---

[1] *The Kingdom's Weekly Intelligencer*, E. 423, 7 ; *Heads of the State
Passages*, E. 423, 11.

[2] *Rushw.* vii. 969, 970 ; *Truth's Triumph*, E. 520, 33 ; *The Triumph
stained*, E. 426, 18 ; *A Whip for the present House of Lords*, E. 431, 1 ;
C.J. v. 435, 437.

[3] See p. 49.

jury, which the Royalists constantly affirmed to have been packed, suffered a traitor's death for the offence of having attempted to liberate one who, in the eye of the law, was still his sovereign.[1]

At every turn, the dominant party was met by difficulties inevitably arising from its attempt to give a constitutional sanction to courses which were essentially unconstitutional. The Lords having liberated the seven impeached Peers, on the ground that no formal charge was before their House, the Commons, on the 28th and 29th, sent up articles of accusation both against the Peers and against the ten survivors of the eleven members. One of the latter, Sir John Maynard, who had remained in England, being brought, on February 5, to the bar of the House of Lords, refused to kneel, pleading that, as a Commoner, the Lords had no jurisdiction over him. The Lords fined him 500*l.* Six of the Peers they admitted to bail. The seventh, Lord Willoughby of Parham, had escaped beyond sea.[2]

*Jan. 28, 29.
Case of the seven impeached Peers.*

*Feb. 5.
Maynard refuses to kneel.*

Escape of Willoughby of Parham.

In the House of Commons, the Independents preserved their majority with the help of those Presbyterians who had been alienated from the King by his rejection of the Four Bills. To retain their support, the Independent leaders were prepared to assist them in the establishment of their church organisation, provided that nothing was done to imperil their own principle of religious liberty. On January 12, a fresh appeal was made to the counties to establish the Presbyterian system.[3] Though this might conciliate some English Presbyterians, it could not possibly conciliate the

Independents and Presbyterians in the House of Commons.

*Jan. 12.
The Presbyterian organisation to be completed.*

---

[1] *Relation of the proceedings against Captain Burley,* E. 1,182, 9. For comments on the jury see an account reprinted from a newspaper of the time in Hillier's *Narrative of the Attempted Escapes of Charles I.* 66. Mr. Hillier ascribed some weight to this curious statement with a confidence which will hardly be shared by those who are acquainted with the inventive tendencies of the Royalist pamphleteers.

[2] *L.J.* ix. 667 ; x. 9, 23, 33.

[3] *Ibid.* ix. 657.

Scots, and on January 2, the Scottish commissioners left London for Edinburgh, having lingered for a time to complete their arrangements for a rising in England in coincidence with a Scottish invasion.[1] Though the details of their plan were unknown to the English Parliament, their general intentions were no longer a secret, and the Houses resolved to send commissioners of their own to Edinburgh to urge the new Parliament, then about to meet, in favour of the English alliance, and to stir up opposition to the Royalist party in Scotland. To hold out a bait to the Scottish leaders, the English commissioners were, on January 29, instructed to offer the payment of an instalment of 100,000*l.* due on February 3 in accordance with the agreement made when the King was surrendered at Newcastle.[2]

Jan. 24.
The Scots
commissioners leave
London.

English
commissioners
to be sent.

Jan. 29.
Instructions
to them.

Already another step had been taken to conciliate the English Presbyterians. On January 26 the Commons resolved to take into consideration a Confession of Faith which had been presented to Parliament by the Assembly of Divines, and further directed that all members of their House who had neglected to take the Covenant should at once make good their omission.[3]

Jan. 26.
The Confession of Faith.

Even an understanding between the Independents and the Presbyterians would not in itself be sufficient to ward off the expected invasion from Scotland or to effect a settlement of the constitutional question; and there are good reasons for believing that Cromwell and St. John, in their eagerness to avert war, made an attempt in the second half of January to open negotiations with the Queen and the Prince of Wales, hoping to induce the latter to take his father's place upon the throne.[4] Whether the King was at

Cromwell
attempts to
substitute
the Prince of
Wales for his
father.

---

[1] Grignon to Brienne, $\frac{\text{Jan. 24}}{\text{Feb. 3}}$, *R.O. Transcripts.*

[2] *L.J.* x. 7. [3] *C.J.* v. 443.

[4] The most direct statement bearing on this affair is that of the Roman correspondent in England. "Si consulta in secreto," he writes, "come si principierà il processo contra il Rè . . . Il processo si farà sopra il morte di suo padre . . . si fingerà di voler dare il corona al Principe, ma si pensa di far Republica." Newsletter, Jan. $\frac{7}{17}$, *Roman Transcripts,*

this time asked to abdicate,[1] or whether the question was reserved till a favourable answer had been received from beyond the sea, it is impossible to say.

In attempting to secure the succession to the Prince of Wales, Cromwell, whose capacity for seeing into the heart of a situation rarely failed him, showed himself alive to the advantage of accompanying a change in the system of government with the least possible shock to the political habits of the nation. His mistake was that he calculated upon others being as placable as he was himself. Not only did his new policy reawaken the serpents of suspicion which were always coiling round the heart of Marten,

Cromwell's policy in the matter.

R.O. The omitted words were thrown in as a blind. I take it that the plans here ascribed to the King's enemies impersonally are a jumble of the intentions of different persons ; but there may have been some who thought of first dethroning Charles—I do not believe that his death was at this time in question—and of then offering the crown to his son. The statement that a communication with the Prince was intended is corroborated by Grignon, who mentions the existence of a design to send Denbigh to France to fetch him, adding that Denbigh hesitated to go, doubting whether he would be well received. This was written on January 31 (*R.O. Transcripts*). On February 1, one of Lanark's correspondents writes (*Hamilton Papers*, 150) that 'the Earl of Denbigh is to go over with some overtures to her Majesty and the Prince.' On February 15, another correspondent (*Hamilton Papers, Addenda in Camden Miscellany*, vol. ix.) says that the Earl of Denbigh's going is a fable, but this may merely mean that the plan had by that time been dropped.

[1] On the question whether there was simultaneously a negotiation with the King, there are several allusions to the existence of some negotiation or another, though nothing definite is said as to its object. "The solicitor," we are told—*i.e.* St. John—"hath made Cromwell his bedfellow, and the army is like them. The treason seems to be awakened and prosecuted against the Lords and Commons by them with all art and violence. . . . Sir H. Vane, Junior, is returned to the Commons House, yet seems unsatisfied, notwithstanding that Cromwell hath bestowed two nights' oratory upon him. Some talk confidently of fresh trinketings with the King, and that Ashburnham is come to London on purpose." (——? to Lanark, Feb. 1, *Hamilton Papers*, 148.) Another writer says on the same day (*id.* 149) that "it is said Parliament intends new addresses to his Majesty, which I believe, because Mr. Ashburnham is in England and will leave no stone unturned to effect any restitution by this army."

but it roused dark thoughts in the heart of him whom he loved
to style his brother, the younger Vane.[1] As to the Prince,

Suspicions of
Marten and
Vane. the suggested understanding with him was hopeless
from the first. He had no mind to set himself
in opposition to his father; still less to submit to
occupy that dependent seat which Cromwell and his friends
styled a throne.

That Cromwell would at this time have been glad, not on
sentimental but on practical grounds, to re-establish the mon-

Cromwell
hopes for a
general re-
conciliation. archy in some form or other is rendered the more
probable if, as is almost certainly the case, a scene,
of which Ludlow has left an account, is to be referred
to the latter part of January in this year.[2] Cromwell, we are
told, invited to dinner the leading members of both parties,
hoping to effect a reconciliation between them. This was fol-

A conference
on govern-
ment. lowed by a conference between 'the grandees of the
House and army'—the name by which important
personages were beginning to be known—on the one
side, and the Republicans or 'Commonwealth's men' on the
other. Amongst these latter was Edmund Ludlow, now a
member of Parliament, to whose surprise and disgust Cromwell and his friends 'kept themselves in the clouds, and would
not declare their judgments either for a monarchical, aristo-
cratical, or democratical government, maintaining that any of
them might be good in themselves, or for us, according as
Providence should direct us.' The Commonwealth-men, on
the contrary, argued at length against monarchy, urging that
as the King had broken his oath to govern according to law, his

---

[1] Besides what has been quoted in the last note, there is evidence of
the continuance of these suspicions well into February. On Feb. 13, a
correspondent writes to Hyde (*Clarendon MSS.* 2,723) that the prevailing party are in great fears and suspicions 'insomuch as Sir H. Vane,
junior, hath left them.' In another letter written to Lanark on Feb. 22
(*Hamilton Papers,* 154), we are told that Cromwell desired a meeting
with Marten that he might be reconciled with him, but that they parted
'much more enemies than they met.'

[2] Ludlow's *Memoirs,* i. 184. The place of this story in the *Memoirs*
would put it somewhat later, but the date seems fixed by the reference to
Cromwell's attempts to reconcile Presbyterians and Independents.

subjects were absolved from their allegiance, and that it was the duty of the representatives of the people to call him to account for the blood shed in consequence of his appeal to the sword.

The old dispute between the men of theory and the men of practice had thus risen to the surface afresh, and Cromwell,

Cromwell throws a cushion at Ludlow's head.

impatient of the letting out of the waters of strife, brought the discussion to a sudden end by flinging a cushion at Ludlow's head and running off downstairs. "But," adds Ludlow triumphantly, "I overtook him with another which made him hasten down faster than he desired."

On the following day Cromwell put his objections to Ludlow's republicanism into articulate language. He was

Cromwell's reply to Ludlow.

convinced, he said, 'of the desirableness of what was proposed, but not of the feasibleness of it.'

Intelligible as this view of the case is at the present day, those to whom it was addressed could find no other explanation than the simple one of Cromwell's ingrained hypocrisy; yet if a republic was not feasible, the Republicans were so far in the right that an understanding with Charles

Feb. 1. He is convinced that Charles will not abdicate.

was still less feasible; and by the end of January or the beginning of February, Cromwell was convinced—this time too, according to one account, by an intercepted letter from the King to the Queen—that Charles, far from thinking of abdication, was planning

Feb. 2. The King's household reduced.

fresh attacks on his opponents.[1] Cromwell and his supporters having at last made up their minds, struck hard and sharp. On February 2 Hammond was

The committee for the Declaration.

directed to dismiss all of Charles's attendants except thirty,[2] and on the same day the committee appointed to prepare a declaration in defence of the Vote of No Addresses set itself seriously to perform its work.[3]

---

[1] "Hanno ancora sopra il medesimo soggetto intercetto delle lettere che S. M. scriveva alla Regina sua moglie." *Newsletter*, Feb. $\frac{4}{14}$, *Roman Transcripts, R.O.*   [2] *C.J.* v. 452.

[3] *Newsletter*, Feb. $\frac{4}{14}$, *Roman Transcripts, R.O.* The writer speaks of this as beginning the process of the King. I take this to mean what I have stated in the text.

On February 4 the temper now prevailing in the House of Commons received an unexpected illustration. Having under

Feb. 4.
A significant
amendment. consideration a clause of the Confession of Faith, which declared that 'infidelity or difference in religion' ought 'not to make void the magistrate's just and legal authority, nor free the people from their just obedience to him,' the House resolved, by a significant amendment, that the phrase should run so as to declare that these defects ought 'not to make void the magistrates' just and legal authority, nor free the people from their just obedience to them;'[1] thus transferring the right to demand the subjects' obedience from the one magistrate who had hitherto borne the name of King to the many who, under the new form of government which was contemplated, were to take his place.

Feb. 5.
Strickland's
mission to
the Nether-
lands. On the 5th Strickland was despatched to the Netherlands to urge the States General to refuse aid to the Prince of Wales[2] and to prevent the Queen from pawning her jewels in the territory of the Republic.[3] By this time it was believed in England that the four English regiments in the Dutch service had placed themselves at the disposal of the Prince of Wales, that the English refugees in France would find 4,000 men to add to their numbers, and that the whole force would be transported to Scotland in Dutch vessels.[3]

From the 5th to the 11th the Declaration upholding the Vote of No Addresses, which was said to have been drawn up by

Feb. 5-11.
The Decla-
ration in
the House. Nathaniel Fiennes,[4] was considered in the House, where it was supported by Cromwell with all the energy at his command. Like the Grand Remon-

Character of
the Declara-
tion. strance it entered into a review of the King's past actions since he came to the crown, in order to maintain that no confidence could be placed in him. Un-

---

[1] *C.J.* v. 456. In neither case is the mark of the genitive case put to the word 'Magistrates.' I have added it in conformity with modern usage.

[2] *Ibid.* v. 457; Grignon to Brienne, Feb. $\frac{7}{17}$, *R.O. Transcripts.*

[3] Newsletter, Feb. $\frac{11}{21}$, *Roman Transcripts, R.O.*

[4] *Merc. Elencticus,* E. 476, 4.

fortunately even the scandal about Buckingham's administering physic to James was raked up in order to charge Charles with indifference to the supposed murder of his father. The old stories of the ships lent for service against Rochelle, of the intention to introduce German horse, of the new liturgy for Scotland, and of the commission supposed to have been granted by the King to the Ulster rebels played their part once more. That which told most against Charles, and which his warmest admirers had most difficulty in meeting, was the narrative gathered from intercepted despatches, and amply confirmed in later times, of his constant attempts to introduce into England troops from beyond the sea. There were, for instance, the tales of the money, arms, and ships demanded from Denmark in 1642, of the applications for foreign troops which had been revealed when the King's cabinet was taken at Naseby and when Digby's cabinet was taken at Sherburn, and of the Glamorgan treaty for bringing in an Irish army. Charles had endeavoured to enslave the kingdom by German, Spanish, French, Lorraine, Irish, Danish, and other foreign forces. In spite of this, Parliament had made a final application to him, but this he had rejected. Consequently the Houses would now use their 'utmost endeavours to settle the present government as may best stand with the peace and happiness of this kingdom.'[1]

On February 11 the Declaration passed by 80 votes to 50. Cromwell, in the course of the debates, had 'made a severe invective against monarchical government.'[2] He had even gone so far as to ask that Selden should be expelled from the House merely because he moved for the omission of the charge about James, on the ground that he had himself been a member of the committee which had examined into the alleged poisoning of James I. by Buckingham, and that nothing had been found reflecting upon the King.[3] Cromwell, it seems, was in that fierce temper

Feb. 11.
The Declaration to be printed.

---

[1] *A Declaration of the Commons of England*, E. 427, 9.
[2] Dr. A. Fraser to Lanark, Feb. 15, *Hamilton Papers, Addenda.*
[3] Letter of Intelligence, Feb. 17, *Clarendon MSS.* 2,723. Nicholas,

which with him always denoted the conclusion of a long
mental conflict. He had chosen his part, and with rude
and unscrupulous thoroughness would sweep aside all who
attempted to bar his way.

however, thought Selden too much 'restrained by fear' (*Clar. St. P.* ii.
393) to state his knowledge of the facts. It is more likely that Nicholas
should have been misinformed than that the account of Selden's speech
given in the text is false.

CHAPTER LIX.

A ROYALIST REACTION.

CHARLES'S persistent refusal to lower his flag would doubtless stand his Cavalier followers in good stead in the future. In the immediate present it exposed them to a persecution from which he might easily have saved them. On none did his rejection of *The Heads of the Proposals* fall more heavily than on his partisans at Oxford. After the attempt made by the Presbyterians in June 1647 to reform the University had been laughed off the stage,[1] week after week was allowed to pass away, without any attempt to uphold the insulted dignity of Parliament against the authorities at Oxford. It was not till August 26, the day on which the Newcastle Propositions were revived at Westminster,[2] that an additional Ordinance was passed, giving to the Visitors the requisite powers to administer the Covenant and the Negative Oath, to send for books and papers, to imprison those who resisted, and to require the magistrates to assist them in carrying out their orders.

*1647.
June.
Results of
Charles's
rejection of a
compromise.*

*Aug. 26.
An additional
Ordinance.*

If Parliament had made even a show of taking measures for the immediate enforcement of this Ordinance, it might reasonably be inferred that its previous slackness had been owing to its time being occupied by its struggle with the army. As, however, fresh delays ensued and the Ordinance was not despatched to Oxford for nearly a month, it is necessary to look for an explanation elsewhere;

*Further
delay.*

[1] See iii. 314.   [2] See iii. 355.

and it is difficult to avoid noticing that it was precisely during the month between the issue of the Ordinance and its trans-

Sept. 24.
The Ordinance sent to Oxford.

mission to Oxford that Cromwell and the Independents were making fresh efforts to come to terms with the King, and that on September 23, the very day before that on which the Ordinance was at last sent off, the House of Commons, in ordering a final application to be made to him, did so without any hope that it would prove successful.[1]

However this may have been, on September 29 the Visitors, having received their new powers, ordered the Heads of

Sept. 29.
A fresh attempt to visit.

Houses to bring in their books, and the Vice-Chancellor to appear before them. Neither did the Heads of Houses produce their books nor did the Vice-Chancellor answer to the summons. On October 8

Oct. 8.
Protest of the Proctors.

the Proctors protested that the Visitation was illegal, on the ground that the King was the sole lawful Visitor of the University. On the 11th the Visitors,

Oct. 11.
The Vice-Chancellor deprived.

overruling this objection, deprived Fell of his Vice-Chancellorship. Resistance, however, did not slacken and it was seen that the only way in which obedience could be obtained lay in the appointment of a Puritan Vice-Chancellor, who by gathering into his hands the threads of authority within the University organisation would save the necessity of coercing it from without.

The first step towards the attainment of this object was to meet the legal objections raised against Fell's deprivation.

Nov. 15.
The University before the committee at Westminster.

On November 15, Fell and his principal supporters attended at Westminster before the Committee of the two Houses entrusted with the supervision of the Visitors. Pembroke, as his manner was in dealing with the weak, overwhelmed them with intemperate abuse, but the majority of the committee, being

Dec. 9.
Sentence of contempt.

less unscrupulous, allowed counsel to the defendants and time to prepare their case. The sentence of the committee was, however, a foregone conclusion, and on December 9 those who had resisted the Visitors

[1] See iii. 368.

were pronounced guilty of contempt in defying the authority of Parliament.

In their struggle against overwhelming power, the University authorities had the support not only of Selden, by whose advice they were guided in the conduct of their case, but also of Vane and Fiennes. "We find," wrote Fell, "the Independents generally favourable to us, and conceive it hard to press us against our consciences." Whether owing to the opposition of the Independents or not, there was again delay, and it was only on December 28 that the sentence of deprivation from the offices of Vice-Chancellor and Dean of Christchurch was pronounced by the committee against Fell. Other deprivations followed in due course. It might have been expected that Pembroke, in his capacity of Chancellor of the University, would have at once proceeded to impose on it a new Vice-Chancellor. Yet, though the authority of the committee was daily set at naught at Oxford, more than seven weeks were allowed to pass away before any such step was taken.

The Independents support the defendants.

Dec. 28. Fell removed from his offices.

Delay in making a new appointment.

Possibly the explanation is in part, at least, to be sought in Pembroke's character. As timid as he was blustering, he may well have been anxious in the midst of the struggle over the Vote of No Addresses to know to which party victory was about to fall. When at last the Independents got the upper hand, they can hardly have been eager, at a time when they were scheming for the succession of the Prince of Wales, to close the door to University preferment in the faces of his supporters. It was not till a week after the Declaration in support of the Vote of No Addresses had cut the last bonds between Parliament and the Royal House that, on February 18, at Pembroke's recommendation, Reynolds was appointed by Ordinance of Parliament to the Vice-Chancellorship and the Deanery of Christchurch.[1]

Probable causes of the delay.

1648. Feb. 18. Reynolds to be Vice-Chancellor.

[1] *L.J.* x. 62, 63. As in the earlier stages of this affair (see vol. iii. 313), I have followed Professor Burrows in his marshalling of the facts brought

It has sometimes been thought, though no evidence exists on the point, that Cromwell had a hand in the selection of
Cromwell and Reynolds.
Reynolds. In any case it is certain that Reynolds was not only a man after Cromwell's own heart, but that his appointment was the outcome of that policy of conciliating the Presbyterians which now occupied the foreground in Cromwell's mind. A persuasive preacher, who in
Character of Reynolds.
an age of controversy made it his rule, so far as it was possible, to keep silence on controversial points, Reynolds was marked out by his piety and integrity for a post in which it was so easy to make enemies and so very hard to conciliate opponents. If there was to be a change in the government of the University—and it is difficult to see how such a change could be avoided—Reynolds was the man to conduct it with the least possible amount of friction.

Under the most favourable circumstances, however, the friction would be enormous. On March 17 the Visitors at
March 17. The Visitation proceeds.
last commenced their proper work, from which time it went on without open resistance. The opponents of Puritanism were swept away and replaced by others more friendly to the ruling powers. One after another, Heads of Houses, Fellows of colleges, and even undergraduates, were called up to answer the crucial question, " Do you submit to the authority of Parliament in this Visitation?" One by one they answered; some absolutely submitting, some attempting by evasive answers to avoid the alternative between material ruin and betrayal of conscience, and others, again, boldly facing consequences and refusing to submit. Only by absolute submission could expulsion be avoided, with all its accompaniments of loss of standing in the world and depriva-
The expulsions.
tion of the means of livelihood. Amongst those expelled were a few men of high intellectual renown, such as Sanderson and Hammond, but the greater number were undistinguished in any way, except by the constancy with which they went forth into the wilderness without hope for the future rather than soil their consciences with a lie.

out in the original evidence. The suggestion of the causes of the delay is, however, mine.

It was the irony of political necessity that this great act of persecution should be carried out when men like Cromwell and Vane were in the ascendant. It was but a bare six months since the Independent leaders who now permitted some hundreds of sufferers to be excluded for conscience' sake from the University of Oxford, had been striving to lay the foundations of a broad system of toleration in *The Heads of the Proposals*, and had even taken into favourable consideration a scheme for extending that toleration to the Roman Catholic priesthood itself. In January they had made use of their authority in Parliament to liberate a Jesuit who had been for three years in prison, and to commute the sentence of death which had been pronounced upon a priest into one of banishment.[1] Like the successor of the Samian despot who was prevented by the rancour of the citizens from laying down the authority which he had received, and 'wishing to be the justest of men failed in his purpose,'[2] the Independent leaders were driven back from accomplishing their schemes of toleration by the intolerance alike of their opponents and of their supporters. The stern fact that English opinion was hopelessly divided, and that no sanguine kindliness could bring those to live together in peace who had war burning in their hearts, would, in one way or another, force itself on the eyes even of the most blind.

(margin: Were they avoidable?)

That which baffled the Independents was the close connection between politics and religion. Those who reverenced the principles and worship of the English Church, also reverenced the authority of the King as the basis of constitutional right. Neither they nor Charles himself would yield on either point. The Visitors at Oxford in vain sought to shelve the difficulty by asking, not for definite confession of religious faith, but for a general acknowledgment of the authority of Parliament. They could not separate things, at that time at least, inseparable. It was impossible to accept either King or Parliament as the final authority in political matters without taking into account the

(margin: Politics and religion.)

---

[1] Newsletter, Jan. $\frac{14}{24}$, *Roman Transcripts, R.O.*

[2] *Herodotus,* iii. 142.

ecclesiastical or religious results which in either case might be
expected to follow. At Westminster as well as at Oxford those
who had striven to restore harmony between the King and his
people found their efforts breaking down. The Royalists had
at least the letter of the law on their side. On February 14

Feb. 14.
Judge
Jenkins in
Chancery,
denounces
the legality
of the
courts.
the Welsh judge, David Jenkins, who had already
suffered imprisonment for his advocacy of the King's
rights, having been summoned before the Court of
Chancery in a private suit, gave a signal of resistance
by denouncing the whole basis of Parliamentary Or
dinances upon which all the courts of law now rested.

Nothing, he declared, had any legality which did
not rest upon the authority of the King. On the
21st, being brought to the bar of the House of
Commons, he refused to kneel, and openly defied the House.
The Commons in anger passed rapidly a Bill of Attainder
against him, and sent it to the Lords for their approval;[1]
but it was impossible to ignore the fact that the indomitable
Welshman had only spoken in public what thousands were
muttering in secret.

The opposition of those who resisted the Parliament and
the army on principle was reinforced by the opposition of
those who resisted them because their own interests or
pleasures were interfered with. What the prohibition of
Christmas games was to the apprentices and the
farm labourers, the closing of the theatres was to
the leisured class amongst the dwellers in London. The
original Ordinance against stage plays had been issued at the
beginning of the war, and had been grounded on the unsuit-
ableness of such frivolous entertainments in a time of distress.[2]
When the war came to an end this motive could no longer be
urged, and plays were again performed though with more or
1647.
July 17.
Order of the
Houses
against
them.
less secrecy. The antagonism of the Puritan spirit
to entertainments too often provocative to vice was
however, as decided as before, and on July 17, 1647,
the Houses revived the Ordinance of 1642, fixing
January 1, 1648, as the date of its expiration.[3]

[1] *C.J.* v. 469.   [2] See vol. i. 14.   [3] *L.J.* ix. 334; *C.J.* v. 248.

Either intentionally or, as is more probable, from sheer negligence, no measures were taken to prolong the Ordinance before the time of its expiration came round, and in January 1648 the theatres, at once taking advantage of the omission, were crowded with spectators. On January 27 it was reckoned that no less than 120 coaches set down spectators at one theatre alone—the Fortune.[1] On February 11 Parliament responded by a savage Ordinance conceived in the very spirit of Prynne, directing that 'all stage-galleries, seats, and boxes' should be destroyed, every actor publicly flogged, and compelled to enter into recognisances 'never to act or play any plays or interludes any more' on pain of being dealt with 'as an incorrigible rogue.' Moreover, all spectators of a play were to be fined five shillings.[2]

Jan.
Theatres opened.

Feb. 11.
Ordinance against stage plays.

To the anger of the pleasure-seekers was added the anger of those who were ready to accept any government provided only that it would give proof of stability, and it was this proof that neither Presbyterians nor Independents were able to give. "Some," wrote a member of the House of Commons, "pray for the Scots; others against them; but whether they come or no, we are in a ready way to be undone; for, without the infinite mercy of God, we shall inevitably run into absolute confusion. The whole kingdom is so full of discontent that I do verily fear it will ere long break out into some disorder."[3]

Call for a stable government.

General discontent.

Nor was it only the sense of uncertainty inspired by the proceedings of the Houses which caused discontent. The Parliament to which Cromwell had been compelled to appeal as the supreme authority in England had neither a consistent policy nor a character for public spirit. It was sufficiently under duress to have lost all self-respect, whilst some at least

---

[1] *The Kingdom's Weekly Intelligencer*, E. 423, 23. At the Bull was played Beaumont and Fletcher's "Wit without Money." *Perf. Occurrences*, E. 520, 32.

[2] *L.J.* x. 41. Headed with the date of Feb. 9, when it was sent from the Commons.

[3] Sir R. Burgoyne to Sir R. Verney, Dec. 30, 1647, *Verney MSS.*

of its members made use of their high position to advance
their private interests.   The Royalists took pleasure in drawing

Charges of corruption. up lists of members of either House who had derived pecuniary advantages from the Civil War, and
though some of the cases alleged were those of men who had
been rewarded for services rendered, there can be little doubt
that in many cases the rewards were higher than the services
justified, and that in others opportunity was afforded of driving
hard bargains at the expense of the State.   Many of those,
moreover, who had seats in the House of Commons found a
ready way of enriching themselves by the sale of the influence
which every member of Parliament then possessed.

Once more the correspondence of the Verney family opens
before us the living image, if not of the whole of the passions

1646.
The Verney family again. and strivings of the age, at least of those personal
grievances and annoyances which never fail to in-
fluence its larger issues, but which are apt to pass
unnoticed and unrecorded.   In January 1646, when Sir

Sir R. Ver-
ney proposes
to send his
wife to
plead for
him. Ralph Verney was still anxiously expecting the
sequestration of his estates,[1] he suggested to his
friend Sir Roger Burgoyne, who was himself a
member of Parliament, that though he was inca-
pacitated by his refusal to take the Covenant from pleading his
own cause in England, he might with advantage send his wife
as his representative.   "Certainly," replied Burgoyne, "it
would not do amiss, if she can bring her spirit to a soliciting
temper, and can tell how to use the juice of an onion sometimes to soften their hearts."[2]

It was not, however, till August 1646, that the danger
appeared imminent.   On the 20th, Dr. Denton[3]—who, though

Aug. 20.
A letter of
Dr. Denton. he was Sir Ralph's uncle, yet, being of much the
same age, had been the companion of his childhood
and was now the most self-sacrificing of friends—
warned him that if Lady Verney was to come to England she
must set out without delay.   "Not," he wrote, "to touch

---

[1] See vol. iii. 211.

[2] Sir R. Burgoyne to Sir R. Verney, Jan. 15, 1646, *Verney MSS.*

[3] See vol. iii. 259, note 3.

upon inconveniences of your coming, women were never so useful as now ; and though you should be my agent and

Women never so useful as now.

solicitor of all the men I know—and therefore much to be preferred in your own cause—yet I am confident, if you were here, you would do as our sages do, instruct your wife and leave her to act it with committees. Their sex entitles them to many privileges, and we find the comfort of them more now than ever. I cannot assure you that she can make up all without your presence, nor you, if you

Oct. 14. Claydon sequestered.

were here neither : but, in my opinion, it is the most probable way can be prescribed or taken." [1]

On October 14 the Claydon estate was sequestered by an order from the County Committee of Bucks. [2]

Accordingly Lady Verney hastened the preparations for her journey, and on November 24 she landed at Rye. It

Nov. 24. Lady Verney in England,

would have been difficult to find a more persuasive pleader. Her native sprightliness, which in her youth had gained for her amongst her husband's friends the nickname of 'Mischief,' had been toned down by years of misfortune and ill-health. She was now expecting to give birth to another child, and the first days of exertion after her arrival in London brought on a fever. Dr. Denton

under medical treatment.

tended her with rare assiduity, physicked her according to the best rules of his art, and drained away the remaining strength of her enfeebled constitution by copious bleedings. When at last her health temporarily improved, he was as ready with advice and practical aid as he had been with his prescriptions.

The first step to be taken towards the removal of the sequestration was to obtain from the Bucks Committee a

A certificate from the County Committee needed.

certificate of the reasons for which Sir Ralph had been adjudged a delinquent, and this the committee refused to give without an order from the Committee of Lords and Commons for Sequestrations, to which in such matters the County Committees were subordinated.

---

[1] Dr. Denton to Sir R. Verney, Aug. 20, 1646, *Verney MSS.*
[2] Order of the Committee of Bucks, Oct. 14, *ibid.*

To obtain this order, Lady Verney had been obliged to gain the support of as many influential personages as possible.

Personal
influence. Mr. Pelham, who afterwards took the chair as Speaker during those ill-starred sittings in which the Presbyterians set the army at defiance, gave her what help and counsel he could, whilst Dr. Denton ran hither and thither amongst the members whose good word it was important to gain. Lady Verney's opinion of lawyers was not a high one. " Lawyers," she wrote in one of those

1647.
Lawyers to
be avoided. voluminous letters in which she poured out her sorrows to her husband by the weekly post, " . . . are very dear, and I find very little satisfaction from them ; for 'tis not law now but favour ; but if it be so that our business must be brought into the House of Commons, then indeed it will be necessary to fee most of those lawyers of the House of Commons ; but I should be very unwilling to have it come there, because 'tis very tedious and very difficult to come off from them." [1]

The legal question at issue soon made itself clear. The mere absence of a member of Parliament from his duties,

The question
at issue. even when he had given no assistance to the King, had been declared to be delinquency by an order of the House of Commons, but that order had not been confirmed by the House of Lords. The point to be decided was whether delinquency could be created by anything short of an

Feb. 25.
An order
from the
Committee
of Lords and
Commons. Ordinance of Parliament. On February 25, 1647, the Committee of Lords and Commons took the preliminary step to bring this question to an issue by ordering the Bucks Committee to make a certificate of the causes of Sir Ralph's delinquency.[2]

The Bucks Committee, however, was not likely to act in a hurry, and Lady Verney was, for the time, in no condition to

March 11.
Church
customs in
England. urge its members on. On March 11 the poor lady wrote to her husband about the christening of her expected child. She would, she said, ' get a minister in the house that will do it the old way ; for 'tis not the fashion

[1] Lady Verney to Sir R. Verney, Jan. 14, *Verney MSS.*
[2] *Ibid.* Feb. 25, 1647, *ibid.*

here to have godfathers or godmothers, but for the father to bring the child to church and answer for it.' Puritans as she and Sir Ralph had been counted before the breaking out of the war, she had no liking for the changes which she now witnessed. " My dear heart," she wrote, "to tell thee how barbarous a place this is would take up more room than this paper ; but truly one lives like a heathen in it. Since I have recovered my health, I have gone to our parish church, but could never but one time get any room there for all the money I offered ; and either I must be at the charge to hire a coach to try all the churches, or else sit at home ; and when one gets room one hears a very strange kind of service, and in such a tone that most people do nothing but laugh at it, and everybody that receives [1] must be examined before by the elders, who they all swear asketh them such questions that would make one blush to relate." [2]

In the midst of her troubles Lady Verney pursued not unsuccessfully her task of making friends. Selden, who was a member of the Committee of Sequestrations, assured her of his support, and other members did the same. For Warwick she as yet angled in vain, though in former days when Lady Warwick was the wife of the Earl of Sussex, Sir Ralph had been on terms of the closest friendship with her, had been the recipient of her confidences on the subject of her portrait by Vandyke, who, as she then complained, had ' painted her too lean,' and had matched the materials for her dresses in the London shops.[3] To do Lady Warwick justice, however, her power rather than her will was wanting, as she had little influence over her husband. One day, when Lady Verney visited her, Warwick came into the room, but he ' sat like a clown ' and offered no civility to his wife's friend.

Members of the Committee of Sequestrations gained.

At last, before the end of March, the certificate from the Bucks Committee arrived, acknowledging that Sir Ralph's delinquency consisted in mere absence from the House. Yet

---

[1] *i.e.* the Communion.

[2] Lady Verney to Sir R. Verney, March 11, 1647, *Verney MSS.*

[3] A small piece of blue damask sent for this purpose is still to be seen in one of the lady's letters preserved at Claydon.

on April 1 Lady Verney still wrote despondingly of the business. " I am sure," she says, " it is very troublesome and
April.
Fresh
delays. chargeable, and I fear will prove a great deal more
tedious than we did expect ; we have the certificate ;
I have given it to Sir Gilbert Gerard with your
letter. He hath promised me to do you all the service he
can, and so hath many others ; but I doubt they will do but
little when they come to it. I have also been with Mr.
Pelham, who was very civil, and told me he would be ready
to do me any service ; but they tell me they believe it must be
referred to the House before I can come off clear, which
torments me to think of ; for, if it must come there, it will
cost us a great deal of money by the tediousness and delays
that I know we shall find there ; it costs me now five and six
shillings in a morning in coach hire those times that I have
gone about it, and one may wait two or three hours and speak
with none of them." [1]

At last, on April 16, the Committee of Sequestrations had
Sir Ralph's case before it, only to find that it was forbidden
April 16.
The House
must be
consulted. by an order of March 23 to meddle with cases of
members of Parliament without special order from
the House.[2] Fresh delay was inevitable. " My
dear," wrote Lady Verney, " I will not tell thee what a trouble
'tis to make friends, for, truly, they all expect more waiting
upon than ever the King did, and will give many promises and
perform nothing." [3]

It was no good time to expect attention. By this time the
Houses were involved in the dispute with the army. On
June 2.
Lady
Verney and
her baby. June 2, before anything had been done in her
husband's affair, Lady Verney was delivered of a
son.[4] In those days it was not customary for ladies
to suckle their own children, or even to keep them with them

---

[1] Lady Verney to Sir R. Verney, April 1, *Verney MSS.*
[2] *C.J.* v. 120. Dr. Denton to Sir R. Verney, April 21, *ibid.*
[3] Lady Verney to Sir R. Verney, April 22, *ibid.*
[4] Dr. Denton to Sir R. Verney, June 3, *ibid.* Lady Verney's postscript is : " This is only to let you know that I thank God I have a great
boy, and wish myself and boy with thee. I can say no more now."

after they were a month old. A young married woman at Claydon was therefore provided as a wet nurse,[1] and at the end of a month from his birth the little Ralph—as his mother had named him in spite of her husband's remonstrances—was removed to Claydon. One of his aunts took him in a coach to St. Albans, after which he was put on a horse in front of his nurse's husband, being tied on to the rider with a garter. It is no wonder that the infant did not survive for many months.

When Lady Verney began slowly to recover strength, the struggle between Parliament and army was passing into an acute stage. "I hope," she wrote on June 24, the day on which the army's demand for the suspension of the eleven members reached Westminster,[2] "your friend[3] will not any longer count it a misfortune that he was turned out of the House ; for I assure you now 'tis the greatest honour that can be to any man to be one of the first chosen members turned out by these old ones. You cannot possibly imagine the change without you saw it. They are grown so humble that Frank Drake[4] hath visited me oftener within this fortnight than ever he did since I came over."[5]

June 24.
Political changes.

Week after week passed away and Lady Verney's petition remained unheard. Till Parliament and army had made up their differences, no one in Parliament had time to remedy a private grievance, however urgent. "I wish," wrote Burgoyne sarcastically at the end of August, when the Presbyterian party had been entirely overthrown, "that my friend's petition were put into the hands of some godly man in the House ; and then without doubt it will be accompanied with a blessed success. I wish that either Fiennes, Vane, or some such worthy patriot would undertake it."[6]

Long delays.

[1] A nurse at that time meant a wet nurse ; a nurse in the modern sense was called a nurse-keeper.

[2] See vol. iii. 304.

[3] *i.e.* yourself, 'your friend' being written to conceal the name of Sir Ralph in case of the letter being opened on the way. The letters themselves are always addressed to Mr. Ralph Smith.

[4] Member for Amersham.

[5] Lady Verney to Sir R. Verney, June 24, *Verney MSS.*

[6] Burgoyne to Sir R. Verney, Aug. 30, *ibid.*

It was not till the end of September that Dr. Denton advised Sir Ralph of his purpose to prepare the ground for the presentation of the petition. Whatever means he took to gain interest, he must have recourse to 'the old way of England—money.' Hope seemed almost at an end. "Truly," wrote Lady Verney to her husband on October 3, "as the case now stands, I apprehend your estate to be in so sad a condition that I cannot see any assurance of subsisting two years to an end. For my part I do not understand anything of the law, therefore I leave it to thee in hope thou wilt think of some way or other that we may be sure of something for ourselves and babies ; but, my dear, I do not distrust, for I am confident God hath so great a blessing for us in store that He will not suffer us to starve, and I thank God I can be content to live with very little so I have but thy company." [1]

Sept. 29.
Dr. Denton's advice.

Oct. 3.
Lady Verney almost despairs.

In October Lady Verney returned to town after a long absence in pursuit of health. By that time Parliament had again settled to business, but she had little hope of a favourable answer to her petition. "Now I am here," she wrote on November 11, "I cannot imagine what course to take ; for everybody tells me that there is no hopes of doing anything in the House of Commons but by bribery, and where I shall get money I vow I know not." "As for the petition," wrote Dr. Denton on the same day, "I delivered it yesterday into a good hand, and I have promised him 40*l.*, and he will give me an account very shortly of it." [2] "I can give you," he again wrote to Sir Ralph on November 14, "no further account of your petition than I did in my last, only, if other counsels alter not, I do think to make my way to the Speaker by feeling his sister-in-law my cousin,[3] and

Oct.
Lady Verney returns to town.

Nov. 11.
Prevalence of bribery.

Nov. 14.

----

[1] Lady Verney to Sir R. Verney, Oct. 3, *Verney MSS.*

[2] Lady Verney to Sir R. Verney, Nov. 11 ; Dr. Denton to Sir R. Verney, Nov. 11, *ibid.*

[3] The wife of Sir John Lenthall, the Speaker's brother. For an earlier charge brought against the two Lenthalls, see vol. ii. 332. The

I am told it is the best way I can take. I intend to-morrow to feel her pulse ; I intend to offer her 50*l*. if within such a time she will get the prayer of my petition granted." [1]

Nov. 25.
Lady
Verney
more
hopeful.

Dec. 17.
The
reference
to the
committee.

It was perhaps from confidence in the efficacy of these means that, in writing on the 25th of November, Lady Verney expressed herself more hopefully than she had done as yet. In a few days, she thought, the House would refer her petition to the Committee of Sequestrations. "Then," she added, " I doubt not but we shall quickly despatch it there ; but this will cost us money." There was weary waiting still, but at last, on December 17, the order of reference was obtained. [2]

The next struggle would be in the committee. Lord Say, who was an influential member of it, was Dr. Denton's uncle and was secured beforehand. Lady Verney put forth all her energy to gain Warwick through his wife. Lady Warwick, though always polite, gave but little hope. At last Lady Verney's persistence was requited. " Lady Warwick," she wrote, " hath at last in some measure played her part ; but I put her soundly to it, for I have been four or five times with her this week." On January 5, 1648, the case was before the committee. Warwick had yielded to his wife's persuasions, and not only attended in person but brought others with him, and the decision was given in favour of withdrawing the sequestration.

Lady Verney was thus at last triumphant, happy in having gained her husband's cause, and still more happy in the prospect of speedily returning to him. The doctor's kindness, she declared, had been beyond expression. " Truly," she wrote, " I think he was more concerned than if it had been for himself. I wish we were able to give him 40*l*., for truly he hath deserved it ; but we must give his

Speaker's indirect gains are reckoned by a hostile witness at 20,000*l*. a year.

[1] Dr. Denton to Sir R. Verney, Nov. 14, *Verney MSS.*
[2] Dr. Denton to Sir R. Verney, Dec. 20, *ibid.*

wife something too, and I think we cannot give her less than the value of 5*l.* in some stuff for a petticoat or the like ; for truly she hath been kind so beyond expression, and hath often made dinners for my occasions ; for every Committee day she hath always had the Parliament men there, that they might go along with us to the Committee ; and that all went out of her purse, and besides she is mighty kind to me. Truly this business hath cost me very dear, and I vow I know not which way I shall get up money enough to defray the charge. To-morrow I must make a dinner for them all ; for indeed we are very much obliged to very many ; and I have no other way to return them thanks. We must give Mr. Pelham some piece of plate unto the value of eight or ten pounds ; for he hath done us service unto the very last ; and being our business hath succeeded well, we must present him ; and now, my dear Rogue, I must needs tell thee that the contentment this hath putt into me is beyond expression ; and I trust in God, I shall be with thee at my appointed time." [1]

The corruption and favouritism which prevailed amongst members of Parliament was probably no worse than that which had stained the Court of James or Charles, but their misconduct was more deeply resented. Habit counts for much, and men who had bribed courtiers without a murmur took it amiss when they were asked to pay for the services of a member of the House of Commons. It was monstrous, it was said, that members of Parliament should grow rich whilst other men

Increase of private expenditure. were growing poor. Expenditure in London society was on the increase. "As long as I have lived in London," wrote Lady Verney to her husband in the spring of 1647, "I never in my life saw half that bravery amongst all sorts of people as is now. Truly I think they have a greater vanity for clothes and coaches than I think was ever in the world. There are those that make every week or fortnight a new gown. I am much wondered at for being so much altered in my humour, but to tell thee the truth, without thou wert here, I care not to trick up myself ; and, besides, I

[1] Lady Verney to Sir R. Verney, Jan. 6, *Verney MSS.*

tell them I have no bye-ways to get money, which many of
them have." [1]

Amongst those who were charged with making their fortune
and the fortune of their families was Cromwell himself. In
the army—to omit more distant relatives—Ireton
was his son-in-law, Desborough his brother-in-law,
Whalley his first cousin, and Robert Hammond the
husband of his first cousin once removed.[2] In 1646, Parliament had voted him a gift of lands out of the confiscated
estates of the Marquis of Worcester to the value of 2,500*l.* a
year. The intention of Parliament was, however, only partially
carried out at the time, and on March 7, 1648, an
Ordinance was passed to make good the deficiency,
by adding land valued at 1,680*l.* a year to complete
the contemplated grant.

Of all this Cromwell's opponents made full use, asserting,
though without offering a shadow of proof, that the land which
thus came into Cromwell's possession was in reality much more
valuable than it was alleged to be. They omitted to say that
the officers of his kindred were amongst the most efficient in
the army. Nor did they ever hint that he was at all times
ready to make personal sacrifices on behalf of the nation which
he served. Yet it appears from a list of military salaries
accepted by Parliament on February 19, that Cromwell's pay was then reduced from 4*l.* to 3*l.* a day,[3]
and on March 21 he further offered to give 'for the
service of Ireland' 1,000*l.* a year for five years, and
to abandon the arrears owing to him which at that
time stood at 1,500*l.*[4] These three abatements, taken together,
amounted within 75*l.* to the income which would accrue to

*Charges
against
Cromwell.*

*March 7.
Grant of
lands to him.*

*Feb. 19.
Reduction of
his pay.*

*March 21.
A munificent
offer.*

[1] Lady Verney to Sir R. Verney, May 6, 1647, *Verney MSS.*

[2] The whole of the Cromwell kindred are dealt with in an article by
Mr. Weyman in the *Eng. Hist. Rev.* for January 1891.

[3] *C.J.* v. 460; *L.J.* x. 66. There is no direct evidence of Cromwell's
consent to the abatement; but if it had been against his will he would
hardly have made the free offer a month later. The abatement was not a
general one.

[4] The free offer is printed by Carlyle after Letter liv.

him during the ensuing five years from the lands which had been granted to him a month before.[1]

To the general causes of dissatisfaction with the existing government must be added special causes of dissatisfaction with the Independents. It is true that moderate men often spoke of the Independents strictly so called without acerbity. "The Independents," wrote Dr. Denton, for instance, in answer to enquiry from Sir Ralph Verney as to their tenets, "have no liturgy as I know of, nor the Scotch a directory. They both do marry, christen, pray extempore, bury, and administer the sacraments alike, both of them without ceremonies of cross or rings, and administer the sacrament to all indifferently, whether they sit, kneel, or stand. The right Independents—*rectiùs* Congregationals—will not willingly administer the sacrament to a mixed congregation; therefore they of their own congregation come to it with tickets; others not of their own congregation, upon recommendation of some of their own congregation, may obtain tickets and receive amongst them. I perceive your humour for Independent books: it jumps with mine, and I shall provide for you as for myself."[2] It was the political teaching of the Independents which did most to raise hostility against them, and that too on those points on which posterity assigns to them the largest share of credit, their democratic tendency, and their doctrine of toleration.

The Independents as a religious body.

The democratic principles to which the Independent leaders had given voice were, in truth, as effectual in welding together Cavaliers and Presbyterians as were the principles of the French Revolutionists in welding together the Tories and the aristocratic Whigs in 1793 and 1794. To the country gentlemen and the traders

Effect of their democratic principles,

---

[1]

		£
Arrears abandoned		1,500
Five years' offer		5,000
Five years' abatement of pay . . .		1,825
		£8,325

Five years' income at 1,680*l.* is 8,400*l.*

[2] Dr. Denton to Sir R. Verney, Oct. 6, 1647, *Verney MSS.*

who had formed the main basis of the Tudor monarchy, but of late had been divided by political and religious differences, the *Agreement of the People* was all that the Social Contract was to the men of the eighteenth century. If Charles had been as capable as Pitt of placing himself at the head of a coalition, the Independents, in spite of their hold upon the army, would hardly have succeeded in maintaining themselves in power.

Equally obnoxious to the governing classes was the persistence with which the Independents clung to the idea of toleration. No doubt they did not entirely agree as to the extent to which toleration was to be carried. Some like Lilburne and Marten held that it should be unlimited. Others like Cromwell thought that it should be confined to such opinions as were not dangerous to the State. All however were of one mind in holding that no religious belief or worship ought to be proscribed simply because it was ridiculous in the eyes of educated men.

and of their doctrine of toleration.

When in 1646 Thomas Edwards, a Presbyterian minister, published a venomous attack on toleration under the title of "Gangræna," he was able to set forth a long list of heresies, some of which were harmless enough, though others cut deep into the very foundations of morality. Truly or falsely he asserted that there were persons living who argued that ''tis as lawful to commit adultery and murder as to baptise a child;' that ''tis lawful for one man to have two wives at once;' whilst others again held opinions which imperilled existing institutions, as 'that children are not bound to obey their parents at all, if they be ungodly,' and 'that 'tis unlawful for Christians to fight and take up arms for their laws and civil liberties.'[1] Others again, according to a list published in March 1648, held 'that the soul of man is mortal as of a beast; that in marriage there are no degrees forbidden, a man may marry his sister or his father's wife; 'that if a man be strongly moved to kill, commit adultery, &c., and upon praying against it again and again it continues, he should then do it.'[2]

1646. Gangræna; its list of heresies.

[1] *Gangræna*, E. 323, 2.
[2] *A true and perfect Picture of our present Reformation*, E. 430, 13.

No sober Independent, it is true, had any wish to protect teaching of this kind, the outcome of unlimited discussion amongst the ignorant class to whom the Bible had been thrown as a book in which every single word was of divine revelation, though every reader was capable of giving to every statement in it a meaning after his own fancy, not only apart from the context, but also apart from the reconciling influence of centuries of human thought. It was, however, but natural that the Independents should bear the blame of all extravagances. This, it was argued, was the unavoidable result of freedom of religion. Only in restricting the teaching of religion to an educated clergy could a remedy be found. It was probably fortunate for the tender plant of liberty that two rival clerical bodies claimed the power of restriction each in their own interest. Between the two, that liberty of speech and thought without which national and ecclesiastical life stagnate, might at last obtain permission to exist

The Independents blamed.

CHAPTER LX.

A GATHERING STORM.

TOWARDS the end of February, the danger which had driven
Cromwell to look for a means of escape from his difficulties in
the substitution of the Prince of Wales for his father,
grew every day more imminent. The discovery of a
plot for the evasion of the Duke of York was ominous of a coming storm. The boy, on being questioned, engaged his honour to have no more to do
with 'such businesses,' and the Houses could but accept his
word.[1]

1648.
Plot for the escape of the Duke of York.

Feb. 22.

The outlook appeared the more dangerous as the Independent leaders had lately gained information through an intercepted letter written by Boswell, the King's agent at
the Hague, how wide-spreading were the ramifica-
tions of the King's designs against them. "I have,"
wrote Boswell to Charles, "perfected my negotiations with
Prince William;[2] and if·the peace between Spain
and the States be declared, which is confidently
said here, he will certainly land a gallant army for
your relief; and I hope you shall have the Irish army and this
meet most successfully. Therefore, as you tender the good of
you and yours, be constant to your grounds. If your Majesty
make laws to strengthen their usurped power, or part with the
Church lands, there can be no hope to restore you, and your
posterity will be for ever undone.[3] All that I or any of your

An inter-cepted letter from Boswell.

Dutch and Irish invasions threatened.

---

[1] *I.J.* 76, 77. [2] *i.e.* the new Prince of Orange.
[3] 'Undone' is conjecturally supplied.

faithfullest servants can say to you is to beg constancy from you." [1]

The knowledge of this despatch was sufficient in itself to convince Cromwell and his allies that they must do everything in their power to smooth away asperities between Parliament
The disbandment of supernumeraries. and army. Difficulties had already arisen in disbanding the supernumeraries, especially as the Houses, after insisting on their dismissal,[2] had refused to pay more than a part of their arrears in ready money. Fairfax, to set an example of obedience, disbanded his own life-guard as unnecessary in time of peace, and in spite of a mutiny, in which the colours were carried off and hidden, succeeded in effecting his object.[3] On March 2, however, serious news
Feb. 22. Poyer's resistance at Pembroke. reached London. It appeared that on February 22 Colonel Poyer, the Governor of Pembroke Castle, had refused to deliver up his charge to Adjutant-General Fleming, who had been sent by Fairfax to take it over. Poyer's plea was that he simply held out till his arrears were paid,[4] but, as Wales was strongly anti-puritanical, a military mutiny might easily develop into popular resistance. The danger was the greater because Laugharne's soldiers, though still in the service of Parliament, were under sentence of disbandment as supernumeraries, and if they followed Poyer's example could hardly be suppressed without the employment of
March 3. Poyer ordered to submit. a strong military force. For the present the Houses met the apprehended danger with words alone. On March 3, they passed an Ordinance declaring Poyer and his adherents traitors if they did not at once submit.[5]

Cromwell, to whom all eyes turned whenever a soldier's

---

[1] The Agent at the Hague to the King, Feb., Deciphers, *Bodl. Lib. Mus.* 203. Dr. Wallis, who deciphered this despatch, says that he deciphered all the intercepted letters of the time.

[2] See p. 45.

[3] *Rushw.* vii. 1,009.

[4] Poyer to Fleming, Feb. 22, *Tanner MSS.* lviii. fol. 721. Carlyle has fixed upon Poyer the nickname of 'drunken Poyer.' See *Rushw.* vii. 1,033 and *A Declaration of divers Gentlemen,* E. 436, 7. On the other hand personal attacks in pamphlets are not always to be trusted.

[5] *L.J.* x. 89.

brain and arm were needed, was at this time so seriously ill that recovery appeared hopeless. On March 7, however, he was

Cromwell's
illness. convalescent. "I find," he then wrote to Fairfax, "this only to be good—to love the Lord and His poor despised people; to do for them, and to be ready to suffer with them; and he that is found worthy of this hath obtained great favour from the Lord." Lilburne's democratic ideal was not Cromwell's, nor did Cromwell imagine it to be his duty to follow in the wake of a Royalist majority. Yet he knew that it would be wise to conciliate that Royalist majority if it could be done without injury to higher interests, and after his re-

Feb.
Revival of
the scheme
for placing
the Prince of
Wales on
the throne. covery, as before his illness, he was ready to lend an ear to any scheme for averting a fresh outbreak of war. As far as can be gathered from imperfect evidence, the proposal to place the Prince of Wales on the throne which had been dropped in January was revived towards the end of February.

"We hear," wrote an Independent on February 28, "that there is an underhand treaty with his Majesty endeavoured by that godly and religious gentleman, Lieutenant-General Cromwell, which we hope will take some good effect; for though we have very much provoked the King, yet we had rather trust him than the rigid Presbyterian yoke which will prove to our party a most antichristian bondage."[1] A Royalist writer shows

March. a few days later what the nature of the overture was. "Shortly," he writes, "the design of the Prince of Wales's crowning in case there be a necessity that monarchical government must continue, is freshly thought upon."[2] It is even possible that the overture here referred to originated, not with the Independents, but with some of the Royalist clergy and laity, who were impatient of Charles's absolute refusal to take part in any satisfactory compromise.[3]

---

[1] *Clarendon MSS.* 2,734.

[2] Bamfield (?) to Lanark, March, *Hamilton Papers, Addenda,* in the *Camden Misc.* vol. ix.

[3] "Mr. Ashburnham and the clergy of England are joined with all their power to make some reconciliation between the King and army." Mungo Murray to Lanark, March 25, probably $\frac{15}{25}$, *ibid.*

Such overtures could not but end in failure. Meanwhile they merely served to increase the exasperation of the Re-

An offer
from
Marten
to the Scots.

publicans. "Mr. Marten," wrote one of Lanark's agents on March 14, "notwithstanding all his severe speeches and writings against the Scots' affairs, sent a great confidant of his to Commissary Copley,[1] entreating him to use his best endeavours to reconcile him to Scotland, and that he and his party which would appear for monarchy might be received into that of the Lords ;[2] and that there was[3] nothing which they would not do to destroy Cromwell and his party, who was the falsest of mankind ; and if Scotland would give him assurance and countenance his actions in Parliament, he doubted not but he should defeat Cromwell and his party, assuring withal that he had four regiments at his service : and, indeed, that party is at this time very mutinous, and expects a fair opportunity to decline Cromwell's commands, hearing Fairfax and Cromwell's resolution is to despatch the chief heads and abettors of that party."[4]

It is unnecessary to take Marten's overture too seriously,

No chance
of an under-
standing
b+tween
Cromwell
and the
Royalists.

but it is certain that he was right in his belief that the bulk of the Royalists had no thought of coming to an understanding with Cromwell. For some time their leaders had been bent on war. When the Scots commissioners left London on January 24,[5] they had already made arrangements for a rising in

---

[1] Copley was a Presbyterian.

[2] I suppose this means the party amongst the Lords which was supporting the King.

[3] 'There was' is not in the MS., the greater part of which is in cipher.

[4] ———? to Lanark, March 14, *Hamilton Papers, Addenda,* in the *Camden Misc.* vol. ix. According to *Westminster Projects,* published on March 23, E. 433, 15, Cromwell asked Marten to join him in purging the House, but Marten, fearing to play into his hands, refused to do so. The authority is not very good, but it is just possible that after his last hopes of getting the King to abdicate were at an end, Cromwell was alarmed at the prospect of marching against the enemy, leaving in his rear a hostile House of Commons, as it might easily become, should the Presbyterian absentees return to their places in the absence of the army.

[5] See p. 56.

England. Kent and the Eastern Association were to take
arms at a given signal. Already, on the 15th, the Queen had
despatched Sir William Fleming to Amsterdam to
pawn her jewels and to buy arms for the equipment
of the insurgents. At the same time it was decided
that the Prince of Wales should remove to Calais,
to be ready for any event.[1]

Jan. 24.
Arrange-
ments for a
rising in
England.

On their return to Edinburgh, the Scottish commissioners
left no stone unturned to rouse the nation in favour of the
King. On February 15, Lauderdale, in an harangue
to the Committee of Estates, sought to stir up the
animosity of his audience against the English Parliament. There were, he said, four things which the English
were unable to endure—the Covenant, Presbytery, monarchical
government, and the Scots. All Hamilton's party were in
favour of war, and on the 16th, when the clergy
petitioned that no forward step might be taken without their knowledge, one of its members declared
that Scotland would come to regret the overthrow of the
bishops now that the clergy took on themselves to interfere in
civil affairs. As, however, Argyle supported the request of the
clergy, the promise demanded was given.[2]

Feb. 15.
Lauder-
dale's
harangue.

Feb. 16.
A clerical
petition
for peace.

The words which had been spoken in the Committee of
Estates were of no light significance. They intimated that the
old alliance between the Scottish nobility and the
Crown, which had supported James VI. in his
struggle with the Presbyterian clergy, had been reconstituted
under Hamilton. Most of the nobles who had deserted
Charles to oppose Episcopacy in 1637 gave him their support
because they wished to humble the Presbyterian clergy in
Scotland, though they deceptively posed as the advocates of
Presbyterianism in England.

Scottish
parties.

On March 2 a new triennial Parliament met at Edinburgh.

---

[1] Grignon to Brienne, $\frac{\text{Jan. 24}}{\text{Feb. 3}}$. *R.O. Transcripts*; Mungo Murray to
Lanark, Jan. 17, *Hamilton Papers, Addenda*, in the *Camden Misc.* vol. ix.
[2] Montreuil to Mazarin, $\frac{\text{Feb. 22}}{\text{March 3}}$, *Arch. des Aff. Étrangères*, lvi. fol.
308.

The representatives of the shires and boroughs were about equally divided between Argyle and Hamilton—or in other

March 2.
Meeting of
the Scottish
Parliament. words, between peace and war.[1] A large majority of the nobles, however, sided with Hamilton, and this was, in a single House, decisive.[2] As far as Parlia-

A Hamilton
majority. mentary action went, Hamilton could do what he chose. It was a great blow to Argyle, who had hitherto held the representative part of Parliament in the hollow of his hands, and he and his partisans, truly or falsely, explained their defeat by alleging that the shifting of the balance at the elections was due not to a change of opinion in the con-

Argyle
supported
by the
clergy. stituencies, but to pressure put upon them by the nobility.[3] Whether this was the case or not, the clergy still regarded Argyle as their leader, and the influence of the clergy was of no slight weight in Scotland.

The knowledge that the victory was less complete than it seemed gave Hamilton pause. Hesitating by nature, and

Hamilton
hesitates. always reluctant to embark on decisive action, he was hardly the man to cut the knot by promptly availing himself of his supremacy in Parliament to push on the invasion of England to an immediate issue. Before the end of February his supporters, Loudoun, Lanark, and Lauderdale, were urging Charles to satisfy the clergy by yielding more than he had hitherto done on the subject of religion, whilst other members of the party were taking steps which made war un-

Langdale
in Edin-
burgh. avoidable. Sir Marmaduke Langdale had recently arrived in Edinburgh, and it was perhaps in compliance with his suggestions that it was agreed that the first step should be the seizure of Berwick and Carlisle.[4]

[1] *Baillie*, iii. 35. Compare Montreuil's despatches.

[2] The Parliament contained fifty six lords, forty-seven representatives of shires, and forty-eight representatives of boroughs. *Acts of Parl. of Scotl.* VI. ii. 1.

[3] See Ross's Letter in *A Declaration of the Kirk*, E. 432, 10.

[4] Lanark, Loudoun, and Lauderdale to the King, *Burnet*, vi. 7. The letter is undated, but it is shown by internal evidence to have been written between Feb. 15 and March 1.

The ministers had for some time been denouncing from
their pulpits all who proposed to make war in favour of a King

Violence of the ministers. who rejected the Covenant. Rumours were indeed
in circulation that the ministers had been bribed

They and Argyle said to have been bribed. by the English Commissioners.[1] Argyle also was
said to have been influenced by offers of money,
and he certainly had a pecuniary interest in maintaining peace, as 10,000*l.* out of the next money payable by
England to Scotland was engaged to wipe out a debt owing
to him by the Scottish Government. So far as the ministers
were concerned, the supposition that they needed money to
stir them to denounce a King who was attempting to advance
the interests of Episcopacy with the help of a Scottish army is
entirely gratuitous, whilst Argyle's political position was too
obviously at stake to make it necessary to seek further explanation of his opposition to his rivals, the Hamiltons. Hereditary
bonds had at that time a far greater hold upon Scotchmen

Loudoun goes over to Argyle. than they had upon Englishmen, and before long
Loudoun, who was also a Campbell, shifted his
ground, and was found once more acting in co-
operation with the head of his family.[2]

In the General Assembly the lay-elders ranged themselves
with Hamilton as the noblemen had ranged themselves with

The lay-elders in the Assembly. James at the Assembly of Perth.[3] With the exception of four, of whom Argyle was one, every
lay-elder in the Assembly voted against the publica-

A clerical manifesto. tion of a manifesto which had been drawn up by
the ministers.[4] The ministers, however, commanded

*March 11.
It is to be kept back for a time.* a majority, and the manifesto was sent to the
press, though on March 11, in consequence of a
strong protest from Parliament, the ministers agreed
to refrain from issuing it, at least for a time.[5]

---

[1] Montreuil to Mazarin, $\frac{Feb. 22}{March 3}$, *Arch. des Aff. Étrangères*, lvi. fol.
308.

[2] *Burnet*, vi. 8.　　　　[3] *Hist. of Engl.* 1603–1642, iii. 237.

[4] Montreuil to Mazarin, March $\frac{8}{18}$, *Arch. des Aff. Étrangères*, lvi. fol.
321.

[5] *Acts of Parl. of Scotl.* VI. ii. 12.

The clerical manifesto was not indeed drawn up in favour of peace in the abstract. The ministers were as ready as the nobles to go to war against the Independent army ; though they objected to assist Charles until he not only took the Covenant himself, but provided for its imposition on his subjects. They also insisted that all Malignants—that is to say all persons hostile to the Covenant—should be excluded from the Royalist forces about to be raised in England.[1] Whatever may be thought of the narrow ecclesiasticism of these Scottish ministers, it must be admitted that they saw clearly that if Presbyterianism was indeed to be established in England, it would not be in consequence of the concessions which had satisfied the Hamiltons.

Every day the conflict between the Scottish factions grew more bitter. On March 13, a projected duel between Argyle

March 13.
An interrupted duel.

and Hamilton's brother-in-law, the Earl of Crawford and Lindsay, was only stopped by the intervention of friends. In the midst of these distractions, the warlike preparations made slow but steady progress. On

March 17.
Report from the Committee of Dangers.

the 17th, a Committee of Dangers which had been appointed a week before, brought into Parliament a report, on the strength of which a second committee was named to concert measures in secret for seizing upon Berwick and Carlisle.[2] Rather than consent, Argyle

Argyle leaves the House, but is brought back.

left the Parliament House, followed by eleven lords and some thirty representative members. Hamilton was fain to call the seceders back. 'Though,' he candidly admitted, 'he had more power in Parliament than they had, yet they had the greater power in the kingdom.'[3] Much valuable time was lost in attempting to produce a union which was in reality unattainable.

The Scottish Parliament and nation were drifting into war. The English exiles, eager to arouse the sluggishness of their new allies, gathered in ever-increasing numbers at Edinburgh.

[1] *Baillie,* iii. 33.

[2] *Acts of Parl. of Scotl.* VI. ii. 13.

[3] Montreuil to Mazarin, March $\frac{21}{31}$, *Arch. des Aff. Étrangères,* lvi. fol. 332.

Langdale was joined by Glemham and by a certain Captain Wogan, who arrived with a body of 200 horse which had been threatened with disbandment by Fairfax. The English commissioners in Edinburgh in vain de-manded his surrender as a deserter. It was im-possible that this state of uncertainty should long continue. It seemed as if matters had reached a crisis, when on March 23, Sir William Fleming arrived, and de-clared that the Prince of Wales was willing to come to Scotland if only he could rely on the Scots being ready to take arms in his behalf.[1]

The English exiles at Edinburgh.

March 23. The Prince offers to come to Scotland.

In England, if writers of Royalist newsletters are to be believed, whole districts were ripe for revolt. The principal persons in Staffordshire and Warwickshire had formed a design for the seizure of Warwick Castle. Notting-ham and Oxford were also to be surprised. Lanca-shire, Cheshire, and North Wales would declare for the King as soon as the Scots crossed the Border. In Essex too there was to be a rising, and a fortress, probably Landguard Fort, was to be seized.[2]

Spread of a warlike feeling in England.

With such hopes, it was all-important to the Royalists that Charles should be once more free to take the field in person. For some time there had been a plot on hand for his delivery, on the understanding that when he was again at large he was to make his way to Scotland.[3] The soul of this plot was Henry Firebrace, who, having been in Charles's service as a page, was allowed to remain in attendance upon his old master. Firebrace had arranged for the conveyance of the secret correspondence,

Plot for the King's escape.

Henry Firebrace.

---

[1] Letters from the Commissioners in Scotland, March 7, 21, 28, *L.J.* x. 111, 127, 172 ; *Packets of letters*, E. 434, 25 ; Montreuil to Mazarin, $\frac{March\ 28}{April\ 7}$, *Arch. des Aff. Étrangères*, lvi. fol. 343 ; Mungo Murray to Lanark, March 25, *Hamilton Papers, Addenda*, in the *Camden Misc.* vol. ix.

[2] ———— ? to Lanark, March 7 ; Byron to Lanark, March 10, *Hamil-ton Papers*, 166.

[3] "I doubt not, if the design fail not, he will make his escape and be with you before you can hope it, so well have I ordered the business as nothing but himself can let it." Firebrace (?) to Lanark, March 7, *Hamilton Papers, Addenda*, in the *Camden Misc.* vol. ix.

which continued to pass between Charles and his friends outside the walls of his prison, and he now, in combination with Mr. Worsley, of Appuldercombe, and Mr. Newland of Newport, and Richard Osborne, one of the King's attendants, was completing the preparations for his escape.

However secret the conspirators might be they could not altogether veil their designs from the eyes of those whose interest it was to penetrate beneath the surface. As early as February 7, the Derby House Committee had information of a plan for breaking into the King's chamber from the floor above him, and of thus conveying him away through rooms in which there were no guards.[1] Later, on March 13, the committee had vague information of another plan which appears to have originated with Firebrace,[2] and their imperfect knowledge led them to direct Hammond to find out the secret by every means in his power.

Feb. 7.
Rumours of a design

An attempt was accordingly made by Hammond to secure further evidence by seizing on the King's papers ; but it came to nothing, as Charles succeeded in thrusting the incriminating documents into the fire. It is possible that there was a scuffle, though the story which obtained currency amongst the Royalists that Hammond struck the King may fairly be set down as a pure invention.[3]

According to Firebrace's plan, the night fixed for Charles's escape was March 20, when he was to slip out of the open casement of his bedroom window, which looked on the inner court of the castle,[4] in which, strange to say, no sentry had been placed. Firebrace would then conduct him to the castle wall and lower him on the other side by means of a rope. Once over the wall Charles would then descend the mound on which the castle was built, after which

Firebrace's plan.

---

[1] The Com. of D. H. to Hammond, Feb. 7, *Letters between Hammond and the D. H. Committee.*

[2] ———? to Hammond, March 13, *ibid.*

[3] Newsletter, March $\frac{11}{21}$, *Clar. St. P.* ii. App. xlvi.

[4] The traditional window, shown to visitors as that through which Charles attempted to escape, has no claims to that distinction. See Hillier's *Narrative of the attempted Escapes of Charles I.* 120.

he would find no further difficulty, except a low counterscarp which could easily be surmounted. On the other side Worsley and Osborne were to be stationed with horses, whilst Newland was to be in attendance at the water's edge 'with a lusty boat' ready to carry Charles wherever he pleased to go.

The only part of this scheme in which Firebrace anticipated difficulty was the initial one. The opening between the side Firebrace's of the casement and the upright bar in the middle suggestions. was, he thought, too narrow to admit of the King's getting his body through, and he therefore urged Charles to

PLAN OF CARISBROOKE CASTLE IN 1648.

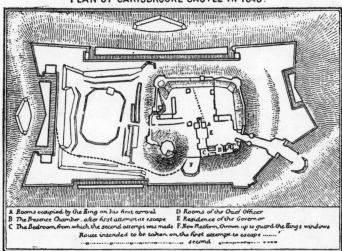

A *Rooms occupied by the King on his first arrival* D *Rooms of the Chief Officer*
B *The Presence Chamber, after first attempt at escape* E *Residence of the Governor*
C *The Bedroom from which the second attempt was made* F.*New Platform thrown up to guard the King's windows*
    Route intended to be taken on the first attempt to escape ....
.... *second* ....

E.S Weller

enlarge it by cutting through a plate at the bottom which seems to have held the upright bar against which the casement shut.[1] Charles however obstinately refused to accept his suggestion. He had, he said, tried the aperture with his head, 'and he was sure where that would pass, the body would follow.' Besides, the cutting of the plate might easily attract observation. Unfortunately for Charles, when the appointed

---

[1] "By cutting the plate the casement shut to at the bottom, which then might easily have been put by." This is by no means clear, but may bear the interpretation given above.

night arrived, Firebrace's anticipation proved to be too well grounded. Charles struggled in vain to force his body through the casement, and, after placing in the window a lighted candle, as a signal that he had failed, retired discomfited to bed. As no word of the attempt reached the Parliamentary authorities for more than a fortnight, it still seemed possible to renew it, and Charles continued to entertain hopes that, when a corrosive substance had been fetched from London, he would be able to remove the bar more silently than if he had filed it through.[1]

March 20. Failure of the attempt.

There can be no doubt that if the King had been really at large, a welcome would have been accorded to him before which even the army would have found it difficult to stand. In London, at least, the overwhelming preponderance of opinion was in his favour. On March 27, the anniversary of the King's accession, more bonfires were lit in the city than at any time since Charles's return from Spain. All who passed along the streets in coaches were compelled to drink the King's health, and shouts for King Charles were mingled with execrations poured out upon Hammond, who was charged with barbarous usage of his prisoner. The butchers vowed that if they could catch him 'they would chop him as small as ever they chopped any of their meat.'

March 27. Royalist feeling in London.

While these scenes were being acted in the streets Marten called upon the House of Commons to 'go through stitch with their work, and to take order about deposing the King.'[2] No wonder that the Independent leaders hesitated to embark on so hazardous a course. Feeling that unless they could gain friends in England their case was desperate, they had for some time been approaching the City with conciliatory offers. They were ready, they said, to restore to the municipal authorities the command over the London militia and the Tower, to withdraw the soldiers from Whitehall and the Mews, and to release the imprisoned aldermen on the sole condition of a

Marten proposes to depose the King.

The Independents negotiate with the City,

---

[1] Firebrace's *Narrative*, printed with Herbert's *Memoirs*, ed. 1702.

[2] Letters of Intelligence, March 30, *Clarendon MSS.* 2,751, 2,754.

hearty support against the Scots.   Their overtures were made
in vain.   Nothing, they were told, would content the City short
of the King's restoration.[1]   Even to that Cromwell and the
Independent leaders had no insuperable objection provided
only that sufficient security could be obtained for his good
behaviour, and there is reason to believe that the English
commissioners had some time before been instructed to

*and make
an offer to
the Scots.*

offer to the Scots, as a condition of peace, that the
King should be set at liberty and restored to the
throne if he would content himself with powers con-

*The King
to be
restored
under con-
ditions.*

siderably less than he had exercised before the civil
war.   The Presbyterians, they added, might have their
share of court offices, but the power over the militia
must be reserved to the Independents.[2]

A security to be obtained by placing the King on the
throne and keeping an army on foot to restrain his actions was

*An illusory
security.*

certain to prove illusory in the end, and that it
should have been proposed at all is to be taken as
evidence of the desperate straits to which the Independent
leaders were driven.   Yet there is reason to believe that over-

---

[1] *Letters of Intelligence*, March 23, *Clarendon MSS.* 2,743; ——? to
Lanark, March 28, *Hamilton Papers*, 169; Walker's *Hist. of Independency*, i. 83.

[2] The Scots were to abstain from interference in England : 'ma però
con conditione di rimettere il Rè in libertà e dentro il suo primo potere,
però con gran modificatione, promettendo a loro parte negl' ufficii della
Corte Reale, ma non nella militia.'   Newsletter, March 24, *Roman
Transcripts, R.O.*   The statement that some negotiation of the kind was
opened is confirmed by a passage in a subsequent letter from Loudoun to
the King : " Lest my deportment may be misrepresented to your Majesty,
I hold it my duty to let you know that the carrying on of the late engagement against the judgment and declarations of the Kirk, refusing to secure
religion . . . and the rejecting of the desires of the commissioners sent
to your Majesty's Parliament of this Kingdom from the Houses of your
Parliament of England, who did offer in their name to join with this
Kingdom in making their applications to your Majesty by treaty upon the
propositions for removing of all differences and giving satisfaction.in all
things which could consist with justice and honour . . . did convince me
of the unlawfulness of that unhappy engagement."   Loudoun to the King,
Oct. 1648.   *MS. in the possession of Mr. John Webster, of Edgehill, near
Aberdeen.*

tures were at this time made to Charles himself. Even Marten seems to have been subdued, for the time, by the imminence of the danger. " If we must have a government," he said, "we had better have this King and oblige him than to have him obtruded on us by the Scots, and owe his restitution to them "[1]

On March 28 Cromwell was at Farnham on private business. A report at once sprang up that he had gone to com-

March 28. Cromwell at Farnham.

municate with Hammond, and it was also said that the Earl of Southampton was at this time urged to

Further overtures to the King.

make himself the medium of a fresh negotiation with the King.[2] Such constant persistence in his efforts to obtain peace with Charles's aid could not

Cromwell will not vindicate himself.

but expose Cromwell to the worst suspicions. Yet he had no thought of freeing himself from blame by any public declaration. " I know," he wrote to an attached friend, " God has been above all ill reports, and will, in His own time, vindicate me. I have no cause to complain."[3]

Neither Cromwell nor his Independent friends could bring themselves to confront the disagreeable truth that nothing short

Persistence of the Independents in seeking peace.

of their absolute submission would avert the impending war. During the last week of March and the first fortnight of April, the effort to bring the King to terms was kept up. Southampton, it is said, refused to act as mediator on the ground that he would thereby expose himself to the penalty threatened in the Vote of No Addresses.[4]

---

[1] —— ? to Lanark, March 28, *Hamilton Papers*, 170.

[2] Walker's *Hist. of Independency*, i. 78.

[3] Cromwell to Norton, March 28, *Carlyle*, Letter lv.

[4] " For the most part of last week Mr. Pierrepont, Mr. St. John, Evelyn, and young Fiennes . . . met Lord Say at Wallingford, where they debated their condition, and concluded it necessary to entertain a treaty with his Majesty, thereby if possible to disengage him from the Scottish interest." —— to Lanark, April 4, *Hamilton Papers*, 174. Walker again states that Cromwell had ' lately had private conference at Farnham with Hammond.' *Hist. of Independency*, i. 78. This must refer to Cromwell's visit to Farnham on March 28. " The Earl of

On April 6, in the midst of these futile negotiations, those who were striving for peace learnt not only that Charles had

April 6.
The King's
attempt to
escape
known.

nearly succeeded in effecting his escape, but that preparations for renewing the effort were still being carried on.[1] Three days later they were once more brought face to face with the problem of maintaining authority which has ceased to be based on good-

April 9.
A riot in the
City.

will. On Sunday, the 9th, during afternoon service, the Lord Mayor sent a party of trained bands to interfere with the amusements of some boys who were playing at tip-cat in Moorfields. A crowd of apprentices and others on the spot took the part of the boys, first pelting

Some of the
trained
bands dis-
armed.

the City forces with stones, and afterwards proceeding to fall on them and disarm them. The possession of arms gave confidence to the mob, now some three or four thousand strong, and, raising a shout of "Now

The mob
rushes
westwards.

for King Charles!" they made their way westwards along Fleet Street and the Strand to drive Barkstead and his regiment out of Whitehall. On their way they passed the Mews, in which a regiment of horse was quartered, and where, as it happened, were Cromwell and

---

Southampton," Walker continues, "hath been courted to negotiate with the King and offered the two Speakers' hands for his warrant." On April 18 a correspondent of Lanark's writes that the negotiation has come to an end. "I hear from a good hand that Mr. Ashburnham hath within fourteen days past been twice from the Independent party with the Earl of Southampton, to get him to go to the King and them; but the Earl refuseth except he have public leave from the two Houses and the King's consent and approbation; neither of which I find they are publicly inclined to do; for one of the chiefest amongst them said lately that they had endeavoured what they could to have a peace, but now nobody would trust them, and they would trust nobody, and therefore were resolved to put it to a battle if ye came in, as they are confident ye will." *Hamilton Papers*, 185. In a newsletter of April 16 from Ford to Hopton, *Clarendon MSS*. 2,763, the message to Southampton is mentioned as having been sent by Say, and the answer returned is given in much the same terms as in the letter of Lanark's correspondent. Something might be said against each of these testimonies if it stood alone. It is the concurrence of so many which carries conviction of their general accuracy.

[1] Cromwell to Hammond, April 6, *Carlyle*, Letter lvii.

Ireton, both of them ignorant of the danger till Fairfax [1] gave them timely warning.

Cromwell at once ordered out his cavalry and charged the mob as it was advancing along the Strand ; two of the crowd were either slain or desperately wounded, and, as too often happens unavoidably in such cases, some of the onlookers suffered together with the actors. By the evening the streets were cleared, and Fairfax retired to bed under the impression that the disturbance was at an end.

A charge in the Strand.

At two in the morning of the 10th, Fairfax was awakened with the news that the apprentices had regained confidence during the night, had secured the City gates at Ludgate and Newgate, had attacked the house of the intrusive Lord Mayor, seizing the small cannon with which it was guarded, and firing shot through his windows. The Lord Mayor, justifiably alarmed, had taken refuge in the Tower. By eight in the morning the whole of the City was in the hands of the rioters, not a man of the trained bands venturing to appear against them. At last Barkstead's regiment accompanied by four or five troops of horse appeared on the scene. Finding Ludgate and Newgate barred against them, they skirted the northern side of the City and were admitted by friendly hands at Moorgate. Pressing on, the soldiers found the insurgents engaged in collecting arms near Leadenhall. Resistance to a disciplined force was impossible, and in a few minutes the crowd was dispersed, unhappily not without the loss of some lives, and the ringleaders led off to prison. An undisciplined mob in the presence of trained soldiers is not really dangerous ; but it was ominous that on this occasion the mob had the sympathy of orderly citizens.[2]

April 10. Renewal of the tumult.

Its final suppression.

To secure the Tower by increasing its garrison, and to insist on the removal by the City authorities of the posts and chains which, at the beginning of the Civil War, had been

[1] He had just succeeded his father as Lord Fairfax in the Scottish peerage.

L.J. x. 188, 190 ; Letter of Intelligence, April 10, *Clarke Papers,* ii. 2 ; Letter of Intelligence, April 13, *Clarendon MSS.* 2,760.

placed in the streets to hinder charges of cavalry, were obvious precautions against a renewal of the danger.[1]　Yet the Independents could not but feel that no display of physical force could be as effective as the establishment of a settled government, and in spite of the Vote of No Addresses, they made one last appeal to Charles to concur with them in the work of peace.　This time the bearer of their message was a woman from the City, who could make her way unobserved to the Isle of Wight.　The result of her employment was that Berkeley and Legge were again despatched from London on a secret mission to the King.[2]

Though the terms now offered to Charles are unknown, there is strong reason to believe that they were accompanied by an intimation that if they were rejected sentence of deposition would be pronounced by Parliament against him, and the Duke of York crowned in his stead as King James II.[3]　The plan of substituting the Duke for his father had been approved by the Council of War ;[4] and the 24th, the day on which there was to be a call of the House

Ap. 10-15. Precautions against its renewal.

The Duke of York to be king.

---

[1] The order to pull down the posts and chains was given by the Lord Mayor on April 10, and confirmed by the House of Commons on the 13th. On the 15th the Commons ordered that the garrison of the Tower should be made up to 1,000 foot and a troop of horse. *L.J.* x. 191 ; *C.J.* v. 529, 532.

[2] "They," *i.e.* Cromwell and his party, "have sent a gentlewoman in Lime Street, with a letter to the King, and after her return Colonel Legge and Colonel Berkeley were despatched to the Isle of Wight ; and because they could not receive the King's answer time enough, they put off the debate of disposing of the King and Kingdom to a longer day ; they have adjourned the Parliament and met at Farnham Castle.　They have ordered the strengthening of the Tower with a thousand foot and a troop of horse, and the taking down of the chains, the drawing of the army nearer the City, &c." *Tricks of the State*, E. 436, 3.　This pamphlet was published on April 29.　Berkeley and Ashburnham probably returned before the 18th, if it is true that the negotiations with the King were broken off before that day.　See p. 96, note 4.

[3] I gather the King's knowledge of this resolve from his anxiety to effect the Duke's escape without delay.

[4] "This army (last April) in their council . . . debated the deposing of the King, disinheriting the Prince and crowning the Duke of York, which was then approved by Cromwell and Ireton." Walker's *Hist. of*

of Commons, seems to have been fixed on for a motion that the King should be dethroned in favour of his second son.[1]

To Charles, therefore, it was of vital importance that the Duke of York should not be found in England on the 24th.

April 21.
Escape of the Duke of York planned.

One obstacle to his escape, the word of honour which the boy had given not to repeat his former attempt to escape,[2] was easily removed by Bamfield, to whom the arrangement of the plan was entrusted. Bamfield told the Duke that as he was under age his promise was not binding without his father's consent, and this sophistry obtained ready credence. The evasion was to be made on the 21st. For some evenings before, the Duke amused himself by playing hide and seek with his brother and sister in the apartments which they occupied at St. James's, in order to accustom his guardians to his absence from the room where he had usually been found at that late hour.

In the meanwhile, Anne Murray, a sister of the well-known Will Murray, had ordered a tailor to make for the boy a lady's

Anne Murray's preparations.

dress. The order almost led to a discovery of the plot, as the tailor was startled by the measurements given to him. He had never, he said, made a dress in which the size of the waist was so large in proportion to the

---

Independency, i. 107. "Shortly," wrote Bamfield in an undated letter, "the design of 622 [the Duke of York's] crowning in case there be a necessity that monarchical government must continue, is freshly thought upon." *Hamilton Papers, Addenda*, in *Camd. Misc.* vol. ix. The same idea is indicated in the King's own letter to Bamfield about the proposed escape of the Duke. "I believe it will be difficult and, if he miscarry in the attempt, it will be the greatest affliction that can arrive to me; but I look upon James's escape as Charles's preservation, and nothing can content me more." *Autobiography of Lady Anne Halkett*, 20. 'Charles's preservation,' I imagine, means the preservation of the rights of the Prince of Wales.

[1] "The citizens . . . see now the army . . . have environed them, on purpose to overawe the Presbyterian members at the great mote on Monday, the 24th instant; but the great design of that day held not since his Highness the Duke of York—wherein it is supposed he was chiefly to be concerned—hath escaped their clutches." *Merc. Elencticus*, E. 437, 10.

[2] See p. 83.

lady's height. The tailor, however, kept counsel, and, on the evening of the 21st, the Duke, saying that he was going off to his game, went into the garden, and opening the gate with a key with which he had been supplied, stepped out into the park, where Bamfield awaited him with a cloak and wig. Thus partially disguised the Duke was taken in a coach to a house in which Anne Murray completed the metamorphosis, clothing him in a ' mixed mohair of a light hair-colour and black,' and a scarlet under-petticoat.

April 21. The escape effected.

In this guise, making as Anne Murray thought a very pretty girl, the boy, still accompanied by Bamfield, who now assumed the character of a brother, took passage in a barge to Gravesend, where the pair found a vessel awaiting them, and put to sea before orders had been given to stop the ports. Two days later they landed at Rammekens, safe from all pursuit. Yet the Duke continued to keep up his disguise after all necessity for it was at an end. On the night after his arrival he shocked the hostess of the inn in which he slept by rejecting the services of her maids when he undressed, and by insisting on occupying the same room as Bamfield.[1]

The Duke conveyed to the Netherlands.

The Houses, as soon as they learnt what had happened, issued orders to transfer some of the servants of the Duke of York to his brother the Duke of Gloucester, now only in his ninth year, and did everything in their power to increase the dignity of the child's position, as if to point him out as a possible occupant of the throne now that his brother was no longer available. For the present, however, the time was unpropitious to such designs, as the signs of approaching war were growing clearer every day. Before the end of April, it was evident beyond dispute that the question was not how the Houses should dispose of the throne, but whether it was to be at their disposal. The news from Scotland was gloomy enough, and scarcely less gloomy was the news from Ireland.

The Duke of Gloucester's household increased.

Bad news from Ireland.

[1] Account of the Duke of York's escape. *Clar. St. P.* ii. App. xlvii. ; *Autobiography of Lady Anne Halkett,* 20. For the date of the escape see *L.J.* x, 219.

CHAPTER LXI.

THE EVE OF THE SECOND CIVIL WAR.

In the winter of 1646, Ormond, finding that the English Parliament refused to accept his surrender of the Lord Lieutenant's office on his own terms,[1] had made a fresh effort to conclude an alliance which might unite the English Royalists with more moderate spirits amongst the Irish Confederates, on the basis of toleration under the King's authority, against Rinuccini on the one hand and the Puritans on the other. On behalf of this scheme Digby, as the King's Secretary of State, and Clanricarde, as a loyal Catholic nobleman, combined in carrying on a negotiation with Preston, the commander of the army of the Confederates in Leinster. Preston, jealous of the influence of O'Neill, and never altogether at his ease in carrying out the Nuncio's behests, listened for a time to their invitations,[2] but in the end broke away from them, and on December 22 signed a declaration throwing the blame of the rupture on the insufficiency of Ormond's offers.[3] After this Rinuccini's triumph seemed complete. When the General Assembly met on January 10, 1647, he consented to the liberation of the members of the Supreme Council whom he had arrested in September,[4] being now strong enough to obtain the

1646. Nov.-Dec. Ormond and the Irish Confederates.

A negotiation with Preston.

1647. Jan. 10. General assembly at Kilkenny,

---

[1] See vol. iii. 187.

[2] The correspondence relating to this negotiation is printed in Carte's *Ormond*, vi. 453–483.

[3] Preston to Rinuccini, Dec. 10, *Lord Leicester's MS.* fol. 1,448; Preston to Ormond, Dec. 19, Carte's *Ormond*, vi. 483; Preston's Declaration, Dec. 22, Gilbert's *Hist. of the Irish Confederation*, vi. 167.

[4] See vol. iii. 159.

consent of the Assembly to a condemnation of the peace
made by the Supreme Council with Ormond,[1] and a general

Feb. 2.
condemns
the peace
with
Ormond.

acceptance of his own principles. Every member
of the Assembly swore not to accept any peace which
did not grant full liberty to the Roman Catholic
religion in the whole of Ireland, the restoration of all
jurisdictions and privileges possessed by the clergy in the
days of Henry VII., the abrogation of all laws hostile to the
Roman Catholic religion, and the restitution of all churches
and benefices not only in the districts now held by the Confederates, but also in those which might be subsequently gained
by them. A new Supreme Council was then chosen, in which
the partisans of the clergy formed a decided majority.[2]

Rinuccini's Parliamentary success could not smooth away
the real difficulties, of his position. The feud between Preston

March-May.
Rinuccini's
difficulties.

and O'Neill was still unappeased. The clergy could
not trust Preston, and the brutalities of O'Neill's
Ulstermen exasperated the laity of the South.[3] The
Nuncio was moreover irritated at the anxiety shown, even by
the clergy, to maintain in all temporal matters their allegiance
to a heretic king.[4] The reluctance of the nobility to submit
to the domination of the clergy was still more strongly marked;
whilst the money which should have been sent from Rome
had not yet arrived. Under these circumstances the Confederate Catholics missed the opportunity of seizing Dublin,
which was offered them by the strife between the Parliament
and army in England.

[1] See vol. iii. 557.　　　[2] Rinuccini, *Nunziatura*, 190–209, 472.

[3] Rinuccini to Panzirolo, May 28, *Id.*, 229.

[4] "Nel giuramento rinnovato in quest' Assemblea vedrà V. E. che il
primo punto è la fedeltà verso il Rè, siccome anco i Vescovi senz' alcuna
difficoltà hanno giurato. Questa cosa è tanto inviscerata in ogni sorte di
persona anco ecclesiastica, che quando il Nunzio si facesse alcun minimo
motivo, enterebbe subito in sospetto d' aver altri fini che di semplice
nunziatura, come i mali affetti anco senza questo cercano alle volte di
persuadere." Rinuccini to Panfilio, March 7, *idem*, 205. The Nuncio
goes on to say that, whenever the sending of 10,000 men to England was
talked of, he took care to express his approbation of the proposal only in
general terms.

Whilst Rinuccini was chafing under the restraints which
hindered the creation of a Papal Ireland, the Queen was
doing what she could to make Ireland Royalist.
In March one of her agents, Father Leyburn, who
travelled under the name of Winter Grant, urged
Ormond to retract the word which he had given to Parliament
and to form a league with Rinuccini in defence of the rights
of the Crown. Leyburn passed from Kilkenny to Dublin and
from Dublin to Kilkenny, but it was not in his power to induce
either Ormond to bend before the Nuncio's terms, or the
Nuncio to accept Ormond's doctrine of the supremacy of the
Royal over the ecclesiastical power.[1]

March.
Mission of
Father
Leyburn.

The precious time thus frittered away could never be
recovered by the Confederates. On June 7 Michael Jones,
appointed by the English Parliament to the command in Leinster,[2] landed in Dublin accompanied
by Parliamentary commissioners, and, what was of
far greater importance, by 1,400 foot and 600 horse. Ormond,
after a protracted negotiation, had no choice but to surrender
unconditionally to the English Parliament. On
July 28 he delivered over the sword of office to the
commissioners, and a few days later sailed for
England. His policy of seeking to bind Ireland to Charles
by the concession of religious toleration under the Royal
authority could not but fail. He never had the material
forces behind him necessary to terrify those who rejected his
offers, nor was it possible for him to inspire those to whom
his policy was in itself acceptable with confidence in a king
who merely sought to make use of Catholic Ireland for his
own ends.

June 7.
Michael
Jones in
Dublin.

July 28.
Ormond
surrenders
the sword.

Whilst Ormond was haggling with the commissioners the
long-expected attack of the Confederates was at last
impending over Dublin. Freed from the rivalry of
O'Neill, who had betaken himself to Connaught,
Preston surprised Carlow in May, and having collected a

May-July.
Preston's
advance.

[1] Notices on this mission are scattered over the *Carte MSS.* of the
time, and Rinuccini's *Nunziatura.*

[2] See vol. iii. 232.

considerable force, was early in July in a position to attack the girdle of fortified posts with which Dublin was surrounded. Naas capitulated on July 15, and Maynooth on the 23rd. Preston then laid siege to Trim. If Trim proved unable to resist, it would next be the turn of Dublin.[1]

Before Trim could be brought to yield, the change of rulers in Dublin exposed Preston to an attack from a commander who, though money and supplies were
still wanting, had a military force sufficiently well
equipped to be available, if only for a short time, for
active service. On August 1 Jones marched out of Dublin ; then striking northwards he effected on the 4th a junction with Sir Henry Tichborne, who, having been one of the King's lords-justices, was now serving the Parliament loyally in his old post as governor of Drogheda. The combined force was reckoned at 5,000 foot and 1,500 horse, whilst Preston had at his disposal at least 7,000 foot and 1,000
horse. On the 8th Jones found Preston's army
posted on Dungan Hill, not far from Trim, and at
once pushed forward to the attack. As at Benburb,[2]
the battle was decided by the result of the encounter of the cavalry. Inferior in numbers and discipline, the Irish horse took to flight on both wings. The foot soldiers alone, stubborn as their resistance was, could do no more than maintain the honour of their race. After more than half their numbers had fallen three thousand survivors took refuge in a bog. Jones at once ordered his horsemen to guard the exits, whilst his footmen pressed in to the slaughter. The Irish officers were reserved as prisoners, but of the private soldiers who entered the bog no more than 228 escaped with their lives. Amongst those who fell were four hundred of the hardy band which had followed Alaster Macdonald in the Highlands under the leadership of Montrose.[3]

Marginal notes:
Aug. 1. Jones leaves Dublin.

Aug. 8. Battle of Dungan Hill.

[1] *Lord Leicester's MS.* fol. 1,708.

[2] See vol. iii. 152.

[3] Relation of Battle of Trim, *Nunziatura*, 243 ; Diary, *Carte MSS.* xxi. fol. 371. In the Relation Macdonald's men are called ' Scoti Iberni,' which seems to settle the question of their race. Colonel Alexander

According to the English accounts no more than 500 of the Irish foot escaped from first to last, whilst the Irish them-

The Irish
loss. selves admitted a loss of 3,000. Preston himself escaped, but his money and baggage, together with his secret correspondence, fell into the hands of the victors. To Jones's hungry soldiers the most valuable prize was 'sixty-four pair oxen' ready to be converted into food. Yet even with this help Jones's commissariat was not in a condition to enable him long to keep the field. He recovered Naas and Maynooth, but on the 10th, only two days after his victory, he was compelled to dismiss Tichborne and to return to Dublin.

Good news met Jones on his arrival at the city gate. A ship had arrived bringing 1,500*l.* from England, an earnest, as the soldiers hoped, of better things to come. The victors, as

Aug. 10.
The con-
querors
enter
Dublin. they strode along the streets of Dublin, were not allowed to display the banners which they had captured. It would savour, said Jones, 'of ostentation and attributing unto man the glory of this great work due unto the Lord only.' [1]

To the Confederate Catholics the blow was, indeed, a heavy one. The Supreme Council summoned O'Neill to

Aug. 12.
O'Neill
summoned
by the
Supreme
Council. their aid, and before long the Ulster chieftain established himself in Leinster, but his followers brought with them an evil reputation as plunderers which rendered a hearty co-operation with the southern Irish impossible. [2] Under any circumstances O'Neill would have found it difficult enough to cope with Jones. His forces were quite insufficient to cope with Inchiquin as well.

Inchiquin, whose savage destructiveness branded him amongst his countrymen with the appellation of 'Murrough of the burnings,' was pursuing his accustomed work of destruction

Macdonald is said to have fallen, but either this must be an error, or the slain man must have been a namesake of the son of Colkitto.

[1] Diary, *Carte MSS.* xxi. fol. 371.

[2] *Lord Leicester's MS.* foll. 1,731–1,738. The charge of plundering is placed beyond dispute by its being made in an account written in Rinuccini's interests.

in Munster. On September 3 he drew near to the Rock of Cashel on which the fortress-cathedral of St. Patrick, the work Inchiquin's ravages. of Norman conquerors, overshadows the lovely chapel of Cormac, the last effort of Irish architectural art in the days before the Irish tribes bowed beneath the yoke Sept. 4. He storms the Rock of Cashel. of the stranger. On the 4th, mounting the ascent, he drove the Irish garrison into the cathedral. Then followed a desperate struggle. Finding the doors blocked against them, the assailants raised ladders to the windows and leapt into the church. For half an hour the fight raged within till some sixty of the defenders, who alone remained alive, took refuge in the bell-tower. Enticed by promise of quarter, they at last descended, to be butchered or retained as prisoners for ransom by the faithless Inchiquin. Five priests were slaughtered as a matter of course. Amongst the slain were some women, whilst others were stripped naked and turned out in their shame. When the destruction of human life was at an end, the soldiers fell upon the great crucifix in the rood-loft, and lopped away the head, the hands, and the feet of the image of the Saviour. That day's work put a barrier between Inchiquin and his countrymen which no subsequent tergiversation on his part ever availed to remove.[1]

After Inchiquin had satisfied his rage and the cupidity of his soldiers at Cashel, his light horse swept the country up to Oct. 2. Jones again leaves Dublin. the walls of Kilkenny. This success encouraged Jones, who had now received fresh support from England, to resume the offensive. Leaving Dublin on October 2, he marched northwards to effect a junction with a soldier of far higher quality than Inchiquin.[2]

That soldier was George Monk. After his capture at Nantwich,[3] in January 1644, Monk was for a long time im· 1644. Monk in the Tower. prisoned in the Tower. He was the very type of a professional soldier, diligent and skilful in the fulfilment of his duties, and entirely uninfluenced by political or religious enthusiasm. As long as Charles was

---

[1] Father Sall's narrative in Murphy's *Cromwell in Ireland*, 388.
[2] *Lord Leicester's MS.* 1,738b.   [3] See vol. i. 295.

in a position to claim his services, Monk turned a deaf ear to the advances of his captors, who would gladly have given employment to so distinguished an officer.   At last, in November

1646.
Nov.
Monk
takes the
Covenant.

1646, when Charles was in the hands of the Scots at Newcastle and the Royal army had ceased to exist, Monk, holding himself free from all further obligation to the King, took the Covenant and accepted service under Lord Lisle,[1] who was then setting off for Munster as Lord Lieutenant of Ireland.[2]

Lisle's appointment proving a failure, Monk returned with him to England in 1647.   His services, however, were too

1647.
July 17.
Monk's
command
in Ulster.

valuable to be readily dispensed with, and on July 17 of the same year he received a commission to command all the Parliamentary forces in Ulster excepting the Scottish regiments under Monro.   As O'Neill was no longer in the North, Monk soon found himself in a position to give assistance to the forces in Leinster, and

Oct. 5.
Junction
between
Monk and
Jones.

on October 5 he brought 1,400 foot and 600 horse to the help of Jones.   Their united army now consisted of 6,000 foot and 1,600 horse—a force which was irresistible as long as it could be fed.   Many fortresses were captured, including the strong town of Athboy, under the very eyes of O'Neill.

---

[1] See vol. iii. 232.

[2] Gumble's *Life of Monk*, 22; *L.J.* viii. 562, 564; ix. 336.   Mr. Julian Corbett holds that Monk did not take the Covenant at this time—though there is evidence that the Committee of Both Kingdoms reported him to be ready to take it—on the ground that the Ulster Scots asked him to take it in 1649, which he thinks they would not have done if he had taken it already.   It appears, however, that, on March 30, 1649, Lord Montgomery of Ards and others wrote to Monk that they did not see how they could 'in conscience join with any new association with such as will not cordially renew the Covenant with us now.'   (*Carte MSS.* xxiv. fol. 332.)   That the Scots in 1649 wanted Monk to take the Covenant a second time is shown still more clearly by the Declaration of the Council of War printed in *The Declaration of the British*, E. 556, 15. The fact is that to take the Covenant in 1646 meant, to a man who cared nothing for ecclesiastical distinctions, a renunciation of the service of Charles I. for that of Parliament.   To take it in 1649 meant a renunciation of the service of the Commonwealth for that of Charles II. and the Scots.

O'Neill was the less able to offer resistance as he had weakened himself by the despatch of Alaster Macdonald into Munster to assist Lord Taaffe, the general of the Confederates, in making head against the victorious Inchiquin.[1]

Nov. 13.
Inchiquin's victory near Mallow.

On November 13, however, Inchiquin defeated the combined army in the neighbourhood of Mallow. As at Dungan Hill, the struggle on the field was followed by a butchery, no quarter being given to any but the officers. Even this distinction did not avail Alaster Macdonald. The strong man whose swashing blows had stemmed the tide of war at Auldearn was negotiating for a surrender, when an officer of Inchiquin's basely stabbed him in the back, and stretched him dying on the ground.[2]

Such a flood of disaster necessarily produced a deep feeling of despondency at Kilkenny, where the General Assembly was again in session. For some time there had been a talk of offering the Protectorate of Ireland to a foreign prince, and for this office Rinuccini would have selected the Pope or some Catholic sovereign acting under the Pope's influence.[3] The old party of peace was, however, too strong for the Nuncio.

Nov. 12.
The General Assembly despondent.

Talk of a Protector of Ireland.

The General Assembly now restored to their places in the Supreme Council many who had been ejected and imprisoned by him a year before. It also insisted, in spite of his objections, on sending three commissioners to France with the twofold object of inviting the Prince of Wales to Ireland, in accordance with a proposal which had been made through Father Leyburn,[4] and of coming to an agreement with the Queen on terms of peace which might supersede those formerly arranged with Ormond.[5]

Commissioners sent to France,

---

[1] *The late Successful Proceedings of the Army*, E. 412, 4; *Lord Leicester's MS.* fol. 1,738b–1,739b.

[2] Inchiquin to Lenthall, Nov. 18, *A True Relation*, E. 418, 6; Rinuccini's *Nunziatura*, 268.

[3] In his letter of Nov. 23 (*Nunziatura*, 265) he does not commit himself so far, but his subsequent letters show what his wishes were.

[4] See p. 104.

[5] See vol. iii. 55.

Rinuccini was the more dissatisfied as two of the commissioners, Lord Muskerry and Geoffrey Browne, were his opponents, and the only one on whose goodwill he could count was the Marquis of Antrim. The influence of the Nuncio, however, was still considerable enough to enable him to exact a promise from the Assembly that, as far as religion was concerned, nothing should be accepted which had not the sanc-

and to
Rome. tion of the Pope, and to obtain the appointment of two other commissioners of his own selection to negotiate at Rome.[1]

It was till February that the two parties of commissioners

1648.
Feb.
Departure
of the
commis-
sioners.

Barry's
mis-ion. left Ireland. At the end of that month Colonel Barry landed at Cork[2] with instructions from Ormond—who had now been for some time in France—to bring the Royalist party in Ireland into active co-operation with that large party amongst the Confederates which was more or less openly hostile to the Nuncio.

Before making for Kilkenny, Barry stopped to have an interview with Inchiquin. In spite of the ferocity he had

Inchiquin
changes
sides. exhibited against his Catholic fellow-countrymen, Inchiquin had for some time been preparing to change sides. He had far more in common with the great Irish landowners who formed the main support of the Royalist party amongst the Confederates, than with Jones on the one hand or Rinuccini on the other. He had also taken alarm at the Vote of No Addresses as implying a defiance to his own class as well as to the King. Accordingly,

March.
A cessation
to be nego-
tiated. he received Barry with open arms, and gave him authority to negotiate between himself and the Confederates a cessation of arms which might afterwards be converted into open co-operation in the King's name.[3]

On March 28 the ominous tidings that negotiations were

[1] Rinuccini's *Nunziatura*, 263–293.
[2] *Lord Leicester's MS.* fol. 1,904.
[3] Philopater Irenæus (*i.e.* John O'Callaghan), *Vind. Cath. Hib.* 58.

on foot reached Westminster.[1]　On April 13 further news

March 28.
The news
reaches
West-
minster. arrived which confirmed the worst fears.　Inchiquin had, on April 3, declared openly for the King and for an alliance with the Scots and the Irish Con-federates, and had also notified to his officers that

April 13.
Inchiquin's
revolt
known. those who refused to support his new policy must leave the country.[2]

Before long news still more depressing arrived from Scot-land.　Whatever hope Cromwell may have entertained of

April 25.
Bad news
from
Scotland. averting an invasion by an understanding with Argyle and the Kirk had now to be definitely abandoned.

April 11.
Demands
of the
Scottish
Parlia-
ment. On April 11 the Scottish Parliament voted that the treaty between the two kingdoms had been broken, and that a demand should be made for the esta-blishment of the Presbyterian religion in England, and the suppression of heresy and the Book of Com-mon Prayer.　It also voted that the English Parliament should be asked to open a negotiation with the King in the hope of obtaining his consent to these terms, and should disband Fair-

April 18.
It names
officers. fax's army of sectaries.　On the 18th the Parliament, in expectation of a refusal of these demands, pro-ceeded to name colonels of regiments about to be raised in the several counties for service against the enemies of religion.[3]

From Wales, too, the news had for some time been alarm-

March.
Proposed
disband-
ment of
Laugharne's
troops. ing.　Early in March hopes had been entertained that the troops raised by Laugharne to fight during the last war on the side of Parliament would suffer themselves to be quietly disbanded.　A consider-

March 23.
Poyer's
sally. able party of them, however, now went off in the direction of Pembroke, giving intimation of their approach to Poyer.　On March 23, Poyer, sure of their support,

---

[1] All that was published was a letter from Inchiquin's officers declaring that they must be fetched home to England unless supplies were sent ; but Grignon, in his despatch of April $\frac{3}{13}$, speaks of Inchiquin as having already joined the Catholics.

[2] *L. J.* x. 161, 189 ; *Papers against Lord Inchiquin*, E. 435, 33.

[3] *Acts of the Parl. of Scotl.* VI. part ii. 23, 30.

sallied out of the castle and chased out of the town the Parliamentary officer, Colonel Fleming, with the soldiers under his command.[1]

Poyer was encouraged by this success to more active operations. Sweeping over Pembrokeshire he levied men and con-

Poyer's activity. tributions, and only just failed in carrying off the Parliamentary commissioners as prisoners to Pembroke. He succeeded in getting possession of Tenby Castle, and was emboldened to issue a proclamation in which he declared openly for the King and the Book of Common Prayer.[2]

THE WAR IN SOUTH WALES.

At Westminster there was grave anxiety as to the attitude

Colonel Horton to disband Laugharne's regiments. of Laugharne's regiments. Colonel Horton was despatched by Fairfax with reinforcements to superintend the disbandment, for, though both soldiers and officers gave fair promises, they might easily be carried away by the enthusiasm of Poyer's good fortune to

---

[1] *A Bloody Slaughter*, E. 433, 5; *The Kingdom's Weekly Intelligencer*, E. 434, 26; *Prince Charles's Letter*, E. 434, 27; *Perf. Occurrences*, E. 522, 11; *Rushw.* vii. 1,039.

[2] *Perf. Occurrences*, E. 522, 17; *The Declaration of Col. Poyer*, E. 435, 9.

resist a government known to them mainly by the taxes which it levied.[1]   As April wore on it became clear that Horton would have more enemies to deal with than the mere garrisons of Pembroke and Tenby.   Laugharne's men took what payment they could get and left their ranks ; but as soon as they were disbanded they for the most part placed themselves under Poyer's orders.[2]   In so doing they were encouraged by Colonel Powel, one of Laugharne's principal officers, though Laugharne himself for the present abstained from action.   On April 17 Horton wrote that he had arrived at Neath, and that an immediate action was expected.

In Wales, as in Ireland and Scotland, Charles hoped to draw to his own profit the not unnatural reluctance of the

A combination against England. population to submit to the predominance of England.   Yet neither his character nor his position fitted him to appear as the champion of overborne

Its inherent weakness. nationalities.   Alike in Scotland and in Ireland the distinctive national feeling had rallied to the representative of the spiritual power—in one case to the Presbyterian clergy, in the other case to Rinuccini.   Hamilton in Scotland and the Confederate lords in Ireland supported Charles's claims in England, because they wished to use his restored authority to support them in opposing ecclesiastical pretensions in their respective countries.   Their most vigorous efforts would be heavily weighted with an ally whose promises no man could trust, and who, when his own objects had been gained, would as readily sacrifice his supporters as his enemies.

To Charles himself the varied nature of the forces taking the field on his behalf was almost certain to be detrimental.

Its effect in England. Cavaliers of the old stock like Glemham and Langdale might cheerfully accept the help of the Scots, as Ormond had accepted the aid of Inchiquin and Muskerry, in confidence that when the victory had once been won their own social position, combined with the favour of the King, would suffice to secure the ascendency of their own principles in the future.   Charles's new allies, the English Presbyterians, were

---

[1] *A Perf. Diurnal*, E. 522, 15.   [2] *Idem*, E. 522, 20.

much less confident, and but few of them were likely to believe that a victory due to the Cavaliers, aided by the less distinctively Presbyterian section of the nobility of Scotland and by the Catholic nobility of Ireland, would really conduce to the attainment of their objects.

If there was a man in England capable of taking advantage of this state of feeling it was Cromwell. All his thoughts made for unity, and after pushing his designs for the conciliation of the King almost beyond the verge of safety, he at last accepted the stern teaching of facts, and betook himself to the conciliation of the Presbyterians. It did not need much clearness of brain to teach him the importance of succeeding here. The army, though comparatively small in numbers, had the advantage of a central position, and might fairly be expected to cope with the large forces threatening it from Scotland and Ireland, because those forces were scattered over a wide circumference, and were ill supported even by the people of the countries which sent them forth. A successful rising in England, and especially in London, would shift the whole balance of the war. The army would, in that case, be deprived at a blow of the support of the machinery of civil government, and would degenerate into a horde of brave and well-disciplined brigands.

The turning point appears to have been reached on April 25. On that day a letter written from Newcastle by Hazlerigg was read in the House of Commons, announcing that a resolution to raise an army had been taken in Scotland.[1] As it happened, the House was unusually full, and in a full House there was always a Presbyterian majority. Yet the effect of this news, even on the Presbyterians, was at once exhibited. Not only did the House resolve to strengthen the fortifications of Newcastle, but to proceed with the least possible delay to the question of the settlement of the kingdom,[2] which had been kept in the background since the Vote of No Addresses, during the time that the Independents had been

April 25. News from Scotland.

Its effect at Westminster.

---

[1] *L.J.* v. 544. The letter is probably the one printed anonymously in the *Perf. Diurnal,* E. 522, 25.

[2] *C.J.* v. 544, 545.

carrying on their secret negotiation for the abdication of the King. On the 27th, before the constitutional debate was opened, a still more pressing question claimed the attention

April 27.
Ill-feeling
between
the City
and the
army.

of the House. The misunderstanding between the City and the army sprung from differences about money quite as much as from differences about religious and political principles. No threats of the soldiers or of Parliament could induce the citizens to pay their assessments, and without the assessments of the City the soldiers must either starve or make themselves unpopular by living at free quarter. Necessarily, therefore, the citizens were in ill odour at head-quarters, and from time to time there was a talk amongst the Agitators of taking the law into their own hands. On the 27th, the City authorities appeared at West-

Everard's
information.

minster, and laid before the Houses information received from an exciseman named Everard, to the effect that, being at Windsor on the 20th, as he lay in his bed, he overheard some officers, of whom Colonel Ewer was one, talking in the next room of disarming the City and forcing it by threats of plunder to advance 1,000,000*l.*

In consequence of this information the City now demanded that the chains taken away from the streets after the late riot [1]

Demands of
the City,

should be restored, that the army should be removed to a farther distance, and that Skippon, who possessed the confidence of both parties, should be appointed to command the trained bands of the whole district within the now demolished fortifications.[2] Cromwell at once perceived

granted at
the request
of Cromwell
and Vane.

that the advantage of coming to an understanding with the City would be far greater than anything that could be gained by the maintenance of irritating precautions against revolt, and, seconded by Vane,[3] he moved that the petition of the City might be granted. The permission to replace the chains and the appointment of Skippon met with no opposition ; the question of removing the army could only be decided with the concurrence of the army itself.[4]

[1] See p. 98.
[3] *Merc. Pragmaticus,* E. 437, 31.

[2] *L.J.* x. 234.
[4] *C.J.* v. 546.

On the 28th the House proceeded to consider the basis of the constitutional settlement of the kingdom. In a division, in which the Presbyterians were supported by Vane and Pierrepont and other leading Independents,[1] it was resolved by the large majority of 165 to 99 that the House would 'not alter the fundamental government of the kingdom, by King, Lords, and Commons.' The question who the King should be was not openly touched, but the House proceeded to resolve that the matter of the propositions drawn up for presentation to the King when he was at Hampton Court should 'be the ground of the debate for the settlement of the peace of the kingdom,' and that any member was to be at liberty in spite of the Vote of No Addresses to propound anything he pleased in the course of the debate.[2]

April 28. King, Lords, and Commons to be maintained.

The Hampton Court propositions to be the basis of the settlement.

There were some who thought that the main object of those who supported this proposal was to cut the ground from under the feet of the Scots. Cromwell, at least, could vote with a safe conscience for a Presbyterian settlement if he could be sure that Parliament would maintain the concession of religious liberty which had been made at the time of the adoption of the propositions intended to be presented at Hampton Court.[3] Most likely, however, he troubled himself for the moment about none of these things. What he wanted now was time in which to beat the Scots, and if Parliament chose to waste time by entering into a fresh negotiation with the King as hopeless as the first, he at least would be the gainer.

Result of these votes.

Having done what he could at Westminster, Cromwell hurried to Windsor. He had there to do with men to whom the very idea of compromise was hateful. On the 24th a body of Agitators had met at St. Albans, where they denounced the ambition of the grandees, and drew up a petition for the immediate adoption of the *Agreement of the People.*[4] This foolish attempt to exasperate

April 24. Meeting of Agitators.

---

[1] ——— ? to Lanark, April 28, *Hamilton Papers,* 190.

[2] *C.J.* v. 547.   [3] See vol. iii. 375.

[4] *The Army's Petition,* E. 438, 1.

nine-tenths of the nation against the army at a moment when
the army had but little good-will to spare was summarily
put down. On the 28th those who had taken part in the
meeting were summoned before a Council of War at Windsor,
and though they ultimately escaped with no more than a
reprimand they were taught that the time was not one for
sowing divisions in the army or the State.[1]

Cromwell could stamp out mutiny, but he could not
conceal from himself that his hold on the army was im-
Cromwell perilled. Everything, it seemed, had gone wrong,
distrusted. and most of all his own sanguine efforts to restore peace by negotiating with the King. It was no secret
that, by many in the army and out of the army, he was regarded as a traitor who had turned aside from the path in
which he had engaged to walk after the suppression of the
mutiny on Corkbush Field. Yet Cromwell's mind was not
troubled merely by the fear of external danger. His failures
always brought with them deep searchings of heart, and stern
questionings of his own conscience to teach him whether he
had in any way strayed from the path of duty. In this he was
not alone, and on the 29th [2] the notables of the army —

---

[1] *Perf. Weekly Account*, E. 438, 8.

[2] The date given in Allen's narrative (printed in *Carlyle* after Letter
lv.) is 'in the beginning of 1648,' that is to say after March 25. Not
only is it impossible to fix the date during Cromwell's negotiations with
the King, but there are other reasons for placing it at the end of April.
Under the date of May 2, *Mercurius Pragmaticus* (E. 437, 31) speaks of
a day of humiliation at Windsor, and Whitelocke fixes it on April 29.
This would bring the third day to May 1, and a Letter of Intelligence of
May 1, in the *Clarendon MSS.* (2,771) says that the Independents in the
House 'will bring the King upon his trial, and make choice of some of
their learned divines to show the lawfulness of it.' The final resolution
at Windsor seems to have been taken after the decision to send off part
of the army to Wales, which was on April 30 or May 1. From this I
gather that the three days of the conference were April 29, 30, and May 1,
especially as we know that Cromwell was at Windsor on April 29, and
it seems unlikely that he should have been absent from Parliament on
the 28th, when the important vote was taken on the settlement of the
kingdom.

both officers and Agitators—met at Windsor to consider the position in which they stood, now when it almost seemed as though the past struggle had been entered upon in vain.

April 29.
A prayer-
meeting.

The first day was spent in prayer with the purpose of 'enquiring into the causes of that sad dispensation.' On the second day 'Lieutenant-General Cromwell did press very earnestly on all those present to a thorough consideration of our actions as an army, as well as our ways particularly as private Christians, to see if any iniquity could be found in them, and what it was, that if possible we might find it out, and so remove the cause of such sad rebukes which were upon us by reason of our iniquities.' Upon this, those who were present carried their inquiry back, searching for the time when the presence of the Lord was amongst them, 'and rebukes and judgments were not as then upon us.' It was a long quest, and those concerned in it were not given to brevity of speech. The time of the meeting sped away as yet without definite result.

April 30.
Cromwell's
urgency.

On the morning of the third day, May 1, news arrived which drove these earnest seekers rapidly to what can hardly have been other than a foregone conclusion. They learnt that in Wales, Fleming, pushing on too far, had been surprised and slain, and that all South Wales was in a state of revolt. Wherever Horton appeared the whole population fled to the hills, and not even a horse-shoe was to be had. At once Fairfax and the Council of War ordered Cromwell into South Wales with two regiments of horse and three of foot, making up together with those under Horton a force of 8,000 men.[1]

April 29.
A check
in Wales.

May 1,
Cromwell
sent to South
Wales.

The renewal of the war, of which so much had been said during the past twelve months, and which the army had, wisely or unwisely, striven so hard to avert, had thus become a grim reality. The sword must again be drawn before peace and settlement could be won. When that Council of War broke up, and officers of whom it was composed joined the Agitators once more to gather up the

The third
day's
meeting.

[1] *A Perf. Diurnal,* E. 522, 26.

conclusions to which they had come since the last day's meeting, the temper exhibited by them was harder than on the day before. Major Goffe led the way, characteristically pointing out their sins of unbelief, base fear of men, and carnal consultations as the fruit thereof; with their own wisdoms, and not with the word of the Lord. For a while his hearers, to whom every success was a sign of Divine intervention in their favour, and every failure a sign of the Divine wrath, listened speechlessly. Bitter tears rolled down their bronzed cheeks as they pondered over their long and fruitless efforts to win the King to the ways of peace. And now their long strivings had an end. Charles's light, insincere talk had culminated in this worst of all offences, the deliberate stirring up of fresh war; not, as in 1642, by placing himself at the head of a party which sympathised with his aims, but by deliberately rousing the hostility of men with whose aims he had no sympathy whatever, and whom he intended, it was impossible to doubt, to cozen and fling aside when they had served his purpose.

Whatever else might be true, the effort to obtain peace with the help of Charles had no shadow of truth in it. Here then was the sin of the army, and this sin must be driven far off if it was again, as in the days of open strife, to be gladdened by the consciousness of the Lord's presence. Some of those present had seen this long ago; all of them saw it now. "Presently," as one who on that day wept and meditated with the rest, told the story long afterwards, "we were led and helped to a clear agreement amongst ourselves, not any dissenting"—this time at least, not even Cromwell—"that it was the duty of our day, with the forces we had, to go out and fight against those potent enemies, which that year in all places appeared against us, with an humble confidence in the name of the Lord only, that we should destroy them; also enabling us then, after serious seeking his face, to come to a very clear and joint resolution on many grounds at large then debated amongst us, that it was our duty, if ever the Lord brought us back again in peace, to call Charles Stuart, that man of blood, to an account for the blood he had shed, and mischief he had done to his utmost, against the Lord's cause and people in these poor nations."[1]

It needs no recourse to the belief in Divine inspiration to account for this stern decision. Charles had played fast and loose with his obligations, till men, such as those who took part in that fierce prayer-meeting at Windsor, had come to think of him as the one root of evil. They had failed to make their way through the tangle of political arguments. They had failed to conciliate their fellow-country-men ; but they had come to the conclusion, not only that there could be no peace for England until Charles had been deprived of his power to stir up never-ending strife, but that he must be called ' to an account for that blood he had shed.'

The decision against Charles.

'That Cromwell agreed with the first conclusion can hardly be doubted ; but if in momentary exaltation of spirit, he gave his assent to the latter, many months had still to pass before he could throw himself heart and soul into the course to which the resolution of his fellow soldiers deliberately pointed.

[1] Allen's Narrative, Somers' *Tracts*, vi. 500.

CHAPTER LXII.

ST. FAGANS AND MAIDSTONE.

From a military point of view everything depended on the possession of the City. The numbers of the army were indeed sufficiently large to keep London down by force, but they were not sufficient to keep down London and to fight the Welsh and Scots as well. Cromwell, clearly recognising this simple truth, had of late been doing everything in his power to induce his brother-officers to abandon their wild talk about a more extended military occupation of the City.[1] It would be time enough when the enemy had been beaten to 'make the City pay for all,' in other words to compel it to pay the assessments which it had hitherto kept back,[2] possibly with such additions as would meet the expenses of the whole of the new war.

1648.
Necessity of conciliating the City.

The act was suited to the word. On May 1 Fairfax, without waiting for orders from Parliament, announced to the House of Commons his intention to despatch Cromwell into

---

[1] See p. 115.

[2] "Before Cromwell went for Wales, it was resolved at a Council of War that the City should have all they could ask or desire, there being no other way for the present to quiet them; and Cromwell then told Fairfax that he did not doubt good success in Wales, and to be with him suddenly in the North . . . to settle those countries, and then they would make the City pay for all." Advices to Ormond, July (?), *Carte MSS.* xxii. fol. 162. The story, it must be remembered, is told by a Royalist, and therefore in a way most unfavourable to Cromwell; and, as a matter of fact, when the army came back it made no attempt to do more than call for the payment of the assessments due to it.

Wales, added that he was about to withdraw the regiments

May 1.
The regi-
ments to be
withdrawn
from White-
hall and the
Mews.

from Whitehall and the Mews, leaving the protection of Parliament to the London forces under
Skippon's command.[1]   The House indeed asked
Fairfax to postpone the execution of his order;
but only till time had been given it to consult the
authorities of the City on the new guard to be provided
for its own safety.[2]

If the City had been heart and soul in favour of a Scottish
intervention these blandishments would have been of little

The Pres-
byterians
distracted.

avail.   As a matter of fact the bulk of the Presbyterians, both in the City and in Parliament, were
beginning to suspect that they were being used as a
catspaw by the Royalists.   "The kingdom," wrote a Cavalier,
"generally desires their King, and the people grows to be un-
quiet, but they are so afraid of a new war as they will hardly
stir.   The Presbyterians are much discontented, and would
willingly be rid of their new masters; yet rather than they will
hazard the coming in of the Cavaliers and the reduction[3] of
Episcopacy, they will sit still."[4]

At Westminster the members composing the Presbyterian
majority were a prey to conflicting emotions.   They were eager

May 2.
Hesitation
of the Pres-
byterians.

to negotiate with the King, and also eager to keep at
a distance the Scots on whom the King mainly relied.
Distrusting the army they were, nevertheless, willing
to make use of it to hold back the flood of Royalism which
threatened to sweep them away.   On May 2 they issued an

Ordinance
against
blasphemy
and heresy.

Ordinance, bristling with death-penalties against
blasphemy and heresy.[5]   Yet, but for the army, the
power to issue such Ordinances would soon pass
out of their hands.   On the day on which this

April 28.
Berwick
seized,

atrocious instrument of persecution was given to
the world, news arrived that on April 28 Sir Marmaduke Langdale, followed by a party of Royalists from Scotland,

---

[1] Fairfax to Lenthall, May 1, Cary's *Mem. of the Civil War,* i. 393.

[2] *C.J.* v. 549; compare a Letter of Intelligence, May 4, *Clarendon
MSS.* 2.773.   [3] *i.e.* the bringing back.

[4] Letter of Intelligence, May 1, *ibid.* 2,771.   [5] *L.J.* x. 240.

had surprised Berwick, and that another party had surprised
Carlisle on the 29th. On May 1, Sir Philip Musgrave, a Cumberland baronet, who had been governor
of Carlisle for the King in the former war, returned
to his old post. Both Langdale and Musgrave entered into
an obligation to surrender to the Scots the places they occupied whenever they were called upon to do so.[1]

April 29, and Carlisle.

This evil news was followed on May 3 by the delivery of a
letter written in the name of the Scottish Parliament, in accordance with its resolutions voted on April 11,[2] with
an intimation that the messenger would wait no
more than fifteen days for a reply. The letter
demanded that all Englishmen might be compelled
to take the Covenant, that the Presbyterian government might
be settled, heresies and schisms, including the Book of Common
Prayer, suppressed, and Popery and prelacy exterminated.
The King, moreover, was to be brought to one of his houses
near London, with a view to the opening of negotiations, whilst
the excluded members were to be re-admitted to their seats,
and the army of Sectaries disbanded.[3]

May 3. Peremptory demands from Scotland.

The Hamilton party, from which this summons emanated,
had acted prudently in refusing to submit it to the scrutiny of
the General Assembly. The demand for the return
of the King suited ill with the proscription of the
Book of Common Prayer. The movement was a dishonest
one from the beginning, cloaking its Royalism in
the disguise of Presbyterian zeal. On May 1
Hamilton and five other lords, one of whom was
Lauderdale, despatched a letter by Sir William
Fleming and Will Murray to the Prince of Wales, formally
inviting him to Scotland.[4]

Their dishonesty

May 1. The Prince of Wales invited to Scotland.

Though the Presbyterians at Westminster, refusing to bow

---

[1] *Perfect Occurrences*, E. 522, 25; *The Declaration*, E. 438; Musgrave's narrative, *Clarendon MSS.* 2,867. I have taken the date of the
seizure of Berwick, which is variously given, from the last source.

[2] See p. 111.

[3] Loudoun to the Speaker of the House of Lords, April 26, *L.J.* x. 242.

[4] Hamilton and others to the Prince of Wales, May 1, *Burnet*, vi. 30.

their heads before the summons addressed to them by the
Scots, merely answered that they would send a reply by their
own messengers, they nevertheless did their best to show that
the interests of Royalism and Presbyterianism were safe in
their hands. On May 6 the two Houses concurred

May 6.
Declaration
of the
Houses.

in a declaration that they would not alter the Government by King, Lords, and Commons ; that they
would maintain the Covenant, and would readily join the Scots
in again presenting to the King the old Presbyterian propositions laid before him at Hampton Court. They however
said nothing about enforcing the universal taking of the Covenant or about the removal of the King to the neighbourhood
of London.[1]

Surely it might be thought that if those who spoke in the
name of the Scottish nation were as seriously Presbyterian

Will the
Scots
accept it ?

as their language implied, they would be satisfied
with these terms. So probable did it appear that
the English and Scottish Presbyterians would agree
that the Independents once more, if report is to be trusted,
made application to the King to treat on the basis of *The
Heads of the Proposals*, thinking them more agreeable to him
than the stringent demands of their opponents.[2]

Whether this report was true or not, Cromwell had no part
in any fresh attempt to re-open negotiations with the King.

May 8.
Cromwell at
Gloucester.

He was already far on the way to Wales. On May 8
he reviewed his forces at Gloucester, telling his men
that ' he had oftentimes ventured his life with them
and they with him against the common enemy of this kingdom,' and that, if they would follow him in this cause,
he was ready to live and die with them. His declaration
was received with applause. No one in the ranks could
doubt that when Cromwell spoke of the common enemy he summoned all who were faithful to him to contend against the King.[3]

Whilst Presbyterian members of Parliament were hesitating,

---

[1] *L.J.* x. 247.

[2] Letter of Intelligence, May 8, *Clarendon MSS.* 2,778.

[3] Hancock to ——— ?, May 8, *A Declaration of Lieut.-Col. Cromwell*,
E. 441, 16

the tide of Royalism was mounting high. The very Eastern

Royalism in
the Eastern
Counties. Counties which had pronounced most strongly against the King in 1642, pronounced with no less strength against military rule in 1648. On April 24 a riot

April 24.
A riot at
Norwich. broke out at Norwich, in resistance to an officer sent to fetch the Royalist Mayor to Westminster.[1] On

May 4.
The Essex
petition. May 4 a petition from Essex was brought to Westminster by a procession of two thousand men on horse or on foot. It was said to represent the wishes of 30,000 of the inhabitants of the county, who prayed that the King might be satisfied and the army disbanded. The City authorities

May 9.
Concessions
to the City. were no less pressing, and on May 9 the Commons agreed to permit the City to nominate its own committee of militia, and even to appoint a new Lieutenant of the Tower, Fairfax's soldiers, who had hitherto

Fairfax to
march to
the North. formed the garrison, being withdrawn from the garrison.[2] On the same day, in consequence of the surprise of Berwick, orders were given to Fairfax to march with all haste to the North.[3]

At head-quarters the Royalist demonstrations caused deep irritation. It is said that the Council of the Army voted on the

May 5.
Ill-feeling at
head-
quarters. 5th, 'That neither this king nor any of his posterity should ever reign kings of England.'[4] There was, however, an impression amongst the soldiers that the questions at issue must be decided by the sword and not by

May 10. votes. "I see," wrote one who was at Windsor when it was known that the Tower and the militia had been abandoned to the City, "no honest men daunted at this news."

Those who sought comfort in the field rather than in the senate were soon to have their reward. On the 11th it was

May 8.
Horton's
victory at
St. Fagans. known in London that there had been a sharp fight on the 8th at St. Fagans, in the neighbourhood of Llandaff, and that the Welsh, of whom Laugharne now openly undertook the command, had been completely

---

[1] *Perf. Occurrences*, E. 522, 23.

[2] *Ibid*. E. 522, 25; ——? to Lanark, May 9, *Hamilton Papers*, *Addenda*.   [3] *L.J.* x. 244, 249; *C.J.* v. 554, 555.

[4] *Merc. Politicus*, E. 442, 2.

defeated by Horton, before Cromwell had come up.[1] The effect of the news in London was the greater on both Parliament and City, as the Presbyterians were beginning to fear the consequences of success. It was evident that England was trembling on the brink of a purely Royalist reaction. The Welshmen at St. Fagans bore the motto "We long to see our King" on their hats. In London the mob was shouting for the King, whilst the Essex petition did not contain a word about Religion or the Covenant. Those who had distrusted the soldiers most now began to think of them as preservers.[2]

May 11. Its effect in London.

In spite of the victory at St. Fagans the pressure of impending danger was hardly lightened. On the 12th the Houses made a weak attempt to avert an invasion from the North by directing their commissioners at Edinburgh to inform the Scottish Parliament that Fairfax's march was directed solely against the Englishmen who had seized Berwick and Carlisle.[3] Wavering as the City was, the Houses could never be secure against a sudden outbreak, and they therefore asked Fairfax to revoke

May 12. A message to Scotland.

Fears of the City.

---

[1] Horton to Lenthall, May 8, *L.J.* x. 254.

[2] "To observe the strange alteration the defeating of the Welsh hath made in all sorts is admirable. The disaffected to the army of the religious Presbyterians now fawn upon them, partly for fear of you, and partly in that they think you will keep down the Royal party which threatened them in their doors in the streets to their faces with destruction, and put no difference between Presbyter and Independent. . . . When the letters were read in the House of the defeat, how many Royalists hung down their heads and went out, not staying the conclusion! From all which you may see clearly how necessary it is to be alway in action with your army, and if not here, yet elsewhere. . . . I find the people have alway been content to—not only part with money - but to be taken with successes ; and the noise of victory running in the ballad is matter for them to prate of. The more wise are put into fear and conformity. This went along with all our victories and wars in France, though they exhausted never so much, so it was fairly carried in raising and faithfully disposed of. The City talk as if they would also join with you against the Royal party, but trust them not, for all that are not fools, except your friends, are for King and Bishops." ——? to ——? *Clarke MSS.*

[3] Instructions to the Commissioners, May 12, *L.J.* x. 254.

his orders for the removal of the two regiments at Whitehall
and the Mews.[1]　Resistance might be expected to
break out in any quarter.　On the 12th there was a
riot at Bury St. Edmunds 'about setting up of a
Maypole,' and on the following day the town was held by six
or seven hundred armed men.　On the 14th the
trained bands of the county appeared on the scene,
and the insurgents submitted.　Yet so uncertain was
the position that Whalley was sent down to maintain order and
a regiment of foot was told off to follow him.[2]

Whatever difference of opinion prevailed amongst the
Londoners the vast majority of them were united in detesta-
tion of the army, and they took care to show their
feelings on May 15, the day appointed for a thanks-
giving for the victory at St. Fagans.　Never had the
City churches been so thinly attended.　A wag taking his
stand at the door of St. Dunstan's called out to the passers-by
that 'if they would come and thanksgive, they should have
room enough.'[3]

On the 16th Surrey followed the lead of Essex.　A procession of petitioners from that county marched through the
City shouting, "For God and King Charles!"　As
they passed Whitehall, where Barkstead's regiment
was quartered, they jeered at the soldiers.　When
they reached Westminster they sent in their petition to the
Houses.　From the Lords they received a brief acknowledgment, but they waited in vain for an answer from the Commons.
Exasperated at this contemptuous treatment, some of them
attacked the sentinels, and attempted to force their
way into the House, with shouts of "An old King
and a new Parliament!"　They were resolved, they said, to
have an answer to their mind.　In the midst of the uproar the
tramp of disciplined soldiers was heard approaching, and at last
Major Briscoe at the head of five hundred men pushed his

---

[1] *C.J.* v. 558.
[2] *Perf. Occurrences*, E. 522, 29 ; Letter from Bury, May **17**, *Perf.
Diurnal*, E. 522, 30.
[3] Letter of Intelligence, May **18**, *Clarendon MSS.* 2,786.

way into Westminster Hall, where the greater part of the crowd was assembled.

For a moment there was an attempt at resistance, and a sword was thrust through the body of a soldier. The troops, however, soon cleared the hall with push of pike. The petitioners, leaving the floor strewed with their wounded, fled into Palace Yard. Some took refuge in boats, whence they pelted their assailants with coal and brickbats. For some time the soldiers, who had been ordered not to use their muskets, bore the storm of missiles patiently, but in the end, their officers having been struck down, they fired at assailants whom they could reach in no other way. The riot was thus brought to a close, about a hundred of the petitioners having been wounded, whilst some eight or ten were either killed outright or died subsequently of their wounds.[1]

There is no doubt that the cause of the Surrey petitioners was popular. In the narratives of the tumult which passed
The cause of the Surrey petitioners popular.
from hand to hand, the soldiers were described as blood-stained butchers, who took pleasure in the slaughter of inoffensive citizens. The cry which the petitioners had raised for an accommodation with the King, the disbandment of the army, and the restoration of the known
May 18. Manifesto of the petitioners.
laws, was widely echoed. Yet even the petitioners, it seems, had not been unanimous in their aims. In a manifesto, published on the 18th, their leaders threw blame on those who had joined their ranks with the design of restoring absolute government, and emphasised their own attachment to the Presbyterian system in the Church and to constitutional monarchy in the State.[2]

---

[1] Each side gave its own account of the affair. For the soldiers we have *A True Relation*, E. 443, 5 ; and *A True Narrative*, E. 443, 29. The petitioners state their case in *The Copy of a Letter*, E. 445, 3 ; and *A Declaration . . . of the County of Surrey*, E. 445, 8. See also on the same side a Letter of Intelligence, May 18, *Clarendon MSS.* 2,786. On the whole I have followed the soldiers' account, which is much more full and definite than the other, and which inspires confidence by the tone in which it is written.

[2] *A Declaration of the County of Surrey*, E. 445, 8.

Amongst the Presbyterians in Parliament the same sentiments prevailed in greater force.   Instead of openly declaring

Policy of
the Presby-
terians in
Parliament.

for the King, they were bent on once more opening
a negotiation with him.   The Independents understood the futility of such a policy far too well to
offer opposition, or to irritate the Presbyterians in such a way
as to drive them into the arms of the Scots.

The key of the situation was in the hands of the City,
which had it in its power to paralyse the army by simply

Attitude of
the City.

maintaining an attitude of passive resistance.[1]
Large numbers of the citizens, however, shared in
the distrust of Charles which prevailed at Westminster.   Men
of business feared with reason that the benefits of a successful
rising would accrue to the Cavaliers, and shrank from placing

Advances of
Parliament
to the City.

themselves unreservedly in the hands of a King
whom even his partisans suspected of dissimula-
tion.[2]   Under these circumstances the City lent an

The militia
and the
Tower
abandoned
to the City.

open ear to the advances made by Parliament,[3] advances which, on May 18, were completed by the
passing of an Ordinance restoring the militia to a
committee, nominated indeed by Parliament, but nominated in

---

[1] See p. 121.

[2] " The Scottish compliance of this city will spoil both themselves and
the kingdom—the kingdom at present, by corresponding with our task-
masters ; and themselves in the end, when for this correspondence they
will be rewarded with slavery ; and this militia which they so dote upon
shall again be taken from them and serve to make rods for their own
breeches.   This hath been often inculcated to them and they seem to be
sensible of such an issue, and promise fair that they will—now their
militia is granted them—give a stroke for his Majesty with the counties
about them, but *credat Judæus Apella, non ego* ; for they are led by the
nose with their own principles by the Kirk of Presbyters in Scotland, by
whose direction it is that they comply thus with the Independent party
that Presbytery may be held up upon any terms in England, whilst they
make their party good at home in Scotland against the Royal engagers,
. . . knowing this, that if the Royalists should prevail in England, then
farewell Presbytery, and therefore they admitted of an Independent compliance as the least evil.   Thus his Majesty is bought and sold still amongst
the factions."   Letter of Intelligence, May 22, *Clarendon MSS.* 2,787.

[3] See p. 125.

accordance with the wishes of the City.   After this the Houses not only ejected Fairfax's soldiers from the Tower, but gave up the charge of the fortress to the citizens under the command of the man of their own choice, the Presbyterian Colonel West.[1]

On May 19 the Common Council welcomed these concessions, declaring its readiness to live and die with Parliament 'according to the Covenant.'[2]   The Royalists attributed the part taken by the citizens to mere cowardice.   "How long," asked one of their pamphleteers, "halt ye between two opinions?   If Mammon be God, serve him; if the Lord be God, serve Him.   If Fairfax be King, serve him; if Charles be King, restore him."[3]

The City had no enthusiasms, and it could not but perceive that the influence of the middle classes was as much endangered by a Royalist restoration as it would be by the success of the democratic Independents.   Accordingly, taking note of the resolution of the Houses to refrain from altering the government 'by King, Lords, and Commons,' the Common Council, on the 23rd, requested Parliament to liberate its imprisoned aldermen and to resume the negotiation with the King.[4]

On the following day the Commons took this request into consideration.   In vain Scott, one of the most decided Republicans in the House, protested against treating with Charles, on the ground 'that it was fitter he should be brought to his trial and drawn, hanged, and quartered than treated with; he being the only cause of all the bloodshed through the three kingdoms.'[5]   The House resolved that Charles should be asked to consent to a settlement of religion and the militia, and to the recalling of his declarations against Parliament on the understanding that, as soon as he had yielded on these points, the propositions which he had rejected at Hampton Court should again be laid before him.[6]   As, however, there was not the slightest chance that he

Marginal notes:

May 19.
The City declares for Parliament,

May 23.
and asks for a resumption of negotiations.

May 24.
The Commons consent.

---

[1] *L.J.* x. 262.
[2] *Id.* x. 272.
[3] *An Eye-salve for the City of London*, E. 445, 7.
[4] *L.J.* x. 278.
[5] *Merc. Elencticus*, E. 445. 23.
[6] *C.J.* v. 572.

would be more yielding now than he had been in the preceding autumn, no one except the Independents, to whom delay was all important, had anything to gain by so fatuous a proposal.

The Royalists, on the other hand, numerous and ardent as they were, were too scattered and disorganised to bring their real strength to bear upon events. Nothing, indeed, could compensate them for their disastrous exclusion from the central position of London. The want of a common leader to whose orders all would be bound to defer was almost equally disastrous. This last defect might indeed be remedied if only the King could regain his liberty. In April, after the discovery of his last attempt, Charles had been removed to another chamber within the castle in which his movements could be more easily watched, as a platform on which sentinels were stationed had been erected beneath his window. Trusty hands, however, conveyed to him instruments with which to cut through the iron bar which would, stop his exit through the window, and nitric acid[1] to dissolve it if this course should be found necessary; whilst three of the soldiers stationed on the platform were suborned to assist him in making his way over the defences of the castle. There were, however, many delays, and the scheme had for some time been known in general terms to the Committee of Derby House. The night of May 28 was at last fixed on for the attempt, but in the course of that very day two of the soldiers whose assistance was thought to have been secured for Charles, gave information to Hammond, and the King's hopes were thus a second time frustrated.[2]

Condition of the Royalists.

April. Charles hopes to escape.

May 28. His plan frustrated.

---

[1] Then known as *Aqua fortis.*

[2] Hillier's *Narrative of the attempted Escapes of Charles I.*; Barwick's *Life of Barwick*, 380. Charles's letters printed by Hillier are in *Egerton MSS.* 1,533. Those printed by Barwick and some others are in *Egerton MSS.* 1,788. For the story told by Osborne against Major Rolph see *Hillier*, 171. I incline to think with Mr. Hillier that the charge against Rolph of having urged Charles to escape with the intention of shooting him was a pure invention of Osborne's, and that the latter, being an accomplice in the plot for the King's escape, wished to save himself by throwing blame on Rolph.

With the King behind stone walls there was no one of sufficient authority to induce the local Royalists to restrain their impatience till the time arrived for simultaneous action. The continued delay in the movements of the Scots was especially trying. It was indeed settled on May 4 that the Scottish army should be 30,000 strong.[1] The incapable Hamilton was appointed to the command in chief, with Callander for his lieutenant-general. Great efforts were made to induce David Leslie to accept the command of the horse, but the man who had contributed so powerfully to the victory of Marston Moor, and who had crushed Montrose at Philiphaugh, refused to take part in an expedition which was unable to secure the blessing of the Kirk.

The Royalists in need of a leader.

May 4. A Scottish army.

Money, too, was hard to get, and the denunciations of the clergy were not without effect on the poorer classes. The levies, though pushed forward by the nobility with all their influence, came in but slowly,[2] and the English who had seized Berwick and Carlisle seemed likely to be left to their own resources for a long time to come.

Slow progress of the levies.

In Wales, too, the course of events was unfavourable to the Royalists. Their defeat at St. Fagans had been effectual, and when, on May 11, Cromwell reached Chepstow[3] he found no army to oppose him in the field. The war in South Wales, in fact, resolved itself into three sieges—those of the castles of Chepstow, Tenby, and Pembroke. On May 24, Cromwell wrote to express his confident expectation that his task would soon be accomplished.[4]

May 11. Cromwell at Chepstow.

May 24. His confidence of early success.

Under these depressing circumstances the Royalist leaders in Kent, having made up their minds that an isolated rising would be an act of madness, resolved to await the Scottish invasion and the consequent withdrawal of Fairfax to the North, in the expectation that London,

Plans of the Kentish leaders.

---

[1] *Acts of the Parliament of Scotl.* VI. part ii. 53.

[2] Montreuil to Mazarin, May 16, *Arch. des Aff. Étrangères,* lvi. fol. 385.

[3] *Perf. Diurnal,* E. 522, 30.

[4] *The Last News from Kent,* E. 445, 9.

when forsaken by its military guardians, would throw in its lot
with the King.[1]

The leaders had taken counsel wisely, but they were always
at the mercy of some accident which might cause an explosion

May 10-11.
A Kentish
Grand Jury.

amongst their excited followers. On May 10 and
11 a special Commission sat at Canterbury to try
prisoners accused of having taken part in the disturbances at Christmas.[2] The Grand Jury, however, not only
threw out the bill against them,[3] but drew up a petition similar
to those presented to Parliament by Essex and Surrey. The

Unpopu-
.arity of the
Co.inty
Committee.

County Committee, which at once took measures to
suppress the petition, had been unpopular before,
and it now found itself exposed to a perfect storm of
indignation.[4] According to a widespread rumour, one of its
members had declared that two of the petitioners ought to be
hanged in each parish, and that horse and foot ought to be
brought into the country to burn and plunder.[5] In the excitement caused by these revelations an impostor, who landed at
Sandwich and declared himself to be the Prince of Wales, was
received with transports of joy.

On May 21 the storm burst. A popular rising swept away
the Parliamentary authorities from the northern and eastern

May 21.
A rising
in Kent.

scaboard of the county. Rochester, Sittingbourne,
Faversham, and Sandwich were taken possession of
by the insurgents in the King's name. On the 22nd

May 22.
Meeting at
Rochester.

a great meeting was held at Rochester, at which many
of the local gentry readily agreed to place themselves
at the head of the movement.[6] The 30th was fixed for an

---

[1] *Clarendon*, xi. 25.   [2] See p. 45.   [3] *Perf. Diurnal*, E. 522, 30.

[4] A letter from a gentleman of Kent, June 15, E. 449, 34.

[5] *A Declaration of the County of Kent*, E. 445, 10; The Mayor of
Rochester to the Houses, May 21, Cary's *Mem. of the Civil War*, i. 422;
Four Gentlemen of Kent to Culpepper, May 30, *Clar. St. P.* ii. 404.

[6] *Clarendon*, xi. 26, 27, tells a story how L'Estrange, who had been
condemned to death for his attempt to seize King's Lynn (see vol. ii. 113),
persuaded young Hales to put himself at the head of the movement.
Most likely this is substantially true, though it can only have been an
episode in the full story. Clarendon omits the important matter of the
Grand Jury and the petition.

armed gathering of the county at Blackheath in support of the petition.[1]

The insurgents did not remain inactive during the days which intervened. On the 26th one party seized on Dartford,

May 26. Progress of the insur- rection. and a second, composed of sympathisers from Southwark, took possession of Deptford, where they carried off some guns from a pinnace lying in the river, and planted them on the high road.[2] Not a moment was to be lost if London was to be saved from being swept away by the movement, which might easily spread to Essex and Surrey, the other two petitioning counties.

Accordingly orders were at once given by Fairfax to provide against the danger. In the evening of the day on which

Southwark secured. Deptford was seized, Rich's regiment of horse from the Mews, and some companies of Barkstead's foot from Whitehall, crossed and secured Southwark, leaving it to the City trained bands to guard the Houses at Westminster.

May 27. Fairfax at Hounslow. On the next day Fairfax held a rendezvous on Hounslow Heath. Abandoning, as he must needs do, his intention of marching into the North, he prepared first to meet the danger nearer home. The mere threat of his approach scared the advanced guard of the insurgents, driving them to abandon Deptford, and to fall back on their main body which was by this time established at Dartford.[3]

On the 29th the Houses received news of an event which seemed likely to convert a local movement into a national up-

May 29. News from the fleet. rising. For some time there had been no good understanding between the army and the fleet, and the displacement of Batten had accentuated the dissatisfaction of the sailors with the growing power of the military commanders.[4] Batten was a decided adherent of the Presby-

---

[1] *Perf. Occurrences*, E. 522, 31.

[2] *The Last News from Kent*, E. 445, 9.

[3] *The Kingdom's Weekly Intelligencer*, E. 445, 13.

[4] " And why after all this . . . I was displaced by a committee at head-quarters at Putney with the advice of their Agitators, I could never understand ; nor why I was sent for up by land, as not to be honoured to come in with the ship threatened . . . to have a charge drawn up against

terian party, and as a good seaman was highly popular with his
men.   On the other hand, his successor, Rainsborough, being
regarded as the nominee of the army, was dreaded and disliked,
and accused of being rough and overbearing, whilst his former
desertion of the sea service for a career on land could not fail
to tell heavily against him.   Unpunctuality in the payment of
wages completed the alienation of the crews ; and on May 27

May 27.
Mutiny of
the fleet. six ships lying in the Downs took advantage of
Rainsborough's absence on shore to declare for the
King, refusing to allow the Parliamentary Vice-Admiral to return on board.   Under the guns of these ships the
Castles of Deal, Sandown, and Walmer were won for the Royal
cause, whilst Dover was straitly besieged, with little prospect of
being able to hold out for any length of time.

On the reception of these evil tidings, Parliament took the
prudent course of appointing the Presbyterian Earl of Warwick

May 29.
Measures
taken at
West-
minster. Lord High Admiral, in the hope that he would
secure the fidelity of the sailors; thus practically
setting Rainsborough aside.[1]   It was not a moment
too soon.   The note of triumph was already sounded
amongst the Royalists.   To-morrow, wrote one of them on the

me, unless I would instantly lay down my commission, though nothing
was objected but my suffering some of the eleven members to go beyond
the seas, when all of them had the Speaker's pass :—this, and because I
was not of the temper of the army were judged sufficient to have me
dismissed, and another—such another—thrust in to be my successor as till
then I never imagined would be vice-admiral of a navy.

"My commission thus surrendered, I was presently turned out of Deal
Castle, and could not obtain leave for two nights longer, though my wife
was then sick and forced from her bed to lie at an alehouse.   But how
this wrought upon my brethren, the seamen, I hope all my life I shall
thankfully remember ; they best knew what service I had done ; and now
beheld mine and their own reward, whereof they expressed a just resent-
ment when all those injuries offered to me were repaid to my new
successor, whom they refused to come on board, sent him back to the
shore and bid him return to the place from whence he came ; it being
most reasonable that that man should hold no command who openly professed himself to be a Leveller." *Declaration of Sir W. Batten*, E. 460, 13.

[1] Rainsborough to Lenthall, May 27, *Tanner MSS.* lvii. fol. 115 ; *The
Kingdom's Weekly Intelligencer*, E. 445, 13 ; *L.J.* x. 577.

29th, there will be 20,000 Kentish men on Blackheath backed
up by the support of the navy.   An equal number was expected

Royalist
hopes.

from Essex to join forces with them, and a bridge of
boats was to be thrown across the Thames to facili-
tate communications between the two counties.   It was not to

FAIRFAX'S CAMPAIGN IN KENT AND ESSEX.

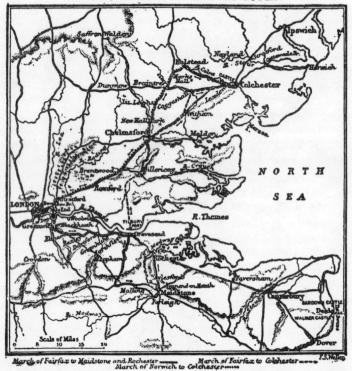

March of Fairfax to Maidstone and Rochester ——   March of Fairfax to Colchester ----
March of Norwich to Colchester······

be supposed—in spite of the concessions recently made by
Parliament—that the City would take part against the insurgents.[1]

In the army itself the advantages on the side of a disciplined
force contending with armed peasants were more correctly
estimated.   "The enemy," wrote Barkstead to Fairfax, "still

[1] Letter of Intelligence, May 29, *Clarendon MSS.* 2,791.

continues at Dartford. They give themselves to be 10,000,
but the countrymen lessen every day. Very many
A soldier's view of the situation. officers and soldiers that have formerly served the King
come in hourly to them. The discourse among them
is that, if the country will not stand to them, they will immediately possess themselves of all the castles and strongholds and
thereby secure landing for the Irish, French, and Danes, of
whose coming they fondly flatter themselves and the malignant
party of the county. These countrymen that are come home
do extremely cry out against the gentlemen that did engage
them, looking upon themselves as utterly undone, which is the
only cause of their coming home, hoping thus to keep their
necks out of the halter." [1] Exaggerated as Barkstead's view of
the case may have been, it had some justification. Many a man
in the hostile ranks had been ready enough to follow his land-
lord to the place of rendezvous, and even to applaud him for
standing up against interference with the local independence of
his county, without having sufficient enthusiasm to carry him
far in resistance to the best-trained army in Europe.

From a military point of view Fairfax's dispositions left nothing to be desired. Having occupied Blackheath, the place
appointed for the rendezvous of the Kentish men,
May 30. Fairfax's dispositions. he sent Major Gibbons through the Weald to the relief of Dover, and placed a strong force at Croydon
to ward off any possible attack on his rear from Surrey. Later
in the day he moved forward with the bulk of
He moves to Eltham. his army, 8,000 strong, to Eltham, on the way to
May 31. The march to Graves-end. Rochester, whither the main body of the insurgents
had retreated. On the 31st, after clearing away the
enemy's outposts occupying the bridge at the bottom
of the hill on which Northfleet stands, he pushed on to Graves-
end, and threw out a reconnoitring party to observe the position
at Rochester. Finding that the drawbridge[2] was
A recon-naissance. raised, and the opposite bank of the Medway strongly
fortified, he gave orders to his army to strike southwards across

---

[1] Barkstead to Fairfax, May 29, *Clarke MSS.*

[2] The drawbridge was at the western end of the bridge. Hasted's
Kent, ii. 17.

the North Downs, by roads entirely concealed from the sight of
the enemy.   After a long and wearisome march he fixed his

A flank
march.

quarters at Meopham for the night.   The next morning, continuing his march in a southerly direction,

June 1.
Fairfax at
Malling.

he reached Malling, where he found it necessary
to halt for some hours to wait for his infantry,
which had necessarily been left in the rear the evening
before.

Fairfax at Malling was still concealed from the enemy by
the undulations of the hills, but if the Kentish leaders could
not see what had taken place, they must either have derived
information from countymen, or formed conjectures of their

The Kentish
men on
Penenden
Heath.

own from Fairfax's inactivity in the neighbourhood of
Rochester.   At all events about mid-day there were
gathered some 7,000 men on Penenden Heath, the
old meeting-place of the shire from immemorial time.   On the
ground on which Lanfranc had once impleaded Odo, the de-
scendants of the men who boasted themselves unconquered by
the Conqueror himself came together to perform—almost in the
presence of the enemy—the elementary work of choosing a
commander.   Any choice from amongst their own ranks would

Preparations
for a general
rising.

probably have inflamed the jealousy of those who
were passed over.   Before, however, any election had
been made a nobleman presented himself claiming the
right to command with credentials beyond dispute.   The arrangements for the general rising which was intended to follow
on the appearance of the Scots in England had been made by
the Queen and Jermyn—the medium of communication between
the Queen on the one side and the English and Scottish

Holland
commander-
in-chief.

Royalists on the other being that veteran intriguer,
Lady Carlisle, who naturally suggested her own
favourite, the Earl of Holland, for the supreme command.   The little Court of St. Germains had been fatuous
enough to accept the proposal, and a commission signed by the
Prince of Wales appointed Holland commander-in-chief of the
army about to be raised in England.

Mere carpet-knight as Holland was, he had sense enough
to know that the premature rising in Kent was a grave misfor-

tune. When, however, the movement had once commenced
Holland furnished it with a leader in the person of the Earl

Norwich to
command
in Kent.

of Norwich, the father of the notorious Goring, and
himself an old courtier of James I., filling up in his
favour a blank commission bearing the signature of
the Prince of Wales. Norwich was no more fit than Holland
himself to command an army, but his claim to lead was at
once admitted.[1]

Norwich took the command about noon. It was four or
five in the afternoon when those on Penenden Heath first

Approach
of Fairfax.

descried, through their 'prospective glasses,' some
of Fairfax's regiments on the western side of the
Medway. The Kentish gentlemen indeed had not been
neglectful of their duty. All that was possible in

Dispositions
of the
Royalists.

purely defensive warfare had been done. A detachment of about 1,000 strong was posted to guard the
river at Aylesford, whilst another of some 3,000 men was thrown
into Maidstone, to guard the bridge against attack. The
remainder of the force, consisting of about 7,000 men,[2]
remained upon the hill ready to carry help to either detachment as occasion might serve.

Fairfax was far too skilful a strategist to attempt to cross
the long bridge which led by the direct road into Maidstone.

A skilful
movement.

Bending southwards he passed the Medway by Farleigh Bridge, which was but slightly defended, and
thus skilfully turned the enemy's left. Once across the river
there was no serious physical obstacle between him and the town.
At one spot indeed, near where the Tovil Brook flows into the
Medway, he had found the lane barricaded and the hedges
lined with musketeers, but after a sharp struggle the opposition

---

[1] *Clarendon*, xi. 5; Hatton to Nicholas, Aug. 29, *Nicholas Papers*,
i. 90. Norwich is invariably styled Lord Goring by the Parliamentarians,
as they did not acknowledge his earldom conferred since the great seal was
carried off in 1642.

[2] Goring's own account says that his army consisted of 'a matter of
7,000 men as they did say,' and 1,000 or 1,500 in Aylesford. He does
not give the number of the garrison of Maidstone. *Clarke Trials*, fol.
66. Fairfax puts the field force at 8,000 and 3,000 in Maidstone. *L.J.*
x. 304.

was beaten down. The bridge over the Len, a little stream which meets the Medway close to the town itself was scarcely defended, and by seven in the evening Fairfax found himself in front of Maidstone itself.

The streets were strongly barricaded, and Fairfax made up his mind to postpone the attack on so formidable a position till the following morning. The impetuosity of his advanced guard, however, brought on a conflict without orders from the General, and the troops could not be held back from supporting their comrades. The resistance was obstinate, and before long the garrison of Maidstone was reinforced by a great part of the force stationed at Aylesford. The soldiers of the New Model, however, carried one barricade after another. The fighting was prolonged till midnight, but by that time Maidstone, and with it the line of the Medway, was in the hands of Fairfax. Norwich with his forces on the hill took no part in the combat, and when all was over he rode off to Rochester. Such conduct is only explicable on the supposition, which finds some support in contemporary narratives, that the country people who formed the bulk of the foot had no heart in the struggle, which was only really popular amongst the gentry and the Londoners.[1] Fairfax, it seemed, had to contend against the majority of the landowners and a

The attack on Maidstone.

---

[1] *Clarendon*, xi. 25; *The Lord General's Letter*, E. 445, 26; *News from Kent*, E. 445, 27; *The Moderate Intelligencer*, E. 445, 30; *Bloody News from Kent*, E. 445, 36. Fairfax to Manchester, June 2, 4, *L.J.* x. 301, 304. See also Carter's *Most True and Exact Relation*, and a letter by I. T. in a pamphlet entitled *A Letter written to Lord Goring*, E. 445, 42

I have reconstructed my account of Fairfax's line of attack in consequence of a note on the subject by Mr. H. E. Malden in the *Engl. Hist. Rev.* vii. 533. More recently Major Martin Hume informs me that in 1848 he delivered a lecture at Maidstone on the subject of the battle. "I took some pains," he writes, "in collecting oral tradition about the fight from aged people whose forbears had been in the town from time immemorial. From this I gathered that no doubt existed that Fairfax crossed Barming Heath, from whence a large body of Royalists were seen on the hills near Kit's Cotty House on the other side of the river between Rochester and Maidstone. These troops took no notice of Fairfax and his army (tradition says from fear, but history shows rather from indiscipline

great part of the middle-class in the towns, not against the bulk
of the country population.

and want of a real leader). The Ironsides are said to have come down
by a road at the side of Barming Rectory, which has been pointed out to
me. There must have been some fighting at Farleigh Bridge, although
Carter says Fairfax ' easily got over,' because on the Farleigh side of the
river, on the left-hand side of a lane, a very short distance from the bridge
there is a field, which not only does tradition point out as the burial-place of
the soldiers who fell, but arms, bones, spurs, &c., are still occasionally
found there. In any case, the men who were supposed to be defending
the pass at Farleigh were not in touch with the Maidstone Garrison, as the
passage of Fairfax was not known in the town until he came into contact
with a body of horse sent out of the town to prevent a surprise. The
encounter took place on the Farleigh Road about a mile from the top of
Stone Street. This was about six or seven in the evening, and an alarm
was at once raised in the town. The first encounter was between an
advance troop of heavy horse on each side, and the Ironsides were beaten
back on their main body at or near Farleigh Bridge, and reinforcements
were hurried up from the town (as they thought) to complete the victory.
Fairfax, however, led his men to the charge himself, and here the first
severe fighting took place ; a large number were killed here and buried in
a field still pointed out, called Postley Field. The Royalists thereupon
retreated, and Fairfax pressed on. The next encounter took place in a
field at the top of Upper Stone Street (just beyond where the Tovil Road
turns off), and a great number are said to have been killed here. The
Royalists were again driven back, and took refuge in the town itself, where
they occupied the houses, and shot from the windows all down Stone
Street and up Gabriel's Hill. (In an ancient house on Gabriel's Hill, years
ago, I was shown some jack-boots, spurs, etc., which the troops had left in
the house after firing upon the Commonwealth soldiers from the windows.)
Stone Street is a very long hill descending to the River Len, which runs
across it. Near the top of Stone Street Hill an earthwork was run across
the road, which was carried with a rush, and lower down, where two side
streets branch off, a stockade of trees was erected, and another was made
on the Gabriel's Hill side (*i.e.* the town side) of the Len Bridge. The
Fairfax army are said to have been nearly two hours storming these
various obstacles, and running the gauntlet of the fire from the houses all
down Stone Street and Gabriel's Hill. At the very top of Gabriel's Hill, *i.e.*
the high town, market-place, &c., there was a strong battery with artillery
run across opposite where is now Wolland's, the fishmonger's, and this
battery, of course, fully commanded Gabriel's Hill. As, however, the
Maidstone people did not know where they were to be attacked, this
battery was extended right across the top of the High Street, and thus

However this may have been, Fairfax had no more serious opposition to fear from the motley forces by which he was opposed. The bulk of the insurgents, on receiving from him promises of good treatment, quietly returned to their homes. Under these circumstances Norwich did not venture to await an attack at Rochester. Crossing the Medway with about 3,000 companions who still remained faithful, he made his way westwards, heading for London, probably in the expectation that the City would even now declare in his favour. On the evening of the 3rd he reached Blackheath. Fairfax, still having on his hands the pacification of Kent, contented himself with despatching Whalley with a party of horse and dragoons in pursuit.[1]

June 2. Dispersal of the Kentish army.

Norwich makes for London.

commanded all the four ways into the town, guns being placed in position.

" All the dead in the town itself were buried in St. Faith's Churchyard, adjoining the present Maidstone Museum, where many relics have been found, some of which are now in the Museum. Judging from the position, Fairfax's loss on Gabriel's Hill must have been very great, and I can only suppose that it must have been a hand-to-hand fight from house to house, and then a final rush for the battery."

I have no doubt that this account is on the whole accurate, but some of its details can hardly be trusted ; for instance, the cavalry charge in which Fairfax's horse is said to have been driven back finds no countenance elsewhere, and I should think it very unlikely that there was any considerable cavalry force in Maidstone. On the other hand, local patriotism would favour the growth of a tradition that the redoubted horse of the New Model had received a check.

[1] Fairfax to Lenthall, June 4, *L.J.* x. 304.

CHAPTER LXIII.

COLCHESTER AND ST. NEOTS.

IF, indeed, the City had opened its gates to Norwich, the course of history would, at least for a time, have been changed. The Presbyterians of the City, however, could not resolve either to trust Charles or to defy him, and fell back upon their old chimera of restoring him to the throne, not on his terms, but on their own. On June 1, before the fight at Maidstone, the City once more called on the Houses to open a personal treaty with the King in which his acceptance of the Covenant would be put forward as an indispensable condition. To this they added a wish that the treaty might be carried on under the protection of the associated trained bands of Middlesex, Essex, Herts, Bucks, Kent, Surrey, and Sussex, that Batten should be restored to the Vice-Admiraltyship, and the imprisoned aldermen released.[1]

On June 3, the day on which Norwich was marching on Blackheath, the Commons, dreading above all things to alienate the City at such a time, voted that they would desist from the impeachment, not only of the aldermen, but also of the ten survivors of the eleven members, thus leaving it open to the latter to return to their seats in the House whenever they felt inclined to do so. They further resolved to take into consideration the treaty with the King at the earliest opportunity.[2] All, however, but the most ardent Presbyterians in the House were too prudent to countenance the proposed association of the

*1648.
Feeling in
the City.*

*June 1.
The City
asks for a
personal
treaty.*

*June 3.
Impeach-
meuts
abaudoned.*

*A treaty
with the
King to be
considered.*

---

[1] *L.J.* x. 295.   [2] *C.J.* v. 584.

trained bands of the home counties, which must, on the one hand, have caused an immediate breach with the army, and, on the other hand, have left Parliament at the mercy of any popular cry for the King's unconditional restoration.[1]

The hesitation of the Presbyterians to throw themselves unreservedly on the King's side virtually gave the control of affairs into the hands of the Independents. When Norwich reached Blackheath he found no sign of welcome. With the gates of London shut against him, and Whalley's troops pressing on his rear, his position was untenable.

A gleam of hope, however, reached him from Essex, where, as he was informed, thousands had risen for the King. Crossing the river alone, he rode off to Chelmsford to ascertain the truth, leaving his deserted followers distracted by panic.[2] The greater part of them fled hurriedly into Surrey, abandoning their horses and casting away their arms to escape observation.[3] About five hundred crossed the Thames in boats, their horses swimming by the side, and on the following morning established themselves at Stratford and Bow, where they were at last rejoined by their commander, who had found no signs of a rising in Essex. Taking possession of Bow Bridge, Norwich cut the communications between Essex and the City, hoping in the first place that London would even yet admit him within its walls, and in the second place that, if that was not to be, he might, by his interposition, give a breathing space to the men of Essex to rally round him.

Norwich soon found that, though many of the King's

Margin notes: Norwich at Blackheath. False information. A panic. Some cross the Thames, June 4. and seize Bow Bridge.

---

[1] "Those at Westminster have done little of late but restored their banished members, and as much as may be pursued the Presbyterian interest, having designed the raising of a new army under the Earl of Denbigh; but in reference to peace or restoring the King, they are as opposite as the Independents." ———— ? to Lanark, June 13, *Hamilton Papers*, 212. They did not, however, take a division on the new army.

[2] *Carter*, 102.

[3] Com. of D. H. to Gerard and Osborne, June 4, *D. H. Com. Letter Book, R. O.*

partisans stole out of London to fill his ranks, no general
Norwich
loses hope
of gaining
the City. movement in his favour was to be expected in the
City. Warner, the intrusive Lord Mayor, had the
threads of municipal authority in his hands, and
Skippon, who commanded the trained bands, was, with all his·
eagerness for peace, prepared to resist to the uttermost a
Royalist movement. On the 4th, Whalley, crossing by London
June 4.
Whalley at
Mile End. Bridge and establishing himself at Mile End, brought
a trained cavalry force to the aid of the party of
resistance. So hopeless did Norwich's enterprise
appear at Westminster that on the 6th it was believed that he
would soon move off to join Langdale in the north.[1]

The news from other parts of the country was on the whole
favourable to the Parliamentary cause. Towards the end of
News
generally
favourable to
Parliament. May Sir Hardress Waller routed a party of insurgents
in Cornwall. Early in June Mitton suppressed a
rising in North Wales headed by Sir John Owen,
who stained his attempt to strike a blow for the King by
singular inhumanity to the Parliamentary sheriff of Merioneth-
shire, whom he caused, in spite of his wounds, to be dragged
from place to place till he died.[2] Another party raising troops
for the King was surprised and overpowered at Woodcroft in
Northamptonshire,[3] and yet another setting out with the same
object met with a similar fate in Lincolnshire.[4] From South
Wales, too, came reassuring tidings—Cromwell had laid siege
to Pembroke, whilst Chepstow Castle had surrendered on
May 25, and Tenby Castle on the 31st.[5] But for the policy,
which had dismantled the greater part of the fortifications in
England,[6] the danger would have been far more serious than it
was.

What that danger might have been was shown by the case

---

[1] Letter of Intelligence, June 5, *Clarendon MSS.* 2,801 ; *The Kingdom's Weekly Intelligencer*, E. 446, 11 ; The Com. of D. H. to Lambert,
June 6, *D. H. Com. Letter Book, R.O.*

[2] *Rushw.* vii. 1,130; *Sir T. Payton . . . with divers others taken
prisoners*, E. 447, 1.

[3] *A Bloody Fight*, E. 447, 2.   [4] *Rushw.* vii. 1,145; *L.J.* x. 313.
[5] *Rushw.* vii. 1,130, 1,134.   [6] See vol. iii. 218.

of Pontefract.   On June 1, Morris, one of Langdale's officers,

June 1.
Pontefract
Castle
surprised. disguising a party of soldiers in the garb of peasants, obtained admission into the castle and secured the stronghold for the King.[1]   A considerable part of Lambert's forces would henceforth be occupied with the siege of Pontefract.   The rising in Kent had hitherto stood in the way of Fairfax's intended march to his assistance, and if the hopes of a rising in Essex entertained by the Kentish insurgents were fulfilled, he might be detained too long in the south to render his army available against the impending invasion of the Scots.

Kent at least was not likely to detain Fairfax much longer. Even before the fight at Maidstone a rumour had spread in the

Fairfax
hopes to
be free. army that Gibbons [2] had succeeded in raising the siege of Dover Castle.[3]   Though the report was

June 6.
Relief of
Dover
Castle. without foundation, the work was accomplished on June 6 by Rich.[4]   On the 8th Canterbury surrendered to Ireton.   The three castles in the Downs

June 8.
Surrender of
Canterbury. —Deal, Walmer, and Sandown—alone held out for the King in Kent.   They were, however, being blockaded by Rich, and Warwick, who had found the crews at Portsmouth loyal to Parliament, was sanguine enough to hope that those of the revolted ships would soon return to their duty, and thus deprive the garrisons of the three castles of all support on the side of the sea.[5]   Fairfax was therefore at last in a position to carry his army out of Kent.

Already, however, the scene had changed in Essex.   On June 4, the County Committee met at Chelmsford, in-

June 4.
The County
Committee
seized at
Chelmsford. tending to take measures to arrest a Royalist movement which had the support of the leading gentry of the county.   The Essex Committee was, however, no

Sir Charles
Lucas rouses
the trained
bands. more popular than the Committee of Kent, and a crowd under the influence of Colonel Farr, an officer of the trained bands, forcing its way into the room where it was sitting, carried off all its members

---

[1] *The Declaration of Sir T. Glemham*, E. 446, 29.
[2] See p. 137.   [3] *Rushw.* vii. 1,136.   [4] *A Petition*, E. 522, 38.
[5] Warwick to Manchester, June 6, *L.J.* x. 313.

as prisoners.[1]   At Westminster the alarm was great, and on

June 5.
An Ordi-
nance of
Indemnity. the 5th the Houses hurriedly passed an Ordinance of Indemnity to all Essex men who had taken part in disturbances in the county, on the direct understanding that the committeemen were to be liberated, and

June 6.
The in-
demnity
meets with a
favourable
reception. on the indirect understanding that no attempt was to be made to protect Norwich and his followers from the vengeance of Parliament.   So little disposed were the country people to side with the extreme Royalists, that when the indemnity was announced at Chelmsford on the 6th the greater part of those gathered in the town showed every disposition to accept the hand held out to them.[2]

To prevent such a catastrophe, Norwich, leaving his troops behind him under Sir William Compton, hurried to Chelmsford

June 7.
Norwich at
Chelmsford. on the 7th.[3]   He there found a powerful advocate in Sir Charles Lucas, a tried and capable soldier who

June 8.
Sir Charles
Lucas wins
the Essex
men. had served in the Low Countries, and had distinguished himself in England in the former war. Lucas now held a commission from the Prince of Wales to lead the forces of the county, and being himself an Essex man, a younger brother of Lord Lucas— whose house hard by the walls of Colchester occupied the site of the ancient abbey—he could speak with a persuasiveness which no stranger could command.   The disgrace of abandon-

June 8.
A rendez-
vous at
Brentwood. ing Norwich and his followers to certain ruin was a powerful incentive to action.[4]   Many members of the trained bands who had made up their minds to accept the indemnity, now consented to remain in arms.

---

[1] The date of this is fixed by the mention of the affair in the Ordinance of Idemnity passed on June 5 (*L.J.* x. 306) in consequence of a letter from Chelmsford dated June 4, *C.J.* v. 585.

[2] *An Exact Narrative*, E. 448, 18.

[3] Carter, *A Most True and Exact Narrative*, p. 115, says that Norwich was at Stratford four days and three nights, which, as he arrived on the 4th, makes the day of his leaving the 7th.

[4] The Siege of Colchester, *Hist. MSS., Com. Rep.* xii. App. part i. pp. 20, 21.

Norwich returned to Stratford to fetch his men, and on the 8th the two parties met at Brentwood.[1]

On the 9th the combined Royalist forces established themselves at Chelmsford. Norwich had brought with him a considerable number of apprentices and water-men from London, some of whom had fought at Maidstone, and also a large party of gentlemen who had slipped out to him, amongst whom was probably Sir George Lisle, another distinguished soldier of the former war.[2] At Chelmsford the Royalists were joined by Lord Capel, who had a commission from the Prince of Wales to command generally in the Eastern Association, and by Lord Loughborough, who had been well known under the name of Henry Hastings as a partisan warrior in the early days of the Civil War. There was good military material at the disposal of the officers, but the force had yet to be subjected to discipline, and more than half of it was still unarmed. Unfortunately for them, Sir Thomas Honeywood, one of the members of the County Committee, who, luckily for himself, had been absent from the meeting at Chelmsford, having gathered together the trained bands from the northern part of the county round his own house at Mark's Hall, near Coggeshall, had swooped down on the county magazine at Braintree, carry-ing off the arms of which his opponents were in such dire need.

June 9.
The Royal-ists at Chelmsford.

Honeywood seizes the county magazine.

On the 10th the Royalists advanced towards Braintree, Whalley following closely upon their movements, but not venturing to attack with his inferior numbers. On the way they turned aside to Warwick's house at Leighs, from which they carried off what arms they could find. The night of the 10th and the greater part of the following day they spent at Braintree, where they organised their little army, and took counsel as to their future movements. Their original plan had been to

June 10.
The Royal-ists at Leighs,

and at Braintree.

June 11.

---

[1] *Carter*, 121–124; *Two Great Victories*, E. 446, 23; *The Moderate Intelligencer*, E. 446, 28; *The Kingdom's Weekly Intelligencer*, E. 447, 10.

[2] There is no definite statement about the time when Lisle joined.

[3] *An Exact Narrative*, E. 448, 18.

push forward into Suffolk and Norfolk, where the gentry were ready to join them, and where it might be possible to secure a sufficient supply of arms and ammunition from their friends beyond the sea.

At Lucas's persuasion, however, the commanders agreed to turn aside to Colchester, not with any intention of taking up a position of defence in the town, but simply in the hope that Lucas's popularity there might secure them recruits before they pursued their march.[1] To reach Colchester, however, was not so easy. Honeywood with his trained bands blocked their way at Coggeshall, and Whalley, who would probably before long be joined by Fairfax, pressed on their rear. To deceive the enemy they started at nightfall, marching some little way in a north-westerly direction, as though they were bound for the Isle of Ely. Then returning into Braintree they halted for a space, and afterwards resumed their march towards the north-east as far as Halstead. Having thus slipped round Coggeshall, they wheeled to the right and made for Colchester, which they reached in the course of the following day.[2] Some attempt was indeed made to resist their entry, but there was a Royalist party in the town, and many of the inhabitants, though not precisely to be spoken of as Royalists, were hostile to Fairfax's army, and the gates were thrown open after a short delay.[3]

If the insurgents expected to continue their march unmo-

Marginal notes:
They resolve to march to Colchester.
Difficulties in the way.
A night march.
June 12. They are admitted into Colchester.

---

[1] *Carter* (p. 129) says distinctly that 'upon Sir Charles Lucas's desire and belief of recruiting there, they concluded to march, but not to stay above a night or two at the most.'

[2] The account of the siege of Colchester (*Hist. MSS. Com. Rep.* xii. App. part ix. 22) for the first time explains how the Royalists reached Colchester without fighting Honeywood. The author thought, when he wrote, that Fairfax and Whalley had already joined Honeywood on the 11th. Whether this was his own mistake or an unfounded belief in the army at Braintree it is impossible to say. This narrative also explains why the Royalists were so long in covering the distance of about fourteen or fifteen miles between Braintree and Colchester.

[3] *An Exact Narrative*, E. 458; *Carter*, 129; *Mr. Round's MS.* p. 77.

lested they omitted to calculate on the swiftness and precision
with which Fairfax struck his blows.   On the morning of Sunday, June 11, the Parliamentary general,
after hearing a sermon at Gravesend, crossed the
Thames at Tilbury Fort with what troops he could gather round
him, and then, racked with gout as he was, led them on to
Billericay.   Impatient of delay, and anxious to hear how it
fared with Honeywood, he himself rode on in advance, reaching Coggeshall, probably on the morning of the 12th, where he
met Honeywood and Whalley.   Then again pushing
on with 1,000 horse, which were very likely Whalley's,
he arrived in the evening at a mile and a half from
Colchester.   On the 13th the remainder of his cavalry came
up, and about noon Barkstead arrived with his brigade of infantry, having covered about fifty miles[1] in little more than
forty-eight hours.   Honeywood's trained bands were already on
the spot, and altogether Fairfax had at his disposition some
five thousand seasoned troops to oppose to four thousand
newly levied men, of whom scarcely more than half were
armed.

Though the command of the Royalists was nominally in the
hands of Norwich as being of the highest rank amongst
the three—himself, Capel, and Lucas—who held
commissions from the Prince, the direction of the
defence fell practically into the hands of Lucas, the only pro-

Margin notes:
June 11.
Fairfax in
pursuit.

June 12.
He reaches
Lexden.

June 12.
Preparations
for defence.

---

[1] The distance is about forty-four miles as the crow flies from Tilbury
Fort to Colchester by Chelmsford.   Taking into account the winding
of the roads of those days, it seems fair to add about six to this number.
In *An Exact Narrative* (E. 448, 18) it is said that 'the General with
four regiments of horse and five regiments of foot came to Chelmsford on
Sunday, and on Monday he marched to Coggeshall.'   *A Perfect Diurnal*
(E. 448, 23) says that on the 11th of June, 'his Excellency with some
half-score of his horse marched from Billobey,' *i.e.* Billericay, 'to Coggeshall, where he found Col. Whalley and Sir T. Honeywood.'   Wilson
(Peck's *Desid. Cur.* ii. 481) says that he met Fairfax, apparently on
the 11th, between Billericay and Chelmsford.   I suspect Fairfax slept
at Chelmsford, reached Coggeshall the next morning, and then pushed
on to Lexden, as I have said, with Whalley's cavalry.   Compare
Carter, 131.

fessional soldier amongst them.   Colchester itself was ill-fitted
to stand a siege.   Its shape is oblong, its walls being built on
Defences of the lines of those of the old Roman city, and except at
Colchester.   one point it had no salient bastion jutting out to allow
the defenders to take the assailants in the flank.   Nevertheless,
an army approaching, as Fairfax's did, by the London Road
would be at a disadvantage.   The road struck the town at
the south-western angle of the town wall, and then ran for
some little way under the southern wall till it reached the
Head Gate, where it turned in.   In this latter part it was commanded by the town wall, and especially by a battery placed
on the south-western angle in St. Mary's churchyard.   Moreover, the ground which falls away below the southern wall
rises again at a short distance outside, and on this higher
ground stood Lord Lucas's house, easily defensible, and forming an admirable outpost for the Royalists.   On the other
hand, the houses of the suburbs spread along the roads and
furnished cover to an assailant who came near enough to make
use of them.

On the 13th Lucas, taking what advantage he could of the
ground, drew up his little army across the London Road ; the
June 13.   foot, according to usage, in the centre, and his scanty
The Royal- following of horse on either wing.   On his right his
ist army.   cavalry was guarded by the sharp dip of the ground
towards the Colne.   On his left the hedges on either side of the
Maldon Road protected his infantry, but his horse which
stretched out beyond the foot had no such defence on their
flank.

To Fairfax it was of the utmost importance not merely to
enter Colchester, but to enter it quickly.   Hoping to repeat the
Fairfax's   achievement of Maidstone and to carry the town with
attack.   a rush, he gave orders for an immediate attack.   To
his surprise Barkstead's foot in the centre was three times repulsed by the steadfastness of the Royalist infantry.   On his
right, however, the Parliamentary cavalry, superior in numbers
and discipline, drove the Royalist horse before them, and
wheeling to the left, attempted to take the Royalist infantry in
flank as Cromwell had taken the King's main body of foot at

The SIEGE of COLCHESTER

By the Lord Fairfax, As it was with the Line and Outworks 1648

Col. Father

Col. Fo...ther

Fe

Horse Guard

Foot Guard

Col. Ewers League

Horse Guard

Horse Guards

Fort Ingolesby

The great Broom Heath

Col Ingolesby's quarters of Foot

Col. Scroop's quarters of Horse

5

Col. Ewers his quarters of Foot at first

14

6

Cambridge Road

London Road

Malden Road

Road into the

Fort Fox

Lexden head quarters

Foot Guard

Horse Guard

Barksteed Fort

Hum

Traine of great Gunns

Col. Cooke Foot quarters

5 Comp. of Col. Barksteeds Reg. quarters

4 Comp. of the Lord of Warwick Regiment

Horse Guard

D...
Gu...
q...

Col. Hannewood's Foot quarters

Col. Harlackenden's Horse quarters

The Generalls quarter of Horse

2 Troops of the Lieut. Generalls Horse

Longmans, Green & C°

York & Bombay.

Naseby. In this, however, they were baffled by the hedges of the Maldon Road, which, being lined with pikemen and musketeers, interposed an impenetrable barrier. The necessity for defending these hedges had indeed so weakened the resistance of the Royalists in front that, after their right wing of horse had also been routed, their whole force was compelled to withdraw into the town. Their retreat was, however, completed, the last ranks alone being overpowered and four or five hundred men killed or made prisoners.

Slight as was the advantage gained it inspired Barkstead with confidence that a complete victory was within his grasp. Barkstead enters the town, Seeing the Head Gate still open, he pressed inside with the front ranks of his victorious infantry only to fall into a trap which Lucas had prepared for him. For some distance within the gate the street rises. From the top of the slope a body of Royalist horse charged down but is driven out. with all the advantage of the ground upon the assailants, whilst a body of Royalist foot advancing along a lane which led from St. Mary's took them in the flank. The result was decisive. The ever-victorious soldiers of the New Model turned and fled. Then, and not before, Lucas ordered the gate to be closed, fastening the bar, for want of a handy peg, with the cane which he carried in his hand.[1]

Far into the night Fairfax continued his attempt to storm

---

[1] The only satisfactory account of this fight is in *Mr. Round's MS.* p. 80. Yet though most of the authorities omit the entrance into the town, there is quite enough corroboration from other sources. The Diary attached to the contemporary map, which is the most distinct military authority on the Parliament side, says that Barkstead 'entered the Head Gate, and being overpowered there and out of the churchyard the King's forces barricaded the gate.' *An Exact Narrative* (E. 448, 18) says that 'they were resolutely charged by the Lord General's van . . . who suddenly beat the enemy from their ground and pursued them into the town, and seven colours of ours entered with them, but . . . our men were forced to give back and the town gates were closed on them.' *Merc. Elencticus* (E. 449, 7) makes Lucas use cannon on the hill, which seems incompatible with his use of horse. Compare also ———? to Lenthall, June 14, *Portland MSS.* ; *Carter,* 131.

the defences. It was all in vain; and on the morning of the

Fairfax's failure.

14th, grasping the truth that a long siege was inevitable, he hastened to prevent the escape of the Royalist horse by placing strong bodies of men on the road leading out of Colchester, and urging the Suffolk trained bands to stop the passages over the Stour by guarding the bridges at Nayland, Stratford, and Catawade.

June 14. He hems in the Royalists.

The Suffolk trained bands.

These Suffolk trained bands had for some time hesitated in their allegiance, and the Royalists had expected to find them on their side. Like so many others of their class, however, they thought of peace first and of party distinctions afterwards, and agreed to prevent the irruption of the Royalists into their country. Some little time afterwards they were actually induced to take their part in the blockade of Colchester, probably thinking it the shortest way to avert the horrors of war from their own county.[1]

In another direction Fairfax was equally successful. He seized Mersea Island with its blockhouse in order to cut off all

Mersea Island seized.

hostile approach by the Colne. On the 19th three vessels laden with provisions for the besieged attempted to force their way up the river, but they were driven back by the garrison of Mersea, whose efforts were seconded by the arrival from Harwich of two ships in the service of Parliament.[2] Nevertheless the provisions in

June 19. An attack from the sea repulsed.

A long siege expected.

Colchester were sufficient to enable resolute men to hold out long, and the besiegers had no resource but to settle down to the work of building forts and repelling sallies.

[1] The writer of the siege of Colchester (*Hist. MSS. Com. Rep.* xii. part ix. p. 26) says that the Suffolk men would have supported the King but that 'there came an order from a person whom . . . the Prince of Wales, commissioned to be General of this County'—perhaps Lord Willoughby of Parham, see p. 195 as Lucas, who held a commission in Essex, cannot be intended—'commanding them not to move upon their allegiance; this was a malignant reflection from the Presbyterian party,' Whether this is true or not, it illustrates the bad feeling between Presbyterians and Cavaliers.

[2] *A Great Victory*, E. 449, 20. The *Diary* attached to the map in the British Museum, of which a reduced copy is given opposite.

It was, however, by no means impossible that from some quarter or other succour might arrive. If Norwich and Capel *Prospect of succour.* were unable to leave Colchester, Fairfax was equally fixed to his lines of circumvallation round it, and either London or any Royalist county so minded might rise without fear of attack from that terrible army the reputation of *State of the navy.* which weighed so heavily on all its enemies. Above all, the power of the sea seemed likely to pass into the hands of the King's partisans. It was true that nineteen ships still remained faithful to the Houses, whilst only nine had declared for the King, but the minds of many of the sailors of the nineteen were trembling on the balance, and it would be most unwise to employ such men on active service against their comrades. Moreover, three of the nineteen were needed to guard the entrance to the Colne, whilst eight of the remainder were either at Portsmouth or in the West, leaving only eight available for service in the Thames.[1]

For the present, though no immediate danger impended from the action of the navy, there was a possibility of an attack *The revolters at Goree.* at any moment. The nine revolted ships crossed to Goree in Holland, where they invited the Duke of York to come on board as their admiral. The Duke *June 29. The Prince of Wales sets out for Holland.* sent them Lord Willoughby of Parham to command as vice-admiral, and held out hopes that the Prince of Wales would soon be with them. On June 25 the Prince left St. Germains for Holland, travelling by way of Calais.[2]

The Derby House Committee naturally took alarm. If the Prince were to land with military stores at Yarmouth or Lynn *Cromwell's siege train wrecked.* it would be hard to find the elements of an army capable of resisting him. Not only was Cromwell still detained before Pembroke Castle, but the vessel which carried his siege train had been sunk at the mouth of the Severn by a sudden storm. All the assistance that Crom-

---

[1] Derby House Committee, *Day Book*, June 13.

[2] Letter of Intelligence, June 21 ; Goffe to Aylesbury, $\frac{\text{June 24}}{\text{July 4}}$, Hyde to Berkeley, July 1, *Clarendon MSS.* 2,817, 2,827, 2,825.

well could render was the despatch of a small force to the aid of Lambert in the North.[1]

It was to the North that the eyes of all English Royalists were now impatiently turning. The cloud long gathering was at last ready to burst. On June 9 the Scottish Parliament gave full powers to its Committee of Estates, and on the next day adjourned its own meetings for two years.[2] Hamilton, who was supreme in the Committee of Estates, had now the whole machinery of Government in his hands, and, supported as he was by the majority of the nobility, was able to defy the opposition of Argyle and the clergy. To destroy his influence it would be necessary to raise an armed force against him, and both David Leslie and Argyle, though they had been sounded on the subject, were too prudent to run the risk of appearing in arms against men who had the support of both King and Parliament.[3] Middleton was now definitely appointed to command the horse and Baillie the foot of the new forces.

Danger in the North.

June 10. Adjournment of the Scottish Parliament.

Hamilton supreme.

Armed with compulsory powers, Hamilton's agents, who usually had at their back the influence of the territorial magnates, found little difficulty in levying men. Fife resisted for a time ; but Fife had been sadly depopulated by the slaughter of Kilsyth, and, in spite of the vigour of its Presbyterianism, its resistance could not be prolonged. In Clydesdale, the other great centre of clerical influence, the opposition was stronger, but gave way before the pressure of military force Sir James Turner, a soldier to the backbone, having been sent to Glasgow to enforce obedience, anticipated the methods by which Louis XIV. afterwards attempted to convert the Huguenots. "At my coming there," to use his own words, "I found my work not very difficult, for I shortly learnt to know that the quartering of two or three troopers and

Useless opposition to the levies.

Fife gives way.

Sir James Turner at Glasgow.

---

[1] Cromwell to Lenthall, June 14 ; Cromwell to Fairfax, June 28. *Carlyle Letters,* lix. lxi. ; *A Wonder, A Mercury Without a Lie,* E. 451, 17.

[2] *Acts of Parl. of Scotl.* VI. part ii. 102.

[3] Montreuil to Brienne, June $\frac{8}{18}$, *Carte MSS.* lxxxiii. fol. 292b.

half a dozen musketeers was an argument strong enough in two
or three nights' time to make the hardest-headed Covenanter
Middleton at in the town to forsake the Kirk and to side with the
Mauchlin. Parliament." A little later a body of 2,000 men
collected at Mauchlin to resist the levies, but were routed by
Middleton without difficulty, after which all open resistance
came to an end.[1]

As to the next step to be taken there was some difference
of opinion amongst the leaders. Lanark proposed that they
Difference should push their advantage home, and crush Argyle's
of opinion party before setting out for England. Lauderdale
amongst the
the leaders. was for an immediate advance southwards, and
A rendez- Hamilton, giving way to his urgency, appointed a
vous ap-
pointed. general rendezvous to be held at Annan on July 4.[2]
An advance into England was indeed necessary if the English
Royalists of the northern counties were not to be driven to
despair. Lambert, who had been recently joined by Ashton with
the Lancashire forces, had driven Langdale into Carlisle, and
was threatening to besiege the place.

Already the double dealing which was at the bottom of
Hamilton's adventure was causing embarrassment. The Com-
Will the mittee of Estates had forwarded to Langdale and
English offi- the other English officers the draft of a letter which
cers take the
Covenant? they called upon them to sign, inviting the Scots to
enter England 'for the ends of the Covenant.' Langdale
refused either to sign it himself or to ask his officers to sign it,
and in the end it was returned with no more than twelve signatures appended.[3]

In spite of these divergences a Scottish invasion, if it could
be made to coincide with a Royalist explosion in England,
would be truly formidable. The Queen, however,
Holland's had rendered this the more difficult by placing the
designs
known. control over the movement in the hands of Holland.
Those by whom the general thus appointed was surrounded

---

[1] Turner's *Memoirs*, 53, 55; *Baillie*, iii. 47.
[2] *Burnet*, vi. 43.
[3] Musgrave's narrative, *Clarendon MSS.* 2,867. Compare Turner's
Memoirs, 57.

had not the art of keeping a secret, and during the last fortnight in June scarcely a day passed without some fresh revelation reaching the Committee at Derby House. It was thoroughly well known that Holland had been issuing commissions for listing men, and that plans had been formed at one time for the surprisal of Windsor Castle, at another for the surprisal of the castles at Winchester and Farnham.[1] It was, however, about his proceedings in the City that the greatest alarm was felt.

July 2. Horses sent out of London. On July 2, it was known that horses were being collected in London and sent out into the country, two or three at a time, in order that they might be in readiness to take part in the coming insurrection. It was expected that in a day or two at least a thousand horses would be smuggled in this manner out of London, and that when this number had been reached an attempt would be made to raise the siege of Colchester. It was also believed that a design had been formed to seize the Tower.[2]

Measures of the Derby House Committee. The Committee promptly issued warrants for the arrest of all who had taken part in these proceedings, and summoned to their aid such forces as they had at their disposition. It happened that Sir Michael Livesey, with a party of soldiers raised in Kent, and Major Gibbons, with some of the men who had been detached by Fairfax for the relief of Dover,[3] were expected to be at Sevenoaks on the evening of the 2nd on their way to quell a disturbance which had broken out at Horsham. Livesey was accordingly directed to hold himself in readiness to meet any danger which might befall, and Captain Pretty, who was in command of a troop of Ireton's cavalry regiment stationed at Windsor, was directed to move eastwards to assist him.[4]

---

[1] *Clarendon*, ix. 102. Details are to be found in the Derby House Committee Books, where, however, Holland's name is not mentioned. The informant of the Committee was a certain Alexander Cotton.

[2] Com. of D. H. to Fairfax, July 2 ; Com. of D. H. to the Lieutenant of the Tower, July 2, *Com. Letter Book*.

[3] See p. 137.

[4] *Com. of D. H. Day Book*, July 2 ; Com. of D. H. to Livesey, July 2 ; Com. of D. H. to Pretty, July 2, *Com. Letter Book*.

On the 3rd, disquieting rumours poured in thickly. The
Committee, fearing that Livesey and Pretty might be over-

July 3.
Disquieting
rumours.

whelmed, wrote hastily to Fairfax to spare at least a
troop of horse, and later in the day a second letter,
telling him that nothing short of a whole regiment
would suffice.[1]

With the Parliamentary authorities thus on the alert, the
Royalist leaders had no choice open to them but to take the

July 4.
Holland
takes the
field,

field prematurely. The Earl of Holland, accompanied by the Duke of Buckingham and his younger
brother, Lord Francis Villiers, left London in the
evening of the 4th and appeared in arms at the head of a party of

July 5.
and appears
in arms at
Kingston.

Royalist gentlemen in the streets of Kingston. After
ransacking the stables of the Parliamentarian gentry,
they rode off with the horses they had thus acquired,
leaving behind a declaration repudiating absolute monarchy, and
declaring for peace and a Parliamentary constitution. Though
their followers were for the present few in number, the highest
estimate being five or six hundred, the course of events in Essex
had shown how easy it was for a small force to swell into an army.[2]

The danger was the greater on account of the dubious
attitude again assumed by the City. On the 4th the Common

July 4.
The Com-
mon Council
asks that the
King may
come to
London.

Council stamped with its approbation a petition in
which the officers of the London trained bands asked
that the King might be brought to London to treat
in person, and not only reiterated the request made
formerly by the City itself, that the London regiments
might be amalgamated with those of the neighbouring counties,

July 5.
Attitude of
the Houses.

but asked that the force thus formed might be
enabled to take the field by the addition of cavalry.
To this petition the Lords heartily consented. The
Commons, on the other hand, postponed their answer to a
more convenient season.[3]

[1] Com. of D. H. to Fairfax, July 3, *Com. Letter Book.*

[2] *L.J.* x. 367 ; D. H. Com. to Livesey, July 4, 5 ; Com. of D. **H. to**
Pretty, July 5 ; Com. of D. H. to Fairfax, July 5, *Com. Letter Book* ;
Cotterell to Denman, July 13, *Clarendon MSS.* 2,832 ; Grignon to Brienne,
July $\frac{6}{16}$, *R. O. Transcripts* ; *The Diary,* E. 453, 40.   [3] *L.J.* x. 364.

The Commons, in fact, had two days before taken up a line which they intended to follow in their negotiation with the

July 3.
Three Pro-
positions
to be pre-
sented. King. On July 3, they resolved that, if Charles was to be admitted to treat, he must first give his assent to three preliminary propositions, thereby engaging to recall his declarations against the adherents of Parliament, and promising the establishment of the Presbyterian government for three years, and the subordination of the militia to Parliament for ten.[1] The Lords, indeed, insisted that the negotiation should be unconditional, but with all their zeal for peace, the Commons refused to abandon their requirement of the King's consent to the three meagre demands which they had now made.[2]

Would the population of the Southern counties give to Charles's supporters in the field the credit for constitutional

Holland's
chances of
success. intentions which the House of Commons refused to himself? Unless this proved to be the case, Holland's appeal to arms was doomed to speedy failure.

Dulbier's
experiences. Conscious of his own deficiencies as a soldier, he had obtained the assistance of Dulbier, the Dutchman to whom all causes were alike, and who had in his time drilled soldiers both for the elder Buckingham and for Cromwell. Dulbier was probably attracted to the present enterprise by the young Duke of Buckingham, whose father he had served. In any case, even if he had been a far better

A horse-race
to supply
recruits. soldier than Holland, he could not accomplish much with 600 horse. His hopes were set on a horse-race, which was shortly to be held on Banstead Downs, as from the concourse attending he could hardly fail to find recruits for the King.

In the meanwhile, horses and arms being still sorely needed, Holland dashed into Reigate on the 6th, hoping to secure the

---

[1] *L.J.* 308.

[2] " Il Parlamento," *i.e.* the House of Commons, " non si vuole fidare del Rè in nessun modo, quando bene gli accordasse tutto quello che li domanda dubitando che in sua presenza possa fare sollevare il popolo in suo favore, et così rimettersi nella sua pristina autorità." Salvetti's News-letter, July $\frac{14}{24}$. *Add. MSS.* 27,962 M. fol. 142.

castle, which was at that time in the possession of a thorough-going Independent, Viscount Castlemaine,[1] usually known in England as Lord Monson. The townsmen showed no inclination to rally to his side, and on hearing that some of Livesey's troops were approaching; Holland withdrew to Dorking. On the morning of the 7th he attempted to return, but finding that Livesey had himself arrived with reinforcements, he rode off hurriedly towards Kingston.

July 6.
Holland at Reigate.

July 7.

Livesey at once gave the word to follow. Holland's rear was overtaken at Ewell ; and a skirmish on the top of the hill was followed by a chase into Kingston. The Cavaliers, to do them justice, quitted themselves like men. As soon as Surbiton Common was passed the horsemen, drawing up in the lane, kept the pursuing cavalry in check, whilst their own foot made their way in safety into Kingston. Lord Francis Villiers, like a gallant boy as he was, had thrown himself into the midst of the rear guard, which bore the brunt of the attack. His horse having been killed under him he continued to defend himself vigorously with his back against an elm tree which rose from a hedge, till one of Livesey's soldiers, slipping to the other side of the hedge, dashed his steel cap off his head and slew him from behind. Few deaths in that blood-stained war struck the imagination of contemporaries with stronger pity than that of the high-spirited youth whose ' rare beauty and comeliness of person ' wrung from Clarendon a lament such as might have beseemed a writer of ancient Greece.[2]

A spirited chase.

Death of Lord Francis Villiers.

Whether the danger was at an end still depended on the temper of the City. Sanguine Royalists had expected that large numbers of citizens, perhaps even whole regiments of the

---

[1] He was Sir William Monson, Lord Monson and Viscount Castle-maine in the Irish peerage. He was usually styled in England Lord Monson.

[2] *A True Relation*, E. 451, 30   Aubrey's *Nat. Hist. and Antiquities of Surrey*, i. 46 ; *Clarke Trials*, fol. 275.

trained bands, would make their way to Kingston and declare
for King Charles.[1]   On the day of the fight the Derby House

Continued
anxiety
at West-
minster. Committee gave orders that all the boats of the horse
ferries over the Thames from Lambeth to Shepperton
should be placed at night under guard on the
Middlesex side, and that by day none should be suffered to
cross except market people and persons employed in the service of the State.[2]   This state of uncertainty was soon brought
to an end.   Not only did no new recruits join Holland, but
most of those already with him slipped away by degrees, seek-

July 8.
Holland
gives up
hope, ing safety in concealment.   On the morning of the
8th Holland himself gave up hope.   Accompanied
by about 200 horse, amongst whom were Buckingham
and Dulbier, he pushed on without any clear object in view
through narrow lanes by Harrow to St. Albans, reaching St.

July 9.
and reaches
St. Neots. Neots on the evening of the 9th.   In the dark hours
of the next morning, Colonel Scrope, despatched by

July 10.
He is sur-
prised and
captured. Fairfax to intercept the fugitives, burst into the little
town.   Dulbier was slain as he stood to arms.   Hol-
land, roused from sleep, took refuge in the archway of
an inn, slamming to the iron gate which barred the entrance in
the hope that he might gain time to effect his escape at the
back.   On this side, however, the broad stream of the sluggish

Escape of
Bucking-
ham. Ouse stopped all passage, and the luckless commander of an abortive insurrection surrendered on
condition that his life should be spared.   Buckingham, more fortunate or more adroit, found his way safely
out of the town in the darkness, and ultimately succeeded in
reaching the Continent.[3]

Contemptible as the whole affair appears to those who are

---

[1] *Clarendon*, xi. 103.   So much may be accepted, especially as it was
stated at Holland's trial that the Earl expected 5,000 men from London
to join him at the horse-race on Banstead Downs.   *Clarke Trials*, fol.
267*b*.   The military details given by Clarendon are quite incor-
rect.

[2] Com. of D. H. to the Ferries, July 7, *Com. Letter Book.*

[3] *Clarke Trials*, fol. 256; *The Moderate Intelligencer*, E. 452, 27;
Prince Charles's Sailing, E. 452, 32.

'wise after the event, Holland's capture was a serious discou-

Discourage-
ment of the
Royalists. ragement to the Royalists. The Scots especially regretted the failure of a diversion on which they had reckoned. Even the prudent Lauderdale wrote of the disaster as the greatest which had befallen the King's cause.[1]

The Derby House Committee was proportionately elated. On the 12th, some prisoners from St. Neots having been rescued

July 12.
The Lord
Mayor
scolded. by a mob in the streets of London, the Committee in right royal style called on the Lord Mayor to keep better order amongst the people, 'who are grown to that insolency as they will be the judges of the actions of their superiors, and take upon them to set at liberty those whom we find just cause to restrain, and openly make themselves parties to that rebellion by defending those who have appeared in it.'[2]

The utter collapse of Holland's attempt to rouse the country revealed the disinclination of that large mass of the population

The
domestic
danger at
an end. which was essentially unpolitical to take arms for the King. From henceforward it was known at West-minster that the domestic danger was at an end. If

Dangers
from
without. the authority of Parliament was to be threatened now it must be by forces from without the realm, by the armies of the Irish Confederates or the Scottish Covenanters, or by the fleet which the Prince of Wales was about to bring over from Holland.

The three commissioners sent by the Irish Supreme Coun-cil to the Queen and Prince[3] reached France in April. Of the

April.
A fresh
negotiation. three, Antrim was steadfast in declaring that no terms of peace would be accepted in Ireland until they had received the approval of the Pope, and that it was absolutely necessary that a Catholic Lord-Lieutenant should be appointed; whilst the other two, Muskerry and Browne,

---

[1] Lauderdale to [the Queen ?], July 19, Wallis's Deciphers, *Bodl. Lib. Mus.* 203. In a letter of the same date to Lady Carlisle he expressed himself in still stronger terms; but this may have been merely to give pleasure to his correspondent.

[2] D. H. Com. to the Lord Mayor, July 12, *Com. Letter Book.*

[3] See p. 109.

urged Henrietta Maria to appoint Ormond lord-lieutenant without waiting for the Pope's approbation, and to sanction

May 4⁄14.

Ormond to go to Ireland

an understanding between Inchiquin and the Confederates. After some hesitation the Queen gave her decision in favour of the latter policy. With the help of the Marquis of Worcester—better known by his earlier title of Earl of Glamorgan—she pawned what jewels still remained in her hands and thereby raised 30,000*l*. in order that Ormond might be well equipped for his duties in Ireland.[1]

Before anything could be done, a crisis occurred in Ireland which made caution necessary. On May 20 a cessation of

May 20.
A cessation with Inchiquin.

Rinuccini excommunicates all who accept it.

arms was signed between Inchiquin and the Supreme Council.[2] Rinuccini, who had already made his escape from Kilkenny, replied by launching an excommunication against all who accepted a cessation made with a man stained by the slaughter of Catholics and the desecration and destruction of churches, and declaring that the new league, if it should prove successful, could only end in handing over Ireland to those Presbyterians to whom Charles had bound himself in Scotland. The Council, in return, charged the Nuncio with splitting Ireland into hostile factions and with making settled order impossible, by rendering eternal the existing feud between the two religions. The Supreme Council, in short, saw that Ireland must be united before she could be free ; whilst the Nuncio saw no less plainly that the English King could form no bond of union.

The Irish generals were as divided as the Irish people. Clanricarde, Preston, and Taaffe placed their swords at the dis-

The Irish generals divided.

Ormond remains in France.

posal of the Supreme Council ; Owen O'Neill threw in his lot with the Nuncio.[3] Through the whole of the summer of 1648 the Irish armies were occupied with their own intestine disputes. There was little likelihood of their being available for service either in England or against the Parliamentary forces in Dublin, and Ormond's mission to Ireland was, in consequence, indefinitely postponed.

[1] *Lord Leicester's MSS.* fol. 2,213b–2,237.   [2] *Vind. Cath. Hib.* 88.
[3] *Lord Leicester's MSS.* fol. 1,949–2,090.

Mazarin, too, upon whose help the Queen had counted, was involved in troubles which rendered it impossible for him to

May ⁷⁄₁₇.
Battle of
Zusmars-
hausen.

assist her. In the spring, indeed, Turenne's victory at Zusmarshausen, which bent the haughty spirit of Ferdinand III., had made it almost certain that the end of the war in Germany could not be long postponed. The Dutch, however, by signing a separate peace with Spain, which had been proclaimed on May 26, had strengthened the Spanish

May 26.
June 25.
Peace
between
the Dutch
and Spain.

government in its determination to persist in its own hostilities with France, now that it was secured against any further attack from the armies and fleets of the Republic. It was of still greater import that an opposition to Mazarin's government was growing up amongst the lawyers of the Parliament of Paris—an opposition which soon afterwards ripened into the political agitation of the Fronde. Anxious as Mazarin might be to weaken the Independent army by sending some small assistance to the Irish or the Scots, it was now evident that he would need for his own purposes all the money he could command.

In another quarter also the English Royalists were doomed to disappointment. The young Prince of Orange, William II.,

Hopes from
the Prince
of Orange.

who had succeeded his father as Stadtholder in the spring of 1647, was ardent and adventurous, and in the hope that he would help in the deliverance of his father-in-law, the Committee of Estates had sent Sir William Bellenden into the Netherlands to plead with him for assist-

Bellenden's
mission.

ance. Bellenden soon found that though the Prince was warlike the commercial oligarchy which held the purse-strings were lovers of peace, and on July 9

July 9.
His report.

reported that nothing beyond fair words was to be had. He had also to tell of a party at the Queen's Court which was eager that the King should owe his deliverance to a Cavalier rising in England rather than to the Presbyterian Scots.[1]

Already, however, the die had been cast. On July 8, only two days before the hopes of the Cavaliers were finally extin-

---

[1] Bellenden to Lanark, July 9, *Hamilton Papers*, 228.

A SCOTTISH INVASION.

guished at St. Neots, Hamilton's army crossed the border and occupied Carlisle.   He had with him about 10,500 men,

July 8. Hamilton enters England. little more than a third part of the force on which he had counted, though Langdale was expected to join him with three thousand more.   Hamilton him-

His defects as a commander. self had none of the qualities of a successful commander.[1]   He suffered himself to be bearded with impunity by Callander, his Lieutenant-General, and only escaped outward humiliation by assuming the appearance of being convinced of the wisdom of whatever proposals

Deficiencies of his army. were made by his subordinate.   His soldiers were raw recruits, and scarcely one out of five amongst the infantry knew how to handle a musket or a pike, whilst the cavalry had yet to learn how to keep their seats.   Artillery he had none, and he was so short of money that his men were driven to plunder the country round Carlisle, thereby alienating the English population on whose help he had counted.[2]

Such an army could not advance rapidly.   Its first forward movement was delayed till the 16th.   Lambert, good officer as

July 16. The Scots advance. he was, fell back with his small force, skirmishing wherever a strong defensive position was to be found.

July 17. Lambert falls back on Bowes and Barnard Castle. Leaving a garrison in Appleby Castle, he quartered his men at Bowes and Barnard Castle, where he hoped to be able to hold the Stainmoor Pass, which rises with a sharp ascent from Westmoreland, and to find support from reinforcements summoned to his aid from Yorkshire.   The Scots, on their part, leisurely established themselves at Kirkby Thore, awaiting the arrival of ammunition and reinforcements.   In addition to the levies still to be raised for them in Scotland, they expected to be joined by 3,000 men who were to be brought from Ireland by Sir George Monro, the nephew of Major-General Robert Monro, the commander

---

[1] "The Duke," says Mrs. Wilson in *Old Mortality* (ch. v.), "that was him that lost his head at London—folk said it wasna a very gude ane, but it was aye a sair loss to him, puir gentleman."

[2] *Burnet*, v. 49-51; *A Declaration from Scotland*, E. 453, 5; *Turner's Memoirs*, 59.

of the Scottish forces in Ulster.[1]   This enforced leisure was
utilised by them in the siege of Appleby Castle.

For some time Hamilton had been in expectation of money
and arms from France, and of the landing of the Prince of

Sir William
Fleming in
Scotland. Wales in Scotland.   About the middle of July Sir
William Fleming arrived from the Queen, with but

Conditions
of the
Prince's
coming. a small supply of arms, and no money at all.   He
announced that the Prince of Wales would only
come on condition that he was allowed to use the
English Prayer Book in his public devotions.   To this were
added other stipulations of which we only know that they
were considered scarcely less obnoxious by the Scottish
leaders.[2]

If these conditions were brought to light, Hamilton's policy
would become untenable in Scotland.   Already the General

Hamilton
condemned
by the
General
Assembly. Assembly, which had met on July 12, was thundering
against him as a traitor to the Covenant.   In vain
Lauderdale, who more than any other man in Scotland represented the insurrection of the lay feeling

Lauder-
dale's hopes. against clerical predominance, struggled to avert
open division.   He was proud of his country and of the part
which he expected to see his country take   " It is Scotland,"
he wrote, " and Scotland only, can save the King and England.
All others have their rise from the expectation of Scotland." [3]
It was not so easy to obtain the consent of the more distinctively
Scottish part of the nation to an alliance with an Episcopalian
king.   Scotland was riven in twain, but the spirit of her people
was not with Lauderdale and Hamilton.

---

[1] *A Perfect Weekly Account*, E. 453, 19; *Bloody News from the Scottish
Army*, E. 453, 24; *A Bloody Fight in the North*, E. 454, 10; *A True
Relation*, E. 454, 14; *Burnet*, vi. 52; Hodgson's Memoirs in *Original
Memoirs*, 113.   For the relationship between Sir George and Robert
Monro, see Grignon to Brienne, $\frac{\text{Sept. 28}}{\text{Oct. 8}}$, *R. O. Transcripts*.

[2] Lauderdale to Lady Carlisle, July 19; Lauderdale and Lanark to
Jermyn, July 19, Wallis's despatches, *Bodl. Lib. Mus.* 203, pp. 53, 55.
These letters were printed on Aug. 16, under the title of *The Design of
the Present Committee of Estates*, E. 459, 5.

[3] *Ibid.*, E. 459, 5.

The time was rapidly approaching when the strength of an army without either discipline or enthusiasm would be tested Hamilton's danger. by an enemy lacking in neither. Cromwell, indeed, had all Lauderdale's dislike of clerical intolerance, June 28. Cromwell's view of the situation. but he had what Lauderdale had not, a perception of the value of free spiritual life to the national well-being. "I pray God," he wrote to Fairfax, whilst he was still detained by the resistance of Pembroke, "teach[1] this nation and those that are over us, and your Excellency and all us that are under you, what the mind of God may be in all this, and what our duty is. Surely it is not that the poor godly people of this kingdom should still be made the object of wrath and anger, nor that our God would have our necks under a yoke of bondage ; for these things that have lately come to pass have been the wonderful works of God ; breaking the rod of the oppressor, as in the day of Midian, not with garments much rolled in blood, but by the terror of the Lord, who will yet save His people and confound His enemies." [2]

Cromwell's hours of weary waiting were at last coming to an end. His guns had been recovered from the mud of the July 4. Pembroke battered, Severn,[3] and on July 4 his batteries opened.[4] On the 11th Poyer surrendered both town and castle. He and three other officers were left to the mercy of the Parliament which they had formerly served, whilst seven- July 11. and forced to surrender. teen more, who in the last war had fought on the King's side, were to go into exile for two years. All other persons were to be protected against plunder, and to be at liberty to return to their homes. Cromwell was now free to hasten northwards to aid Lambert in his unequal struggle.

---

[1] Carlyle misread this word as ' that,' and consequently inserted ' may discern' afterwards without MS. authority in order to make sense.

[2] Cromwell to Fairfax, June 28, *Carlyle*, Letter lxi.

[3] See p. 154.   [4] *Perf. Occurrences*, E. 525, 5.

CHAPTER LXIV.

PRESTON.

WHILST Cromwell was on his northward march, opinion at Westminster was divided on the elementary question, whether the Scots were enemies or friends. Whatever the cause may have been, the feeling of the Presbyterian majority in the House of Lords was far more un-compromising in its Royalism than that of the Presbyterian majority in the House of Commons. On July 18 the Peers rejected a declaration in which the Commons had qualified the invaders as enemies.[1] The clashing between the Houses on the subject of the three propositions[2] had not abated, and on the 20th the Commons insisted upon the danger of entering on a negotiation with the King without previous security. Those, they said, who having taken part in the recent insurrections were now clamouring for an uncon-ditional treaty, would upon that pretence, 'if such a treaty should be yielded unto, press the Parliament to yield up all in that treaty, to the end they may set up an absolute tyranny, that they as instruments' might 'share therein, and repair themselves with the spoil of the Commonwealth.'[3]

1648.
Difference of feeling between the two Houses.

July 18.
The Lords refuse to call the Scots enemies.

July 20.
The Commons insist on the three propositions.

There is some reason to think that the idea of placing the Duke of Gloucester on the throne was under these circumstances revived, as the shortest way out of the difficulty if the attempt to open negotiations with the King should prove abortive.[4] The Lords would hear of none of these things. On the 21st they not

Proposal to make the Duke of Gloucester King.

---

[1] *L.J.* x. 384.   [2] See p. 159.   [3] *L.J.* x. 386.
[4] Salvetti's *Newsletter*, July $\frac{21}{31}$, *Add. MSS.* 27,962, M, fol. 144.

only persisted in their rejection of the proposal to declare
the invaders enemies, but associated themselves further
with the Scottish cause by ordering the publication of a manifesto issued by the Scottish Committee of Estates against toleration either of the
sects or of those who used the Book of Common
Prayer.[1] On the 22nd the Commons replied by
sending to press their own declaration that the
Scots were enemies, without waiting longer for the
approbation of the Lords.[2]

July 21
The Lords
support the
Scots.

A Scottish
manifesto.

The Scots
declared
enemies.

Obviously the Scottish manifesto was intended to conciliate
the support of the English Presbyterians, not to give voice
to a policy which no serious man can ever have
expected to carry out with Charles upon the throne.
Lauderdale indeed could write to Lady Carlisle as if
he approved of it in his heart. " I dare," he asserted, " both
answer for the honesty of the matter of it, and for the rudeness
of the form and language,[3] for truly it was the work of very
few hours, not above four and twenty."[4] More of his real
opinion is doubtless to be found in a conversation which he
held about this time with Robert Baillie. "Lauderdale," wrote Baillie, "continues kind to me, and
regrates[5] much the difference between us ;[6] fears it
become a fountain of great evils, either the overthrow of the
design for the King against the sectarists, or the putting up of
the malignant party so high that they will hardly be gotten
ruled, at best the making of the government of our church, as
we exercise it, to be abhorred by all in England and abroad,
and intolerable to our own State at home."[7] Lauderdale's
was the voice of the irreligious statesman attempting to rule
the enthusiasms of the world by humouring them. Other
men, far less able than himself, perceived that if Hamilton's enterprise succeeded, it would be to the advantage

Lauder-
dale's view
of the
manifesto.

His conver-
sation with
Baillie.

---

[1] *Declaration of the Committee of Estates*, E. 453, 32.

[2] *C.J.* v. 644.   [3] Did he write it himself?

[4] Lauderdale to Lady Carlisle, July 8, *Bodl. Lib. Mus.* 203, p. 50.

[5] *i.e.* regrets.   [6] *i.e.* between the nobles and the clergy.

[7] *Baillie*, iii. 64.

of the pure Royalists and not to that of the Presbyterian Constitutionalists. "Whatsoever you hear of the Duke Hamilton declaring," wrote an English Cavalier, "be confident he is for Episcopacy, and will in time make their kirkmen to know it." [1]

Lauderdale was already appointed to a mission on which his special arts were likely to avail him more than on a public
Lauderdale stage. He was to visit the Prince of Wales in the
to go to the hope of inducing him to come to Scotland, without
Prince.
imposing those conditions which had been declared
July 9? indispensable in the message brought by Fleming. [2]
The Prince
leaves Calais The young Charles was now almost in an indepen-
for Helvoet-
sluys. dent position. He had sailed from Calais on or
about July 9, and on his arrival in Holland had been enthusiastically welcomed on board the fleet awaiting him at Helvoetsluys. [3]

In the Prince's council no good understanding prevailed. Culpepper and Hopton headed one party which was ready to
Parties in his make the utmost possible concessions to the Presby-
council. terians, and it had been by their influence that Willoughby of Parham had been named Vice-Admiral. [4] A second party, which gathered round Hyde, wished to see no wavering on the subject of Episcopacy and no concession to the Scots. The supporters of this policy had been treated with studied rudeness whilst still in France by Jermyn, who took the side of their opponents, and Hyde himself had been left to find his own way to Holland as best he might, instead of being allowed to accompany the Prince. Yet, though Hyde was as yet absent, he had the satisfaction of knowing that the cause which he had at heart had found a champion in Prince Rupert.

Between these conflicting factions it was hard for the Prince, now a youth of eighteen, to steer his course. The question

---

[1] *Rushw.* vii, 1,197.

[2] Lauderdale to [the Queen ?], July 19, *Bodl. Lib. Mus.* 203, p. 61.

[3] *Clarendon,* xi. 32.

[4] The Duke of York being officially Lord High Admiral. Hatton to Nicholas, Aug. 29, *Nicholas Papers,* i. 90.

of his relations with the Scots might, however, be deferred till after Fleming's return, and on the 16th he announced his intention of putting to sea.[1] On the 17th he gave orders for the issue of a Declaration to the effect that he had taken arms to settle religion in accordance with the terms of the Engagement between his father and the Scots, to restore the King to his throne, and to bring about an act of oblivion and the disbandment of all armies.[2]

July 16.
The Prince resolves to put to sea,

July 17 and orders a Declaration to be issued.

On the 22nd the Prince's fleet was in Yarmouth roads. If he could have established himself in the town so as to form a nucleus for a rising of the gentlemen of Norfolk, things would have gone hard with Fairfax, who was still detained before Colchester. The Prince, however, had no land force with him, and though a large party amongst the townsmen was willing to admit him, the magistrates, supported by a small body of troops, were able to suppress the movement in his favour. Finding that nothing was to be gained by longer stay, he sailed for the Downs,[3] where he found that, though Walmer Castle had surrendered, the castles of Deal and Sandown continued to hold out for the King.

July 22.
The Prince off Yarmouth.

July 23. and makes for the Downs.

The Prince's approach did not fail to give encouragement to his partisans in London. On July 22, at the request of the City, the Lords revoked an order given by the Houses to Skippon to raise troops for the defence of Parliament independently of the Committee of Militia.[4] The Commons, on the other hand, stood by the order given to Skippon ; but on the 28th they agreed to a compromise on the more important question of the negotiation with the King, consenting to waive their three propositions if the Lords were

Dispute between the Houses on an order given to Skippon.

July 28. Proposed compromise on the treaty.

---

[1] The Prince of Wales to Hamilton, July $\frac{16}{26}$, *Hamilton Papers,* 232.

[2] Order by the Prince, July $\frac{17}{27}$, *L.J.* x. 399 ; *Declaration by the Prince,* E. 547, 14

[3] The Bailiffs of Yarmouth to the Com. of D. H. July 29, *L.J.* x. 399 ; Com. of D. H. to Hammond, July 27, *Com. Letter Book.*

[4] *L.J.* x. 379, 389 ; *C.J.* v. 651.

willing to fix the place for the treaty in the Isle of Wight instead of in London or the neighbourhood.[1] It was said at the time that this compromise was suggested by the Independents, who feared lest if they continued to oppose the treaty they would be swept away by popular indignation.[2]

The chance that this compromise would be accepted was much increased by the publication of an intercepted letter

July 31.
An intercepted letter.

from one of Hamilton's agents in London. "We are in this City," declared the writer, "generally right; only Skippon makes some disturbance by listing horse and foot, which, though inconsiderable to what we have listed for us, yet we hope not only to null his listing, but out him from his being General of this City. The Lords have already done something, but wait for some further encouragement from hence; to which purpose the Common Council are about framing a petition." [3] This letter reminded the citizens of the danger of bloodshed within their own walls, and without their support the Peers were unable to hold out.

Aug. 1.
The Lords accept the compromise.

On August 1, the day after the letter was read to the Common Council, the Lords accepted the compromise of the Commons.[4] By fixing the place for the treaty in the Isle of Wight the Commons had at least succeeded in keeping the King at a sufficient distance from London to prevent his throwing himself into the City to head an insurrection against their own authority.

July 31.
Charles declares himself not bound by the Scottish manifesto.

Charles at least had no intention of being bound by the manifesto of the Scots. On July 31 he wrote to the Committee of Estates, telling them that though he could not assent to all that they had put forth, he was confident that 'upon a calm and friendly debate an agreement was easy.' [5] As usual, he bound himself to nothing.

---

[1] *C.J.* v. 649.　　　[2] Grignon to Brienne, Aug. $\frac{7}{17}$, *R.O. Transcripts.*
[3] W. G. to Sir A. Gibson, July 26. *The Letters . . . and other Papers, which were communicated to the Common Council,* E. 456, 31.
[4] *L.J.* x. 405.
[5] The King to the Committee of Estates, July 31, Cary's *Mem. of the Civil War,* i. 443.

Warwick had not yet completed his task of weeding out all the disaffected seamen from the ships under his command,[1] and

.The two fleets.

it is possible that an immediate attack by the Prince of Wales would have laid London bare on the side of the sea. The Prince, however, was short of money, not having wherewithal to pay his crews. He accordingly resorted

Merchant-men seized by the Prince.

to the desperate expedient of seizing merchantmen on their passage through the Downs, and, on the 29th, having secured several prizes—one alone being

July 29. A letter to the City.

valued at 20,000,[2] he wrote to the Common Council asking for that sum to be paid him in support of his patriotic enterprise, adding that on receipt of it he would liberate the captured vessels.[3]

On reading this letter the City drew up a spasmodic petition to the Houses, asking for the speedy liberation of the King, and

The City asks for a cessation.

for an immediate cessation of arms.[4] The Commons were not likely to humour the City merchants by granting so unreasonable a request, and on August 4

Aug. 4. The Commons' declaration against those who help the Prince.

they declared all who aided the Prince to be guilty of high treason, not before one member at least had asked that the Prince himself might be included in this condemnation.[5] After a while, the feeling in the City grew less cordial towards the Prince, who, while posing as a friend, blockaded the Thames and stopped the course of trade.

Though the Prince was not yet in a position to make the

The Prince's presence encourages declarations for the King.

attack on the Thames which he had in contemplation, his presence in the Downs served as an encouragement to those who in various quarters were hesitating to declare openly for the King. Before the end of July, Boynton, the Governor of Scarborough,

---

[1] Warwick to the Com. of D. H., *L.J.* x. 414.

[2] *Whitelocke*, 327.

[3] The Prince of Wales to the City, July 29, *The Declaration of his Highness*, E. 457, 14.

[4] *L.J.* x. 427.

[5] *C.J.* v. 661; Salvetti to Gondi, Aug. $\frac{4}{14}$, *Add. MSS.* 27,962, fol. 151; ——? to Joachimi, Aug. $\frac{11}{21}$, *Add. MSS.* 17,677, S, fol, 176,

announced his defection from his Parliamentary masters.[1] It
was scarcely less of a calamity that Batten, who had been

July 28 ?
Defection
of Scar-
borough.

Batten
escapes to
the fleet.

detained in London by the Derby House Committee, had made his escape, carrying with him
to the Prince in the Downs 'The Constant Warwick,'
one of the best of the Parliamentary ships.[2] As might
have been expected, the Prince received the old
sailor graciously and conferred on him the honour of knight-
hood. The vessels comprising the Prince's fleet now reached
the number of eleven.[3]

In other parts of England the Parliamentary authorities
were sufficiently circumspect to avert impending danger. At

An attempt
on Ports-
mouth.

A plot at
Oxford.

State of the
West.

Portsmouth an attempt made by some sailors to seize
the place in collusion with some of the soldiers of the
garrison was detected and baffled, and a similar plot
discovered amongst the soldiers at Oxford was likewise suppressed. The attitude of the population of
Devon and Cornwall was so menacing that, at the
request of the Commons, Fairfax countermanded orders which
he had given for the withdrawal of two regiments quartered in
the West under Sir Hardress Waller.[4]

That such schemes of revolt should have been even unsuccessfully entertained was sufficiently alarming, and it was

Parliament
needs an
army in the
field in the
South.

hardly possible to guard entirely against them as
long as Parliament had no army capable of taking
the field in the South of England. As there was
little expectation of Fairfax's speedy release, the
hopes of Independents and of all who wished ill to the King's
cause were fixed on Cromwell, whilst the Royalists took the
opportunity of his absence to redouble their machinations
against him. When, on August 1, a numerously signed

---

[1] The Mayor of Hull and others to Lenthall, Aug. 3, enclosing a
narrative, *Tanner MSS.* lvii. fols. 167, 169.

[2] *The Resolution of the Prince of Wales*, E. 456, 2

[3] The eleven ships measured 3,690 tons, and carried 274 guns and
1,200 men.

[4] *The Kingdom's Weekly Intelligencer*, E. 456, 8 ; *The Moderate*, E.
457, 21.

petition for Lilburne's release was presented to the House
of Commons it was supported in that House with singular

Aug. 1.
The
Commons
vote for
Lilburne's
liberation. unanimity, and on the 2nd the Lords, no less
unanimously, concurred with the Commons.[1] That
the two Houses, agreeing in nothing else, should
have agreed in this, can hardly be explained, except

Aug. 2.
The Lords
concur. on the supposition that the Presbyterians expected
Lilburne, when once at large, to prove a thorn in the
side of Cromwell.[2]

The Lords' vote on Lilburne's freedom was promptly
followed by the appearance of Major Huntington, who had

Major
Huntington
before the
House of
Lords. formerly been in Cromwell's confidence, but who,
having persisted in supporting the King after Crom-
well had found it hopeless to continue negotiations,

His narra-
tive. had resigned, or probably had been compelled to
resign, his position in the army. He now came
forward to tell the story, as he understood it, of the relations
of Cromwell with the army and the King in the preceding
year, drawing the inference that Cromwell had all the time been
aiming at supreme power for himself, and had no sincerity in
him. Cromwell, he said, had asserted that 'every single man
is judge of just and right as to the good and ill of a kingdom ; that the interest of honest men is the interest of the

---

[1] *C.J.* v. 657 ; *L.J.* x. 408.

[2] "John Lilburne . . . at length is come off with credit, his
greatest credit being his late moderation, which wrought so far on the
moderate party of both Houses that they all joined together against
Cromwell's faction, and voted him a present enlargement. . . . Now then,
seeing honest John is got loose, it will not be long ere Mr. Speaker and
Noll Cromwell be both brought to the stake; for he means to have a bout
with them to some purpose, I can tell you." *Merc. Pragmaticus*, E. 457,
11. "I could," wrote Lilburne in 1649, "at my pleasure have been
revenged of him . . . either by divisions in his army . . . or by joining
in impeaching him with Major Huntington ; which I had matter enough
to do, and was earnestly solicited to it again and again, and might have
had money enough to boot in my low and exhausted condition to have
done it ; yet I scorned it." *Legal and Fundamental Liberties*, p. 32, E.
567, 1. As to the quarter from which Lilburne received support we have
a statement that Sir John Maynard, one of the eleven members, begged
strongly for his liberation. *A Speech by Sir J. Maynard*, E. 458, 2.

kingdom ; . . . that it is lawful to pass through any forms of government for the accomplishing of his ends ; and, therefore, either to purge the Houses and support the remaining party by force everlastingly or to put a period to them by force is very lawful and suitable to the interest of honest men ; that it is lawful to play the knave with a knave.'[1]

Huntington's narrative was probably somewhat distorted, but there is no reason to doubt that it was substantially accurate. Cromwell's mind was not cast in a rigid mould, and his expressions uttered at different times and under different circumstances were not to be reconciled with any one political formula. He was never a rigid Parliamentarian, and even when he deferred most humbly to the two Houses, it was because he regarded them rather as a necessary source of authority than, as Eliot might have styled them, the mouthpiece of the national will. He would never have urged that 'the interest of honest men' ought in any case to be postponed to the national will, however clearly expressed. As for the startling assertion that Cromwell held it to be 'lawful to play the knave with a knave,' more information than we now possess is needed before any sober judgment can be pronounced upon it. Cromwell was certainly not one of those simple-minded men who wear their hearts upon their sleeves, and he undoubtedly did not think it in accordance with his duty to inform his political opponents what means he was about to adopt to countermine their machinations.

Its general accuracy.

Those who had hoped to make Lilburne an instrument for the destruction of Cromwell were not long in discovering their mistake. Lilburne at once declared Huntington to have acted basely in accusing another of crimes in which he himself participated, and of attacking one who was absent in the service of his country. "A coward," said Lilburne in conclusion, "lies upon advantage."[2]

Lilburne attacks Huntington.

Lilburne was not to be induced to damage a man who was fighting against the Scots. With amusing self-sufficiency he

[1] Huntington's Narrative, Aug. 2, *L.J.* x, 408,
[2] *The Moderate,* E. 457, 21.

wrote a patronising letter to Cromwell, 'lending,' as he said, 'a hand to help him up again, as not loving a Scotch interest.'

CAMPAIGN OF PRESTON.

March of Cromwell ——; March of Hamilton ‥‥; March of Lambert ‥‥·   F.S Weller

"To demonstrate unto you," he wrote to Cromwell regardless of grammar, "that I am no staggerer from my first principles that I engaged my life upon nor from you, if you are what you ought to be, and what you are now strongly reported to be; although if I prosecuted or

Aug. 3.
His letter to
Cromwell.

desired revenge for a hard and almost starving imprisonment,
I could have had of late the choice of twenty opportunities to
have paid you to the purpose ; but I scorned it, especially when
you are low ; and this assure yourself that if ever my hand be
upon you, it shall be when you are in your full glory, if then you
shall decline from the ways of truth and justice."

"This letter," added Lilburne in his account of the affair,
"as I have been told by the bearer,[1] was very welcome to
him."[2]   Cromwell, without being inordinately grate-
ful, may well have been pleased to find that when an
old friend was doing his best to mangle his reputation, an old enemy had stepped forward to take his part.
though in a somewhat uncouth fashion.

Cromwell's reception of it.

Whilst the Presbyterians were intriguing at Westminster,
Cromwell was steadily pressing on. Sending the bulk of his
cavalry forward to strengthen Lambert, he followed with three
regiments of foot, one of horse, and a small party of dragoons.
On August 1 he reached Leicester. "Our brigade,"
wrote one who served under him, "came hither to-
day. Our marches long, and want of shoes and
stockings gives discouragement to our soldiers, having received
no pay these many months to buy them, nor can we procure
any,[3] unless we plunder, which was never heard of by any
under the Lieutenant-General's conduct nor will be, though
they march barefoot, which many have done, since our advance from Wales."[4]   Before long, probably at
Nottingham on the 5th, the sufferings of the weary
soldiers were alleviated by the arrival of 2,500 pairs
of shoes from Northampton, and of 2,500 pairs of stockings
from Coventry.[5]

*Aug. 1.
He arrives at Leicester,*

*Aug. 5.
and at North-ampton.*

As yet Cromwell had no train of artillery with him, and his
brigade had therefore to remain at Doncaster from the 8th to

---

[1] *i.e.* Sexby.   [2] *The Legal Fundamental Liberties*, p. 32, E. 567, 1.
[3] 'nor any can procure' in text.   [4] *The Moderate*, E. 457, 21.
[5] The shoes and stockings had at least arrived before the brigade
reached Doncaster on the 8th. *The Moderate Intelligencer*, E. 459, 19.
According to *The Moderate*, E. 457, 21, they were expected to be found
at Nottingham.

the 11th, awaiting its arrival from Hull.[1] He utilised the delay
by bringing help to the besiegers of Pontefract, driving the

Aug. 8.
Cromwell at
Doncaster.
Royalists out of the town and cooping them up in
the castle.[2] He had also to conduct an operation
from which considerable benefit was likely to accrue
to his own command. He left behind him some new levies
which had lately joined him from the midland counties, and in
their place took away with him the old soldiers who had hitherto

The name of
Ironsides.
been carrying on the siege. It was at Pontefract
that Cromwell's men were first called by the nickname of Ironsides, a term which had hitherto been appro-
priated to himself.[3] It was not, however, an epithet which
came into general use for some time to come.

The approach of Cromwell was the more welcome to the
few friends of Parliament in the North, as a recent event had

Hidden
dangers
brought clearly before their minds the impossibility
of trusting in the fidelity even of men who had

Aug. 9.
Henry
Lilburne's
defection at
Tynemouth.
hitherto been forward in the Parliamentary cause.
On August 9 Henry Lilburne, the Lieutenant-
Governor of Tynemouth Castle, a brother of John
and Robert, declared for the King. He had been disgusted
at the real or alleged plot of some amongst the Levellers to
murder the King whilst still at Hampton Court, and was subsequently charged with having given information against his
brother John as being concerned in the design.[4] Whatever
may have been the motives of his defection, he did not live to

Aug. 10.
He is slain.
tell his own story. In the night, Hazlerigg despatched a party from Newcastle to recover the castle.
The assault was successful, and in the dark hours of the
morning of the 10th, Henry Lilburne met a soldier's death in

[1] Com. of D. H. to Fairfax, Aug. 2, *Com. Letter Book.* At that time
Cromwell appears to have expected to reach Doncaster on the 14th, a date
which he anticipated by six days.

[2] *The Moderate Intelligencer*, E. 459, 19.

[3] *The Resolution of the King's Subjects*, E. 456, 18.

[4] *The Second Part of England's New Chains Discovered*, p. 6, E. 548,
16 ; see also a petition to Fairfax from other incriminated persons, who
charge Henry Lilburne with bringing false accusations against them, Nov.
28, 1647, *Clarke Papers*, i. 419.

defending the post against those by whom it had been entrusted to him.

It was not, however, by the loss or the maintenance of a
single fortress that the great issue could be decided. On
July 31.   July 31 Appleby Castle surrendered to the Scots on
Appleby
Castle   honourable terms, and Hamilton, who had at last
surrenders.   received reinforcements and artillery from Scotland,
and who was expecting soon to be joined by the further reinforcements which Sir George Monro had brought over from
Ireland,[1] felt himself in a condition to advance. On August 2
Aug. 2.   he reached Kendal, from which place he threw out
Hamilton
at Kendal.   parties of horse to forage and plunder as far as Dent
                  and Sedbergh. As the way past Dent led into
Lambert
compelled to   Wensleydale, Lambert, whose position at Bowes and
fall back.   Barnard Castle was thus completely turned, fell back
on Richmond in order to guard Yorkshire against attack.
Here, however, he received information which convinced him
Aug. 3.   that it was not through Wensleydale that the Scots
He posts   would advance.[2] He now thought it certain that
himself at
Richmond,   they would either march directly southwards through
Lancashire, or cross into Yorkshire from Ribblesdale by the
valley of the Aire, in order to break up the siege of Pontefract
with the help of the Yorkshire Cavaliers.[3] Holding that the
latter movement was far more probable than the former, Lam-
                  bert retreated from Richmond and took up a posi-
and falls
back on   tion between Knaresborough and Leeds, in which he
Leeds.   would be able to await the arrival of Cromwell, and
at the same time to check the advance of the Scots against
Pontefract so far as it was possible for his scanty forces to hold
them back.

To fall on Lambert before Cromwell reached him was entirely out of Hamilton's power. He lingered at Kendal, where,

---

[1] See p. 165.

[2] *The Moderate*, E. 457, 21 ; *The Moderate Intelligencer*, E. 457, 33.

[3] The first mention of the supposed intention of the Scots to pass into
Yorkshire is in a letter written from Richmond on Aug. 3, *Perfect Occurrences*, E. 525, 15 ; but Lambert would not have fallen back unless he had
suspected it a day or two sooner.

being still without horses and artillery, he seized from the country people such baggage horses as he could find, thereby

Aug. 8.
Hamilton
still at
Kendal. arousing a feeling of hostility which was not favourable to a speedy advance. The season, too, was against him. The rain poured down incessantly, and brooks easily crossed in other years were now raging torrents.

Langdale's
projects. Langdale, impatient of the delay, pushed on to Settle, hoping to win over the governor of Skipton to betray the castle to him, and probably intending, in case of success, to relieve Pontefract. If he could carry with him the sluggish Scots, he might even make his way to the eastern coast, and set free the hard-pressed Royalists at Colchester. "God," wrote Hamilton to him on the 1st, "increase the distraction of London, and send you Skipton, and preserve our friends in Colchester."[1]

In the meanwhile the Scottish army was suffering from internal distractions, which Hamilton was powerless to appease.

Monro's
arrival. Monro arrived at Kendal with intelligence that he had brought his contingent from Ireland across the border. His veterans would have been well employed in stiffening the raw levies which constituted the bulk of the main army; but Monro refused to take orders from Callander or Baillie, whilst Callander objected to receive him as an independent commander. Hamilton, after some hesitation, could find no other remedy but to direct Monro to tarry behind, and to form a separate army of four or five thousand men, in conjunction with Musgrave's English force. For all practical purposes Monro might as well have remained in Ireland.[2]

On August 9 Hamilton advanced towards Hornby,[3] and

[1] Hamilton to Langdale, Aug. 7, *Clarke Trials*, fol. 148. An intercepted letter in which Langdale expressed to Lucas his intention of coming to his aid was printed at the time (E. 457, 20).

[2] Musgrave (*Clarendon MSS.* 2,869) sets down the combined army as being 'above 7,000' after he and Monro had been joined by the fugitives from Preston. They must, therefore, at this time have numbered about four or five thousand.

[3] *A Letter from Holland*, E. 467, 21. This is a long account of the whole expedition written by an English Royalist who accompanied the

there settled down once more.   He was still there on the 13th
when he received a visit from Langdale, who had ridden over

Aug. 9.
Hamilton
moves to
Hornby.
from Settle to tell him of the gathering of the Parliamentary forces in Yorkshire, though whether he
was aware that Lambert had been joined by Crom-

Aug. 13.
A council
of war.
well must remain uncertain.   At a council of war
Middleton and Turner recommended a movement
into Yorkshire to meet the enemy in front ; whereas Hamilton
and Baillie were in favour of continuing their southern advance

A march
through
Lancashire
decided on.
through Lancashire.   Hamilton held to his own
opinion, and as Callander professed himself neutral,
the commander-in-chief for once carried his sub-
ordinates with him.   He seems to have been influenced by the
hope that Manchester would declare in his favour, and that
Lord Byron, who, after the failure of many schemes for getting
the neighbouring fortresses into his hands, was waiting at
Llanrwst for the approach of the Scottish army, would prove
a valuable ally to the invaders.[1]   Of any suspicion of danger
from Cromwell's lion-spring across the Yorkshire fells no hint
has reached us.

After this decision Langdale returned to Settle, drew in his
forces, and directed them towards Preston, where he was to

Langdale
moves
towards
Preston.
join Hamilton.   On the night of the 16th, according
to his own statement, he received intelligence that
Cromwell was but three miles off.   According to the

Aug. 16.
Tidings of
Cromwell's
approach.
Scottish authorities, Langdale persistently asserted
that he had to do merely with Colonel Ashton and
the Lancashire levies.   Certainty is in this case unattainable, but it is more probable that the Scottish version

army, but could not get employment in it on account of his former activity
against the Covenant.

[1] Hamilton's advance to Hornby on the 9th is gathered from a letter
written by him on the 8th announcing his intention of moving there.
Clarke Trials, fol. 146b.   See also Langdale's relation, *Chetham Soc.
Civil War Tracts of Lancashire*, 267 ; Turner's *Memoirs*, 62.   The
writer of the *Letter from Holland* (E. 467, 21) puts the decision to march
through Lancashire at Kirkby Thore.   Very likely it was discussed at
Hornby a second time.

is correct, and that Langdale treated the rumour at the time as an idle tale.[1]

However this may have been, the rumour was absolutely true. On the 11th Cromwell, having at last received his artillery from Hull, was at liberty to move, and having had ample opportunities of conferring with Lambert during the last few days, he joined forces with him on the 13th between Knaresborough and Wetherby.[2] Even with the addition of the Lancashire forces under Ashton, Cromwell had now under his command no more than 8,600 men, as he was compelled to leave behind two regiments to block up the newly-revolted Scarborough.[3] He afterwards reckoned the Scots, probably not without exaggeration, at 21,000, or even at 24,000.[4] It was, however, no time to count heads. If Hamilton could join hands with Byron, North Wales and the Midlands might be expected to rise to support him, and even the suppressed fires in London might blaze up once more. Terrible stories of Scottish inhumanity, growing in enormity as they passed from mouth to mouth, stung Cromwell to the quick. Hamilton's plunderers, it was said, had stripped the cottages on their line of march to the very

Aug. 13. Cromwell sets out.

[1] Compare Langdale (*Civil War Tracts of Lancashire*, 268) with Turner's *Memoirs*, 63, and *Burnet*, vi. 58. Incapable as Hamilton was, it seems incredible that he should have taken no steps to provide against Cromwell's attack, if he had been positively informed that he was close at hand. Burnet says that on the 16th—the 18th is an obvious misprint— 'Callander got some hint of Cromwell's joining Lambert.' The writer of he *Letter from Holland* (E. 467, 21) says on the morning of the 17th there was 'no knowledge of any enemy to be near us as yet, only some intelligence came the night before that part of the forces were quartered within less than twelve miles, the which in less than an hour after was contradicted by an eminent person, and so the former discredited.'

[2] Cromwell to Lenthall, Aug. 20; Cromwell to the Committee at York, Aug. 23, *Carlyle*, Letters lxiv., lxv. In *Perfect Occurrences*, E. 525, 17, and *The Moderate Intelligencer*, E. 457, 33, we hear of meetings between Cromwell and Lambert on the 10th and 11th. No doubt Lambert rode over to see his commander and to take his orders before the junction of the forces.

[3] *The Bloody Battle of Preston*, E. 460, 20.

[4] *Carlyle*, Letters lxiv., lxv.

pothooks, had seized children as hostages for ransom, and had butchered them when their parents were unable or unwilling to pay the sum demanded.

Cromwell's march was conducted in far other guise than Hamilton's. Leaving behind him the artillery, which it had cost him so much trouble to secure, he made his way *Cromwell's march.* through the rough Craven country, and on the third *Aug. 15. He reaches Gisburn.* day, picking up Ashton's forces on the way, quartered at Gisburn in the Valley of the Ribble. On the 16th, *Aug. 16. A council of war at Hodder Bridge.* a short council of war was held by the side of the road at Hodder Bridge. Should the army, it was asked, cross the Ribble to the south bank in order to block Hamilton's way across the river as he left Preston, or should it keep on the north bank, and fall upon the enemy in Preston itself? The latter course was adopted on the ground that there was more likelihood of bringing on an engagement this way, as it was supposed that Hamilton would halt at Preston to await the arrival of Monro.[1] Neither here nor anywhere else is there the slightest hint of Cromwell's having formed the strategical plan of attacking Hamilton in flank which has been liberally ascribed to him by modern writers.[2] In war, as in politics, Cromwell never rose above the

---

[1] "It was thought that to engage the enemy to fight was our business; and the reason aforesaid"—*i.e.* that Hamilton was likely to halt at Preston to await Monro—"giving us hopes that our marching on the north side of Ribble would effect it, it was resolved we should march over the bridge." Cromwell to Lenthall, Aug. 20, *Carlyle*, Letter lxiv.

[2] In the first place Cromwell had to go into Yorkshire to meet his artillery; and, in the second place, he must have received his information from Lambert, all of whose movements point to a belief that Hamilton would advance to relieve Pontefract. Lambert fell back on Richmond on August 3, and from that time at least the expectation that he would have to defend Yorkshire must have been foremost in Lambert's mind. It is impossible to show that Cromwell did not provide for the alternative of Hamilton's choosing to advance through Lancashire, but there is no evidence that he did so, and he never takes credit for any plan of the kind. In the passage quoted in the last note stress is laid on the importance of bringing on a fight, whilst nothing is said about the advantage of attacking Hamilton on the flank.

simple strategy of finding out the enemy wherever it was
most easy to give him battle. That evening he fixed his
quarters in Stonyhurst Park. The next day he was to 'put it
to the touch, to win or lose it all !'

On the 16th,[1] whilst Cromwell was approaching Stonyhurst,
the news of his approach, whether credited or not,[2] was carried
to Langdale and Hamilton. The Scottish army was
loosely dispersed for foraging purposes, and on that
day Callander and Middleton led the cavalry towards
Wigan, some sixteen miles to the south of Preston.
Hearing, however, a rumour that Cromwell was not
far off, Callander, instead of bringing back his whole
force to the support of the infantry, merely retraced
his own steps towards Preston to consult with Baillie
and the Duke.

Dispersion of Hamilton's army.

Aug. 16. The Scottish horse advance to Wigan.

Callander returns.

On the morning of the 17th Hamilton himself arrived at
Preston. Regardless of his danger he directed Baillie with
the infantry to cross the Ribble in continuation of
the forward march in which the army was engaged.
Before Baillie had time to carry out these orders,
news arrived that Langdale—who had drawn up his own force,
consisting of about 3,000 foot and 600 horse amongst some
enclosed fields lying on the north-west of the town in the line
of Cromwell's approach—was being assailed by the enemy.
Hamilton accordingly at once countermanded the order given
to Baillie, who had not yet crossed the bridge, bidding him
remain on the north side of the Ribble to support Langdale,
and sending a messenger to Middleton to bring the cavalry
back as speedily as possible.

Aug. 17. Preparing for battle.

On this Callander, always ready to dispute the prudence of
his general's orders, intervened. The infantry, he urged, would
be exposed to destruction if they attempted to with-
stand the enemy without the cavalry. By reverting
to the original plan, and sending Baillie with the whole body
of the foot across the bridge, the junction of the infantry with
the cavalry returning from Wigan under Middleton would be
hastened, and the whole Scottish army would then have the

Callander's advice.

[1] Burnet's 18th must be a misprint.   [2] See p. 182.

advantage of fighting with the Ribble in front instead of behind. That this plan would place Langdale and his Englishmen in imminent peril was perhaps of little moment in the eyes of the Scottish nobleman. Either, he argued, the enemy's attack was in force, or it was a mere demonstration. In the latter case Langdale would easily hold his own. In the former, he could easily fall back through Preston and join the Scottish army across Ribble Bridge. Hamilton, as usual, gave way to his overbearing lieutenant, and the Scottish infantry marched across the river, leaving Langdale to his fate. Hamilton was, however, a brave man though a bad general, and, gathering round him a small body of horse which had formed the rearguard of his army, and was still in Preston, he rode out to the help of Langdale.[1]

[1] According to the *Letter from Holland* (E. 467, 21), "though not suspecting that the whole strength of the enemy was so near hand, he," *i.e.* the Duke, "presently despatched order that Lieut.-Gen. Middleton . . . should with all expedition march there to us with the cavalry, and gave command to Baillie . . . to draw them all in order on the moor, and not to pass the bridge, intending to fight the enemy if need required it. . . . Lieut.-Gen. Baillie causes the foot to stay accordingly; which the Earl of Callander perceiving, he earnestly adviseth that it was safest the foot should forthwith march to their quarters, where they might the sooner receive succour from the cavalry which was on the same side of the river; that the enemy probably had but an inconsiderable force there wherewith Sir Marmaduke Langdale's forces would be able to deal with the help of part of our horse, that was beginning to advance towards us— not those with Middleton; that in case the enemy had there his whole force he might easily with his horse come about and overrun the foot if they stayed on the moor, they wanting our cavalry to assist them, but if they passed the water, not only they would be in safety, but also Sir Marmaduke—whether the enemy had his whole strength there. or not— would by degrees be able to draw off his men to our foot on the other side, and then both forces might join to make good the bridge and fords till our whole horse came thither. These reasons being so weighty, and proceeding from a commander of such repute and long experience in war and Lieut.- General of that army, were assented to by the Duke; so the foot passed the river." This passage makes the affair intelligible. It agrees with the narrative given by *Burnet*, vi. 60, though the latter avoids all mention of Callander's advice, making him order Baillie to cross the river, and over- hear Hamilton's objections by sheer personal determination.

Thus it was that Langdale's 3,600 Englishmen, unsupported except by Hamilton's small body of horse, were exposed to the

The battle of Preston.

attack of more than double their number of the best soldiers in the world. His outpost on the moor was soon driven in, and his only chance of holding out with the main body lay in the hedges of the enclosed fields in which he had taken his stand. These hedges interposed an insuperable obstacle to any repetition by Cromwell of his tactics at Marston Moor and Naseby. There was indeed a narrow lane through the middle of Langdale's position, at the entrance of which

THE BATTLE OF PRESTON.

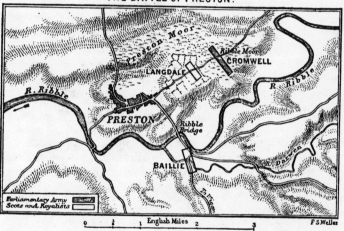

Cromwell posted his own regiment of horse and a second regiment under the fiery Harrison, hoping in the end to send them both by that route to break up Langdale's force when it had once been dislodged from its position. First, however, the enclosed fields on either side must be cleared, and against Langdale's infantry, protected by the hedges, Cromwell hurled his foot regiments as to the storm of a fortress, guarding them with horse on the flanks in view of possible sallies of the enemy. After repeated attempts had been made without success, Cromwell's regiments on the left showed signs of flinching, and Ashton's Lancashire levies were ordered up to restore the fight.

By the admission of friend and foe Langdale and his Englishmen fought like heroes. Yet, after four hours' struggle, they were at last compelled to give way and to fall back upon the town. When the hedges were at last cleared the two regi-
Langdale's ments of horse which Cromwell had set apart for the
retreat. service, dashing through the lane, followed them
into the town, and cleared the streets. Though Langdale personally got safely to Baillie's quarters across the Ribble, the greater part of his infantry surrendered, whilst his horse, together with those who fought under Hamilton, fled north-wards and joined Monro. Hamilton himself, who had refused to abandon Langdale as long as he kept the field, only reached
The bridge the south bank of the river by a ford. Cromwell's
gained. musketeers then, posting themselves on the high
bank which slopes down on the north side of the Ribble, com-manded the bridge, and under the protection of their fire a charge soon cleared it of the enemy. Later in the evening Baillie and the whole of the Scottish infantry were driven still further south over the Darwen, a smaller stream which joins the Ribble somewhat lower down, and the bridge over the Darwen, as well as that over the Ribble, was occupied by Cromwell.

When the Scottish army lay down that night its condition was practically hopeless. Not only had it, if Langdale's Englishmen
Condition of be counted in its ranks, lost 1,000 killed and 4,000
the Scottish prisoners, but it had ceased to feel confidence in its
army. commanders. The self-sufficient Callander had done
as badly as the impressionable Hamilton. He had neither allowed Baillie to support Langdale, nor had he brought up the cavalry
A night from Wigan in time to support Baillie. In the council
council. of war hastily summoned in the night time, Baillie
and Turner alone argued for fighting it out where they stood. Callander, who had caused the mischief, was for slipping away in the dark, and his proposal was supported by the other officers.

The adoption of this course was fatal to the army which Hamilton still nominally commanded. It was without means
A fatal of transport, as the peasants who had been com-
resolution. pelled to furnish horses had stolen away with them
in the dark, and no other baggage-animals could be procured

by a beaten army. Each soldier was therefore ordered to take with him as much powder as his flask would hold, and directions were given to blow up what remained after the army was so far on its way that the explosion would not betray its movements. In that army, however, orders were seldom obeyed, and the whole of the ammunition fell uninjured into Cromwell's hands.[1]

Hamilton was already three miles on his way before Cromwell discovered his retreat. Cromwell at once ordered

A night march.

Ashton to hold Preston with 4,000 men against Monro and Musgrave. So imminent did an attack

Ashton left at Preston.

from the north appear that Cromwell directed Ashton to put his 4,000 prisoners to the sword if the enemy assailed him. Fortunately for them, Monro, in spite of Musgrave's pleadings, refused to stir.[2] Cromwell himself, who had been reinforced after the battle,[3] followed Hamilton with 5,500 men, though he reckoned the enemy's force to be still twice that number.

In the pursuit Cromwell had to deal, not with Baillie's disorganised infantry, but with Middleton's horsemen, who had at

The pursuit.

last arrived from Wigan after Hamilton had moved off and now covered the retreat of their comrades. Facing round again and again they drove back the English cavalry, losing, it is true, many prisoners, amongst whom Hurry was one, but inflicting some damage on the pursuers; Colonel Thornhagh, one of Cromwell's best officers, being amongst those killed in one of these attacks.[4]

The rain had been pouring in torrents throughout the day,

[1] *Carlyle*, Letter lxiv. ; Turner's *Memoirs*, 63 ; *Burnet*, vi. 60 ; Langdale's Narrative, *Civil War Tracts of Lancashire*, 267 ; Hodgson's Memoirs in *Original Memoirs*. The narrative in Burnet reads as if it were either drawn up by Turner or afterwards used by him.

[2] *Carlyle*, Letter lxiv. ; Musgrave's relation, *Clarendon MSS.* 2,867.

[3] There is no direct mention of these reinforcements, but among the regiments left with Ashton were some not named as taking part in the battle. Cromwell and Ashton had now about 1,000 more men than are said to have been with them on the 17th.

[4] *A Letter from Holland*, E. 467, 21.

and the whole Scottish force was wet and half starved when it reached Wigan on the evening of the 18th.   The hungry men

Aug. 18. Hamilton at Wigan. fell on the town, Royalist as it was, and stripped it bare.   The moon then shone out and Hamilton ordered another night march, hoping to secure the bridge over the Mersey at Warrington and so to gain time

Aug. 19. The fight at Winwick. to join Byron in North Wales.   On the morning of the 19th Cromwell, still pursuing, was upon them at Winwick.   Fighting in desperation, the Scottish army held out for some hours.   After a loss of 1,000 killed and 2,000 prisoners, they left the field and continued their retreat.

On went the chase.   At Warrington Hamilton had still with him 3,000 horse and 4,000 foot, and was thus still superior in

Hamilton at Warrington. numbers to his pursuers, but his men were forlorn and spiritless, and he himself with shattered nerves was even less capable of taking a resolution than he had been at Preston.   Callander, representing to him that a beaten force of infantry, with a small stock of powder soaked with rain, was a hindrance rather than an assistance, induced him to give, or to allow others to give, orders to Baillie to surrender without making any attempt to defend the bridge.   Baillie,

Baillie surrenders. when he received the command, was as one distracted. Would not some brother soldier, he asked, put a bullet into his head and save him from this disgrace?   Resistance was, however, practically hopeless.   Half, at least, of his soldiers had flung away their arms, and those who had retained them were without powder and shot.   Baillie, indeed, gave orders to defend the bridge, but his orders were obeyed by no more than 250 men.[1]   In the end Baillie did as he was bidden, and 4,000[2] more captives, together with Warrington and its bridge, passed into Cromwell's hands.[3]

Hard service and miry ways had worn out the pursuers almost as much as the pursued.   The Scots, wrote Cromwell,

---

[1] Attestation, Aug. 22, *Baillie*, iii. 456.

[2] Baillie says that he had only 2,600 or 2,700, but Cromwell no doubt picked up many stragglers.

[3] *Carlyle*, Letter lxiv. ; *Burnet*, vi. 62 ; Turner's *Memoirs*, 64 ; Hodgson in *Orig. Memoirs*, 120.

'are so tired, and in such confusion, that if my horse could but; trot after them I could take them all ; but we are so weary we

The effects of hard service. can scarce be able to do more than walk after them. . . . They are the miserablest party that ever was. I durst engage myself with 500 fresh horse and 500 nimble foot to destroy them all.　My horse are miserably. beaten out, and I have 10,000 prisoners.' [1]

Despatching Lambert in pursuit of the remaining Scottish, horse, Cromwell himself turned back northwards to deal with

Aug. 20. Cromwell turns north- wards. Monro, and to stifle in Scotland any preparations which might be made for prolonging the war.　Before he left Warrington he had a warning to address to the

His warning to Parlia- ment. Parliament at Westminster.　"Surely, sir," he wrote to Lenthall, "this is nothing but the hand of God ; and wherever anything in this world is exalted or exalts itself, God will put it down ; for this is the day wherein He alone will be exalted.　It is not fit for me to give advice, nor to say a word what use you should make of this ; more than to pray you, and all that acknowledge God, that they would exalt Him, and not hate His people who are as the apple of His eye, and for whom even kings shall be reproved ; and that you would take courage to do the work of the Lord, in fulfilling the end of your magistracy, in seeking the peace and welfare of this land ; that all that will live peaceably may have counten- ance from you, and they that are incapable and will not leave troubling the land may speedily be destroyed out of the land." [2]

A sterner note was here mingled with the pleadings for liberty of conscience which had sprung to Cromwell's lips after

Cromwell not vin- dictive. the rout of Naseby and the surrender of Bristol.[3] Yet there was nothing vindictive in his call for the destruction of those who continued to trouble the land.　No cry for vengeance or for retributive punishment of any kind was heard from him.

Nor did the political side of the strife escape Cromwell's

---

[1] *Carlyle*, Letter lxv.

[2] Cromwell to Lenthall, Aug. 20, *Carlyle*, Letter lxiv.

[3] See vol. ii. 252, 319.

notice. "The greatest part by far of the nobility of Scotland,"
The Scottish he wrote, "are with Duke Hamilton."[1]   In Scotland,
nobility. as in England, the question of the supremacy of King
or Parliament was giving way to a strife of classes.

Hamilton at least was no longer in case to be the champion
of any cause.   His wearied horsemen staggered on as best they
A disastrous might.   At first they thought of making their way to
retreat. Byron.   Their next hope was to join Sir Henry
Lingen, who had, as they believed, risen in Herefordshire.
Abandoning this plan after leaving Malpas, they wheeled round
to the east, hoping to return to Scotland by fetching a compass
wide enough to avoid falling in with their pursuers.   As they
pressed on they were harassed by the trained bands of the
counties through which they passed, Middleton, the most
capable of their officers, being taken prisoner on the way.

On the 22nd, with rapidly diminishing numbers, Hamilton
reached Uttoxeter.   There the soldiers mutinied, refusing to go
Aug. 22. farther.   On the 25th Hamilton offered to capitulate
Hamilton at to the governor of Stafford.   Before the terms had
Uttoxeter. been agreed on, Lambert appeared on the scene.
Aug. 25. Commissioners on both sides were appointed, and
His capitu- articles of surrender were agreed on and signed.
lation. Then Lord Grey of Groby rode in with a body of horse from
Leicestershire and seized on Hamilton as his prisoner.
Lambert, however, insisted on the observance of the articles
signed.   Hamilton and all with him were to be prisoners of
war, having 'the lives and safety of their persons assured to
them.'[2]

The day before this catastrophe Callander and Langdale,
with such of their followers as they could persuade to ac-
Callander company them, separated themselves from Hamilton
and Lang- and rode off towards Ashbourne.   Callander's Scottish
dale ride off. horse, however, soon mutinied and refused to go
Langdale farther, whilst Langdale and a small party of English
captured. continued their journey alone, hoping to escape unnoticed.
They were, however, detected not far from Nottingham, and

---

[1] Cromwell to Lord Grey of Groby, Aug. 20, *Clarke Trials,* fol. 124.
[2] *Burnet,* vi. 64 ; Turner's *Memoirs,* 70 ; *Clarke Trials,* fol. 107b.

were taken prisoners and lodged in Nottingham Castle. Callander was more fortunate. He succeeding in reaching London, and in due time he made good his escape into Holland.[1]

Callander escapes.

The mass of Scottish prisoners captured in Lancashire were a sore burden upon the resources of Parliament, and on September 4 the House of Commons appointed a committee to make a distinction between those who had taken service under Hamilton by compulsion and those who had taken it voluntarily. Those who belonged to the former—that is to say, the great majority —were to be released on an engagement never again to enter England as soldiers without the leave of the English Parliament. Those who belonged to the latter were to be shipped to the plantations beyond sea—that is to say, to be bound to servile labour either in Virginia or Barbadoes. When no more were required by the plantations, the remainder were to be despatched to Venice to serve under the Republic.[2]

Sept. 4. The Scottish prisoners to be released or transported.

[1] Langdale's narrative, *Chetham Soc. Civil War Tracts of Lancashire,* 270 ; *Burnet,* vi. 64.

[2] *C.J.* vi. 5.

CHAPTER LXV.

THE SURRENDER OF COLCHESTER.

EVERY Royalist in England knew that the blow struck at Preston had crushed his last hopes. Local risings, even if successful, would no longer be able to look for a delivering army round which to rally. Alone they could accomplish nothing. Lingen, from whom much had been expected, had risen prematurely in Herefordshire, had been chased into Montgomeryshire, and had there been routed on August 17,[1] the day on which Cromwell burst on Langdale from Ribble Moor. A few days later Byron, on his reception of the news from the North, drew back hastily to Anglesea, whence he ultimately made his way to the Isle of Man.[2]

1648.
Aug. 17.
Rout of
Lingen.

Byron's
retreat.

On no one can the rout of Preston have fallen more heavily than on Lauderdale, who, on August 10, reached the Downs, full of confidence in his own powers of persuasion to remove the obstacles which had hitherto stood in the way of the Prince's journey to Hamilton's headquarters. On his arrival he found the Royalists in good heart. The castles in the Downs had been relieved, and news had arrived that the London citizens were collecting money to ransom the captured vessels.[3] On the 14th, however, a force which had 'landed to drive off

Aug. 10.
Lauderdale
in the
Downs.

Aug. 14.
A repulse
before
Deal.

[1] *L.J.* x. 686. Webb, in the *Civil War in Herefordshire*, ii. 422, prints Lingen's proclamation with the date of Aug. 22. This must be a misprint for Aug. 12.

[2] Byron's Relation, *Clar. St. P.* ii. 418.

[3] See p. 173.

the besiegers under Colonel Rich from before Deal, was itself
driven back to the ships with heavy loss.[1]

In the meanwhile Lauderdale was urging the Prince to
submit to the Scottish terms. With the lad himself, eager
as he was for action, he found little difficulty. The
Prince readily consented to come to Scotland unaccompanied by his proscribed followers, and,
though he pleaded hard that an exception might be made in
favour of Rupert, Rupert himself declined to be made a bone
of contention, and it was finally arranged that he should remain
in Holland till the Scots had accepted his professions of friendship. Lauderdale's next proposal that the Prince, as long as
he remained in Hamilton's army, should conform to the
Presbyterian worship, excited more resistance, Hopton and
Gerard declaring strongly against its acceptance. Lauderdale
was consequently informed that the Prince could not give the
required promise without his father's permission, and that some
time must elapse before that permission could be obtained.
Lauderdale, who was too shrewd an observer of human nature
to be easily baffled, replied that the negotiation with which he
was charged admitted of no delay, and that if he
could not have an immediate answer he would return
to Scotland on the morrow. The future Charles II.
was not prepared to sacrifice his inclination to a
religious scruple, and on the 16th he formally announced his
acceptance of the whole of the Scottish terms.

*A nego-
tiation with
the Prince.*

*Aug. 16.
The Prince
accepts the
Scottish
terms.*

It was now arranged that the Prince should sail for
Berwick with as little delay as possible, and should make his
way from that point to Hamilton's head-quarters,
wherever they might happen to be. Lauderdale saw
with pleasure that the partisans of the Scottish alliance had
gained an ascendency over the Prince, and that Lord Willoughby
of Parham, one of those who pronounced most strongly in its
favour, received, in addition to his command of the fleet as
vice-admiral, a commission which placed him at the head of
the land-forces in Suffolk, Norfolk, Lincolnshire, and in two

*Presbyterian
designs.*

[1] Instructions to Lauderdale, July 2; Lauderdale to Lanark, Aug. 10,
Hamilton Papers, 232, 237; *L.J.* x. 685.

other counties.[1] Lauderdale's pleasure was the greater as
Willoughby assured him that he intended to employ none but
Presbyterians, and named the Presbyterian Poyntz as his
major-general. Another force, composed of the men of the
English regiments discharged from the Dutch service after the
peace, was to be despatched to Scarborough to raise the
Royalists of Yorkshire, and of these Newcastle was to be the
general and Wilmot the lieutenant-general.[2] It is true that
neither Newcastle nor Wilmot professed to be Presbyterians,
but they both declared their readiness to favour the Presbyterians and to support the alliance with the Scots.

The success of Lauderdale's mission was bitterly felt by the
old Cavaliers, who, after shedding their blood for Church and

King, found that they had no favour to expect at the
Court of the heir-apparent. "Sir Marmaduke," wrote
Lauderdale on the 20th, in ignorance that but three
days before the man whom he despised had alone of all
Hamilton's officers won honour at Preston, "is not at all valued
here." The great Marquis of Montrose was regarded with
equal scorn. "James Graham," continued Lauderdale, "is
no acceptable Prince in this Court." It was perhaps well for
the King that he was immured in Carisbrooke, where such
voices could not trouble him. He little thought when he gave
his assent to the Engagement that his son would take its empty
phrases as a real declaration of policy.

In the City, too, the Presbyterian merchants were again stirring. It was firmly believed on board the fleet in the Downs that
what London had failed to do for Norwich or Holland
it would do for the Prince of Wales when he unfurled
his father's banner in the North. The commanders of the City
forces were already named. Major-General Browne, who had
recently been chosen Sheriff, was to command the London
trained bands. Massey, who had returned to England,[3] was
to be placed in charge of a new body of infantry which was
being secretly levied, and Graves in charge of the cavalry which

*Disappoint-
ment of the
Cavaliers.*

*Preparations
in the City.*

---

[1] Their names are not given.
[2] Lauderdale to Lanark, Aug. 26, *Hamilton Papers*, 248; Sir E.
Verney to Sir R. Verney, Sept. $\frac{6}{16}$, *Verney MSS.*   [3] See vol. iii. 349.

was being got together in a similar way.[1] "The Lords and the City," wrote one of Rupert's correspondents, "understand each other, as also the Reformadoes, that are considerable—8,000 in number."[2] A simultaneous explosion of all the Royalist forces was, in short, to sweep away the army of Fairfax and Cromwell, and to complete the work which had hitherto failed through the premature and isolated outbursts of individual localities.

Prospects of the Royalists.

To this hopeful scheme a death-blow was given by the news from Preston and Warrington.[3] "The Lord," wrote Lauderdale on the 20th, "send me a good account of our army, for I must confess at this distance they go very near to my heart."[4] A day or two later Lauderdale knew that that army had ceased to exist, and that English Presbyterianism had no longer a rallying-point round which to gather.

Effect of the news from Preston.

When the tidings from Preston reached Lauderdale the long agony of Colchester was almost ended. For some days after his repulse on June 13,[5] Fairfax busied himself in raising forts to complete the isolation of the besieged. His weak point was on the northern side of the Colne, as the Suffolk trained bands, which had been ready enough to occupy the bridges over the Stour, in order to prevent a Royalist invasion of their county, were by no means anxious to take part in offensive warfare. It was not till the 24th that, being at last persuaded that in this case their best defence lay in joining Fairfax's attack, they marched into Essex and occupied the high ground commanding the bridge over which the road leads from Colchester in the direction of Suffolk.[6] On July 2 the work of circumvallation was completed.[7]

Progress of the siege of Colchester.

June 24.
Fairfax joined by the Suffolk tiained bands.

[1] Lauderdale to Lanark, Aug. 19, 20: Declarations by the Prince of Wales, Aug. 16, 17, 18, *Hamilton Papers*, 239, 250.

[2] W. Steward to Rupert, Aug. 20, *Rupert Transcripts* in the possession of Mr. Firth.

[3] *Burnet*, vi. 71.

[4] Lauderdale to Lanark, Aug. 20, *Hamilton Papers*, 248.

[5] See p. 152.   [6] The *Diary*, see p. 153, note 2.

[7] *Mr. Round's MS.* p. 87.

All that military art could achieve was done by the besieged under the skilful guidance of Lucas.   There were constant sallies, and the artillery within the town did no slight mischief. The temper of the besiegers grew embittered at the prolonga-tion of the struggle, and they freely accused their opponents of using roughened [1] or even poisoned bullets, judging from ap-pearances which were probably the result of the want of proper appliances for casting.   In the teeth of desperate resistance, Fairfax steadily pressed on, drawing the toils more closely

July 14.
Fairfax
gains the
Hythe and
Lucas's
house, round the town.   On July 14 he gained the Hythe, the landing-place for boats arriving from the mouth of the Colne, and on the same day he seized on Lord Lucas's house.   On the 15th he stormed the gate-

July 15.
and wins the
gate-house. house of the old abbey.[2]   The importance of the possession of this post, which commanded the southern wall of the town,[3] was acknowledged by the desperate but futile efforts made from time to time by the

Attempts to
escape. besieged to cut their way out through the hostile lines,[4] and by the constant stream of deserters which began to slip away in spite of all that the Royalist commanders could do to keep them back.

On the 17th the besiegers were gratified with the news that

July 17.
News that
Pembroke
Castle is
taken. Pembroke Castle had at last been taken, and that, though they were themselves tied to the ground on which they stood, Cromwell was at liberty to betake himself to the North.[5]   By the beginning of August the grim spectre of famine had come to the aid of Fairfax.

---

[1] 'Chewed bullets' according to the language of the day.   One of these is 1 ow in the Museum in Colchester Castle.   On a second complaint, made later, the Royalist commanders answered 'that for rough cut things they must excuse them, as things stood with them at that time.'   *Mr. Round's MS.* p. 90.

[2] *Mr. Round's MS.*, p. 87, is quite clear on this point.   The *Diary* speaks of a battery being raised 'against St. John's from the Lord Lucas' House.'   The latter authority says nothing about the taking of the house, and I presume that battery was raised after the gate-house was taken on the 15th.   The house was in the grounds of St. John's Abbey, but the St. John's which was attacked must have been the church of that name.

[3] See p. 151.   [4] *Mr. Round's MS.* p. 88.   [5] The *Diary.*

Inside Colchester the bodies of dogs and horses, swarming as
they were with maggots, were greedily devoured, and after the
Famine in   second week in August even this loathsome food
Colchester.   began to fail. As usually happens in such cases, the
civilian population suffered far more than the soldiers of the
garrison. Starving men who, with arms in their hands find
themselves in the midst of an unarmed population, seldom fail
to provide first for their own necessities.[1] Whatever latent
Royalism there may have been in Colchester, and it is not
likely that there was very much,[2] was quenched amidst the
misery of the famine and the insolence of the soldiers, and by
the beginning of August the citizens could but look forward
with longing to the day of surrender.

Neither Norwich nor Fairfax would give these miserable
ones relief so long as Hamilton kept the field. On August 16
Aug. 16.   a crowd gathered round Norwich, bringing with
Norwich   them their children in the vain hope that the sight
urged to
surrender.   of the wan faces and wasted frames of the little ones
would melt his heart. Norwich would not abandon the King's

---

[1] *Mr. Round's MS.* p. 96. I do not mention the specific acts of
outrage recorded in *Colchester's Tears*, E. 455, 16, as that pamphlet was
published in London, and, though it professes to derive its information
from escaped townsmen, deserves no more credit than other catchpenny
productions of the day. The assertion made in it that Lucas was
interrupted by the Earl of Norwich in an attempt to ravish a woman
throws doubt on the accuracy of its other statements. If there had been
any truth in a story most improbable in itself, it would have been pleaded
by the Puritan soldiers in justification of Lucas's execution.

[2] The political sentiments of the population are probably fairly
indicated in a statement that 'The chief minister of this place, Mr.
Harman, that not long before stirred up the people against the army,
branding them with the names of heretics and schismatics, and the people
of the town who affronted and abused our soldiers when they quartered
there, now both ministers and people have longed for their deliverance
by the hands of those whom they so much despised before.' *A True
and Correct Relation of the Taking of Colchester*, E. 461, 24. The
inhabitants, in short, were for the most part Presbyterian and anti-
military, ready to get rid of the army if they could, but not enthusiastic for
the King. That there was a Royalist party amongst them is, of course,
not denied.

cause on account of private sorrows, and on his rejection of the petitioners, the Mayor wrote to Fairfax, begging him to allow civilians to pass his lines.   Fairfax replied that 'he pitied their condition, but it did not stand with his trust to permit it.'   On the 17th the Royalist commanders showed signs of exhaustion, proposing to Fairfax to surrender in twenty days if they were not relieved within that time.   Fairfax replied ' that he hoped, in much less time, to have the town without treaty,' and ordered preparations to be made for storming the walls, though his purpose was probably rather to intimidate the besieged than to cast away unnecessarily the lives of his soldiers.

Fairfax refuses to let civilians pass.

Aug. 17. Proposal to surrender.

Inside the walls, Norwich had hard work to stem the tide of mutiny.   It is even said that he angrily bade the women, who were crying for bread, 'to eat their children,' and that the women threatened in return to tear out his eyes, secure of the concealed sympathy of the soldiers, who were hardly less hungry than themselves.   On the 19th, Norwich, driven to extremities, sent to ask Fairfax for terms.   On the 20th Fairfax declared that, with the exception of deserters, all soldiers and officers under the degree of a captain would be allowed to depart unharmed.   Superior officers and gentlemen were to surrender at mercy.   The conditions were hard, and Norwich could not yet bring himself to submit to them.   On the 21st, pressed hard by a famished crowd of women and children, Norwich ordered the gates to be thrown open, and bade them go to the enemy with their complaints. Many did as he bade them and the remainder were thrust out by his orders.   When the poor creatures reached Fairfax's sentries they threw themselves on their knees imploring that mercy might be shown at least to their children.   It was not to be. The sentries were ordered to fire shots over the heads of the women to frighten them back, and when this proved of no avail, they told them that, if they did not return, they would be stripped of their clothing and driven back in their nakedness. Before this threat—it can hardly have been intended to be more—the poor gaunt creatures recoiled and found shelter for

A cry for bread.

Aug. 19. A demand for terms.

Aug. 20. Fairfax's terms.

Aug. 21. Women turned out.

the night in a mill outside the walls, known as the Middle Mill.[1] On the following morning they were readmitted within the gates.

One more attempt was made by the besieged to obtain better terms. Fairfax was, however, inexorable, and the news of Cromwell's victory at Preston gave him assurance that time was no longer of consequence. He at once took measures to spread the news within the town, with the result that the commanders of the besieged, learning that they had held their ground as long as their constancy could serve the King's interest, resolved on the night of the 25th to provide for their own safety by one more desperate effort to break through Fairfax's lines. The horsemen, who were for the most part gentlemen, were eager for the venture. The foot-soldiers, believing that the horse would outstrip them and leave them to the mercy of the enemy, not only hung back, but even threatened to kill their officers if they passed the gates. On the morning of the 26th they declared that, if resistance were further prolonged, they would deliver them up to Fairfax.[2] After this the commanders had but one course to pursue, and before the day was far spent, commissioners from both sides met to agree on the articles of capitulation.[3]

Aug. 22. News from Preston.

Aug. 25. An attempt to break out.

Aug. 26. The final negotiation.

Fairfax and his Council of War now insisted on harder terms. The privates and subaltern officers, instead of being allowed to return to their homes with all they possessed, were admitted simply to quarter for their lives. The lords and gentlemen, as well as the captains and other superior officers, were, as before, to submit to mercy.[4] To a question as to the meaning of submission to mercy, an answer was given 'that they

[1] The *Diary* gives the dates day by day. The contemporary pamphlets and newspapers are too numerous to quote. The account of the women turned out is from *The Kingdom's Weekly Intelligencer*, E. 461, 14. See also *Mr. Round's MS.* p. 92.

[2] *Clarke Trials*, fol. 23b.

[3] *Perf. Occurrences*, E. 526, 1; *A True and Perfect Relation*, E. 462, 16. [4] *Perf. Occurrences*, E. 526, 1.

be rendered or do render themselves to the Lord General or whom he may appoint without assurance of quarter, so as the An explanation. Lord General may be free to put some immediately to the sword if he see cause ; although his Excellency intends, chiefly and for the generality of those under that condition, to surrender them to the mercy of Parliament, and of the mercy of the Parliament and General there hath been large experience.' [1]

On the 27th the articles of capitulation thus explained were at last signed, and on the 28th the Parliamentary army marched into the town. In the meanwhile a Council of War Aug. 27. The capitulation signed. met to select the persons to be put to death. At first voices were raised for the execution of Norwich and Capel as the highest in rank. Fairfax, however, Aug. 28. Colchester occupied by Fairfax. urged that it would be more fitting to leave peers to 'be proceeded upon by the power of civil justice, and that the other persons, being more near to the condition of soldiers of fortune, and less eminent, should be set apart for Lucas, Lisle, and Gascoigne to be shot. the military execution.[2] Fairfax's suggestion found acceptance, and the fatal vote fell upon Lucas, together with Sir George Lisle and Sir Bernard Gascoigne, a Tuscan soldier, whose real name was Bernardo Guasconi.[3]

The sentence was passed at two in the afternoon, but time

[1] I have followed almost entirely the form printed in *The Lords' Journals*, x. 478. The last phrase as there printed is, however, manifestly corrupt, 'to surrender them to the mercy of the Parliament and General. There hath been large experience.' The phrase has been altered above in accordance with the version given by Ireton in evidence at Capel's trial, *Clarke Trials*, fol. 22. Ireton then expressly stated that to the best of his belief the form usually circulated was erroneous.

[2] *Clarke Trials*, fol. 33b. The words 'should be set apart' are conjecturally added to fill a hiatus in the report. The phrase 'soldiers of fortune' has sometimes been treated as if it conveyed a sneer. At that time it merely meant 'professional soldiers,' as opposed to lords and gentlemen who, like the three peers who fell at Newbury, served the King with the intention of returning to a civil life as soon as the King's authority was restored.

[3] For further information about him, see *Nozze Guasconi-Gardini*, Firenze, 1886.

was given to the condemned to confer with a minister, and to partake of the communion.   About seven in the evening [1] the

The con-
demned men
in the castle-
yard.

three prisoners were brought into the grassy castle-yard on the southern side of the vast keep, which had been reared by Norman hands, building as none but the sons of Rome had built before them.   Lucas and Gascoigne embraced one another mutually, protesting their innocence of any crime deserving death.   "Though I do not believe in predestination," chimed in Lisle, "yet I believe it is God's will, and truly I should have thought myself a happy person if I could live to have a longer time of repentance, and to see the King, my master, on his throne again, whom I beseech God to send to all the happiness that is due to so just, so good a man."   Then Lucas turned to Ireton, who had been appointed, together with Whalley and Rainsborough, to see the sentence carried out, asking by whom and on what grounds he had been condemned.   Ireton told him he had been condemned by Parliament, which had pronounced all who engaged a second time in war to be traitors and rebels.[2] The soldiers, he added, were but the instruments of Parliament to suppress its enemies and to execute its judgments. "I do plead before you," replied Lucas, "all the laws of this kingdom.   I have fought with a commission from those that were my sovereigns, and from that commission I must justify my action."

To this tragic issue had the question of sovereignty been brought.   A few more words were spoken, a few more prayers were said, and then Lucas took his stand in the ap-

The execu-
tion of Lucas
and Lisle.

pointed place on a stone, round which, according to the belief prevalent in Colchester, the grass refuses to grow.[3]   The soldiers fired, and Lisle, starting forward, caught in his arms the body of his slaughtered friend and kissed the dead man's face.[4]   Then he took his own station

---

[1] *Packets of Letters*, E. 461, 29.

[2] Declaration, June 20, *L.J.* x. 338.

[3] Possibly there are stones from the old walls buried at no great distance from the surface.

[4] An account of the death of Sir C. Lucas, *Clarke MSS.*

where Lucas had stood before him, and called to the firing-party to come nearer. " I'll warrant you, sir," said one of the men, " we'll hit you." Memories of the battle-field crowded on the mind of the soldier in his last moments. " Friends," he smilingly replied, " I have been nearer you when you have missed me." The fatal shots were fired, and Lisle spoke no

Gascoigne
reprieved. word again. Gascoigne, who had already taken off his doublet to die with his comrades, was told that he was reprieved. His foreign extraction, combined it is said with the devoutness of his preparation for death,[1] had saved him.

No wonder the Royalists looked on the execution of Lucas and Lisle as an act of brutal ruffianism. Both of them, it

Indignation
of the
Royalists. was alleged, had fought like soldiers, and had done nothing whilst they were in command to make them unworthy of the treatment usually accorded by soldiers to a brave and high-spirited foe. What was more, they had fought in defence of the legal authority of the King against a rebellious and usurping Parliament.

On the Parliamentary side it was pointed out that a garrison refusing to surrender an untenable position had, by the

The Parlia-
mentary
view. laws of war, forfeited its right to quarter.[2] Yet the main stress was laid on the difference between the second and first wars. In the first, whatever lawyers might say, soldiers had agreed to treat the struggle as one carried on for honourable ends on either side, in which those who fell into the enemies' hands were entitled to the treatment accorded to prisoners taken in a war between hostile nations. There was no such feeling in Fairfax's ranks in regard to the second war. " The ground of it all," a Royalist had written nearly three months before the surrender of Colchester, " is that the kingdom is weary of the war, and it is generally believed that the King desires peace more than the Parliament."[3] The exasperation amongst the soldiers was caused

---

[1] *Clarendon,* xi. 107 ; Newsletter, Sept. $\frac{1}{11}$, *Roman Transcripts, R.O.*

[2] Rare instances in which Royalists had acted on this principle were quoted, and Lucas was himself charged with having threatened to do so at Stinchcombe in revenge for the refusal of quarter to Royalists at Canon Froome. See *Clarke Papers,* ii. 38.

[3] Letter of Intelligence, June 1, *Clarendon MSS.* 2,796.

by the belief that Charles and the Royalists were unfairly using this desire for peace to throw the kingdom into confusion, and ultimately to reintroduce the old condemned system of government in Church and State. Nor were other circumstances wanting to strengthen the feeling of anger in their breasts. The long fruitless negotiations in which Charles had baffled their sincerest efforts, and more especially the duplicity with which he had brought the Scots into England when he was making overtures to Parliament, drove them to regard the cause for which Lucas and Lisle had fought as one for which no honourable man should draw his sword.

Though such arguments may serve to explain the motives of Fairfax and the Council of War, they do not serve to justify their deed. It was done, as Fairfax explained, 'for some satisfaction to military justice, and in part of avenge for the innocent blood they have caused to be spilt, and the trouble, damage, and mischief they have brought upon the town.'[1] If the minds of the members of

The deed not to be justified.

---

[1] Fairfax to Lenthall, Aug. 29, *Rushw.* vii. 1,243. It will be seen that no question was raised of the condemned men having violated their parole. They were shot as traitors to the established authority of Parliament. Yet as the question has been often raised it may be well to consider it. Mr. Firth in a note to his edition of *The Life of William Cavendish, Duke of Newcastle,* App. 366, points out that the sole evidence for the belief that Lucas had given his parole to Fairfax after his capture in 1646 is the correspondence exchanged between them on June 19, 1648, in which Fairfax charges Lucas with forfeiting his parole, and Lucas replies that after making his composition he had informed Fairfax that he had punctually performed his engagement, 'as they stood in relation to his Lordship,' and that Fairfax had been satisfied. Lucas then proceeds as follows : "But, my Lord, beside my inclinations and duty to the service I am in at present, be pleased to examine whether the law of nature hath not instigated me to take my sword again into my hand, for when I was in a peaceable manner in London, there was a price set upon me by the Committee of Derby House, upon which I was constrained to retire myself into my own country, and to my native town for refuge."

Mr. Firth shows that Lucas by no means cleared himself of the obligation of the parole. "The Committee of Goldsmiths' Hall," he writes, "to which this composition was paid, exacted from delinquents the taking of the Covenant and an oath not to assist the King against the Parliament, 'nor any forces raised without the consent of the two Houses of Parliament

the Council of War had been less clouded by anger, they would surely have perceived that it was for a civil rather than for a military tribunal to unravel the question of the guilt of the prisoners. It was thus that Cromwell had dealt with Poyer and his companions at Pembroke, and it is hardly possible to doubt that if Cromwell, and not Ireton, had been the guiding spirit in the council which sat in judgment before Colchester, Lucas and Lisle, like Norwich and Capel, would have been reserved for the sentence of Parliament.[1]

Before the evening closed, Fairfax sent Ireton, Whalley, and Ewer to Norwich and Capel, to assure them that they and the other superior officers would have quarter for their lives. Capel's short answer was that they would have given better thanks if their own lives had been taken and Lucas's and Lisle's spared.[2] Further than quarter for life, Fairfax's assurances did not go. The officers were relegated to various prisons to await the judgment of Parliament. The gentlemen who had served as soldiers

Norwich and Capel assured of quarter for their lives.

---

in time of war.' . . . The action of Sir Charles in taking up arms again in 1648 was a distinct breach of this engagement." This appears to be indisputable. Nor can the other point raised by Lucas about the price set on his head be pleaded in his favour. Mr. Firth indeed does not give an opinion on it, but I can see no reason to doubt that what Lucas refers to is some action taken by the Committee of Derby House in putting in force an Ordinance of May 23, 1648, enjoining all who had served on the King's side in the former war, with certain specified exceptions, to leave London. If the Committee believed Lucas to be hiding, it might very well have offered a reward for his apprehension, and, by his own showing, all that happened to him was that he had to retire to his own house in Essex. It was monstrous to assert that a mere police measure of this kind justified him in breaking his oath.

[1] "Indeed," said Hamilton at his trial, speaking of Cromwell, "he was so very courteous and so very civil as he performed more than he promised, and I must acknowledge his favour to those poor wounded gentlemen that I left behind, that were by him taken care of, and truly he performed more than he did capitulate for." *Clarke Trials*, fol. 116b.

[2] *Idem*, fol. 24b, 32 ; *Carter*, 201, 202 ; *Clarke Trials*, fol. 32. It was disputed at the trials of Norwich and Capel whether this promise exempted them from proceedings in a civil court, but there can be no doubt that it covered as much as is given above.

were delivered over to Fairfax's officers, who picked them out in turn, that they might hold them to ransom.[1] To the subalterns and private soldiers was assigned a heavier lot. They were first shut up in one or other of the churches in the town, where they were pillaged by the soldiers, and for the most part stripped to their shirts. After a few days they were marched off to Bristol and other western ports, where such of them as reached their destination alive were shipped off, either, according to the example set in the case of the Scottish prisoners taken in Lancashire, to serve as unwilling labourers in the burning heat of the West Indies, or to enforced military service in the employment of the Venetian Republic.[2]

Harsh as was this treatment of the captives, the treatment of the townsmen was even more unjustifiable. If Colchester Treatment had erred in admitting the Royalists into the town, of the town. its inhabitants had had cause enough to regret their error. Yet Fairfax had promised his soldiers 14,000*l.* in lieu of the plunder to which they claimed a right, apparently on the ground that they might have stormed the place if they had

---

[1] "For the officers," writes Carter, "he," *i.e.* Fairfax, "distributed to every regiment a certain number of gentlemen that were prisoners, as slaves to the gallies or to ransom themselves. The officers whereof came to the pound, as the manner of graziers is by their cattle, and called them first out of that into another, and then drove them away for the market, to make the most of them ; so most of them afterwards, as they were able, and according to the civility of those they were distributed to, bought their liberties and returned home." *Carter*, p. 203.

[2] *Ibid.* ; Fairfax to Moore, Sept. 6, 1649, *Hist. MSS. Com. Rep.* x. part iv. 93. The whole arrangement is clearly stated in *The Moderate Intelligencer* (E. 462, 18): "The prisoners taken in this town are disposed after this manner : the Lords, with two men apiece attending them, and twelve other officers, are to march with the General s regiment to-morrow, . . . the other officers are to be sent, some to the Mount, some to Pendennis, some to Cardiff, Oxford, Arundel, and divers other strengths, but none beyond Trent ; the common soldiers, prisoners, return not to London to their masters to be ready for a new business, but will be conveyed West, in relation to Bristol and other sea-towns, that so they may pass to America, Venice, or as shall be appointed ; the gentlemen, not soldiers, are committed to the care of troopers and others until further order be taken.

been allowed to do so. Colchester was, however, impoverished
by the siege, and upon its pleading the impossibility of raising
so large a sum, Fairfax remitted 2,000*l.*, offering at the same
time to distribute amongst the poor another 2,000*l.* out of the
money raised. He then wrote to ask the House of Commons
to give him 4,000*l.* to make up the deficiency, and the House,
to ensure that there should be nothing lacking, voted him 5,000*l.*
to be paid out of the estates of delinquents in Colchester, or, in
case these proved insufficient, out of the estates of delinquents
in other parts of Essex.[1]

The truth is that a savage spirit of exasperation filled the
soldiers against those whom they regarded not as legitimate
enemies, but as unprincipled breakers of the peace.

Exaspera-
tion in the
army.

Even Cromwell shared, though in a very modified
degree, in this feeling. To him the victories gained

Cromwell
holds victory
a sign of
Divine
favour.

were not simply the result of the superiority of a
small but disciplined army over forces scattered
and untrained, they were the visible tokens of the
presence of God vindicating the cause of His chosen ones by
the destruction of His enemies, and condemning the hesitations of Parliament. Even Vane himself, it seems, had not
sufficiently appreciated this appeal to the God of Battles. Not
many days after the victory of Preston Cromwell sent him a
message that he was as little satisfied with his ' passive and
suffering principles' as Vane was with his own active ones.[2]
" Remember my love," wrote Cromwell to St. John, a few days
later, " to my dear brother H. Vane ; I pray he make not too
little nor I too much of outward dispensations."[3]

---

[1] Morant, *Hist. of Essex*, i. 73. There was raised

		£
From the Dutch Congregation		5,980
From the Head and North Wards		3,928
		9,908

leaving 2,092*l.* to be raised from the other two wards, 2,000*l.* being return-
able to the poor. Of the money thus got, only 2,000*l.* was paid to the
Essex and Suffolk Trained Bands, leaving the whole of the rest for distribution amongst Fairfax's own soldiers.

[2] *The Proceeds of the Protector*, p. 5, written by Vane in 1656.

[3] Cromwell to St. John, Sept. 1, *Carlyle*, Letter lxvii.

Cromwell had on his side an idealist as pure as Vane, and less apt to distrust the power of force to solve moral and social problems. "Fairfax!"[1] wrote Milton:—

Milton's
sonnet to
Fairfax.

" —whose name in arms through Europe rings,
 Filling each mouth with envy or with praise,
 And all her jealous monarchs with amaze,
 And rumours loud that daunt remotest kings,
Thy firm unshaken virtue ever brings
 Victory home, though new rebellions raise
 Their hydra-heads, and the false North displays
 Her broken league to imp their serpent wings.
O yet a nobler task awaits thy hand :
 (For what can war but endless war still breed ?)
 Till truth and right from violence be freed,
And public faith cleared from the shameful brand
 Of public fraud. In vain doth valour bleed,
 While avarice and rapine share the land."

Between the violence and rapine of the Cavalier and the fraud and avarice of the Presbyterian member of Parliament, Fairfax was to advance the standard of truth and right. To Vane, compelled to seek for truth and right by Parliamentary methods, the achievement seemed less easy of attainment. On August 14 Holles, following the example of others of the excluded members, took his seat once more at Westminster. Even the victories in Lancashire and Essex produced in the Houses no such exultant mood as to lead them to break with the King. During the late troubles, Skippon had earned an evil name amongst the Presbyterians of the City by the resolution with which he anticipated all attempts to give armed help to the Royalists. Yet, when Cromwell's triumphant

Vane's Parliamentary position.

*Aug. 14.
Holles takes his seat.*

*Aug. 23.
Skippon pleads for peace.*

---

[1] The title in Milton's own hand is "On the Lord Gen. Fairfax at the Siege of Colchester." This looks as if the sonnet was written before the town was actually taken, though virtually certain to surrender, and therefore in August rather than September, to which latter month it is usually ascribed. In this case the words 'ever brings victory home' must mean 'is accustomed to do it, and therefore is certain to do so now.' See Masson's *Life of Milton*, iii. 688

despatch from Warrington was read in the House of Commons, it was Skippon who warned the members not to be so elated

Aug. 24.
Repeal of
the Vote of
No Ad-
dresses. with success as to neglect the way of peace.[1] On the following day the repeal of the Vote of No Addresses passed both Houses, and the preparations for the proposed treaty with the King were thus enabled to proceed without further hindrance.[2]

Before long, too, what embers of war were still alight in southern England were trodden down. On August 25 Deal

Aug. 25.
Surrender of
Deal Castle. Castle surrendered, and Sandown Castle was the only one of the three fortresses in the Downs remaining

Aug. 26.
The Prince
proposes to
go to
Holland. in the hands of the Royalists. On the following day the Prince, finding himself short of provisions, and having no immediate chance of support on land, determined to return to Holland to revictual. As soon as

Mutiny of
the crews,
who insist
on sailing up
the Thames. his resolution was known the crews broke into mutiny, insisting upon sailing up the Thames, where they hoped to defeat the Parliamentary fleet under Warwick if they did not at once prevail on his crews to desert him. What they wanted was to be the English sailors of an English King, not to threaten England from a basis of operations in a foreign country. They would rather, they said, live on half rations than go back to Holland without striking a blow. The opportunity now offered might never recur. Eight of Warwick's ships were still on their way from Portsmouth to join him, and would easily be cut off by a Royalist fleet holding the mouth of the Thames.[3] In the absence of this detached portion of the Parliamentary navy the two fleets were about equal in fighting powers, but it was understood that the Parliamentary crews had no heart in the cause for which they were asked to fight.[4]

The behests of the sailors were promptly obeyed, and on

---

[1] ——? to Joachimi, *Add. MSS.* 17,677, T, fol. 191b. The letter is dated Sept. 1, *i.e.* $\frac{Aug. 22}{Sept. 1}$, but this is an evident mistake, the date being probably transferred by the copyist from that of the preceding letter.

[2] *L.J.* x. 454.

[3] ——? to Joachimi, Aug. $\frac{21}{31}$, $\frac{Aug. 22}{Sept. 1}$, *Add. MSS.* 17,677, T, fols. 182. 186.

[4] *The Copy of a Letter*, E. 464, 23.

the 29th the Prince, sailing up the estuary of the Thames,

Aug. 29.
The Prince
catches sight
of Warwick.

caught sight of the enemy.   On the 30th, when both fleets were off the Medway preparing for action, they were separated by a sudden storm from the north-

Aug. 30.
A storm
separates
the fleets.

west, which made it impossible for the Prince to attack.   The next day the gale still blew, whilst on board the Royalist fleet there remained but one butt

Aug. 31.

of beer and not a single drop of water.   There was

Sept. 3.
The Prince's
fleet in
Holland.

no choice now but to make with all speed for a Dutch port.   By September 3 the whole of the Prince's fleet was anchored in neutral waters off

Sept. 2.
Warwick in
the Downs.

Goree.   On September 2 Warwick, having effected his junction with the Portsmouth squadron, anchored in the Downs [1] and on the 5th Sandown Castle surrendered to its besiegers.[2]   Parliament was now master of every foot of

Sept. 5.
Surrender of
Sandown.

ground in southern and central England.   An insurrection conducted not only without unity of military direction, but without concurrence amongst its leaders in the political objects at which they aimed, could hardly, in the presence of a compact and disciplined army, have ended otherwise than in complete disaster.

[1] *A True Relation by Sir W. Batten,* E. 458, 8 ; Warwick to the Com. of D. H. Aug. 31, *L.J.* x. 483 ; Dr. Steward's Relation, Sept. $\frac{7}{17}$, *Clarendon MSS.* 2,878 ; A Relation of the Fleet, *Clar. St. P.* ii. 414.

[2] *Perf. Occurrences,* E. 526, 5.

CHAPTER LXVI.

THE TREATY OF NEWPORT.

THE events of the last few weeks had led, outwardly, at least, to a marked change in the relations between the Houses and the City. On August 31 the Common Council forwarded to Parliament a paper which, though it contained the usual demands for a Presbyterian settlement, a treaty with the King, and the disbandment of the army, also contained a denunciation of the late war, and an invitation to come to an understanding with the army.[1] No doubt the change of language is in the main to be ascribed to the successes of Cromwell and Fairfax, but, in part at least, it may also be traced to annoyance at the seizure of London ships and interference with London trade.[2]

The wave of dissatisfaction with those who had stirred up unsuccessful war, which made even the citizens of London desire to come to terms with the army, made the stauncher Independents in the House of Commons anxious to hinder any futile endeavour to come to terms with the King. As the mouthpiece of these Ludlow travelled to Colchester—either when the town was on the point of surrendering, or not long after it had surrendered—in order to urge Fairfax to bring his army to Westminster, and to put an end by force to the proposed negotiation. As might have been

Marginal notes:
1648.
Aug. 31.
Change of tone in the City.

Opposition to the proposed negotiation with the King.

Ludlow urges Fairfax to hinder it.

---

[1] *L.J.* x. 478.

[2] Grignon to Brienne, $\frac{\text{Aug. 31}}{\text{Sept. 10}}$, *R.O. Transcripts.*

expected, he received from Fairfax the vaguest possible answer.
Ireton, to whom he next applied, was more definite. Though

Ireton advises a postponement of action. he agreed with Ludlow in thinking that military interference would ultimately be necessary, he considered it advisable to postpone action till the negotiations had been so far developed as to divulge the objects of both parties, and thereby to render unpopular both the King and those who had confidence in his word.[1]

An argument against immediate military intervention was no argument against petitioning the House of Commons in

Sept. 11. The petition of the London Levellers. opposition to the course which it seemed bent on adopting ; and accordingly, on September 11, a petition, to a great extent at least the work of Lilburne,[2] was laid before the House by the London Levellers. It maintained the doctrine that the House of Commons was the supreme authority in the realm, and called for the abolition of the negative voices of the King and the House of Lords, and generally for reforms of the nature of those demanded in the *Agreement of the People*. In the end the petitioners asked the House to consider 'whether the justice of God be likely to be satisfied, or His yet continuing wrath appeased by an act of oblivion.'[3]

---

[1] Ludlow's *Memoirs*, i. 203. He says that he went 'to the army which lay at that time before Colchester.' It is inconceivable that he expected Fairfax to come to London before Colchester was taken, and I see no reason to doubt that he really went either whilst the army was before Colchester just after the surrender, or during the last two or three days of the siege when it was quite certain that Colchester would surrender. Ludlow can never be trusted about dates, but I do not think he would have written that he went to Colchester if his visit had been at a later time when the army was at some other place. If he did go to Colchester his visit cannot have been later than about Sept. 6, as it was known in London on the 8th that Ireton was no longer there. *Perf. Occurrences*, E. 526, 5.

[2] Lilburne says that he 'was compelled by conscience to have a hand in' it. *Legal Fundamental Liberties*, p. 29, E. 560, 14. It has also been ascribed to Marten, *Merc. Pragm.* E. 464, 12. Marten, however, was not at this time in London.

[3] *Parl. Hist.* iii. 1,005.

On the deliberations of either House this petition of the London Levellers had no influence whatever. The prepara-

Sept. 18.
Opening
of the Treaty
of Newport. tions for treating with the King were rapidly pushed forward, and on September 18 the negotiation itself was opened at Newport, it being understood that it was to last forty days and no longer. Charles, liberated on parole from his confinement at Carisbrooke, was allowed to occupy the house of William Hopkins in the little town, whilst the actual meetings between himself and the commissioners were held in the Town Hall.

The fifteen commissioners chosen by Parliament to con-duct the negotiations had been selected from both parties ; the

The Par-
liamentary
commis-
sioners. most conspicuous amongst them being Northumber-land, Holles, Say, and Vane. They were instructed to present each of the old Hampton Court propo-

The recall
of declara-
tions sitions [1] in order ; the first containing a demand that Charles should withdraw all his declarations against Parliament. To the body of this proposition Charles made no objection, but he not unreasonably shrank from accepting a statement in the preamble to the effect that 'both Houses of Parliament' had 'been necessitated to undertake a war in their

Sept. 25.
accepted by
the King. just and lawful defence.' On the 25th, however, he withdrew his opposition, stipulating that nothing to which he agreed should have any validity unless a com-

Charles
stipulates
that no con-
cession shall
be valid
without a
complete
agreement. plete understanding were arrived at on every point, and thus convincing himself that whatever con-cessions he might make would be merely nominal. As Charles had himself no expectation that an under-standing would ever be reached, he was thus enabled to promise whatever he found convenient, without regarding himself as in any way bound by his words.[2]

On the 26th there was a warm discussion in the House of Commons on the admission of this stipulation. As might have been expected, the Independents protested against it

---

[1] See vol. iii. 355.

[2] Walker's *Perfect Copies of all the Votes . . . in the Treaty held at Newport*, bound with his Hist. Discourses, 1–25 ; The King to the Prince of Wales, Nov. 6, *Clar. St. P.* ii. 425–31.

as having a merely dilatory object. It happened, however,

that the debate fell on a day fixed for a call of

Sept. 26.
Debate in
the House of
Commons on
the King's
stipulation.

the House, when the Presbyterians trooped up in large numbers to avoid the fine imposed on absentees. Consequently their opponents did not even venture to divide against them ; and an attempt

Sept. 28.
It is
accepted.

made by the Independents to reopen the question in a thinner House on the 28th was promptly suppressed.[1]

In the army, Charles's delay in accepting the first article caused the greatest irritation. The regiments at Newcastle

Sept. 21.
Feeling
of the regi-
ments in the
North.

and before Berwick were the first to appeal to Fairfax in support of the petition of the London Levellers,[2] and their opinions were certain to find an echo in the ranks of Fairfax's army, the head-quarters

Ireton urges
the purging
of the
House,

of which were on September 21 removed to St. Albans. It was still more significant that Ireton

Sept. 27,
and offers to
resign his
commission.

abandoned the expectant attitude which he had maintained in his conversation with Ludlow at Colchester, and urged Fairfax to put an end to the treaty by purging the House. On the 27th he wrote to Fairfax a long letter, in which he set forth his views, and

His probable
motives.

in the end offered to resign his commission.[3] It is probable that the explanation of his change of view is to be found in the events passing at Newport

---

[1] *Merc. Pragmaticus*, E. 465, 19.   [2] *The Moderate*, E. 467, 1.

[3] This letter has not been preserved, but Mr. Firth tells me of a note written on a newsletter of Sept. 26 in the *Clarke MSS.* " Comm. Gen. Ireton wrote a long letter to Ld. Fairfax with reasons for laying down his commission, and desiring a discharge from the army, which was not agreed unto v[id]e l[ette]rs dated 27 Sept." In *Merc. Pragmaticus* of Oct. 3 (E. 469, 19), there is a statement (Sign. Nn. 2) that there was a talk of petitioning Fairfax for ' a new purge . . . and truly in Com. Ireton's opinion it is high time.' On the last page, indeed, a contrary disposition is attributed to Ireton, but this is evidently a mere rumour brought in when the newspaper was going to press, as it is contradicted in the following number, in which, under the date of October 7, it is said that certain ' devilish letters ' stirring up the army to resistance ' had their frame from Ireton, and countenance from his father Cromwell.'

and Westminster. Charles's long delay in sanctioning the withdrawal of hostile declarations must have struck Ireton as affording ground for an appeal to the people against a King whose heart was not set upon peace ; whilst the vote of the Commons on the 26th, by which they accepted Charles's merely dilatory stipulation, was sufficient evidence that the Presbyterians were not to be trusted with the conduct of a negotiation in which they allowed themselves to be so easily befooled. As neither Ireton's views were adopted, nor his resignation accepted, it is to be presumed that Fairfax found sufficient support amongst the officers to resist Ireton's urgency, but was nevertheless induced to agree to some compromise,[1] the exact nature of which cannot now be ascertained. What-

Ireton retires to Windsor.

ever may have been the reason of Ireton's withdrawing his resignation, he retired to Windsor for a time, either to dissociate himself from Fairfax's action, or simply to watch events till the interference for which he had been pleading should become inevitable.

Sept. 25. The question of Church government.

Aug. 29. The Presbyterian system established by Ordinance.

In the meanwhile the crucial question of Church government had been reached at Newport. On August 29, nearly three weeks before the opening of the negotiations, Parliament had taken care to pass a comprehensive Ordinance, establishing a complete Presbyterian system without the slightest stain of toleration,[2] and the King was, therefore, met with at least

---

[1] Fairfax, it was alleged, was ready to stand to the agreement to be made between the King and both Houses, 'the consideration whereof is said now to be the true cause why Ireton left the head-quarters and retired to Windsor.' *Merc. Pragmaticus*, E. 466, 11. "Can it be," writes Mr. Firth to me, "that Fairfax proposed standing by the treaty, that Ireton then proposed to resign—that Fairfax then promised, in order to induce Ireton to withdraw his resignation, to demand certain specified securities from the King—that Ireton accordingly withdrew it, and retired to Windsor to watch the progress of the negotiation, returning to head-quarters after it had failed?" Mr. Firth also suggests that Ireton may have obtained the consent of the extreme party to delay by representing to them that Fairfax would ultimately join them, and that his resignation was caused by the discovery that Fairfax insisted on defending the treaty made by the Houses with the King whatever it might be.

[2] *L.J.* x. 461.

the semblance of an accomplished fact. In the first days of
the treaty two of the Presbyterian Commissioners, Holles and

*The Pres-
byterians
urge Charles
not to
waste time.* Grimston, being fully alive to the danger of military
intervention, threw themselves on their knees before
Charles, entreating him to yield at once all that
was possible without wasting time in useless dis-

*Vane
pleads for
toleration.* cussions. Vane, on the other had, did his best to
persuade Charles, through his Episcopalian supporters, to accept the scheme of toleration set forth in *The
Heads of the Proposals.*[1] Charles gave no heed to the pleadings
of either party. The old thought of wearing out his adversaries
by engaging them in mutual strife was ever present to his mind.
Some, indeed, of his advisers recommended him to grant all
that was asked, and when he was again on the throne to break
his promise, as having been made under duress ; but Charles,
though he had sometimes played with this idea, preferred a less
direct method of gaining his ends.[2]

Accordingly, on the 25th, Charles had to listen to a proposal from the commissioners that he should assent to a whole

*Sept. 25.
Charles
asked to
establish
Presby-
terianism.* string of acts, not only abolishing Episcopacy and
the Prayer Book, and establishing the Presbyterian
system and the Directory in their place, but also enjoining the taking of the Covenant on all persons
in the realm, including himself.[3]

To this exorbitant demand Charles replied on the 28th by
proposing his old expedient of a three years' Presbyterianism

*Sept. 28.
The King's
reply.* with toleration, not only for himself 'and those of
his own judgment,' but also for 'any others who'
could not 'in conscience submit themselves thereto.'
To this he added a scheme for satisfying the purchasers of

---

[1] Burnet's *Hist. of his Own Time*, i. 44. So much as appears in the
text may, I think, fairly be accepted, but when Burnet adds that Vane
made this proposal merely to spin out the time till Cromwell could return
with his army, he appears to be attributing motives of the existence of
which he had no means of knowing.

[2] A long letter of a Royalist in Newport (E. 464, 29), in which this
assertion is made, looks very like a forgery. See, however, Grignon to
Brienne, $\frac{\text{Sept. 28}}{\text{Oct. 8}}$, *R.O. Transcripts.*   [3] *Walker*, 26.

bishops' lands by granting them leases for ninety-nine years at
low rents, thus avoiding the absolute alienation of Church
property. As for the Covenant, he would neither swear it
himself nor enjoin it on others. Then, taking up the second
main point at issue, he declared himself ready to abandon the
militia to Parliament, not, indeed, as he was asked to do, for
twenty years, but for ten. He was, moreover, ready to allow
the Houses to do as they pleased with Ireland, to appoint the
chief officers under the Crown for ten years, and also to
allow the City, for the like space of time, to control its own
militia, and to have the custody of the Tower. He then expressed a hope that, as he had conceded so much, he would
be allowed to come to Westminster in 'a condition of absolute freedom and safety.' He also asked for the restitution
of his revenue, and for an act of oblivion to apply to both
parties.[1]

On the allegation of the commissioners that they were
precluded by their instructions from accepting any reply which
was not a direct answer to the propositions, Charles,
on the 29th, sent this proposal to the Houses by an
independent channel.[2] Whilst awaiting a reply, he
engaged in a controversy with the commissioners and
the Presbyterian divines by whom they were accompanied.[3] With a keen eye for the weak points of an opponent,
Charles was at his best in discussions of this nature. "The
King," said Salisbury to one of the secretaries, "is wonderfully
improved." "No, my Lord," was the prompt answer, "he was
always so, but your Lordship too late discerned it."[4]

Polemical skill is, however, little apt to conciliate opponents.
That Charles's proposal in itself was far more rational than the
one to which the Houses expected him to subscribe
will hardly be denied at the present day. The real
question was whether the three years of grace which
he engaged to allow to the Presbyterian government were to be
utilised by him for the purpose of bringing about a rational

Sept. 29.
It is sent to
the Houses.

Charles as
a contro-
versialist.

The real
question
at issue.

---

[1] *Walker*, 29.
[2] *Idem*, 34.
[3] *Idem*, 35–48.
[4] Warwick's *Memoirs*, 324.

compromise after full and free discussion, or for the purpose of recovering sufficient power to enable him to overthrow Puritanism altogether when the fourth year arrived. Nothing can indicate more plainly the prevailing distrust of Charles than the fact that on October 2 the House rejected his proposal without a dissentient voice.[1] "The army and well-affected abroad," said Sir John Evelyn, "would think very strangely that the King should be at liberty, and no further security given for their liberties than his bare word, and, therefore, I humbly conceive that if the King's offers were so large as we desire, yet in no case ought we to yield that he should come hither till they were passed into acts."[2] Evelyn was an Independent, but even the Presbyterians did not vote against him.

Sir J. Evelyn's speech.

Charles had therefore to throw himself on the defensive, arguing with no slight skill of fence against the Parliamentary proposition as it stood. On October 6, being hard pressed about the Covenant, he replied that it was so interwoven with Scottish interests 'that if they were taken out it would be as thin as my Lord Say's country cheeses.'[3] That he was in earnest in his championship of Episcopacy is undeniable. The tears which dropped from his eyes when he believed himself to be unobserved are an evidence of the sharpness of the internal struggle.[4] The arguments of the Presbyterian ministers who accompanied the commissioners made absolutely no impression upon him, and he was as proof, as one of his successors afterwards showed himself to be, against the

Charles on the defensive.

Oct. 6.

His championship of Episcopacy.

---

[1] *C.J.* vi. 41. [2] *Merc. Pragmaticus*, E. 466, 11.

[3] "The cheeses alluded to," says Mr. Bruce, who gives this account from a MS. in the possession of the Earl of Verulam (*Archæologia*, xxxix. 113) "were those of Banbury. . . . Bardolph terms Slender 'You Banbury cheese' (*Merry Wives of Windsor*, Act i. sc. 1) in allusion to the same characteristic attributed by the King, in a certain possible case, to the Covenant." Mr. Bruce dates Charles's remark on the 5th, but the conversation which gave rise to it appears to have taken place on the 6th. See Oudart's diary in Peck's *Desiderata Curiosa*, 390.

[4] Warwick's *Memoirs*, 326.

political argument that he was not bound in his legislative power by his coronation oath.[1]

Once more, finding his position intolerable, Charles planned an escape from the island, this time with the assistance of his

Oct. 7.
Charles plans an escape,

host, Hopkins.[2] It is true that he had given his parole to remain at Newport, but his mind was fertile in explanations, and not later than October 7 he had

and determines to spin out the negotiation.

determined that in this matter he was not bound by his plighted word.[3] All that remained was to spin out the negotiation as long as possible. Accordingly

Oct. 9.
His answer about Episcopacy,

he informed the commissioners on the 9th that he was ready to give way in some degree. The Episcopacy, he explained, on the maintenance of which he insisted after the three years of Presbyterianism came to an end, was the primitive Episcopacy of which so much had been heard in 1641. Bishops were 'to have counsel and assistance

and about the mi itia and Ireland.

of Presbyters in ordination and jurisdiction, and in the last were and are limitable by the civil power.' On the same day Charles promised to concede the militia for twenty years, and to settle Ireland in such a way as Parliament might decide.[4]

It is unnecessary to consider whether these concessions, if honestly granted, ought to have proved acceptable. " I pray

Charles explains his condition.

you," wrote Charles in the evening to Hopkins, "rightly to understand my condition, which, I confess, yesternight I did not fully enough explain, through want of time. It is this : notwithstanding my too great concessions already made, I know that, unless I shall make yet others which will directly make me no King, I shall be at best but a perpetual prisoner. Besides—if this were not, of which I am too sure—the adhering to the Church—from which I cannot depart, no, not in show—will do the same : and, to deal freely with you, the great concession I made this

[1] The King to the Prince of Wales, Nov. 6, *Clar. St. P.* ii. 435.

[2] Hillier, *Narrative of the attempted Escapes of Charles I.* 270.

[3] The King to Hopkins, Oct. 7, Wagstaffe's *Vindication* (ed. 1711), 160.

[4] *Walker*, 49–54.

day—the Church, militia, and Ireland—was made merely in order to my escape, of which if I had not hope, I would not have done ; for then I could have returned to my strait prison without reluctancy ; but now, I confess, it would break my heart, having done that which only an escape can justify. To be short, if I stay for a demonstration of their further wickedness, it will be too late to seek a remedy ; for my only hope is that now they believe I dare deny them nothing, and so be less careful of their guards." [1]

Having thus eased his conscience, Charles lightly accepted one proposition after another till, on October 13, he reached the one on delinquents, in which he was asked to except from pardon thirty-seven of his chief supporters and all recusants who had taken arms on his behalf, as well as to subject an immense number of his undistinguished followers to lesser penalties on a graduated scale. [2] Even the prospect of being able to nullify all his concessions in the end was insufficient to induce Charles to assent to this demand, and, on the 17th, he rejected it, though he offered to except from pardon all who had taken part in the Irish rebellion, and to exclude from office, or even to banish for a time, all persons named to him by the Houses. He further expressed his readiness to require all the so-called delinquents to pay a moderate composition, and to exclude them from Parliament for a term of three years. [3]

Propositions lightly accepted.

Oct. 13. The proposition on delinquents

Oct. 17. rejected by the King.

In the meanwhile the Presbyterian majority in both Houses had concurred in the rejection of the King's last proposal on Episcopacy. [4] So hopeless did the chance of an agreement appear that on the 17th the Independents carried a motion for adjourning the House of Commons to the 23rd. On the 27th the forty days to which the negotiation was limited would have elapsed, and thus only a few days would be left after the reassembling

Oct. 11–17. Votes in Parliament.

---

[1] The King to Hopkins, Oct. 9, Wagstaffe's *Vindication* (ed. 1711), 160. For the King's Parole, see instructions to Hammond, Aug. 24 ; and Hammond's letter to Manchester, Aug. 28, *L.J.* x. 454, 474.

[2] *Walker*, 57.   [3] *Idem.* 61.   [4] *C.J.* vi. 49.

of the House for the discussion of any new proposals.

Oct. 21.
Charles
offers to
grant
limited
Episcopacy.
This motion, however, was afterwards rescinded at the instance of the Lords,[1] and on October 21 the King gave in what he declared to be his final answer on the subject of the Church, in which he proposed that at the expiration of three years of Presbyterianism ordination should be conferred by bishops, but only with the 'counsel and assistance of Presbyters,' and episcopal jurisdiction exercised in such a way as Parliament might approve.[2]

Oct. 24.
Efforts of
the Lords
to prevent
a breach.

Oct. 26.
An expe-
dient pro-
posal.

Oct. 27.
The King's
offer
rejected.
The Lords, eager as ever to avert a breach, voted on the 24th that no more than seven persons should be excepted from pardon. On the 26th they agreed to 'an expedient,' which would at least have allayed all anxiety as to the use of the King's negative voice. Presbyterianism was to remain in force at the end of the appointed three years until some other arrangement was made, legal presumption being thus given to the Presbyterian and not to the Episcopal system.[3] The Commons on the other hand preferred to meet the King's offer with a direct negative, and on the 27th they rejected the whole of his proposal.[4]

Significance
of this vote.
The treaty was indeed continued for some weeks longer, as the Houses from time to time prolonged it far beyond the forty days to which it was originally limited. The vote of October 27 was nevertheless its death-blow. The King had yielded all that he could reasonably be expected to yield, and the Presbyterian majority, which had pressed so earnestly for a treaty, had only succeeded in showing its incapacity for understanding the most elementary conditions of human nature, and in giving to Charles a stage on which he could display his own apparent moderation and fairness of mind.

Whether Charles was as fair-minded as he appeared to be may indeed be doubted. All through October he was urging

---

[1] *C.J.* vi. 53 ; *L.J.* x. 547.   [2] *L.J.* x. 559.
[3] *Idem*, x. 564.   [4] *C.J.* vi. 62.

Hopkins to carry out that plan for his escape which was to render all these concessions futile. "I shall hold out as long as possibly I may," he wrote on the 16th, "but it cannot be long, for the businesses of the Church and my friends come so fast upon me that I cannot promise you a week. Therefore lose no time." "I assure you," he wrote again on the following evening, "that I shall have but few days free to act my part; I need say no more, but let me know what is possible to be done, and then it is for me to judge. I assure you, my friends abroad desire my freedom if it be possible more than myself, being confident thereby in a great measure to alter the face of affairs." "Believe me," he wrote again on the 30th, "I shall speedily be put to my shifts, or cooped up again; wherefore, if you can conveniently I would speak with you this night after supper." [1]

Oct. 16.
Charles continues anxious to escape.

Oct. 17.

Oct. 30.

Charles indeed had need of haste. With his full knowledge the Queen had been weaving plans for a renewal of war, enough of which came to light to cause irritation against her husband as well as against herself. In one respect, indeed, her hopes proved delusive. She had for some time expected that whenever peace was restored to the Continent Mazarin would make it his first object to assist Charles to regain his throne. At last the long-hoped-for day arrived. On October 14, the Treaties of Westphalia were signed, that between France and the Empire at Münster, and that between the Empire on the one hand and Sweden and her Protestant allies on the other at Osnabrück; France thus gaining that predominance in Germany for which Richelieu and his successor Mazarin had long been striving. If, however, the war in Germany was ended, the war between France and Spain was not; and, what was even more fatal to the Queen's expectation of receiving pecuniary aid from the French Government, barricades were raised in the streets of Paris, and the Queen-Regent was obliged to capitulate to the insurgents. In the midst of the troubles of the Fronde, Mazarin had no power,

The Queen's schemes.

Oct. ¹⁴⁄₂₄
The Peace of Westphalia.

The Fronde.

---

[1] Wagstaffe's *Vindication* (ed. 1711), App.

even if he had the will, to aid in the recovery of Charles's crown.

Nevertheless Henrietta Maria continued to hope. It was true that her son's fleet had, ever since September 19, been

The Prince's fleet at Helvoet-sluys.

blockaded at Helvoetsluys by Warwick,[1] but the Prince of Orange was favourable to his cause, though unable openly to support him.[2] For money the Queen

A negotiation with Lorraine and Venice.

sought far and near. She had a negotiation with the Duke of Lorraine for a loan of troops, and another with Venice for a loan of money.[3] Even Mazarin, she fancied, hard pressed as he was, might be induced to advance money if he were allowed to import into France Irishmen who could be converted into soldiers.

It was, indeed, the growing strength of the Royalists in Ireland which, while it seemed to be the strongest, was in

The Queen's hopes from Ireland.

reality the weakest, point in the hazardous game which the Queen was playing. Early in October Ormond landed at Cork,[4] once more as the King's Lord-Lieutenant, with instructions to knit closely together the bonds already forming between Inchiquin and the Confederates, and thus to construct out of the followers of both religions a united Royalist party, which might not only win Ireland for the King, but might, in the end, win England as well. To keep up the communication between Ireland and the fleet at

The Prince to go to Jersey.

Helvoetsluys, the Prince was to winter in Jersey.[5] The garrison of Scilly having recently declared for the King, one more link was added to the chain which connected Ireland with the Dutch port in which the Royal Navy was lying. As far as can be gathered from existing evidence, the Queen and her advisers intended that in 1649 Ireland should play the part which in 1648 had been assigned to Scotland.

[1] Summons by the Lord Admiral, Sept. 19, *L.J.* x. 522.

[2] Memorandum by the Prince of Orange, Groen van Prinsterer, *Arch. de la Maison d'Orange Nassau*, ser. 2, iv. 267.

[3] Digby to Ormond, Oct. $\frac{11}{21}$, *Carte MSS.* lvi. fol. 431.

[4] Ormond to Sir A. Blake, Oct. 4, *Carte MSS.* xxii. fol. 298.

[5] Nicholas to Ormond, Oct. $\frac{12}{22}$; Jermyn to Ormond, Oct. $\frac{16}{25}$, Nicholas to Ormond, Oct. $\frac{19}{29}$, *Ibid.* xxii. foll. 360, 402, 438.

It is impossible to doubt that Charles was cognisant of the plan of operations which was intended to restore him to power in the course of the coming year. " Now," he wrote to the Queen on the 10th, "lest the rumour of my concessions concerning Ireland should prejudice my affairs there, I send enclosed letter to the Marquis of Ormond, the sum of which is to obey your command, and to refuse mine till I certify him I am a free man." [1]

Oct. 10.
A letter from Charles to the Queen.

On October 27 Ormond's arrival in Ireland was known at Westminster, and on the following day the House of Commons came to the knowledge of a letter in which the King's Lord-Lieutenant offered to conclude peace with the Supreme Council,[2] as well as of other letters which showed that he was preparing in conjunction with the forces of the Confederates to attack Jones's army. Copies of these letters were at once forwarded to Charles with the request that he would publicly disavow them.[3] On the day on which this summons was despatched Charles wrote again to Ormond. "Though," he informed him, "you will hear that this treaty is near, or at least most likely to be concluded, yet believe it not ; but pursue the way you are in with all possible speed." " Lastly," he wrote in another letter of the same date, " be not startled at my great concessions concerning Ireland, for that they will come to nothing."[4]

Oct. 27.
Ormond's landing known at Westminster.

Oct. 28.
Charles asked to disavow Ormond.

Charles writes to Ormond.

On November 1 Charles returned an evasive answer to the request of the Houses that he should disavow Ormond. He said that since the opening of the treaty he had never transacted business relating to Ireland with any but the Parliamentary commissioners, and that he had already consented that upon the conclusion of the treaty the Houses should have the sole management of

Nov. 1.
Charles's evasive answer to Parliament.

---

[1] Extract from a letter from the King to the Queen, Oct. 10, *Ibid.* xxii. foll. 330 and 334. I have substituted 'I,' 'my,' for 'King of England,' and so forth, which are mere translations of ciphers.

[2] *C.J.* vi. 63.   [3] *Walker*, 71 ; *L.J.* x. 569.

[4] The King to Ormond, Oct. 28, Carte's *Ormond*, v. 24 ; Carte's *Orig. Letters*, i. 185.

the Irish war. He therefore considered it unreasonable that he should be pressed to make any public declaration on the point submitted to him.[1]

Though the details of Charles's communications with Ormond were unknown in London, the general impression

Oct. 28.
Danger of a new combination.

produced by his attitude was in accordance with existing facts. "It is the opinion of wise men," wrote some one from Newport on October 28, "that if the King be resolved not to agree with Parliament he will escape hence to the Prince's fleet, leaving the Parliament and the army to their divisions, and to the discontents and hatred of the distracted people ; his Majesty hoping by the next spring to have as fair a game to play over again as he had this summer."[2]

To anxiety resulting from knowledge of the personal character of the King was added anxiety caused by the

Oct. 20.
A permanent settlement demanded.

temporary nature of the constitutional restraints hitherto proposed. A pamphlet issued on October 20 pointed out that even if Charles abandoned the control of the militia for twenty years the whole question of authority would be reopened at the end of that term, whoever might be on the throne at the time. "Grant him this," wrote the anonymous author, "and grant him all. Grant him but this to remain according to his request unquestionably in the Crown, and his negative vote also, and grant him to be a tyrant *in perpetuum*, both him and his . . . from generation to generation."[3] The necessity of making a permanent change in the constitution in the direction of Republicanism, and of executing justice on Charles as the cause of the late bloodshed, were ideas which now took root in many vigorous minds on which they had made no impression

Petitions from soldiers and civilians.

when they were first brought forward by the Levellers in the autumn of 1647. Demands of such a kind, and more especially the demand for justice, formed the staple of petitions which were beginning to come in

---

[1] *Walker*, 73.   [2] *Packets of Letters*, p. 5, E. 469, 21.
[3] *The Royal Project*, E. 468, 22.

both from soldiers and civilians,[1] and which culminated in an outspoken appeal from Ireton's regiment to Fairfax, asking him

Petition from Ireton's regiment. to stand up against those who had repealed the Vote of No Addresses, and to see that impartial justice was 'done upon all criminal persons,' and 'that the same fault' might have the same punishment in the person of King or Lord as in the person of the poorest commoner.[2]

Ireton prepares a demand for justice on the King. It was moreover understood that Ireton himself in his retirement at Windsor was drawing up an argumentative defence of the demands which formed the subject of these petitions. A conflict was evidently impending between Ireton and Fairfax, the result of which could not fail to be influenced by the course taken by Cromwell.

It was now known that Cromwell would soon be free to throw the weight of his presence and his sword into the *Cromwell's return expected.* balance of events in England. After turning back from Warrington Cromwell had still to deal with the *Sept. 8. Sir G. Monro retreats into Scotland.* forces under Monro and Musgrave, making in all about 7,000 men. Monro, however, not being on good terms with his English allies, made his way through Durham to the Borders, and, crossing the Tweed into Scotland on September 8, left Musgrave to his fate. Lanark and the Committee of Estates, anxious to hold Cromwell back from carrying the pursuit across the Border, gave orders that no Englishman who had been in arms in conjunction with Hamilton or Monro should be admitted into Scotland.[3]

By this time Cromwell was at Durham pushing steadily northwards. He soon learnt that he would not be without potent allies in Scotland itself. Argyle had seen in Hamilton's

---

[1] See, for instance, the petitions from Oxford and Leicestershire brought before the House on Sept. 30, that styled *The Declaration of the Army* on Oct. 3, and those from Newcastle and from Sir W. Constable's regiment on Oct. 10. *The Moderate,* E. 465, 25 ; 466, 10 ; 468, 2.

[2] *The True Copy of a Petition . . . by . . . the Regiment under the Command of Com.-Gen. Ireton,* E. 468, 18. It was published on Oct. 19.

[3] Musgrave's relation, *Clarendon MSS.* 2,867 ; *Burnet,* vi. 78, 79.

defeat an opportunity for recovering the power that he had lost. The ministers preached in his favour from one end of the country to the other. Lord Eglinton roused the stern Presbyterians of the west, who were known in Edinburgh as Whiggamores,[1] it is said, from the cry of Whiggam with which they encouraged their horses. The crowd of half-armed peasants who followed in Eglinton's train, and to whose incursion the name of the Whiggamore Raid was given, had the popular feeling behind them. They easily possessed themselves of Edinburgh, where old Leven secured the castle for them. David Leslie, who had refused to fight for Hamilton, placed his sword at the disposal of Argyle, and the Chancellor Loudoun, who had been long hesitating between the two parties, now openly deserted the Committee of Estates and being himself a Campbell brought what authority he possessed to the support of the head of his family.[2]

The Whiggamore Raid.

The Committee of Estates, thrust out of Edinburgh, took refuge under Monro's protection at Stirling, where they found themselves again opposed by the Whiggamores,[3] who were now reinforced by Argyle's Highlanders, and by the followers of the few Lowland noblemen who adopted their cause. Lanark and the officers of Monro's army argued strongly in favour of fighting the insurgents, believing that it would be easy to gain a victory over their heterogeneous force. The members of the Committee of Estates were, however, too conscious of their political isolation to approve of such a course. They promptly opened negotiations, and on September 26 abandoned all claim to the government of the country. It was agreed that Sir George Monro's soldiers should return to Ireland, and that all persons who had taken part in the defence of the Engagement should resign whatever offices and places of trust they held in Scotland.[4]

Monro at Stirling.

Sept. 26. The Whiggamores triumphant.

That the agreement was seriously intended can hardly be

---

[1] This name is, as is well known, the origin of the later ' Whig.'

[2] See Loudoun's explanation of his change of front, p. 95, note 2. An explanation discreditable to Loudoun is given in Burnet's *Hist. of his Own Time*, ed. 1823, i. 75.   [3] Burnet's *Lives of the Hamiltons*, vi. 81-83.

[4] *Idem*, vi. 81-94 ; *Bloody News from Scotland*, E. 465, 22.

doubted. In Ireland, however, it was no longer possible for
Scottish soldiers to take an independent part. On September 16 Monk, who distrusted Robert Monro and
suspected that he intended to support his nephew in
maintaining the authority of the Hamilton party,
after its disaster at Preston, won over some of the
Scottish officers and with their help surprised Belfast,
Carrickfergus, and Coleraine, Robert Monro himself being sent
as a prisoner to England and lodged in the Tower. When,
therefore, Sir George Monro's soldiers in Scotland were making
ready to cross into Ireland, they learnt that the landing-places
were all in the hands of English garrisons, and that it had
become impossible for them to gain a footing in that country.
Wandering aimlessly about the Scottish Lowlands, they were
attacked and sadly maltreated by the Whiggamore peasants.[1]

Sept. 16.
Monk
surprises
Belfast,
Carrick-
fergus and
Coleraine.

On September 15, whilst the negotiation between the
Scottish parties was still in progress, Cromwell summoned
Berwick,[2] and receiving a dilatory answer from the
commander of the garrison, applied formally to
the Committee of Estates in a letter in which
he set forth at length how God had at Preston
decided the controversy between them, and asked
for the restitution of Berwick and Carlisle, 'the
ancient rights and inheritance[3] of the kingdom
of England.' If this demand was not granted Scotland must
take the consequences. More hopefully did Cromwell ac-
credit messengers to Argyle and his party, who had
already on the 13th declared for the restoration of
these fortresses to England.[4] By the 21st he had
brought his whole army across the Tweed, giving strict orders
against plunder.[5]

Sept. 15.
Cromwell
summons
Berwick.

Sept. 16.
Cromwell
applies to
the Com-
mittee of
Estates,

Sept. 21.
and crosses
the Tweed.

---

[1] *Burnet,* vi. 95, 96; *The Earl of Warwick's Summons,* E. 465, 15;
C.J. vi. 41.

[2] Cromwell to the Governor of Berwick, Sept. 15, *Carlyle,* Letter lxx.

[3] Carlyle is certainly wrong in interpreting these words to imply ' the
right to choose our own King or No-King, and so forth.'

[4] Cromwell to the Committee of Estates, Sept. 16, *Carlyle,* Letter
lxxii.; Instructions from the Committee, Sept. 13, *Thurloe,* i. 100.

[5] Cromwell to Lenthall, Oct. 2, *Carlyle,* Letter lxxv.

On the following day a conference was held at Mordington, on the Scottish side of the Tweed, between Cromwell on one *Sept. 22.* side and Argyle on the other, the result of which *A conference at Mordington.* was an order to Ludowick Leslie, the governor of Berwick, to surrender the place. Leslie, however, declined to take orders from anyone but Lanark, and it was not till the 29th, after the agreement had been effected at Stirling, that Lanark confirmed the orders of Argyle. On *Sept. 30.* September 30 Cromwell entered Berwick, and Car- *Berwick surrendered.* lisle surrendered a few days later. Musgrave, about the same time, gave up Appleby, and except Scarborough and Pontefract no post in England held out any longer against Parliament.

The surrender of Berwick and Carlisle was not the only subject treated on at Mordington. Argyle, whilst his opponents still held out at Stirling, was anxious to secure the services of an English force to countenance the transference of authority which he meditated. Cromwell accordingly bade *Lambert sent forward.* Lambert advance in all haste towards Edinburgh with six regiments of horse and one of dragoons, whilst a body of foot was ordered to follow as far as Cockburnspath in support.[1] Thus encouraged, the Whiggamore leaders constituted themselves without Parliamentary authority into a Committee of Estates.[2]

Having received permission from the English Parliament,[3] Cromwell followed Lambert, arriving at Edinburgh on October 4, *Oct. 4.* where he was honourably received and lodged in the *Cromwell in Edinburgh.* Canongate in the house of the Earl of Moray. Argyle and Johnston of Warriston supped with him that evening. What passed between Cromwell and Argyle we have no means of knowing. The head of the English party of

---

[1] Cromwell to Lenthall, Oct. 2, *Carlyle*, Letter lxxv.

[2] They had been named by Parliament to sit on the original committee (see p. 155), but with express injunctions not to do so unless they would acknowledge the proceedings of Parliament in support of the Engagement. This condition they now threw aside, at the same time excluding their rivals in virtue of the stipulations made at Stirling. *Burnet*, vi. 97.   [3] *L.J.* x. 520.

toleration could hardly long remain on good terms with the head of the Scottish party of intolerance ; but for the present the alliance between the two was firmly enough cemented by their common enmity to Hamilton and the Engagers.

Oct. 5.
His demands,

On the 5th Cromwell presented to the new Committee of Estates a demand that, in accordance with the compact at Stirling, all who had supported the late Engagement should be removed from offices of trust in Scotland.

Oct. 6.
are agreed to.

On the following day he received an unconditional promise from the committee that they would do what after all was no more than their interest required.

Oct. 7.
Cromwell leaves Edinburgh.

On the 7th Cromwell left Edinburgh on his return to England, leaving Lambert with two regiments of cavalry to protect Argyle and his committee from the Engagers.[1]

Before leaving Scotland Cromwell gave a letter of recommendation to Colonel Robert Montgomery, who was about to start for England, begging the House of Commons to grant the bearer an order for 2,000 Scottish prisoners.[2]

Oct. 8.
A recommendation to Col. Montgomery.

Montgomery's intention was to sell them to the King of Spain for service in the Low Countries. When, however, he reached England he found that two ship-loads of the prisoners had more or less voluntarily engaged to go to the foreign plantations,[3] a phrase which was probably in this case a euphemism for Barbadoes. As large numbers of their comrades had been allowed to run home to Scotland in order to save their keep, it was not without difficulty that Montgomery got together the 2,000 he required. His next difficulty was that the Spanish Government, which never had much money to spare, omitted to make the expected remittance, and after some time Montgomery, wearied with its delays, proposed to transfer his recruits to France. The sum which he demanded for them was, however, regarded as exorbitant by Grignon, the French ambassador, and the negotiation dragged on without result till the catastrophe arrived which put

---

[1] Cromwell to the Committee of Estates, Oct. 5, *Carlyle*, Letter lxxvii. ; *L.-G. Cromwell's Letter*, E, 468, 19 ; *A True Account*, E. 468, 26. [2] Cromwell to Lenthall, Oct. 8, *Carlyle*, Letter lxxviii. [3] *L.J.* x. 572.

an end for the time to the residence of French ambassadors in England.[1]

On October 14 Cromwell was at Carlisle.[2]   After a short delay he marched into Yorkshire, where he took up his quarters at Knottingley, to enforce if possible the submission of Pontefract and Scarborough.   Hopeless as was their position the garrisons of these two fortresses had no thought of surrender.   Desperate men are ready for any deed of violence, and the knowledge that Rainsborough, who was known as having been one of the first to advocate a trial of the King, had now reached Doncaster with his regiment, whetted their desire for vengeance.

*Oct 14.
Cromwell
at Carlisle.*

*He advances
on Knot-
tingley.*

*Oct. 29.
Rains-
borough
murdered.*

On October 29 a party sallied out of Pontefract and rode into Doncaster, where they gained admission into Rainsborough's lodgings on the pretence that they brought him a message from Cromwell.   On his refusal to accompany them as a prisoner they shot him dead   Slipping away before the alarm was given the murderers regained Pontefract in safety, rejoicing in a deed which did more than anything else to quicken a cry for blood in the hearts of the Independents.[3]

[1] Grignon's despatches constantly refer to this affair.

[2] *C.J.* vi. 57.

[3] *A Full and Exact Relation*, E. 470, 4; *The Moderate*, E. 470, 12; *Packets of Letters*, E. 470, 17.

CHAPTER LXVII.

THE REMONSTRANCE OF THE ARMY.

ABOUT the middle of October the cry for justice without respect of persons had been raised more definitely than ever
before in the petition of Ireton's regiment.[1] The
general approbation accorded that cry by the soldiers
strengthened the hands of Ireton, who by that time,
or at least not long afterwards, had completed the
long manifesto which for brevity's sake is usually
known as *The Remonstrance of the Army.*[2]

*1648
Oct.
A demand
for justice
without
re-pect of
persons.
Ireton
completes
The
Remon-
strance
of the
Army.
Danger of
continuing
the nego-
tiation with
the King.*

The whole argument of this Remonstrance ranges
round two theses : the danger of continuing to treat
any longer with the King, and the justice and expediency of bringing him to trial.   On the first head
the Remonstrance pointed out that by stirring up
internal war and by inviting the Scots into England
the King appeared to have had no other aim than that of convincing the nation that it could have no peace till he was
himself restored to power.[3]   To negotiate with him after this
would be to acknowledge that his position was independent of
the nation, and of such acknowledgment he was sure to take

---

[1] See p. 227.

[2] *A Remonstrance of his Excellency, Thomas Lord Fairfax, General of
the Parliament's Forces, and of the General Council of Officers held at St.
Albans, the 16th of November*, 1648, E. 473, 11.   The date is that of the
meeting of the council of officers.   The Remonstrance itself was finally
adopted on the 18th.   The form printed in Rushworth is a mere abstract.

[3] *A Remonstrance,* 18.

advantage, assuming that all reforms to which he gave his consent were merely 'concessions from his will.' It might further be doubted whether the King would consider himself bound by any engagements he might make. He had violated all those into which he had hitherto entered, and had been at all times ready to revenge himself upon his opponents, as in the cases of the members whom he imprisoned in 1628, and of the members whom he attempted to seize in 1642.[1]

Moreover, there was no form of words which Charles would hold to be binding. "We know besides, what Court maxims
Difficulty of binding him.
there are amongst the King's party concerning some fundamental rights of the Crown which the King cannot give away, and their common scruple whether a King granting away such or any other hereditary crown rights can oblige his heirs and successors, or exclude their claim ; but if all other pretexts fail, their non-obligation to what is wrested from them by force in a powerful rebellion, as they count it, will serve such a King's conscience for a shift to make a breach where he finds his advantage." [2]

Such was the language of a man, who having, like Ireton, watched Charles's acts and words, had the penetration to
What will happen if the King is restored?
deduce from them correctly the secret workings of his mind. Suppose, he continues in effect to say, the King has been restored under the present treaty, has submitted to all the obligations you are seeking to put upon him, will he not have the credit of bringing back peace, and will not he thereby become immensely popular ? How then can he be restrained from breaking his word, except by keeping up the existing army to compel him to observe it. In that case, however, the taxation needed for the purpose will weigh the army down with an irresistible burden of unpopularity, thus making it unnecessary for the King to resort to force to gain his ends.[3] Each Parliamentary party will endeavour to have the King on its side in its struggle with its opponents. The small boroughs easily accessible to influence will be mainly in his hands and in the hands of the

---

[1] *A Remonstrance*, 29.　　　[2] *Idem*, 32.　　　[3] *Ibid.*

Cavaliers, and he will thus have the majority of the House of Commons at his disposal.[1]

It was, however, easier to point out the dangers of a restoration than to provide a substitute for monarchical government. In making the attempt, Ireton started with the doctrine afterwards known as that of 'the Sovereignty of the People.'[2] The Supreme Council or Parliament, he declared, ought 'to consist of deputies or representaives freely chosen by' the people, 'with as much equality as may be, and those elections to be successive and renewed either at times certain and stated, or at the call of some subordinate officer or council entrusted by them for that purpose.' This Supreme Council was to make laws and to exercise judicial power over public offenders, 'either according to the law where it has provided, or their own judgment where it has not.'[3]

The Sovereignty of the People.

Then turning to the question of subjecting the King to such judicial power, Ireton urged that Charles had been guilty of an attempt to convert a limited into an absolute monarchy, and had thereby shown himself to be a traitor in the highest degree. Nor was the question merely one of inflicting punishment for past misconduct. Ther never could be any safety against tyranny, unless it were shown to future generations of kings that no king was above human law, and therefore practically irresponsible.[4]

Question of the King's trial.

On this reasoning Ireton based five demands : 'That the capital and grand author of our troubles, the person of the King,—by whose commissions, commands or procurement, and in whose behalf, and for whose interest only, . . . all our wars and troubles have been, with all the miseries attending them,—may be speedily brought to justice for the treason, blood, and mischief he is therein guilty of;' that the Prince of Wales and the Duke of

The King to be brought to justice.

[1] *Ibid.* 42-46. This is a curious anticipation of the Parliamentary system of George III.

[2] No doubt in speaking of the people he limited his meaning to those who had a stake in the country. See vol. iii. 388.

[3] *A Remonstrance*, 15, 16.   [4] *Idem*, 20, 27.

York should be summoned to surrender for trial on pain of being declared incapable of governing, and sentenced to die without mercy if found in England or its dominions; that capital punishment might be executed on a sufficient number of the King's instruments in both wars; that other delinquents should be moderately fined; and, finally, that the soldiers might receive payment of their arrears.[1]

It may well have been that in the beginning of November Ireton considered that the time was come to lay his draft

Ireton and Fairfax.

A Council of Officers to meet.

before the representatives of the army, and though there is no evidence on the subject, it is probable that he urged Fairfax to summon once more the full Council of the Army to take it into consideration. What Fairfax did was to summon a Council of Officers alone, to meet at St. Albans on November 7, thus excluding the Agitators whose voices might be expected to be given in Ireton's favour rather than in his own.

On the appointed day the sittings of this Council were opened in the old Abbey Church of St. Albans. The first

Nov. 7-9. Its first meeting.

day's meeting was mainly occupied with prayers and a sermon; the meetings of the 8th and 9th with complaints of the niggardliness of Parliament in withholding the soldiers' pay, and in omitting to provide for the widows and orphans of those who had fallen in its service.

Nov. 10. Ireton's draft considered.

It was not till the 10th that the main question was reached, and it is probable—though here again direct evidence is wanting—that Ireton's draft was then laid before the council. If so its drastic proposals did

---

[1] *A Remonstrance*, 62–65. Thus far *The Remonstrance* was mainly if not entirely the work of Ireton. Not only are the thoughts his, but there is contemporary evidence to that effect. " This Declaration was both hatched and penned by his," *i.e.* Cromwell's, " son Ireton against the consent of the General." Letter of Intelligence, Nov. 20, *Clarendon MSS.* 2,920. Lilburne, too, speaks of great ones at head-quarters ' whose high and mighty Declaration, drawn by Ireton at Windsor, when he pretended to lay down his commission.' *Legal, Fundamental Liberties*, p. 31, E. 560, 14. According to *Merc. Pragmaticus* (E. 473, 35), Ireton was assisted by Hugh Peters. How a later addition was made to the Remonstrance will appear farther on.

not fail to stir opposition, many of the colonels taking alarm lest the army should be discredited as being the chief fomenter

Opposition
of the
colonels.

of the troubles of the nation, and combining in expressing a 'wish that the hearts of King and kingdom' might be knit together in a threefold cord of love.'[1]

It was, perhaps, to counteract this unexpected demonstration that, when the council met again on the 11th, a strongly-

Nov. 11.
A petition
from three
regiments.

worded petition from the three regiments of Fleetwood, Whalley, and Barkstead was presented to Fairfax.[2] Fairfax was not to be thus intimidated.

Fairfax
declares
his mind.

Nothing, he said, 'was so dear to him as the complete settling of the liberties and peace of the kingdom.' He would, therefore, 'proceed to such things as may give most hopes of justice and righteousness to flow down equally to all, without any overture tending to the overthrow of the government of the kingdom,' and would 'clearly commit his share of interest in this kingdom into the common bottom of Parliament, and when his Majesty' should 'give his concurrence to what is tendered, and what else shall be proposed by the Parliament necessary for procuring the rights and liberties of the people,' he would 'to the utmost of his endeavour maintain and defend his Majesty and his Parliament in that just, long-desired agreement.'[3]

Under any circumstances such a declaration would have carried weight. As matters stood it was absolutely decisive.

A com-
promise
agreed to.

It was impossible for Ireton and his supporters to confront King and Parliament in opposition to their own general. In order to find a way out of the difficulty a compromise appears to have been agreed to. On the one hand, when the question was put 'whether they should acquiesce in the results of the treaty,' it was carried in the affirmative, only six votes, it is said, being given to the contrary.

---

[1] *The Representations and Consultations of the General Council of the Army,* E. 472, 3. The name General Council was frequently used from habit of this council of officers.

[2] *A Petition from several Regiments,* E. 470, 32.

[3] *The Representations and Consultations, &c.,* E. 472, 3.

On the other hand, it was resolved that the army should in
tervene in the negotiation, by submitting to Charles certain
indispensable conditions, which, if he accepted them, were
afterwards .to be laid before Parliament.   On this the council
adjourned to the 16th, apparently in order to afford time for
the consideration of the proposed conditions before
they were finally adopted [1]   On the 15th an informal
meeting of officers was held at the Bull's Head Inn,
which ended in their declaring 'their most pious and unanimous resolutions for peace.' [2]

Nov. 15.
Meeting of
officers.

That Ireton expected that the overture about to be made
would be attended with successful results is in the highest
degree improbable, and he had been for some time
in communication with Lilburne, from whom he
hoped to find support.   It had been at Cromwell's
suggestion that conferences had recently been held between a
number of the Levellers and the more thoroughgoing Independents of the army, including, as may fairly be presumed,
many of the Agitators who had been excluded by Fairfax from
the council.

A conference
b tween
Levellers
and soldiers.

The first conference elicited an unexpected difference of
opinion.   The first thing to be done, according to the soldiers,
was 'to cut off the King's head, and force and
thoroughly purge, if not dissolve, the Parliament.'
To this Lilburne took exception.   It was true, he said, that
the King was 'an evil man in his actions, and divers of his

A difference
of opinion.

---

[1] Letter from St. Albans, Nov. 14, *Packets of Letters*, E. 472, 9 ;
———? to Joachimi, Nov. $\frac{17}{27}$, *Add. MSS.* 17,677, T. fol. 283.   That
there was practical unanimity in the council is known from a letter written
on the 17th to Hammond by Ireton and three other colonels.   " It hath
pleased God, and we are persuaded in much mercy, even miraculously to
dispose the hearts of your friends in the army, as one man . . . to inter-
pose in this treaty, yet in such wise, both for matter and manner as, we
believe, will not only refresh the bowels of the saints and all other faithful
people of this kingdom, but be of satisfaction to every honest member of
Parliament when tendered to them and made public, which will be within
a very few days."   *Letters between Hammond and the Committee . . . at
Derby House,* 87.

[2] *A Remonstrance from the Army,* E. 472, 13.

party as bad,' but that was no reason for trusting the army with political power. It was the people's interest 'to keep up one tyrant to balance another,' and not 'to devolve all the government of the kingdom into the wills and swords of the army.'

After this explosion, those present at the conference quieted down, and it was resolved that a committee of both sections should be appointed to meet the difficulty. This committee accordingly met in London, at the Nag's Head Tavern, on November 15, the very day on which the officers at St. Albans were giving expression to their desire for peace with the King. The committee came to the conclusion that an agreement, apparently on. the lines of the old *Agreement of the People*, should be drawn up, and that it would meet again at head-quarters to give effect to this purpose. Accordingly, either on the 16th or 17th, it moved to St. Albans, where, finding that time was pressing, as there was little likelihood that the King's answer to the overtures from the army would be long delayed, it determined that it would be sufficient for the present to add some paragraphs to the draft of the Remonstrance. These paragraphs were to point in the direction of the proposed agreement, on the understanding that until both sections of the committee were at one in this matter, no attempt should be made by the army to dissolve Parliament by force.[1]

Marginal notes:

Nov. 15. A committee at the Nag's Head.

Nov. 16 (?). A temporary measure.

Even if this circumstantial statement had never reached us, it would have been easy to discover, from internal evidence alone, that much in the concluding paragraphs of the

---

[1] The story is mainly taken from Lilburne's *Legal, Fundamental Liberties*, pp. 29, 30, E. 560, 14. Lilburne speaks there of the necessity of making the addition at once, and though he gives no reason for haste, it is obvious that he must have been thinking of the necessity of being ready when the King's answer arrived. On the 15th some Agitators wrote to the citizens of London protesting against the idea of their being against the treaty ' provided that we may be assured of security for the future, our arrears paid, the great burden of the kingdom removed and taken off, religion settled, and the subject freed from all tyranny and oppression either from Prince or representatives.' *A Remonstrance from the Army*, E. 472, 13. The writers were probably those who sat on the Nag's Head Committee.

Remonstrance in its final shape either proceeded from some
other pen than Ireton's, or were at least written by him under
the influence of the Levellers. The constitutional provisions bear the appearance of a compromise between
the author of the *Heads of the Proposals* and the
authors of the *Agreement of the People.* Parliament
is to be required, after fixing a date for its own
dissolution, and providing for its biennial successors, to
ordain that all who had fought on the King's side should be
excluded from voting at elections or sitting in Parliament for
a competent number of years,' and the same condition was
to be imposed on all who should 'oppose or not join in agreement to this settlement.' Parliaments thus chosen
were to have supreme power with two reservations :
first, that they might not question anyone for the
part taken by him in the civil war, except so far as had been
determined by the existing Parliament ; and, secondly, that
they might not take away 'any of the foundations of common
right, liberty, or safety, contained in this settlement or agreement.' Further, any representative in Parliament was to be at
liberty to enter his dissent, that the people might have an
opportunity of judging how far he had been faithful to his
trust. Moreover, no future king was to be admitted 'but upon
the election of, and as upon trust from the people, by such
their representatives, nor without disclaiming and disavowing
all pretence to a negative voice against the determinations of
the said representatives or Commons in Parliament.' [1]

'These matters of general settlement' were to be proclaimed by Parliament or 'by the authority of the Commons
therein, and to be further established by general
contract or agreement of the people with their subscriptions thereunto.' No one, moreover, was to
'benefit by this agreement who shall not consent and subscribe

An addition to the Remonstrance.

A constitutional compromise

Restrictions on future Parliaments.

An Agreement of the People demanded.

---

[1] Apparently some of these constitutional provisions are taken from
Ireton's original draft, others from the suggestions of Lilburne and his
followers. There is no clearly cut line between the two parts of the
Remonstrance. It would be curious to know who first suggested the idea
of an elective monarchy.

thereunto ; nor any king be admitted to the crown, or other person to any office or place of public trust, without express accord or subscription to the same.'[1]

Between the earlier and the later parts of the Remonstrance there is an evident breach of continuity. In the one the basis

Contrast between the two parts of the Remonstrance.

of the constitution is the sovereignty of the people ; in the other, the acceptance of a certain constitutional scheme not yet accepted by any legal or popular authority. In this, as in other respects, such as the absence of a House of Lords and the establishment of an elective monarchy without a negative voice—this

The Instrument of Government foreshadowed.

part of the Remonstrance foreshadowed *The Instrument of Government* which, four years later, was issued as the constitutional charter of the Protectorate. On the other hand, the Council of State which played so important a part both in *The Heads of the Proposals* and in *The Instrument of Government* is here passed over in silence.

On November 16, whilst Ireton and the Levellers were working together in amending and completing the Remon-

Nov. 16. The army's final overture to the King.

strance, the Council of Officers despatched to the King the proposals which had been put into shape since its last meeting on the 11th.[2] In these Charles was asked to grant no merely temporary concessions to last for ten or twenty years, but a permanent constitutional settlement. A period was to be fixed by statute to the sitting of the existing Parliament, and its place was to be taken by biennial Parliaments in which the House of Commons was to be elected under an improved system as far as the distribution of seats was concerned, though no provision was made for lowering the franchise. The militia was to be superintended by a Council of State, and the great officers of the crown to be appointed by Parliament for ten years, and after that by the King, whose choice was, however, to be limited to selection out of three names submitted to him by Parliament. Only five Englishmen were to be excepted from pardon, the compositions of all other Royalists being fixed at a moderate sum.

[1] *A Remonstrance from the Army*, 65–67.   [2] See p. 238.

The army was for the present to be kept on foot, and a fixed establishment provided for it, but only till two months had elapsed after the meeting of the first biennial Parliament, to which would thus be given a free hand in all matters relating to the defence of the realm.

Such were the main conditions on the acceptance of which the Council of Officers professed its readiness to restore the

On accept-
ance the
King to be
restored. King, the Queen, and their royal issue 'to a condition of safety, honour, and freedom in this nation, without diminution to their personal rights, or farther limitation to the exercise of the regal power.'[1] Like the Four Bills, presented twelve months before, this overture omitted all reference to the ecclesiastical questions in dispute, and did not directly touch on the burning question of the negative voice. Practically, however, by depriving Charles of control

Nature of
the changes
required. over the armed force and the appointment of officials, it made it impossible for him, if he once accepted the conditions, to set the will of Parliament at defiance, and virtually asked him to substitute a monarchy of influence for a monarchy of authority. Nurtured as he had been in the traditions of the Tudors and the Stuarts, Charles was, in short, required to anticipate, in all essential points, the system which prevails in the reign of Victoria.

Though Ireton had consented to the transmission of these proposals to Newport, it is most unlikely that he anticipated

Ireton does
not expect a
favourable
answer. anything else than their summary rejection. For some days news had been arriving from the Isle of Wight which gave little reason to expect that the King would be found in a yielding mood. On the 12th Charles again wrote to Hopkins[2] to inquire about the tides and the

Charles
again
prepares to
escape. stations of the guards which he would have to evade after succeeding in getting clear of the Castle.[3] As had happened before, his project was betrayed to the Committee of Derby House, and on the 13th the committee wrote to inform Hammond that the King intended to

---

[1] *His Majesty's Declaration*, E. 473, 5.   [2] See p. 223.

[3] The King to Hopkins, Nov. 12, Wagstaffe's *Vindication* (ed. 1711), App. 163.

escape and to make for Gosport on the night of the 16th or 17th.[1]

If there was nothing now disclosed to indicate Charles s further intentions, a belief was abroad that if he were once free he would put himself at the head of the force

His supposed projects.

which Ormond hoped to gather together in Ireland in the following year. Moreover, there had been, soon after the overthrow of the Scots at Preston, a complete change in the management of the fleet in Holland. The Presbyterian Vice-Admiral, Lord Willoughby of Parham,[2] had been discarded, and Rupert appointed in his place.

The fleet under Rupert.

There was no mystery about Rupert's intention to act in combination with Ormond. "The seamen," according to a London newspaper, "report that, if they are not all pleased when the treaty comes to a period, they can prevail with . . . . Tromp to conduct them out of the harbour, and when they are on the main, they'll get away in an Irish mist, which is now thicker than a Scottish."[3]

Under these circumstances Ireton, knowing as he did that, if Charles succeeded in getting away, all constitutional arrange-

Nov. 17. A letter from four colonels.

ments would be made in vain, joined three other colonels, Harrison, Desborough, and Grosvenor, in writing a letter to Hammond on the 17th, the day on which the overtures from the army were being brought under Charles's eye. After touching on the excellence of these overtures and on the desire of everyone in the army that peace might be secured,[4] the four colonels turned to a subject

Hammond not to allow the King to escape.

which would brook no delay. "Considering," they wrote, "of what consequence the escape of the King from you in the interim may prove, we haste this despatch to you, together with our most earnest request that, as you tender the interest of this nation, of God's people, or of any moral men, or as you tender the ending of England's troubles, or desire that justice and righteousness may take place, you would see to the securing of that person from escape,

---

[1] Com. of D. H. to Hammond, Nov. 13, *Letters between Hammond and the Com. of D. H.* 85.   [2] See p. 170.

[3] *The Perf. Weekly Account*, E. 472, 10.   [4] See p. 238, note 1.

whether by returning him to the Castle, or such other way as in thy wisdom and honesty shall seem meetest." Then follow words significant of the relations now existing between Fairfax and the writers. " We are confident," they proceed,

The four colonels expect to be supported by the army.

" you will receive in a few days the duplicate of this desire, and an assurance from the General and Army to stand by you in it ; and, in the meantime, for our parts, though it may not be very considerable to you, we do hereby engage to own you with our lives and fortunes therein, which we should not so forwardly express, but that we are impelled to the premises in duty and conscience to God and man." [1]

Evidently Ireton was secure of the acceptance of the Remonstrance by the Council of the Army in the event of Charles's rejection of the last overture. On the

Charles rejects the overture of the army.

17th, the day on which the letter of the four colonels was written, Charles briefly, though in characteristically indirect fashion, rejected the terms laid before him. He was willing, he replied, writing either to Fairfax or to the Council of Officers, to annul all declarations against Parliament and to consent to an act of oblivion embracing all his subjects. It would, however, be necessary for him to come to London if he was to put into formal shape his other concessions. "These," he added, " being perfected, his Majesty believes his two Houses will think it reasonable that the proposals of the army concerning the succession of Parliaments and their due elections should be taken into consideration." Not only had he, by implication, acknowledged the nullity of the concessions already offered by him at Newport, but by ignoring all the demands for security made by the Council of Officers, and by offering to submit its constitutional proposals to a Parliament which detested the army, he practically set both Parliament and army at defiance.

By this time Charles's favourite plan of balancing one party against another was thoroughly discredited. Even the Houses had not been moved by the proceedings at St. Albans to

[1] Ireton and others to Hammond, Nov. 17, *Letters between Hammond and the Com. of D. H.* 87.

throw themselves into his arms. It is true that on the 13th the House of Lords, being in desperate straits for money,

Nov. 13.
Hamilton
to be
liberated.
agreed to liberate Hamilton on payment of a fine of 100,000*l.* Yet on the 15th the two Houses con-

The King
to accept
the pro-
positions as
they stand.
curred in a vote that Charles himself should be 'settled in a condition of honour, freedom, and safety' only upon his agreeing to accept without alteration the propositions which he had rejected or amended at Newport.[1]

The Council of Officers was likely to take still more active measures. Charles had made the path easy to those who were

Nov. 18.
The
Council of
Officers
adopts *The
Remon-
strance of
the Army.*
compassing his destruction, and when, on the 18th, his reply was read in the council, the only dissentients to the acceptance of the Remonstrance were Colonel Rich and Captain Cecil.[2] Fairfax, resolute in the field, had no intellectual initiative, and was therefore no match for Ireton in council.

On the 20th the Remonstrance was presented to the House of Commons by Colonel Ewer and some other officers in the

Nov. 20.
It is pre-
sented to
the House
of Commons.
name of the whole army.[3] It was only natural that an attempt to cut the constitutional knot by the intervention of the army should be resented by a body of men who still hoped, however unreasonably,

Attitude of
the House.
to solve all difficulties by argument. It is true that the Commons could not regard the question from the purely Royalist point of view, as they believed as firmly as the army that the King had attempted for the sake of power to change a limited into an absolute monarchy, and that he must in some way or other be subjected to Parliamentary control. Yet they detested the idea of making parliaments democratic, and still more the idea of allowing the army in any way to influence the decisions of the Houses. It was no blame to the majority of the members that they shrank instinctively from the proposal to bring the King to trial, not only as subversive of the traditional respect for monarchy, but also as tending to overthrow that respect for law upon which their own claim to reverence was based.

[1] *L.J.* x. 587, 592.   [2] *Merc. Militaris*, E. 473, 8.   [3] *C.J.* vi. 81.

Whether the House of Commons had any means of offering permanent resistance to the army may well be doubted, but it

Logical defects in the position of the House. is certain that it would be unable to gain even a tactical success unless it opened its eyes to those radical facts to which it had long been blind. The root of the matter lay in the acknowledgment by the army that, from good motives or bad ones, Charles never would consent to those changes in the constitution which Presbyterians and Independents concurred in desiring, and that he must therefore either be restored on his own terms—that is to say, with no more than a temporary abandonment of his right of appointing officials, controlling the armed force, and hindering legislation by his possession of a negative voice—or he could not be restored at all. It was indeed possible that if the House promptly concurred with the demand of the Remonstrance by dethroning the King, it might win over to its side Fairfax and those who had supported him in the first meetings of the Council of Officers, and thus reduce the army for a time to impotence by dividing it in twain.

That the Commons should take so bold a step was not to be expected. Large bodies of men are incapable of sudden

The Commons postpone consideration of the Remonstrance. changes of position, and the House, on receiving the Remonstrance, obeyed its instinct of inertness by simply postponing its consideration to the 27th. On the following day it proceeded to discuss the treaty with the King, as though he could ever be won to adopt the constitutional views which were accepted at Westminster.[1] In one respect, indeed, the Houses hoped to give

Nov. 18. Names of those to be banished, satisfaction to Charles. On the 18th they had concurred on the names of seven persons to be banished, namely, Norwich, Holland, Capel, Loughborough,

Nov. 21. and of those to be excepted from pardon. Lingen, Laugharne, and Owen,[2] every one of whom had been a promoter of the recent insurrections. On the 21st, the day after the Remonstrance had been presented, they also concurred on the names of seven persons to be absolutely excepted from pardon. Of these only one, Judge Jenkins, was within their power, whilst the other six,

---

[1] *C.J.* vi. 82.   [2] *L.J.* x. 590, 596.

Newcastle, Digby, Byron, Langdale, Grenvile, and Dodington, had already escaped to the Continent, so that in their case the sentence was merely equivalent to one of banishment for life.[1]

If the Houses expected to win Charles by any concessions short of absolute submission, they were soon undeceived. On

Nov. 17.
Charles
stands
firm about
Ormond, the 17th, the day on which he defied the army, he defied the Houses by again refusing to change his answer on the subject of his directions to Ormond.

Nov. 21.
and about
the Church. On the 21st he declared that he would not go a step beyond his former offer relating to the Church. Episcopacy might be suspended for three years and

limited when the three years came to an end, but it must not be abolished, nor were the bishops' lands to be alienated in

Nov. 25.
The nego-
tiation
prolonged. perpetuity.[2] When these answers reached London the Houses could not resolve on any definite course, and on the 25th they contented themselves with ex-

Charles's
letter to
Ormond. tending the time of the negotiation to the 27th. Before that day arrived Charles threw a sop to them

by placing in the hands of their commissioners a letter to Ormond requiring him to desist from any further dealings with the Irish confederates.[3]

On November 27 the commissioners took leave of Charles,

Nov. 27.
The com-
missioners
take leave
of Charles. carrying with them his final answers, and the letter to Ormond, which, as he had previously instructed the Lord Lieutenant to disregard anything he might write in captivity, was absolutely valueless.[4]

Though this particular act of duplicity remained for the present undiscovered, the army had knowledge enough of

The army
impatient.

Cromwell
agrees with
Ireton. Charles's double dealing to render it increasingly impatient of the persistence with which the Houses were attempting to set him again upon the throne. It was, moreover, by this time known at St. Albans

that Cromwell was at last prepared to support the main contention of the Remonstrance—the demand for the execution of justice upon all offenders without respect of persons.

[1] *L.J.* x. 587, 595, 599.

[2] *Walker*, 81 ; Peck's *Desid. Curiosa*, 404.

[3] The King to Ormond, Nov. 25, *Walker*, 95.   [4] See p. 225.

Enough of Cromwell's correspondence of this time has been preserved to enable us to some extent to follow the growth of this resolve in his mind. A letter written by him to Hammond on November 6,[1] before the meeting of the Council of Officers at St. Albans, bears evidence of Cromwell's inability as yet definitely to make up his mind on the great question of the trial of the King. It appears from this letter that Cromwell had heard that a party amongst the Independents, including Vane,[2] Pierrepont, and Hammond, in their alarm at the thoroughgoing reforms demanded by the Levellers, were anxious to come to an understanding with the King on the basis of moderate Episcopacy and toleration. It was to this state of opinion that he now addressed himself.

Nov. 6. Cromwell's letter to Hammond.

Some of the Independents wish to restore the King.

"Dear Robin," wrote Cromwell, "I trust the same spirit that guided thee heretofore is still with thee. Look to thy heart ; thou art where temptations multiply. I fear lest our friends should burn their fingers, as some others did not long since, whose hearts have ached for it.[3] How easy it is to find arguments for what we would have ; how easy to take offence at things called Levellers, and run into an extremity on the other hand, meddling with an accursed thing. Peace is only good when we receive it out of our Father's hand, most dangerous to go against the will of God to attain it. War is good, when led to it by our Father ; most evil when it comes from the lusts that are in our members. We wait upon the Lord who will teach us and lead us, whether to doing or suffering. Tell my brother Heron[4] I smiled at his expression concerning wise friend's[5] opinion, who thinks that the

Cromwell's distrust of Charles.

He deprecates offence being taken with Levellers,

---

[1] Cromwell to Hammond, Nov. 6, *Clarke Papers*, ii. 49. This letter is signed Heron's Brother. Heron stands for Vane, whom Cromwell constantly styles his brother. It begins ' Dear Robin ' like all Cromwell's letters to Hammond, and the language is unmistakably Cromwell's.

[2] For Vane's anxiety to come to terms with the King, see p. 217.

[3] Probably alluding to his own and Ireton's efforts to win the King in 1647.   [4] *i.e.* Vane.

[5] Probably Pierrepont. Both Vane and Pierrepont were at Newport as commissioners for the treaty.

enthroning the King with Presbytery brings spiritual slavery, but with a moderate Episcopacy works a good peace. Both are a

and objects to accepting the King's restoration with moderate Episcopacy.
hard choice; I trust there's no necessity of either, except our base unbelief and fleshly wisdom make it so; but if I have any logic it will be easier to tyrannise having that he likes and serves his turn, than what you know and all believe he so much dislikes;[1] but, as to my brother himself, tell him indeed I think some of my friends have advanced too far, and need make an honourable retreat."

Cromwell was influenced by his own experience in Scotland. If he had come so easily to an understanding with

An alliance with the Presbyterians preferable.
Argyle, why should it be difficult to come to an understanding with the Presbyterians in England? "I hope," he continued, "the same experience will keep thy heart and hands from him against whom God hath so witnessed, though reason should suggest things never so plausible. I pray thee tell my brother Heron thus much from me, and if a mistake concerning our compliance with Presbytery perplex an evil business—for so I account it—and make the wheels of such a chariot go heavy, I can be passive and let it go, knowing that innocency and integrity lose nothing by a patient waiting upon the Lord."

Evidently some of Cromwell's Independent friends had been blaming him for coming to terms with Argyle. "Our

Cromwell justifies his alliance with Argyle.
papers," he continues in self-justification, "are public. Let us be judged by them. Answers do not involve us.[2] I profess to thee I desire from my heart—I have prayed for it—I have waited for the day to see union and right understanding between the godly people—Scots, English, Jews, Gentiles, Presbyterians, Independents, Anabaptists, and all. Our brothers of Scotland—really[3]

---

[1] *i.e.* easier for the King to tyrannise with Episcopacy than with Presbytery.

[2] *i.e.* We are bound by our own words, not by the answers made by the Scots. Cromwell perhaps refers to the answer made by the Committee of Estates on Oct. 6, in which they speak of 'these covenanted kingdoms.' E. 468, 19. [3] *i.e.* not merely politically.

Presbyterians—were our greatest enemies. God hath justified us in their sight—caused us to requite good for evil—caused them to acknowledge it publicly by acts of State and privately, and the thing is true in the sight of the sun ; it is a high conviction upon them. Was it not fit to be civil, to profess love, to deal with clearness with them for the removing of prejudice ; to ask them what they had against us, and to give them an honest answer ? This we have done, and no more ; and herein is a more glorious work in our eyes than if we had gotten the sacking and plunder of Edinburgh, the strong castle into our hands, and made a conquest from the Tweed to the Orcades ; and we can say, through God, we have left such a witness amongst them, as if it work not yet, by reason the poor souls are so wedded to their government,[1] yet there is that conviction upon them that will undoubtedly have its fruit in due time."

One lesson more Cromwell drew from his experience in Scotland. The new Committee of Estates had taken on itself to dissolve the late Parliament and to order fresh elections. "I have," wrote Cromwell, "one word more to say. Thy friends, dear Robin, are in heart and profession what they were ; have not dissembled their principles at all. Are not they a little justified in this, that a lesser party of a Parliament hath made it lawful to declare the greater part a faction, and made a Parliament null and called a new one, and to do this by force, and this by the same mouths that condemned it in others ? Think of the example and of the consequence, and let others think of it too, if they be not drenched too deep in their own reason and opinion." To cut the knot of the constitutional difficulty in England not by a mere forcible expulsion of members, but by a forcible dissolution followed by new elections, was the expedient which, at least for the moment, commended itself to Cromwell's mind.

New elections in Scotland.

The example one to be considered.

In this letter, written by Cromwell on November 6, there is no indication whatever of any wish to bring the King to trial, and no definite indication of any wish even to dethrone him. A fortnight later all was changed. On the 20th, after Cromwell

[1] *i.e.* the Presbyterian government of the Church.

had had time to digest the answer given by Charles on the 17th to the army's demand for security,[1] he forwarded to Fairfax

Nov. 20. Cromwell's change of tone.

He asks for justice without respect of persons.

a bundle of regimental petitions couched in what was now the usual style. "I find," he wrote, "a very great sense in the officers . . . for the sufferings and the ruin of this poor kingdom, and in them all a very great zeal to have impartial justice done upon offenders ; and I must confess I do in all, from my heart, concur with them, and I verily think and am persuaded they are things which God puts into our hearts."[2]

By this time, too, Cromwell was growing impatient of the proceedings of the Presbyterians at Westminster. Amongst

Order for the removal of Sir John Owen.

the prisoners in his custody was Sir John Owen, who had headed a rising in North Wales,[3] and had in consequence been voted a traitor. Cromwell now received an order to send this man up to London that he might, in accordance with the vote of the 18th,[4] be banished on making his composition. He at once flamed up in wrath.

Cromwell's angry remonstrance.

"If I be not mistaken," he wrote to two members of the House, "the House of Commons did vote all those traitors that did adhere to or bring in the Scots in their late invading of this kingdom under Duke Hamilton ; and not without very clear justice, this being a more prodigious treason than any that had been perfected before ; because the former quarrel was that Englishmen might rule over one another, this to vassalise us to a foreign nation ; and their fault who have appeared in this summer's business is certainly double to theirs who were in the first, because it is the repetition of the same offence against all the witnesses that God has borne, by making and abetting a second war."[5]

Here, then, and not in any constitutional ideas about limited monarchy, lay the root of Cromwell's cry for justice on delinquents, n which, after long hesitation, he had at last included a

---

[1] See p. 244.

[2] Cromwell to Fairfax, Nov. 20, *Rushw.* vii. 1,339. The letter is reprinted by Carlyle (Letter lxxxiii.) with unnecessary changes of form.

[3] See p. 145.   [4] See p. 246.

[5] Cromwell to Jenner and Ashe, Nov. 20, *Carlyle*, Letter lxxxii.

cry for justice on the King. The men who had invited foreigners 'to vassalise us' must die without respect of persons, in expiation of so great a crime. In a second letter to Hammond, written on the 25th, Cromwell strove to justify his change of ground in the spirit of one who argues because he has made up his mind, not in that of one who has resolved to follow the argument whithersoever it may lead him. With the Remonstrance itself he deals somewhat slightingly, not being much concerned with constitutional considerations, though he is thoroughly in accordance with its general conclusions. "God," Hammond had argued, "hath appointed authorities among the nations, to which active or passive obedience is to be yielded. This resides in England in the Parliament. Therefore active or passive resistance is forbidden."[1] "All," replies Cromwell, "agree that there are cases in which it is lawful to resist." The only question is 'whether ours be such a case.' Then follow suggestions rather than arguments. Is *Salus populi* a sound position? Secondly, does the treaty carried on at Newport violate the engagements made by Parliament with the army ; and, if so, is it likely to provide for the safety of the people? "Thirdly," asks Cromwell, "whether this army be not a lawful power called by God to oppose and fight against the King upon some stated grounds ; and being in power to such ends may not oppose one name of authority for these ends as well as another name?"

It was an audacious suggestion, against which Cromwell himself had once protested with all his might, and from which even now he soon draws back in alarm. "Truly," he proceeds, "these reasonings may be but fleshly." He then falls back on providences as supporting his position, and on the steady growth of a feeling amongst the people of God, doubtless by His inspiration. "If the Lord," he writes, "have in any measure persuaded His people, as

Marginal notes:

The root of Cromwell's cry for justice on delinquents.

Nov. 25. Another letter to Hammond.

Hammond's argument.

Cromwell's reply.

The authority of the army.

The testimony of providences.

---

[1] "is forbidden" is only suggested as representing "&c." in the original.

generally He hath, of the lawfulness, nay, of the duty :—this persuasion prevailing upon the heart is faith, and the more the difficulties there are, the more the faith." There must therefore be no longer hesitation. Neither fear of the Levellers and of their destructive principles, nor the hesitations of those who cling to the doctrine of non-resistance, holding that 'the people of God may have as much or more good the one way than the other,' must be a hindrance to resolute action. "Good," bursts out Cromwell, "by this man, against whom the Lord hath witnessed, and whom thou knowest ! Is this so in their hearts, or is it reasoned, forced in ? "[1]

Cromwell cared more for the thing to be done than for the way in which it was done. Far into the future he could not look, and he had no appreciation of the instinctive horror with which the English people regarded an army which counted its impulses as the revelation of the will of God. He might be able to remove the immediate obstacle in the way of peace, but it was beyond his power to lay broad the foundations of the peace for which he sighed.[2]

[1] Cromwell to Hammond, Nov. 25, *Carlyle*, Letter lxxxv.

[2] Whilst these pages are passing through the press the new volume of Mr. W. D. Hamilton's Calendar of Domestic State Papers (1648-1649) has brought to my knowledge the letters of Crewe to Swinfen recently presented to the Record Office. The one dated Nov. 6 is a good example of the view of the ordinary timid Presbyterian, without any grasp of the political situation. Crewe, who was one of the commissioners at Newport, writes thus : "We shall use our utmost endeavours here to bring the King nearer the Houses, and you will do good service at London in persuading the House to come nearer the King. A breach is likely to hazard the Navy and to lose Ireland, where the Papists gain what we lose ; and no man knows what will become of religion and the Parliament if we have not peace. Future troubles will be laid to the charge of the Presbytery, and the people will be apt to hinder and oppose that which they conceive to have been the occasion of their miseries, and so, instead of abolishing Episcopacy, we may beget an enmity to Presbytery in those who might otherwise have been made friends. . . . I entreat you to further a satisfactory answer to the King's propositions ; he expects it, and therein hath great reason on his side."

CHAPTER LXVIII.

PRIDE'S PURGE.

BEFORE Cromwell's last letter reached its destination, Hammond's views and opinions had ceased to influence the course
1648.
Military
opinion
at St.
Albans. of events at Carisbrooke. The vote of November 20,
by which the Commons postponed the consideration
of the Remonstrance,[1] was held at St. Albans as
intimating a resolution to continue the negotiation
with the King. As it was known on the 18th that Charles
The King to
be secured. was still bent on leaving the island,[2] there was all
the more reason to secure his person in such a
manner as to make escape impossible.

To effect this object it would be necessary to remove
Hammond, who had replied either to the letter from the four
Hammond
refuses to
secure him. colonels or to a later one from Fairfax by a repetition of his offer to resign his post, whilst he refused
blankly to make any change in the King's position,
and declared himself bound in honour to take orders from
Parliament in this matter and not from the General. Fairfax
replied on the 21st, recalling Hammond to head-quarters on
the plea that he hoped to be able to remove his scruples,
informing him at the same time that Colonel Ewer had been
appointed to take charge of the Isle of Wight in his absence.[3]

---

[1] See p. 246.

[2] Com. of D. H. to Hammond, Nov. 18, *Letters between Hammond
and the Com. of D. H.* 90.

[3] Fairfax to Hammond, Nov. 20, *L.J.* x. 610 ; Ireton to Hammond,
Nov. 22, *Letters between Hammond and the Com. of D. H.* 95. Hammond's letter containing his refusal to imprison the King has not been
preserved, but the two replies to it leave no doubt about its purport.

By the bearer of Fairfax's despatch Hammond also received a letter from Ireton, in which an attempt was made
even at that late hour to convince him that the path
of duty lay in obedience to his military superiors.
Upon the receipt of these letters, the distracted
governor attempted to comply at the same time with his civil
and his military obligations. Having made preparations for
leaving the island, he notified his intention to the Speaker
of the House of Lords on the 26th,[1] and on the
27th gave over his charge during his absence to
Major Rolph and two other officers, Captain Boreman and Captain Hawes, with instructions to prevent the removal of the King from the island
'unless by direct order of Parliament,' and authorising them in case of necessity to call upon the
two regiments of trained bands belonging to the
island to support the soldiers of the garrison.[2]

Hammond distracted by opposing duties.

Nov. 26. He prepares to start,

Nov. 27. and instals three officers in his place, instructing them to resist the King's removal.

Meanwhile measures were being taken to counteract any
such movement on Hammond's part. Head-quarters had
been moved to Windsor on the 24th, and on the
following day the Council of Officers held long
debate, at the end of which Ewer was finally despatched to the island. When he arrived at Carisbrooke on the 27th he found that Hammond had
not yet commenced his journey, and at once placed
in his hands a warrant from Fairfax and the Council
directing him to secure the King's person in Carisbrooke Castle until Parliament had taken action upon the
Remonstrance, of which, as the warrant itself stated, one of
the objects was 'that the person of the King' might 'be proceeded against in a way of justice.'[3] Ewer added
that if Hammond refused to comply with this order,
he was himself instructed to summon forces from
the mainland in order to carry it out. On Hammond's declaration that he would resist to the uttermost,

Nov. 24. Head-quarters at Windsor.

Nov. 25. Ewer sent to the Isle of Wight.

Nov. 27. His altercation with Hammond.

Ewer and Hammond to go to Windsor together.

---

[1] Hammond to Manchester, Nov. 26, *L.J.* x. 610.
[2] Orders by Hammond, Nov. 27, *id.* x. 615.
[3] Warrant, Nov. 25, *L.J.* x. 614.

Ewer agreed that they should both betake themselves in company to Windsor.

Ewer had gained all that he really wanted in withdrawing Hammond from his post. On the 28th, when the pair reached Farnham, Hammond was met by orders from the Houses to return to the Isle of Wight, but before he could comply with them he was arrested and taken to Windsor, where he was charged with remissness in carrying out his orders, and sent to Reading on his parole being given not to leave the place till he received permission from his superior officers.[1] Things were about to be done which could not safely be intrusted to a punctilious, scrupulous man, beyond measure anxious to do his duty both to Parliament and army, but without initiative or decision.

Nov. 28. Hammond arrested.

It is probable that Ewer accompanied Hammond to Windsor : at all events he did not return to the Isle of Wight. On the 27th, before his departure from the island was known at head-quarters, Fairfax and the Council of Officers sent him instructions to remove Charles to Hurst Castle, apparently on the ground that Parliament was suspected of a design to remove him elsewhere,[2] but on the 28th or 29th, for some reason now unknown, they resolved to send Lieutenant-Colonel Cobbet and Captain Merryman in Ewer's place, with orders merely to confine the King again within the walls of Carisbrooke Castle.[3]

Nov. 29 (?). Cobbet and Merryman sent to the Isle of Wight.

The two officers arrived at Newport on November 30, and at once entered upon a conference with the three deputy governors. Before anything had been settled fresh orders arrived from Fairfax directing

Nov. 30. Their arrival at Newport.

---

[1] Hammond to Manchester, Nov. 28, 29, *L.J.* x. 616 ; *Votes in Parliament*, E. 475, 16.

[2] The reason given is that there appears 'to us here some danger in his continuance within the island, which perhaps is not so visible to you there.' The Council of Officers to [Ewer], Nov. 27, *Clarke MSS.*

[3] *A Declaration of the Three Deputy Governors*, E. 476, 8. It appears from this declaration that Cobbet and Merryman had their instructions directly from the General and Council, not from Ewer, and the most likely explanation is that Ewer was detained at Windsor.

Cobbet and Merryman to secure the King and to remove

Are ordered to remove the King to Hurst Castle. him to Hurst Castle, and requiring the deputy governors by name and in general all other officers and soldiers in the island to assist them in the execution of this order.

For the three deputy governors it now became a question whether they owed obedience to Fairfax or to Hammond. Rolph declared himself bound to obey Fairfax, whilst Boreman held that, though his duty was to carry out Hammond's instructions, he was not strong enough to resist the commands of Fairfax. The third, Hawes, agreed with Rolph as to his duty, but was unwilling to take part in offering violence to the

They assure themselves of Rolph's help. King.[1] In this discrepancy of opinion, Rolph was practically master of the situation, especially as the soldiers of the garrison were clearly on his side. A company of foot and a troop of horse which had crossed the Solent in the day arrived at Newport after nightfall, as did also the soldiers of the garrison of Carisbrooke, whose places were taken by a company of the local trained bands.[2]

The secret of the intentions of the officers had been intrusted to too many persons to be well kept, and one of

The plan betrayed. Charles's servants heard from an informant in disguise that the King was to be carried off in the night. Charles at once sent for Richmond, Lindsey, and for a certain Captain Cooke, who, though he served in the Parliamentary army, had been won over to pity him in his mis-

Cooke sent to Rolph. fortunes. Cooke was despatched to inquire the truth of Rolph, who had a lodging in the town. "You may assure the King from me," was Rolph's answer, "that he may rest quietly this night, for, on my life, he shall have no disturbance this night." Cooke, noticing the stress laid

---

[1] *A Declaration of the Three Deputy Governors*, E. 476, 8.

[2] According to a letter from a certain Vaughan printed in *A True and Certain Relation* (E. 475, 19), Charles had summoned the trained bands of the island to his help, and on this very day large numbers had come into Newport to help him. I fancy that if this story had been true we should have heard something of these men when the crisis arrived. It is not unlikely that the whole letter was invented in London.

on the words 'this night,' suspected that something was wrong, and carried his report to the King, who, during his absence, had heard a rumour that 2,000 men were collected at Carisbrooke.

It was a dark and rainy night, and Charles, though anxious to ascertain the truth of the news, was with some difficulty induced to allow Cooke to face the storm by going to Carisbrooke to make inquiries. On his arrival Cooke found himself in the presence of several newly arrived officers, and he ultimately wrung from Boreman —the one of the deputy-governors who commanded in the castle—an admission that a design against the King was in contemplation. Hurrying back to Newport, he found the King's lodgings beset with guards, some of whom had even penetrated within the doors of the house. By this time it was nearly midnight, and it was with some difficulty that Cooke obtained the removal of the soldiers to a little distance from the house, on the plea that the smoke from their lighted matches incommoded the King.

Cooke inquires at Carisbrooke.

Guards placed about the King's lodgings.

After listening to Cooke's report, both Richmond and Lindsey urged Charles to make his escape while yet there was time. Charles, however, characteristically hesitated now that the moment for action had come. The attempt, he argued, would almost certainly fail, and would exasperate the soldiers. He even persuaded himself that he would be no worse off in the hands of the army than he had been at Hampton Court. If the officers, he argued, should seize him, they must preserve him for their own sakes, as no party could secure its own interests without his help, as long as his son was out of reach. "Take heed, sir," replied Lindsey, "lest you fall into such hands. All will not steer by such rules of policy. Remember Hampton Court, where your Majesty's escape was your best security."

Charles urged to escape, but refuses to do so.

Lindsey's argument,

Lindsey's common-sense made no impression on Charles, and it was equally in vain that Cooke sought to prove that escape would be easy. He had the password, and to show how little difficulty there was in the matter,

supported by Cooke.

he took Richmond as his companion and passed out through the guards and came back without hindrance. After his return, Cooke assured Charles that he had horses and a vessel ready for him as soon as he had cleared the guards. Charles, who for the last two months had expressed on paper his readiness to break his parole, now fell back on his conscience. "They have promised me," he said, "and I have promised them, and I will not break first." Cooke reminded him that his promise had been given to the Houses, not to the army. This argument had no effect, and an attempt to terrify Charles by representing the greatness of the danger likewise failed. "Never let that trouble you," replied the King; "I would not break my word to prevent it." When it came to the point, the dishonour of uttering a deliberate falsehood, as distinguished from an evasion or equivocation, stood up clearly and unmistakably before Charles's mind.

Charles pleads his conscience,

and refuses to be terrified.

Charles had formed his resolution. Dismissing Lindsey and Cooke at one o'clock in the morning, he kept Richmond with him, and lay down to rest. At daybreak a loud knock was heard at the door. As soon as it was opened, several officers pushed into the room, and, telling the King that he was to be removed to Hurst Castle by orders from the army, they hurried him off to a carriage waiting below, without giving him time even to eat.[1] As soon as Charles was seated, Rolph attempted to follow him into the coach. Charles at once leapt to his feet, "It's not come to that yet," he said, angrily. "Get you out," and, suiting the action to the word, thrust the intruder back, and motioned to his own attendants, Herbert and Harrington, to take their places. Rolph mounted his horse and, riding by the side of the coach, showed how deeply he felt his discomfiture by reviling the King as he went.[2]

Dec. 1. Charles carried off to Hurst Castle.

[1] Cooke's Narrative, printed with Herbert's *Memoirs*, ed. 1702. Cooke is throughout spoken of as a colonel, by his later title. In the same volume is a letter from Firebrace written in 1675, and therefore of less value than Cooke's account, which was written immediately after the events described, his own title only being subsequently changed.

[2] Firebrace's letter in Herbert's *Memoirs*, p. 199, tells the story of

In this manner Charles was conducted to a point on the coast a little beyond Yarmouth, where he was placed in a boat

Charles landed at Hurst Castle.

and landed at Hurst Castle, a block house raised by Henry VIII. to defend the Solent, surrounded by the sea except where a long and narrow spit of shingle joins it to the Hampshire coast. Black and desolate must the scene have appeared on that December morning, when Charles, stepping out, was received by an officer, whose stern looks and rough appearance, combined with his uncourtier-like demeanour, startled the King's attendants. A word, however, from Cobbet frightened him into propriety of demeanour. Not long afterwards the governor, Captain Eyre, who had been absent, returned to his charge, and from him Charles received nothing but consideration. The accommodation of the lonely fortress was, of necessity, poor, and in December even the room assigned to the King for his meals was so dark as to require the illumination of candles at midday.[1]

The army would have gained little by possessing itself of

An understanding with the Levellers necessary.

the King's person, unless it could also bring the Houses under its control. Yet, if this was to be done, it would be necessary to come to an understanding with the Levellers, whose influence amongst the soldiers was great, and who had received from Ireton a promise

---

Rolph. Herbert (p. 83) tells the same story of Cobbet, but Herbert is anything but trustworthy in matters of detail, and the civil behaviour of Cobbet at Hurst Castle leads me to think that Rolph was the intruder. He would consider that, as the senior of the deputy governors, he had Charles under his charge as long as he was in the island. He must, moreover, have been very sore on account of the charge brought against him by Osborne. See p. 131, note 2.

[1] Herbert's *Memoirs*, p. 84. The newspapers of the time make sad havoc of names, and hopelessly confuse Eyre with Ewer. The mistake has naturally found its way into that collection of newspaper cuttings which bears the name of the Fourth Part of *Rushworth's Collections*, and Mr. Goodwin, who wrote the life of Ewer in *The Dictionary of National Biography*, has unfortunately fallen into the trap. A reference to *C.J.* v. 96 shows where the truth lies. Eyre seems to have borne the local rank of colonel. Herbert speaks of a rude person who received Charles as the governor himself. It appears, however, from a letter printed in the *Clarke Papers*, ii. 66, that Eyre was not present at the time of Charles's arrival.

that no force should be used against Parliament till both parties had so far agreed upon a constitutional settlement as to avert the danger of establishing a military despotism.[1]

Accordingly on November 28, the day on which Hammond was arrested at Farnham, Lilburne, attended by a few of the

Nov. 28. Lilburne at Windsor.

more prominent members of his party, appeared at Windsor, anxious to induce the officers to accept a modified *Agreement of the People*,[2] as the only bulwark against Royal despotism on the one hand, and military despotism on the other. After a long discussion, in which

Differences between him and Ireton.

Ireton spoke in the name of the army, it appeared that only two points of importance remained to be settled. In the first place, Lilburne held that there ought to be unrestricted liberty of conscience, whereas Ireton thought that certain extreme opinions ought to be repressed. In the second place, Ireton assigned, and Lilburne refused to assign, to Parliament a right to inflict punishment in certain cases not punishable by law. Lilburne, who saw behind Ireton's arguments a settled intention to erect a Parliamentary despotism, broke up the conference, and was about to return to London in dudgeon, when Harrison appeared to plead with him for further consideration of the points at issue.

If there was an officer in the army likely to have influence over Lilburne that officer was Harrison. Harrison, it is true,

Harrison and Lilburne.

thought more of establishing the reign of the saints than of establishing the reign of law, but exceptional measures, such as those which Ireton advocated, would bear as hardly upon the saints as upon the sticklers for legal procedure, and in the recent conference Harrison had shown in no uncertain tones his dislike of some of Ireton's

Harrison announces the plan of the army.

proposals. He now plainly told Lilburne that the army had made up its mind to put the King to death even if it was necessary to have recourse to martial law. He then expounded the means which they intended to adopt to obviate that necessity. They intended, it seems, 'totally to root up' the existing Parliament, and 'to invite so

[1] See p. 239.

[2] *His Majesty's going from the Isle of Wight*, E. 475, 5.

many members to come to them to manage businesses till a
new and equal representative called by an Agreement be settled.'
It seemed as though the officers at Windsor had been struck,
as Cromwell had been struck,[1] by the example of Argyle.   A
certain select number of members of the House of Commons
were, according to this programme, to play the part of Argyle's
new Committee of Estates.   There was, however, this important difference between the two cases, that in Scotland only a
new Parliament had to be summoned, whereas in England a
new constitution had to be proclaimed.   It is scarcely possible
to doubt that communications, now lost, had passed between
Cromwell and Ireton on the subject.

By this statement, Lilburne's objections were by no means
removed.   Thinking, it may be presumed, that the main
question for him was what manner of Agreement
should be ultimately adopted, he proposed that its
preparation should be confided to a committee of
sixteen members, four being from the army, four
civilian Independents, four Levellers, and four Independent
members of Parliament.   In his generous enthusiasm Lilburne
even added that he would be ready to admit four Presbyterians
if they were willing to attend.   Harrison leapt at the proposal,
and on the morning of the 29th, when Lilburne called early
on Ireton to receive his approval, he was informed by Harrison
that Ireton, who was still in bed with his wife and could not
see him, had not only given his approval to the
proposal, but unless, as is exceedingly probable,
Lilburne was mistaken as regards this part of the
message, had even agreed that the decision of the committee
on all points should be received as final.[2]   It seems hardly
possible that Ireton should have proposed to bind his brother
officers to the details of a scheme on which their opinion had
not been taken.

Now that Lilburne's opposition was removed, it became
possible for the predominant party in the army to carry out its
design without fear of divided counsels.   The situation in the

*Lilburne
proposes a
committee
on the
Agreement.*

*Nov. 29.
Ireton
accepts it.*

---

[1] See p. 250.

[2] Lilburne's *Legal, Fundamental Liberties*, p. 31, E. 560, 14.

House of Commons was menacing. On the 27th, the day
fixed for the discussion of the Remonstrance, the debate was
adjourned to December 1,[1] and, for all that appeared, it was
likely to be adjourned indefinitely. Accordingly,
Nov. 27.
Debate on   on the 29th, after Lilburne had left Windsor, the
the Remon-   Council of Officers determined to insist on the House
strance ad-
journed.   accepting three demands : the impartial administration of justice, the regular payment of the soldiers with a view
to putting an end to the system of free quarter, and the speedy
enactment of salutary laws. To secure these things the army
was to enter London.[2]

The march of the army from Windsor was preceded by the
issue of a declaration bearing the date of November 30, which
Nov. 30.   showed that the three demands had been made with
A declara-   no expectation that they would be accepted. It was
tion from
the army.   hopeless, according to this declaration, to argue
further with the existing Parliament, and the army, therefore,
proposed to appeal 'unto the extraordinary judgment of God
and good people,' the sense of the latter being manifested in a
succession of reformed Parliaments. The existing Parliament
was to be immediately dissolved, and to bridge over the
interval before fresh elections could be held, those members
who had remained faithful to their trust—in other words those
who agreed with the army—were to withdraw from the House,
placing themselves under the protection of the army. Upon
this they would be treated by the army as a kind of provisional
government employed to direct the course of affairs till a
Parliament elected by the reformed constituencies had been
brought into existence. As soon as this had been happily
accomplished the army would willingly disband.[3] On the

[1] *C.J.* vi. 90.

[2] *His Majesty's Letter*, E. 474, 12.

[3] *The Declaration of . . . the Lord General Fairfax and his General
Council of Officers*, E. 474, 13. The most important sentence is the
following : "We . . . desire that so many of them," *i.e.* of members of
the House of Commons, "as God hath kept upright, and shall touch with
a just sense of those things, would by protestation or otherwise acquit
themselves from such breach of trust and approve their faithfulness by
withdrawing from those that persist in the guilt thereof, and apply them-

same day Fairfax announced to the Lord Mayor that he was
about to enter London, and expected an immediate payment of 40,000*l.* out of the arrears of the
City assessments.[1]

A Letter to
the Lord
Mayor.

On the following day, December 1, Prynne, who had
recently been elected for the first time, and had taken his seat
on November 7, made an urgent call on the House
to vote the army rebels.[2] To this appeal, however,
the Commons turned a deaf ear, attempting to avert
the danger by authorising the Lord Mayor to send
the required sum to Fairfax. At the same time they directed
the Speaker to request the General to keep at a distance, on
the ground that his approach would be dangerous to the City
and the army. It was only after a division that the Commons
abstained from adding that it would also be 'derogatory to the
freedom of Parliament.'[3]

Dec. 1.
The Com-
mons hope
to appease
the army.

It little mattered what form of words the House might see
fit to use. On the 2nd the streets of Westminster and
London once more resounded with the tramp of
armed men other than their own citizen soldiers.
Fairfax took up his quarters at Whitehall,[4] and
Parliament and City were at his mercy, or rather at the mercy
of that Council of Officers under whose tutelage he in reality
acted.

Dec. 2.
The army
enters
London.

selves to such a posture whereby they may speedily and effectually prosecute those public ends . . . and, for so many of them whose hearts God
shall stir up thus to do, we shall therein in this case of extremity, look
upon them as persons having materially the chief trust of the kingdom
remaining in them ; and though not a formal standing power to be continued in them, or drawn into ordinary precedents, yet the best and most
rightful that can be had, as the present state and exigence of affairs now
stand ; and we shall accordingly own them, adhere to them, and be guided
by them in their faithful prosecution of that trust, in order unto and until
the introducing of a more full and formal power in a just representative to
be speedily endeavoured."

[1] Fairfax to the Common Council, Nov. 30, *L.J.* x. 618.

[2] Lawrans to Nicholas, Dec. 1, *Clarendon MSS.* 2,964.

[3] *C.J.* vi. 92 ; Lenthall to Fairfax, Dec. 1, *Tanner MSS.* lvii. fol.
448.

[4] Lawrans to Nicholas, Dec. 4, *Clarendon MSS.* 2,964.

On December 1, the day before the entry of the army, Holles had reported to the House of Commons the final

Dec. 1.
The King's
answer
reported. answer made by the King to the Parliamentary commissioners before they left Newport. In the discussion which ensued Vane bitterly criticised the

Vane
attacks, and
Fiennes
defends it. King's offers, but the Presbyterians found an unexpected ally in Fiennes, who argued that the King had yielded all that was necessary 'to secure religion, laws, and liberties.' He was quite ready even to accept the establishment of Presbyterianism with the limit of three years. Presbyterianism, he said, must be weak indeed if it could not stand upon its trial for three years. Fiennes's change of front was deeply resented by the Independents, who asserted that he had been bribed by Charles with an offer of a 'Secretaryship of State, and his father, Lord Say, by the promise of the Lord Treasurer's staff.'[1] It is unnecessary to resort to such an explanation, as a reasonable man might easily, by leaving out of sight the question of Charles's trustworthiness, come to the conclusion that, under the circumstances, the best course was to accept his offers.

It had been expected in the House that the discussion on the King's answer would take place on December 2, but the

Dec. 2.
Further
delay. entry of the army into London on that day distracted the attention of the members, and the debate was again adjourned. The 3rd was a Sunday, and before the House entered upon business on the morning of the 4th,[2] it was officially informed that the King had been removed by force to Hurst Castle. All through that day and the follow-

Dec. 4.
An all-night
sitting. ing night there was hot debate on the question whether the House should merely affirm that 'the removal of the King was without the knowledge of the House'—a form of words upon which both parties could

---

[1] Lawrans to Nicholas, Dec. 4, *Clarendon MSS.* 2,964; ——? to Joachimi, $\frac{\text{Nov. 24}}{\text{Dec. 4}}$, *Add. MSS.* 17,677, T, fol. 293.

[2] The writer of the Newsletters in the *Roman Transcripts* in the Record Office puts the arrival of the letter at 5 P.M.; but it seems impossible that a letter dated at Carisbrooke on Dec. 1 should not have been received at Westminster till the afternoon of the 4th.

agree ; or, should adopt an amendment, supported by the Presbyterians, declaring that the King had been removed without the House's knowledge or consent. It was not till

Dec. 5.
The action of the army repudiated.

eight o'clock on the morning of the 5th that the Presbyterians finally carried their amendment. Then some earnest lover of peace amongst them moved that the King's answers to the propositions should be ac-

The debate cn the King's answers adjourned.

cepted. The Independents, anxious to see this question settled in the sense of their opponents in order to give an excuse for the intervention of the army, wished the question to be put. The Presby-terians, however, preferred delay, and carried a motion for adjournment by the decisive majority of 144 to 93.[1]

It was not merely because the House was jaded that the Presbyterians, in spite of their assured majority, had adjourned

Reasons for the adjourn-ment.

the discussion. They would now, too late for them-selves, have welcomed Charles's compromise, but feared to alienate the Scots by accepting even mode-rated Episcopacy.[2] When the House met again somewhat

The King's answers de-clared to be a ground of settlement.

later in the day, the majority, still disinclined to accept the King's answers as a whole, contented themselves with carrying, by 129 to 83, a resolution that they were 'a ground for the course to proceed upon for the settlement of the peace of the kingdom.' In order to make this dilatory proposal palatable to the army, a committee was appointed to confer with Fairfax, in the hope of keeping 'a good correspondency between the Parliament and the army.'[3]

At some time in the course of the two days' debate Prynne

Prynne's argument.

delivered a long and ponderous oration, in which he urged the House to accept the King's offers as satis-factory. In so doing, he contrived to surmount what was, to

---

[1] *C.J.* vi. 93 ; Grignon to Brienne, Dec. $\frac{7}{17}$, *R.O. Transcripts.*

[2] The Commons, writes Grignon, resolved ' de ne point agiter si les responses dudict Roy etoient satisfactoires ; ce que fut faict par les Pres-byteriens, qui les eussent bien pu faire lors declarer telles, affin de ne point offenser les Escossois qui avoient declaré n'en estre pas satisfaicts. *Ibid.*　　　　　　　　　　　　　　　　　　　[3] *C.J.* vi. 93.

him, a considerable difficulty—the King's refusal to abandon Episcopacy—characteristically remarking that he had himself written a book, which had never been refuted, on the unbi-shopping of Timothy and Titus. He was, therefore, quite certain that, if he were brought into the King's presence, Charles would himself acknowledge the Presbyterian argument to be conclusive. On the more practical question of the power of the Houses to keep the King to his engagements, Prynne argued that the stipulations about the militia and official appointments would make it impossible for him to throw off the bonds under which he would be placed.[1]

This was not the view taken in the army. There the eagerness for the most drastic measures, which had shown

The army eager to interfere. itself in the Remonstrance and the declaration, remained unabated Nor was it likely that, in the heat of the struggle, practical men would abide by the letter of any promise made personally by Ireton to Lilburne, and thus suffer an opportunity for grasping power to slip away, whilst an ideally perfect form was being discovered for the new

Lilburne's committee. constitution. Lilburne, indeed, satisfied with Ireton's engagement, had, even before the army moved to London, brought together at Windsor thirteen out of the sixteen members of his committee. After some discussion, Lilburne and the three other Levellers locked themselves into a

A new Agreement of the People. room with Marten, and before they left it completed the draft of a new Agreement of the People. When the army arrived in London the committee transferred itself to the head-quarters at Whitehall; and though

---

[1] *The Substance of a Speech* by W. Prynne. No doubt, as Professor Masson argues (*Life of Milton*, iii. 695), the speech was shorter in delivery than in print. There is a further difficulty, that it is said to have been delivered on Dec. 4, whereas the question whether the King's offers were satisfactory to which it is addressed was not discussed, according to the journals, till Dec. 5. Possibly this subject may have been held to be germane to the question whether the House approved of the King's seizure, which was before it on the 4th. Besides, we cannot tell how much the speech was altered for publication. If we could accept the authority of the *Roman Newsletter* (see p. 265, note 2) there would be no difficulty at all.

Ireton and Lilburne opposed one another vigorously, the draft was finally adopted in an amended form by a majority.

It was significant that the three absentees were all members of the House of Commons, Marten being the only one of the four named who was present at the meetings either at Windsor or Whitehall.[1] Marten had left Westminster in August, and, without orders from any one in authority, had raised a troop of horse in Berkshire, mounting his men by the simple process of breaking into the stables of the gentlemen of the county.[2] An outcry was soon raised, and, to avoid punishment, he and his troop moved off to the north, where he remained till the attitude of the army towards Parliament tempted him to Windsor. The three absentee Parliamentary members of the committee—Alexander Rigby, Thomas Chaloner, and Thomas Scott—were certainly not likely to err from any sympathy with the Presbyterians.

Marten's recent escapade.

The absence of these men is to be accounted for by their rooted objection to that which was common to Ireton and the Levellers. Though the Levellers wished to postpone the forcible dissolution of Parliament till the Agreement of the People was completed, they concurred with Ireton in desiring that such a dissolution should take place at no long interval of time. Partly, no doubt, from the promptings of private interest, but, it may fairly be urged, still more by public motives, the Republican members of Parliament objected to the scheme set forth in the recent Declaration of the army,[3] in accordance with which they were to leave Westminster under protest whilst the army dissolved Parliament. They seem to have thought that if once they abandoned Westminster they would lose the prestige conferred by sitting in the historical House of Commons, and would cease to be regarded as the legitimate possessors of authority. They therefore urged that there should be no dissolution, but that those who voted for continuing the negotiations with the King should be ejected from the House.[4]

Opposition to the proposed dissolution.

[1] *Legal, Fundamental Liberties*, p. 34, E. 560, 14.

[2] Marten to Lenthall, Aug. 15 ; Account of the Conduct of the Soldiers, Aug. *Tanner MSS.* lvii. foll. 197, 199.

[3] See p. 263.   [4] Ludlow's *Memoirs,* i. 206.

The vote of the House of Commons on the 5th brought matters to a point. In the afternoon of that day a meeting was held at Whitehall, at which both officers and members of the House were present. In vain Ireton and Harrison pleaded for the dissolution of Parliament in accordance with the Declaration of the Army issued by the Council of Officers at Windsor. The existing House, they urged, 'had forfeited its trust,' and 'if they did not totally dissolve it, but purge it, it would be but a mock Parliament and a mock power.' "Where," they added, " have we either law, warrant, or commission to purge it, or can anything justify us in doing it but the height of necessity to save the kingdom from a new war that they with the conjunction with the King will presently vote and declare for, and to procure a new and free representative and so successive and free representatives, which this present Parliament will never suffer, and without which the freedoms of the nation are lost and gone?" [1]

Nothing, in short, the officers argued, would justify a forcible purge unless it were followed by a dissolution and an immediate appeal to the people to elect a new Parliament. The arguments used on the other side have not been handed down, but it may very well have been pointed out that a general election would probably lead to results very different from those on which the hearts of all who took part in the meeting were set. In the end the meeting adopted the colourless resolution that Parliament having forfeited its trust, it was 'the duty of the army to endeavour to put a stop to such proceedings.' [2] The question at issue was really settled by the appointment of a joint committee of three officers and three members of Parliament, who were to consider the course to be pursued to carry this resolution into effect.[3] As it is certain that the three civilians were

Marginal notes:
Dec. 5. A meeting at Whitehall.

Ireton and Harrison plead for a dissolution.

Conditions of a purge or dissolution.

Arguments for a purge.

A colourless resolution.

A Committee appointed.

---

[1] *Legal, Fundamental Liberties*, p. 34, E. 460, 14.

[2] Ludlow's *Memoirs*, i. 209. Ludlow gives the result, Lilburne the arguments; but it can hardly be doubted that both refer to the same meeting. [3] *Idem*, i. 210.

unalterably opposed to a dissolution, recourse to a purge was a foregone conclusion, as, even on the not very probable hypothesis that all the three officers preferred a dissolution, they would undoubtedly prefer a purge to a dissolution carried out in opposition to those members of Parliament who had hitherto acted in agreement with the army.

In accordance with the determination of this committee, Westminster Hall and the approaches of the House of Com-

Dec. 6. The House of Commons beset with soldiers.

mons were, without any authority from Fairfax, beset by soldiers at seven o'clock in the morning of the 6th. Colonel Pride, who commanded the guard stationed in the lobby of the House, had in his

The Purge.

hands a list on which were the names of certain members, whilst Lord Grey of Groby, himself a member of the House, stood at his side, ready to point out to him the mem-

Those who resist are placed in confinement.

bers in question. As each one of these approached the door of the House he was turned back, and in case of resistance was removed by the soldiers to a room known as the Queen's Court, and there placed in confinement. In addition to those who were merely turned back, the number of those put under restraint amounted to forty-one.

The first step taken by those members who were permitted to pass the doors of the House was to send the serjeant-at-

The House orders their liberation,

arms to liberate the prisoners.[1] It is probable that many who concurred in this step took it merely in order to save appearances; but there must have been not a few, perhaps a majority, of those present who, though they had hitherto voted with the Independents, were irritated by the subjection of the House to military violence.[2]

[1] *C.J.* vi. 93.

[2] Ludlow, in his *Memoirs*, i. 211, says that the House 'was moved to send for those members who were thus excluded from the army; which they did, I presume, rather out of decency than from any desire they had that their message should be obeyed.' This, no doubt, represents his own feeling; but, according to *Merc. Elencticus* (E. 476, 4), there were, on Dec. 11, only about thirty members who thoroughly agreed with the army. The authority is not a good one; but the statement is more likely to be exaggerated than entirely false.

However this may have been, the serjeant brought back an
answer from the officer in charge of the prisoners, that he
would obey no one except his own military superiors, and upon
this the House directed the committee, which had been ap-
and sends to   pointed on the preceding day for the purpose of
Fairfax.   opening communications with Fairfax, to wait upon
the General with a request that he should at once give the
required orders.

Fairfax, either unable or unwilling to act alone, replied, in
conjunction with the Council of Officers, by sending a charge
Charge by   asking for the resumption of the proceedings against
the officers. Holles and the remaining survivors of the eleven
members, and for the trial of Major-General Browne, who was
accused of bringing in the Scots.   The officers also asked that
all who had voted for the re-admission of Holles and his companions, or had opposed the vote declaring those who had
invited the Scots to be traitors,[1] should be permanently excluded from the House, whilst others who had voted on various
occasions in a way obnoxious to the army should be excluded
till they had given satisfaction.   It is probable that in these
two categories all those whose names were on Pride's list were
included.

Finally, the officers expressed a hope that those who
remained faithful to their trust would speedily 'take order for
the administration of justice,' fix a period for a dissolution,
and 'provide a speedy succession of equal representatives.'[2]
Throughout this charge the King's name was never mentioned.

Upon this message the House, before bringing its sitting to
The General   a close, merely reiterated its order to the committee
to be asked   to 'confer with the General for the discharge of the
to discharge
the mem-   members.'[3]   The prisoners gained no benefit by
bers.   the intervention of their colleagues.   In the afternoon Hugh Peters, indeed, arrived in the Queen's Court and

---

[1] 'To the number of ninety and odd, as upon the division of the
House appeared.'   This vote, however, passed on July 20 without a
division.   *C.J.* v. 640.

[2] *The Articles and Charge of the Army*, E. 475, 30.

[3] *C.J.* vi. 94.

released Fiennes and Rudyerd, giving to those who inquired by what authority they had been detained the short answer,

Two of the pisoners liberated. 'By the power of the sword.' The remaining thirty-nine were then taken to a neighbouring tavern, familiarly known as 'Hell,' where they passed the night in two upper chambers, affording no resting-place except benches and chairs. Seven of the oldest amongst them were offered permission to go home on giving their parole to return in the morning. They, however, refused even so far to acknowledge the authority by which they were detained.[1]

In the evening of the day on which the arrests were effected, Cromwell, who had left Lambert behind him to prosecute the

Cromwell's return. siege of Pontefract, rode into Westminster. He had not, he said, 'been acquainted with this design; yet,

He disclaims knowledge of Pride's Purge. since it was done, he was glad of it, and would endeavour to maintain it.'[2] There can hardly be a doubt that Cromwell had been consulted as to the proposed interference of the army; but the special form which it took had been rapidly determined, almost certainly only on the preceding day, so that there had been no time to obtain his opinion on the adoption of a purge in place of a dissolution.

On the morning of the 7th he took his seat, and received the thanks of the House for his victories.[3] Marten, who came

Dec. 7.

Marten's return. in at the same time, signalised his entry by a jest significant of his own feelings. "Since Tophet," he said, "is prepared for kings, it is fitting their friends should go to Hell!"[4]

It was in vain that, on the preceding day, the Commons

The House orders the demands of the army to be considered. had urged Fairfax to set free the imprisoned members. They were now informed by the Council of Officers that no answer would be given to their request till they had replied to the last demands of the army. The House first directed that these demands

---

[1] *A True and Full Relation*, E. 475, 14.

[2] Ludlow's *Memoirs*, i. 211.

[3] *C.J.* vi. 94.   [4] *Merc. Pragmaticus*, E. 476, 2.

should be considered on the 9th, but on the 8th, apparently shrinking from the humiliation, adjourned to the 12th.[1]

On the 7th the prisoners, with one addition to their number, were taken to Whitehall. On their arrival they were not allowed to see Fairfax, but, after being left for four hours in a room without a fire, were ultimately removed to various inns in the Strand. Omitting the names of Rudyerd and Fiennes, who had been liberated after a short detention, and adding those of a few who, like Major-General Browne, were arrested some days later, the total number of members in confinement was forty-five, whilst ninety-six others who had offered no resistance had been simply turned back by the soldiers and forbidden to enter the House, making in all one hundred and forty-three affected by Pride's Purge. In the end the prisoners were set free on giving their parole to make no attempt to return to their places in the House.[2]

The prisoners at Whitehall.

They are removed to the Strand.

After this act of violence all interest in Parliamentary proceedings is for a time at an end. The sitting members had been strong enough to hinder an appeal to the people, but they now found themselves unable to obtain serious recognition as the legitimate holders of supreme authority. To England at large they seemed, what in reality they were, the mere creatures of military violence. The army was their master, and, through them, the master of the State.

Weakness of the remaining members.

Whatever might be the political results of their deed, it was necessary, if discipline was to be maintained, to satisfy the soldiers by providing them with the arrears of their pay. Accordingly, Fairfax wrote, on the 8th, to the Lord Mayor and Common Council demanding 40,000*l.* as an instalment of the unpaid assessments of the City. To show that neither Parliamentary nor municipal authority would stand in his way, he sent troops to seize upon the money belonging to Parliament in the treasuries of the Committee for

Dec. 8.

The arrears of pay demanded from the City.

[1] *C.J.* vi. 95. These proceedings strengthen the view that the demand of the House for the liberation of the prisoners was not made merely to save appearances.

[2] *A True and Full Relation,* E. 476, 14 ; *Parl. Hist.* iii. 1,248.

Compounding at Goldsmiths' Hall, and of the Committee for Advance of Money at Haberdashers' Hall. From these sources he obtained little, but from Weavers' Hall, where a sub-committee of the Committee for Advance of Money had its place of meeting, he carried off, it is said, no less than 28,000*l.* As a more direct measure against the City itself, he quartered soldiers in the citizens' houses with the intimation that there they would remain till the whole sum demanded had been paid.[1] In a few days, however, he so far relented as to remove the men into some empty houses, on the undertaking of the City to provide them with beds to sleep on.[2] It was understood, however, that more stringent measures would be taken unless the money required was found speedily.

Money seized.

The House of Commons, too, felt the pressure of the army. When it reassembled on the 12th it was found that many of the members who still took the part of their imprisoned colleagues had resolved to absent themselves, and the House was thus, as it were, by a second and voluntary purge, at last reduced to a condition in which those who supported the course taken by the army were numerically preponderant. So poor was the attendance that Royalist news-writers were able, truly or falsely, to report that business was frequently delayed by the difficulty of making up the necessary quorum of forty members.[3] On the 12th the House, thus thinned, made no difficulty in re-expelling the survivors of the eleven members ; and, afterwards, on the 13th, revoked the repeal of the Vote of No Addresses as having been dishonourable to Parliament ; and annulled the votes authorising the Treaty of Newport, as well as those imposing a fine on Hamilton, and

Dec. 12. Thinness of the attendance in the House.

Repeal of recent votes, Dec. 13.

---

[1] *The Moderate*, E. 476, 5 ; *Whitelocke*, 362. Two regiments of foot and one of horse were quartered in the city. *Perf. Occurrences*, E. 526, 40*. Other sums are mentioned in various newspapers as having been seized at Weavers' Hall.

[2] *Ibid.*

[3] On Dec. 7 a division showed the presence of eighty-two members, including the tellers. The next division, taken on the 14th, showed only fifty-seven ; and the next again, on the 20th, only fifty-five.

banishing Norwich and the other leaders in the second war.

Dec. 14.
The House
asks for the
restoration
of its mem-
bers.

On the 14th a message was sent to Fairfax asking him to state 'upon what grounds the members of the House are restrained from coming to the House by the officers and soldiers of the army.'[1]

The question was not likely to meet with a favourable response. On the 12th the army leaders had arrested Browne,

Dec. 12.
Browne
and others
arrested.

Clotworthy, Waller, Massey, and Copley on the charge of having participated in an invitation to the Scots to invade England.[2] It was, however, difficult

Dec. 14.
Cromwell
goes to
Windsor.

to find evidence against them, and on the 14th Cromwell, in accordance with a request from Hamilton, who was now confined at Windsor, rode down to visit him. Hamilton's object was no doubt to enlist the sympathies of the powerful Lieutenant-General in his favour, whereas Cromwell was anxious to draw from him, as the price of his life, information which would lead to the conviction of those Englishmen who had invited him across

Dec. 15.
Hamilton
refuses
to give
evidence.

the border. Hamilton had many faults, but he refused to betray his associates, and Cromwell gained nothing by his journey.[3] In the meanwhile, the remnant of the Commons settled down into the acceptance of the consequences of Pride's Purge, and on the

A protesta-
tion of the
excluded
members
voted
scandalous.

15th they put the crown to their subserviency by branding as scandalous a protestation, drawn up by Waller and others in the name of the excluded members, against the violence to which they had been subjected.[4] Of the five who had been last seized, Massey succeeded in effecting his escape. The other four remained for some years in prison, untried and uncondemned.

[1] *C.J.* vi. 95–97 ; ——? to Joachimi, Dec. $\frac{15}{25}$, *Add. MSS.* 17,677, T, fol. 306. This writer attributes the request to the shame of the members at being seldom able to form a quorum.

[2] *Perf. Occurrences*, E. 526, 40*. According to one writer, Browne acknowledged writing a letter of invitation to the Scots ; ——? to Joachimi, Dec. $\frac{15}{25}$, *Add. MSS.* 17,677, T, fol. 306. This is, however, exceedingly unlikely, and is probably only an enlargement of Browne's declaration that the accusation against him was 'for nothing else but loyalty to the King and Parliament.'   [3] *Merc. Pragmaticus*, E. 476, 35.

[4] *C.J.* vi. 97 ; *A Declaration*, E. 476, 33.

CHAPTER LXIX.

THE PRELIMINARIES OF THE KING'S TRIAL.

ON one point the mutilated House of Commons stood firm even against the army—every suggestion that it should fix a date for its own dissolution fell on deaf ears. Yet, though Ireton and his supporters had been forced to substitute a purge for a dissolution, they had not freed themselves, nor, as far as it appears, had they any wish to free themselves, from their obligation to support in some form or other an agreement of the people which should substitute within a very short time a Parliament elected on new principles for the little group of members now sitting at Westminster.

1648.
Ireton favourable to an early dissolution.

By December 10 Lilburne's committee [1] had done its work. As he believed Ireton to have promised that whatever received the approbation of the committee should be accepted without further inquiry, he was sanguine enough to suppose that his scheme would at once be submitted for signature—first to the officers, then to the soldiers, and finally to the people in general. He was grievously dis-appointed when he found that it was to be, as a preliminary step, laid before the Council of Officers for approval.[2] It was perhaps in consequence of this rebuff that he sent to the press the Agreement [3] as it had approved itself to his committee, in order that the nation

Lilburne's disappoint-ment.

Dec. 10.
Lilburne's Agreement of the People sent to the press.

---

[1] See p. 267.   [2] *Legal, Fundamental Liberties,* p. 35, E. 560, 14.
[3] *Foundations of Freedom, or an Agreement of the People,* E. 476, 26. This was actually published, according to Thomason's date, on the 15th, but the prefatory letter in his copy is dated Friday, Dec. 10. Dec. 10, however, was not a Friday, and as the letter is dated in a copy in Mr. Firth's possession Dec. 15, which was on a Friday, I have no doubt that the 15th is correct. Yet the book must have been sent to the press a few

might know what constitutional blessings he had striven to obtain for it.[1]

On December 11 a discussion was opened, in which Lilburne and some of his followers were permitted to take

Dec. 11.
The *Agreement of the*
People
before the
Council. part. The clauses most open to dispute in the new *Agreement of the People* were those relating to the so-called reservations—that is to say, to the list of questions to be reserved or exempted from the control of Parliament. Of these the most important, that

Dec. 14.
The reservation on
religion. prohibiting all interference with religion, was reached on the 14th ; and, in the debate which was expected to arise on this point, Hugh Peters, Nye, John Goodwin, and other Independent divines were invited to take part, Fairfax himself being in the chair. In the course of the debate Ireton expressed himself strongly on its being the magistrate's duty to punish offences against the first table ; but the whole question was postponed for more mature con-

Dec. 21.
A com-
promise
arrived at. sideration. On the 21st a compromise was arrived at. The Parliament or Representative was to have 'the highest and final judgment concerning all natural[2] things,'[3] whilst it was to be interdicted from interfering with the worship of such Christian societies as did not disturb the public peace, with the wide exception of those addicted to 'Popery and Prelacy.'[4] A question raised by Ireton as to the duty of Parliament to suppress blasphemy

days earlier, and probably on Lilburne's discovery that he was to submit his plan to the officers for revision. This Agreement is identical with the form in *Rushw.* vii. 1,358, except that two long clauses are there omitted, one of which contains the number of the members to sit for each constituency, the other a proposal for dividing constituencies returning more than three members into electoral divisions returning one member each.

[1] See p. 262.   [2] *i.e.* not divine.   [3] *Clarke Papers*, ii. 71, 140.

[4] *The Moderate Intelligencer*, E. 536, 18. Walker, in his *History of Independency* (ii. 50), states that, on December 25, 'the Council of War voted a toleration of all religions.' The vote of the 24th must be referred to, though the *Clarke Papers* (ii. 144) do not give any debate on the subject for that day. These papers do not notice a meeting on the 25th, though their silence is not conclusive. Ultimately the clause was still further modified, and the liberty was declared not to extend necessarily to Popery or Prelacy.

was passed over in silence. A second point on which Ireton

The right of
Parliament
to punish
officials. and Lilburne were at issue, whether Parliament might inflict punishment not authorised by law, was solved by restricting its right to cases of 'public officers failing in their duty.'[1]

It was not only on the future constitutional arrangements that the Council of Officers took the lead. On the 15th,

Dec. 15.
The King to
be brought
to Windsor. whilst Cromwell was still absent on his mission to Hamilton at Windsor, they voted 'that the King be forthwith sent for to be brought under safe guards to Windsor Castle, and there to be secured in order to the bringing of him speedily to justice.' In accordance with this resolution, Fairfax wrote to Cobbet and the other officers who had conducted the King to Hurst Castle, informing them that

Dec. 16.
Harrison
sets out. he would be fetched away by Harrison.[2] On the morning of the 16th, Harrison, at the head of a large body of horse and dragoons, rode off to fulfil his mission.[3]

The King's stay at Hurst Castle had been rendered as agreeable to him as circumstances would allow of. Cobbet

The King
at Hurst
Castle. had shown him what kindness and civility lay in his power. The King's lodging was rough at the best, and the daily walk along the shingle, with the wintry sea on the one side and the shallow mud-flats on the other, monotonous enough. Charles, however, did what he could to be cheery, chatting with the officers, and his own attendants, and interesting himself in the passing shipping.[4]

---

[1] *Clarke Papers,* ii. 148.

[2] Fairfax to Cobbet and others, Dec. 15, *ibid.* 146.

[3] *Merc. Pragmaticus,* E. 476, 35.

[4] Herbert, in his *Memoirs,* 39, speaks of Harrington having been dismissed from attendance on the King whilst he was at Hurst Castle for commending the King's replies to the Presbyterian divines at Newport. On the other hand, *The Kingdom's Moderate Intelligencer* (E. 536, 33), of Jan. 2, 1649, states that Harrington was dismissed from Windsor because, though he promised not to help the King to escape, he would not promise to denounce anyone else who might do so. Herbert's *Memoirs,* 91-94. As there can hardly be any doubt that the contem-

Late in the night of the 17th Charles was roused from his sleep by unwonted sounds, and Herbert, being sent forth to make inquiry, returned with the information that the noise was the clank of the drawbridge let down to admit Harrison. Charles, at the time when he was preparing to fly from Hampton Court, had been told that Harrison had advocated his assassination, and he now imagined that his murder in this lonely spot had been determined on, and that Harrison had been selected as the fitting instrument of crime. Further inquiries having elicited the fact that Harrison was sent to conduct him to Windsor, Charles was completely reassured. Windsor, he knew, was a pleasant place, and he could not imagine that the army in removing him had any purpose except to deal kindly with him.

Dec. 17. Harrison's arrival.

The King fears assassination.

Harrison had visited Hurst Castle to give orders, not to execute them, and he, therefore, rode away on the evening of the 18th, without asking for a personal interview with the King. On the morning of the 19th Charles was conducted by Cobbet to the mainland, where he found a party of horse appointed to guard him. He slept at Winchester, where he received a hearty welcome from the Mayor and the citizens. The night of the 20th he passed at Farnham. Three or four miles short of the place he descried a fresh party of horse drawn up to receive him. The officer in command was 'gallantly mounted and armed, a velvet montero was on his head, a new buff coat upon his back, and a crimson silk scarf about his waist, richly fringed. Charles's attention was at once arrested by so splendid a figure, and being told that this was the dreaded Harrison, replied that 'he looked like a soldier, and that having some

Dec. 18. Harrison leaves the Castle.

Dec. 19. Charles removed to Winchester,

Dec. 20. and Farnham.

He meets Harrison.

porary account is the true one, we have here a means of measuring the amount of confidence that can be reposed in Herbert's handling of details. Most likely Harrington was taken to task about his language; and Herbert, writing about thirty years after the event, fancied it to have been the cause of his dismissal, antedating it so as to place it at Hurst Castle.

judgment in faces, if he had observed him so well before, he should not have harboured that ill opinion of him.'[1]

After supper, Charles, standing by the fire, beckoned to Harrison, and, taking him into a recess by one of the windows,

A conversa-
tion with
Harrison. told him that he had been informed of his intention to murder him at Hampton Court. Harrison, as might have been expected, peremptorily disclaimed the truth of the charge. What he had really said, he declared, was 'that the law was equally obliging to great and small, and that justice had no respect of persons.' On this, Charles broke off the conversation, though he did not, even now,

Dec. 23.
Charles
fails to
escape, realise the danger in which he was. On the 23rd he continued his journey, dining at Lord Newburgh's house at Bagshot, where, as he had been told, the fleetest horse in England awaited him, in order that, should an opportunity present itself, he might escape on its back. The first news that Charles heard on his arrival was that the horse

and arrives
at Windsor. had fallen lame,[2] and he had therefore no choice but to pursue his way as a captive. He arrived at Windsor in the evening.[3]

By this time the Council of Officers, having settled the most controverted points in the *Agreement of the People*, had

Opinions in
the army on
the disposal
of the King. leisure to turn its attention to the disposal of the King's person. Amongst the officers the prevailing opinion was that which had been set forth in the early part of the Remonstrance. In their straightforward simplicity they believed that the King had caused all the evil that had befallen the nation, and that, for this treason—they counted it nothing less—he ought to suffer a traitor's death. Some, on the other hand, though probably a very few, whilst accepting to its uttermost the charge against the King, held that there was no authority in existence which could bring him legally to his trial, and that, if he was to be put to death at all, he should be put to death by the power of the sword, which was at that time in fact predominant in England.[4]

---

[1] Herbert's *Memoirs*, 95–98.   [2] *Clarendon*, xi. 222.

[3] Herbert's *Memoirs*, 98, 99.

[4] *Clarendon*, xi. 226 ; Major Francis White to Fairfax, Jan. 22, 1649,

It was inevitable that, when once the King's trial appeared actually within reach, some even of those who had eagerly clamoured for bringing him to justice should ask themselves whether it was necessary or even desirable that his blood should be shed. On December 11, an alternative *Agreement of the People* had been laid before Ireton by certain Common Councilmen and other citizens of London. Though it began with attributing to the King all the bloodshed in the late war, its authors did not even ask for his deposition. They contented themselves with demanding 'that if any King of England shall hereafter challenge to himself a negative voice to the determinations of the Representative in Parliament,' or shall refuse the royal assent to laws tendered him by the Commons 'after consultation with the Lords, . . . he may be deposed by the same Parliament, and that any subject assisting him therein was to be treated as guilty of high treason.'[1]

There was too little practical knowledge of the world in this scheme to secure its acceptance; but evidence exists which points to Ireton as withdrawing from the extreme position which he had taken up in the Remonstrance. His view now seems to have been that it would be well to bring the King at once to trial, and then to leave him in prison till he consented 'to abandon his negative voice, to part from Church lands,' and 'to abjure the Scots.' Cromwell even went further than this. In opposition to Ireton, he now asked that the King's trial might be deferred until the subjects, such as Norwich and Capel, who had stirred up the last war[2] had been brought to trial. On or before the 21st the Council of Officers itself rejected, though by only five votes, a

The Copies of several Letters, E. 548, 6. Clarendon's idea is that these men wanted to assassinate Charles. Major White's opinion is as stated in the text.

[1] *Several Proposals*, E. 477, 18.

[2] A letter, dated Jan. 8, 1649, says that :—" Our Councils will not

proposition the actual tenor of which is unknown, but of which the general sense aimed at the taking away of Charles's life.[1]

A letter, written on the 21st by a Royalist agent who was possessed of good information, strengthens the belief that Cromwell was at this time still anxious to save the King's life. It was, writes this person, whose name, real or assumed, was John Lawrans, 'the petty ones of the levelling conspiracy' who were most eager for the death of the King ; 'for now— which is strange to tell—I have been assured that Cromwell is retreating from them, his designs and theirs being incompatible as fire and water, they driving at a pure democracy and himself at an oligarchy ; and it will appear that the wild remonstrance and the present design of taking away the King's life is forwarded by him only to make the Levellers vent all their wicked principles and intentions ; that, having declared themselves, they may become the more odious and abominable, and so be the more easily suppressed, when he see the occasion to take them off and fall openly from them.' The writer's views on Cromwell's motives have but little value. The important point is that he believed Cromwell to be on the side of lenity. He further tells us that when the Council of War was discussing the question of the King's trial, Pride, as

A letter brought in by Pride. he believed at Cromwell's instigation, brought in 'a strange, ranting letter' to the effect that it was irrational to kill Charles I. when Charles II. would be at large—to 'exchange a King in their power for a King out of their power, potent in foreign alliances and strong in the affections of the people.'[2]

---

endure any mediations, no, not hear again of Ireton's proposals—viz., 'that it were perhaps safer to have the King live prisoner for to dispose him a while to abandon his negative voice,' &c." A copy of a letter, Jan. 8, *Carte MSS.* xxiii. fol. 425. Writing on Dec. 21, Grignon states, 'que le différend d'entre Cromwell et Ireton n'est que pour sçavoir si l'on commencera par luy "—*i.e.* the King—"comme veut ce dernier, ou si l'on fera le procès auparavant aux seigneurs et autres personnes principales que l'on tient prisonniers, qui est l'advis de Cromwell.' Grignon to Brienne, Dec. $\frac{21}{31}$, *R.O. Transcripts.*

[1] Grignon to Brienne, Dec. $\frac{21}{31}$, *R.O. Transcripts.*

[2] Lawrans to Nicholas, Dec. 21, *Clarendon MSS.* 2,968. These

A totally different piece of evidence points in the same direction. If there were any two men engaged in public business who were unlikely to countenance violence against the King, they were Whitelocke and Sir Thomas Widdrington, the two legal commissioners for the custody of the Great Seal. Both had abstained from sitting in the House after Pride's Purge. Yet it was with these cautious lawyers and with Lenthall, a man no less cautious, that Cromwell and Colonel Deane had an interview on the 18th. The next day the visit was returned to Cromwell, 'who lay in one of the King's rich beds at Whitehall.' On the 21st Cromwell, this time unaccompanied by Deane, met Lenthall, Widdrington, and Whitelocke, when they 'discoursed freely together about the present affairs and actions of the army and the settlement of the kingdom.' On the 22nd the two lawyers proposed that, with a view to the restoration of the excluded members, the Council of Officers should be requested to give an answer to the messages sent by the House, and that, on the other hand, 'heads for a declaration' should be drawn up to be subsequently embodied in a manifesto, if they could first secure the approval of the Council of Officers as well as of Parliament itself. It can hardly be doubted that the chief condition on which the authors of the proposed manifesto intended to insist was the abandonment of any intention to bring the King to trial.[1]

Dec. 18. Whitelocke and Cromwell.

Dec. 19.

Dec. 21. A conference with the lawyers.

Dec. 22. A proposed manifesto.

It can hardly be doubted that Cromwell and his allies amongst the officers desired at this time to save the King's life, if it was possible to do so without injury to the cause for which they had fought. It is true that, on the 23rd, the House

---

sentiments are so like those of Major White (see pp. 280, 301) that I suspect him to have been the author. If so, Cromwell's complicity is more than doubtful.

[1] *Whitelocke*, 362, 363. Whitelocke, in giving an account of these proceedings, says that he and Widdrington hoped that 'the courses of the army' might 'be moderated—as. it was in some measure at this time— though it brake out again into violence afterwards.'

of Commons appointed a committee to consider how to proceed by way of justice against the King.[1] Lawrans, however,

Dec. 23.
A committee
to consider
the pro-
cedure
against the
King.

A bargain
being
driven.

states that this was no more than a threat, held out with the object of driving a better bargain with Charles. "This," he writes, "is evident by what the Speaker said to a friend of mine in discourse on Saturday night [2]—that if the King came not off roundly now in point of concession, he would be utterly lost ; which saying implies thus much— they have applied themselves, and are now bartering with his Majesty." There would, thought Lawrans, be a trial, but the charges brought against the King would, if these concessions were made, be such as he could answer without difficulty. As for the appointment of the committee by the House of Commons, too much must not be made of it. One of its members, Nicholas Love, had told a friend 'that the charge would be nothing but what he knew the King could clearly acquit himself of.' "Truly, sir," concludes Lawrans, "I have it from good hands—some of them Independents— that what I have here represented is a true draft of their intentions ; but whether his Majesty will comply with them so far as to part with his negative voice and be no more—as I have often said—than a Duke of Venice, which I hear is the hard condition they intend to impose upon him, is not known, and it is very hard to believe." In the end the writer expresses his opinion that, if the negotiation failed, it would be wrecked on this question of the negative voice, and on the demand made for the surrender of the bishops' lands.[3]

Although accuracy of detail is no longer attainable, we are not left wholly in the dark as to the manner in which this last

How the
demand
was made.

overture was made to Charles. Since Pride's Purge, the small number of members attending the House of Lords had become still smaller. Fifteen peers had been present on December 5. On December 6 there were

---

[1] *C.J.* vi. 102.   [2] *i.e.* Dec. 23.

[3] Lawrans to Nicholas, Dec. 25, *Clarendon MSS.* 2,972. Compare the extract given at p. 281, where a third point is added—that Charles shall 'abjure the Scots.'

but seven, and between the 12th and the 19th the highest
number of attendances was seven, and the lowest three. Of
this little group of peers, all of them no doubt seriously
disquieted at the course of events, four—Pembroke,
Salisbury, Denbigh, and North—visited Fairfax on
the 19th. In referring to this visit, the Royalist
Lawrans declares that 'Pembroke, in the name of
the rest, said they came to cast down their honours at his
Excellency's feet, and protested their desire is not to maintain
peerage, or any other privilege whatsoever that might be conceived prejudicial to the public interest.' The officers, added
this writer disdainfully, both scorned and jeered at them ; and
when Fairfax mounted his horse, Denbigh held the stirrup.[1]

Attendances in the House of Lords.

Dec 19. A visit to Fairfax.

No doubt the motives here assigned for the visit of the
peers had their origin in the lively imagination of political
opponents. Its real object may safely be conjectured to have
been the overture about to be made to the King, and this view
of the case is corroborated by the fact that one of the four
peers, the Earl of Denbigh, was chosen to carry that
overture to Charles, as well as by the fact that on
the 21st the Lords fixed a call of their House for
the 28th, the day on which the result of Denbigh's mission
was likely to be known at Westminster.[2] That this mission
had the approval of Cromwell is shown by the urgency with
which the Lieutenant-General, speaking on the 25th,
exhorted the Council of Officers to spare the King's
life as a pure matter of policy, upon his acceptance
of the conditions now offered.[3]

Denbigh's mission to the King.

Dec. 25. Cromwell pleads for the King's life.

For information on Denbigh's proceedings we have to
fall back on the despatches of the French agent, Grignon.
Denbigh, he tells us, was selected because his family
connection with Hamilton [4] enabled him to conceal
the real object of his mission to Windsor under the pretext of

Denbigh at Windsor.

---

[1] Lawrans to Nicholas, Dec. 21, *Clarendon MSS.* 2,968.

[2] *L.J.* x. 636.

[3] So much may be gathered from the hostile account in *Merc. Melancholicus,* E. 536, 27.

[4] Hamilton's wife had been Denbigh's sister.

a visit to the Duke. He seems on his arrival to have expected
Charles to send for him with a view to the discussion of the
terms. As it can hardly be doubted that Charles
had been made cognisant of their general purport,
his omission to invite Denbigh into his presence
may be taken as tantamount to a rejection of the overtures
which he brought.[1]

The King will not see him.

Charles's refusal to admit Denbigh into his presence had
much the same effect on the Council of Officers as the reply
given by him on November 17 to their earlier overtures. On the 25th, after Cromwell's appeal, only a
very small minority—composed, it is said, of no
more than six [2]—had declared in favour of pushing
the conflict with the King to extremities. On the
27th Charles was left entirely without supporters in the same
council. There are no signs of opposition to an order given
on that day that the King should no more be served
upon the knee, that all ceremonies of state to him be
left off, and his attendants be much fewer and at less charge.[3]

Dec. 27. Effect of the King's rejection of their terms on the Council of Officers.

The King's state cut off.

Cromwell's motives for engaging in this last attempt to come
to terms with the King are matter for conjecture only. Yet
apart from his usual habit of hesitating long before
he sanctioned the employment of force to cut knots
which might be disentangled by mutual agreement,
he could not but know that the pleadings of his own
heart were reinforced by every motive of policy. The party
amongst the officers which in November had followed Fairfax

Cromwell's motives for engaging in the nego-tiations,

---

[1] Grignon to Brienne, $\frac{\text{Dec. 25}}{\text{Jan. 4}}$, $\frac{\text{Dec. 28}}{\text{Jan. 7}}$, *R.O. Transcripts.* In the letter
of Dec. 28, Grignon writes that Denbigh had not seen the King, 'quoy-
qu'en effect, ce fust son dessein, qu'ils couvroient de celuy d'aller parler
au Duc d'Hamilton son beau-frère, pour pouvoir mieux laisser croire que
les ouvertures qu'il vouloit faire audit Roy n'estoient point premeditées, et
pour ce il attendoit que le dit Roy le fist appeller : ce qu'il ne voulust pas
faire ainsi qu'il a mandé sans en avoir fait sçavoir la raison ; mais encore
que Cromwell luy veuille faire parler d'accommodement, il est difficille de
croire qu'il desire.' It is inconceivable that Denbigh did not allow a hint
of the subject of his mission to reach the King.

[2] *Merc. Melancholicus*, E. 536, 27.

[3] *Whitelocke*, 365.

CHARLES AND CROMWELL 287

in resisting Ireton's Remonstrance had to be met, whilst outside the army the demand for the King's death was splitting
the party of the political Independents in twain. Vane, who
had been staunch in approving of Pride's Purge, objected to
the King's death, whilst Pierrepont ' expressed much dissatisfaction at those members who sat in the House, and at the
proceedings of the General and army.'

On the other hand, Charles's refusal even to consider the
overtures now made through Denbigh must have put an end
and for to every remnant of hesitation remaining in Crom-
breaking well's mind. The political situation was at least
finally with
the King. cleared, as Charles, by insisting on the retention of
his negative voice, and on the inviolability of the property of
the bishops, had fallen back on his doctrine of his own inde-
feasible sovereignty in the barest possible form. Cromwell
was not one to comprehend the finer shades of Charles's character, or to recognise in the obstinacy with which he clung to
the institutions of the past a conscientious desire to do his best
for the Church and nation. Still less was he likely to discover
that, whatever might have been Charles's duplicity and ignorance of mankind, he was, nevertheless, contending after his
own peculiar fashion for the continuity of settled order, which
the predominance of an army in political affairs must in all
circumstances weaken. It is not in the nature of political strife
to take note of those shades of character and intention which
mitigate the judgment of posterity. At times of crisis the
essential differences appear to stand alone, and when those
differences come to be embodied in two opposing personages, the
battle is joined as between two deadly and irreconcilable foes.

That the battle would end in Cromwell's favour might have
been foretold by anyone capable of entering into the charac-
Charles and ters of the two men. The distinction between the
Cromwell. strength of Cromwell and the weakness of Charles
can hardly be better expressed than in the following words of
a writer who has a deep insight into the recesses of the human
mind :—" A purpose wedded to plans may easily suffer shipwreck ; but an unfettered purpose that moulds circumstances
as they arise, masters us, and is terrible. Character melts to

it like metal in its steady furnace. The projector of plots is but a miserable gambler and votary of chances. Of a far higher quality is the will that can subdue itself to wait and lay no petty traps for opportunity." [1]

Now that the army was again of one mind, the scene of action was transferred to the House of Commons. Here, too,

Dec. 28.
An Ordinance for the King's trial in the Commons.

Dec. 29.

1649.
Jan. 1.

Jan. 2.
Sent to the Lords, accompanied by a resolution. Charles's rejection of the last overture from the army destroyed all opposition, and on the 28th, the House, carrying out the will of the army, read the first time an Ordinance which instituted a special court for the trial of the King. The second reading quickly followed on the 29th, and the Ordinance was finally passed on January 1.[2] On the 2nd it was sent to the Lords, accompanied by a resolution that 'by the fundamental laws of this kingdom, it is treason in the King of England for the time being to levy war against the Parliament and kingdom of England.'[3] The Ordinance itself appointed Chief Justices Rolle and St. John, together with Chief Baron Wilde, to act as judges, and associated with them, to take the place of a jury, 150 commissioners, of whom twenty were to form the quorum.

Before this Ordinance was despatched to the Lords, Cromwell stood up to explain his position. "If any man whatsoever," he is reported to have said, "hath carried on

Cromwell defends his conduct. the design of deposing the King, and disinheriting his posterity ; or, if any man had yet such a design, he should be the greatest traitor and rebel in the world ; but, since the Providence of God hath cast this upon us, I cannot but submit to Providence, though I am not yet provided to give you advice."[4] The reference to Providence was with Cromwell an infallible indication of a political change of front ;

[1] George Meredith's *Evan Harrington*, ch. vii. The words were written without the slightest reference either to Charles or Cromwell.

[2] *C.J.* vi. 105, 106.   [3] *Ibid.* vi. 107.

[4] *L.J.* x. 641 ; Blencowe's *Sydney Papers*, 47 ; *Heads of a Diary*, E. 356, 34 ; *Merc. Pragmaticus*, E. 537, 10. Lawrans to Nicholas, Jan. 8, *Clarendon MSS.* 2,996. Walker told the same story in his *Hist. of Independency*, ii. 54, but it is only from Lawrans that we get the date of the speech.

but it usually needed some strong opposition to put him quite
at his ease in the new position which he was taking up.

Such an opposition at once manifested itself when the
Ordinance reached the House of Lords. Manchester urged

Opposition in the House of Lords.

that the resolution declaring the King to be a traitor
was in contradiction with the fundamental principles
of the law. "Not one in twenty of the people in
England," said Northumberland, "are yet satisfied whether
the King did levy war against the Houses first, or the Houses
first against him ; and, besides, if the King did levy war first,
we have no law extant that can be produced to make it treason
in him to do ; and, for us, my Lords, to declare treason by an
Ordinance when the matter of fact is not yet proved, nor any
law to bring to judge it by, seems to me very unreasonable."
Pembroke declared himself neutral. He loved not, he said, to
meddle with matters of life or death. Denbigh vowed that he
would rather 'be torn in pieces' than sit as a commissioner at
the trial. In the end both Ordinance and resolution were
unanimously rejected, and the House then adjourned for a
week in the expectation that, in the absence of the Lords, the
Commons would find it impossible to proceed.[1]

No merely formal obstacle, however, was sufficient to keep
back from their purpose the men who were now scattered over
the empty benches of the House of Commons. On the 3rd,

1649. Jan. 3. The Commons reject a letter from the Queen.

after summarily rejecting a letter from the Queen, in
which she asked leave to visit her husband in his
misfortunes,[2] they gave a first and second reading to
a new Ordinance creating a High Court of Justice,
and once more passed the resolution thrown out by

A new Ordinance creating a High Court of Justice.

the Lords. It is possible that they had by this time
discovered that the services of the three judges
named in the former Ordinance were not to be
obtained; at all events, no attempt was now made to secure
the assistance of any of the judges. The court was simply to
consist of one hundred and thirty-five commissioners, who
were to assume the functions of both judge and jury.

[1] *Merc. Pragmaticus*, E. 537, 20.
[2] Grignon to Brienne, Jan. $\frac{4}{14}$, *R.O. Transcripts.*

On the 4th the Commons passed three additional resolutions which were strangely democratic as proceeding from so unrepresentative a body:—"That the people are, under God, the original of all just power: that the Commons of England, in Parliament assembled, being chosen by and repres nting the people, have the supreme power in this nation; that whatsoever is enacted or declared for law by the Commons in Parliament assembled, hath the force of law, and all the people of this nation are concluded thereby, although the consent and concurrence of King or House of Peers be not had thereunto." [1]

Jan. 4.
*Three reso-
lutions.*

On January 6 the Act—the name of Ordinance being now dropped [2]—was finally passed.   Its preamble declared it to be notorious 'that Charles Stuart, the now King of England, not content with those many encroachments which his predecessors had made upon the people in their rights and freedoms, had a wicked design totally to subvert the ancient and fundamental laws and liberties of this nation, and, in their place, to introduce an arbitrary and tyrannical government; and that, besides all other evil ways and means to bring this design to pass, he hath prosecuted it with fire and sword, levied and maintained a cruel war in the land against the Parliament and kingdom, whereby the country hath been miserably wasted, the public treasure exhausted, trade decayed, thousands of people murdered, and infinite other mischiefs committed; for all which high and treasonable offences the said Charles Stuart might long since justly have been brought to exemplary and condign punishment.   Whereas also the Parliament, well hoping that the restraint and imprisonment of his person, after it had pleased God to deliver him into their hands, would have quieted the distempers of the kingdom, did forbear to proceed judicially against him, but found by sad experience that such their remissness served only to encourage him and his com-

Jan. 6.
*Passing of
an Act for
a High
Court of
Justice.*

*Its
preamble.*

---

[1] *C.J.* vi. 110, 111.

[2] *C.J.* vi. 113.   The Act itself is printed in the *State Trials*, iv. 1,046.   There is a MS. copy of it in the Thomason Tracts (E. 357, 35), dated Jan. 3, and still styled an Ordinance.

plices in the continuance of their evil practices and in raising of new commotions, rebellions, and invasions; for prevention therefore of the like or greater inconveniences, and to the end no chief officer or magistrate whatever may hereafter presume traitorously and maliciously to imagine or contrive the enslaving or destroying of the English nation, and to expect impunity for so doing,' certain persons were appointed 'for the hearing, trying, and adjudging the said Charles Stuart.'

Unlike the resolution which accompanied the first Ordinance, this preamble, passing rapidly over the legal and constitutional aspect of the case, lays stress upon the practical consideration that a nation cannot suffer itself to be subjected to the will of one man, still less to be kept by that man in a perpetual turmoil. Charles was to be brought to trial mainly because, as long as he lived, England could have no peace, and because his successors needed to be taught that they would be held responsible if they imitated his example.

Though there is not a tittle of evidence, one way or the other, it is not unlikely that the practical character of this Act was in some way owing to the influence of Cromwell. Outside. Parliament, at least, he was showing his dislike of theoretical solutions of political difficulties. On the day on which the Act creating a High Court of Justice passed the House, the Council of Officers, again taking up the *Agreement of the People*, discussed the clause fixing the date of the dissolution on April 30, 1649. Ireton, always prone to abide by constitutional theory, supported the retention of the clause as giving the only possible security for a speedy return to a system of representative government, whilst Cromwell declared that it would ' be more honourable and convenient for' the members of the House 'to put a period to themselves.'[1] The majority of the Council of Officers indeed sided with Ireton, and the clause was therefore retained ; but the course of events was soon to teach those who now voted against Cromwell that the cause to which they were devoted would suffer shipwreck if

[1] *Clarke Papers*, ii. 170.

the possessors of whatever shred of legal authority still remained in existence on the Parliamentary side were alienated by a threat to deprive them of a power to which, for reasons selfish and unselfish, they clung with desperate tenacity. It would be easy for them to argue that, in the midst of the crisis evoked by the trial and execution of the King, it would be fatal to the cause of which they were the champions to plunge the country into the turmoil of a general election.[1]

[1] Cromwell, in short, in act if not in words, anticipated the well-known advice of President Lincoln, not to swop horses when crossing a stream.

CHAPTER LXX.

THE HIGH COURT OF JUSTICE.

How strongly opinion was running against the course taken by the House of Commons became manifest on January 8, when the High Court of Justice met for the first time in the Painted Chamber. Out of the hundred and thirty-five persons named as commissioners or judges, only fifty-two appeared. Fairfax, indeed, was there, as well as Cromwell and Ireton. Amongst the colonels of the New Model Army in attendance were Sir Hardress Waller, Pride, Whalley, Harrison, Ewer, Hewson, and Goffe. Lord Grey of Groby, Ludlow, Marten, and Hutchinson, who were also present, had, indeed, never served in that army, but they had, in one capacity or another, held commands on the side of Parliament. The civilian members were less conspicuous. It was probably on account of the thinness of the attendance that the Court without proceeding to business adjourned itself to the 10th, first ordering proclamation to be made of its next sitting. This order, however, bore no more than thirty seven signatures. Fairfax not only abstained from signing, but he never appeared in the Court a second time.[1]

It is not unlikely that the Lords, when they met on the 9th, after a week's adjournment, were encouraged by these abstentions to take up a position of their own. They appointed a committee to draw up an Ordinance to the effect 'that whatsoever King of England shall hereafter levy war against the Parliament and Kingdom of England shall be guilty of high treason and be

1649.
Jan. 8.
First meeting of the Court.
A poor attendance.

Jan. 9.
The Lords take the question in hand.

[1] *State Trials*, iv. 1,052.

tried in Parliament.'[1] As, however, the course thus proposed left Charles still King of England, it did not offer even as much security as would result from his deposition, and the minority who now swayed the House of Commons had no mind to content themselves even with his deposition. They had come to the conclusion that ' stone dead hath no fellow,' and that as long as Charles lived there would be no peace in the land.

It was, moreover, unlikely that any suggestion made by the Lords, whatever its nature might be, would meet with favour in the Commons. Though they had hitherto kept up intercourse with the other House, the Com-mons had claimed the right of passing Acts of Parliament without its sanction, and when some Ordinances relating to public business were now sent down to them, it was only by a majority of 31 to 18 that the messengers were admitted, and by a majority of 33 to 19 that a formal answer was returned that the House would send an answer by messengers of its own. That answer was never sent, and day after day the Lords contented themselves with business of such a nature as not to necessitate application to the other House. On their part, the Commons gave a clear indication of the direction in which they were tending by order-ing that a new great seal should be engraved in which all share in government was implicitly denied to the House of Lords. On one side was to be a map of England and Ireland, with the arms of the two countries ; on the other a representa-tion of the House of Commons with the inscription : " In the first year of freedom, by God's blessing restored, 1648." [2]

The Commons having thus asserted their claim to supreme Parliamentary authority, left the field open for the action of the High Court of Justice. When the Court met again on the 10th, forty-five members only being present, it chose as its president Serjeant Bradshaw, one of the very few lawyers who were prepared to countenance

Communi-cation be-tween the Houses broken off.

A new great seal.

Jan. 10.
Bradshaw President of the Court.

---

[1] *L.J.* x. 642. The suggestion has a certain resemblance to that made on December 11 by some London citizens. See p. 281.

[2] *i.e.* 1648/9.

the revolutionary proceedings against the King.   Various preliminary arrangements were made on the 12th and 13th, and
on the 15th the number of attendances having risen

Jan. 12-25.
Preliminary
sittings of
the Court.
to fifty-six, a draft of the charge against the King
was read.   On the 17th it was ordered that Charles

Jan. 17.
The King to
be brought
to Cotton
House.
should be lodged in Cotton House—formerly the
residence of Sir Robert Cotton—on account of its
close proximity to Westminster Hall, the place appointed for the trial.   It was also ordered that during
the sessions of the Court, the Hall should be guarded by a
strong force of soldiers, and that barricades should be set up to
keep off the pressure of the crowd.   It was finally decided that
the trial should begin on the 20th.[1]

In the presence of this great resolve it was impossible to
obtain the attention of practical men for those questions relating to the ultimate depository of constitutional authority which
had appeared all-important to theoretical politicians like Lil-

Jan. 15.
The *Agree-
ment of the
People* com-
pleted,
burne.   On the 15th, indeed, the Council of Officers
completed the *Agreement of the People*; Lilburne,
however, having discovered that the officers intended
to present the document to the Commons instead of
circulating it for signature amongst the people and compelling its
adoption by the House, had for some days past withdrawn from
the discussion.   He justly regarded a mere request to a body
of the nature of the existing House of Commons that it should
make way for another elected on more popular principles as

Jan. 20.
and laid
before the
House.
little better than a farce.   When on the 20th the
officers laid the Agreement before the House, they
humbly begged the Commons to take it into consideration and to circulate so much of it as they thought fit
amongst the people, adding a request to the well-affected
amongst them to notify their acceptance of it by appending
their signatures.[2]   The officers obviously intended to create a
new constituency of 'the well-affected' only.   But they were
in no mood to press their point, and when the House returned

---

[1] *State Trials*, iv. 1,055–1,063.

[2] *An Agreement of the People*, E. **539, 2**; *Legal Fundamental Liberties*, p. 35, E. **560, 14**.

the purely dilatory answer that the Agreement should be taken
into consideration as soon as 'the necessity of the present
weighty and urgent affairs would permit,'[1] they ac-
quiesced without a murmur.   Cromwell's prevision
that it would be impossible to induce the House to attend
to the formation of a new constitution whilst the life and death
of the King hung in the balance was justified by the event.[2]

A dilatory
answer.

On the actual question of the day Cromwell's mind was no
less fully made up.   The idea that it would be wiser to dethrone Charles than to put him to death had naturally found favour in many quarters.   Even amongst
the more zealous members of the sects this idea was
not entirely absent.   On December 29 a certain
Elizabeth Pool made her way into the room in which
the Council of Officers was sitting, to tell them that she had
learnt by a vision that the army was the chosen instrument of
God for the healing of the nation ; and on January 5
she reappeared, to inform the officers that, though
God had permitted the army to imprison the King,
He forbade them to put him to death.[3]   What was
more serious was that a large number of the Independent statesmen, who had shared with Cromwell
the burden and heat of the late struggle, would have
nothing to do with the King's execution.   What
Cromwell said to his 'dear brother' Vane we do not know ;
but when young Algernon Sidney made the purely legal objection that 'first, the King can be tried by no court ; secondly,
no man can be tried by this court,' Cromwell dashed away the
appeal to mere constitutional legality.   "I tell you," he re-
torted fiercely, "we will cut off his head with the Crown upon
it."[4]   The legal formulas which had fenced the majesty of the
King had ceased to be applicable.

Question of
deposing the
King raised.

1648.
Dec. 29.
Elizabeth
Pool's vision.

1649.
Jan. 5.
She wants
the officers
not to put
Charles to
death.

Jan. 20.
Views of
some of the
Independent
statesmen.

On January 19 Charles was brought from Windsor to
St. James's Palace.   The secret of his removal had been so

[1] *C.J.* vi. 122.   [2] See p. 291.
[3] *Clarke Papers*, ii. 150 ; *A Vision*, E. 537, 24.
[4] A. Sidney to Leicester, Oct. 12. 1660.   Blencowe's *Sydney Papers*,
237.

well kept that nothing was known of it till his actual arrival.
On the morning of the 20th, the day on which the trial

Jan. 19.
The King
brought to
St. James's. was to begin, he was carried in a sedan chair to
Whitehall, whence he was subsequently taken to
Cotton House by water, with the evident intention

Jan. 20.
and to Cot-
ton House. of evading a popular demonstration in his favour.[1]
When he landed at the foot of the steps which led
up from the river to the garden of the house, the court by

A session of
the Court in
the Painted
Chamber. which he was to be tried was already sitting privately
in the Painted Chamber, engaged in settling the best
mode of dealing with eventualities which might occur
in the course of its proceedings.   It is said that Cromwell,
catching sight of the King passing from the river through the
garden of Cotton House, reminded his fellow-commissioners
that they must be ready with an answer if Charles should
demand by what authority they sat ; and that Marten, after an
interval of silence, gave the reply : " In the name of the Commons in Parliament assembled, and all the good people of
England." [2]

Whether these words were actually used or not, the Court
almost immediately after Charles's arrival adjourned to West-

The Court in
Westminster
Hall. minster Hall, where seats were set for its members
on the raised daïs at the upper or southern end.   A
bar had been fixed across the Hall also on the daïs,

Prepara-
tions for the
trial. and in front of this, after some hesitation, Bradshaw
directed that a chair, covered with crimson velvet,
should be set for the King immediately facing the judges.
Behind this chair was a space reserved for the guards under

---

[1] Grignon to Brienne, $\frac{\text{Jan. 22}}{\text{Feb. 1}}$, *R.O. Transcripts*.   On the morning of
the 20th Vane, who had of late absented himself ' by scruple of conscience,
as it was said, came again and sat in the House of Commons.'   Leicester's
Diary, *Blencowe*, 54.   He may have come in order to use what influence
he had against a death-sentence.

[2] The story was told by Sir Purbeck Temple at Marten's trial after
the Restoration (*State Trials*, v. 1,201).   Temple said that he witnessed
the scene through a hole in the wall, and that Cromwell ran back from
the window ' as white as the wall.'   Neither of these statements is very
probable, but the story, if it be not true, was at least well invented.   As
printed Marten's answer runs, ' The Commons and Parliament.'

WESTMINSTER HALL AND THE SURROUNDING BUILDINGS.

A.A. Windows, from one of which Cromwell saw the King coming through Cotton Garden.

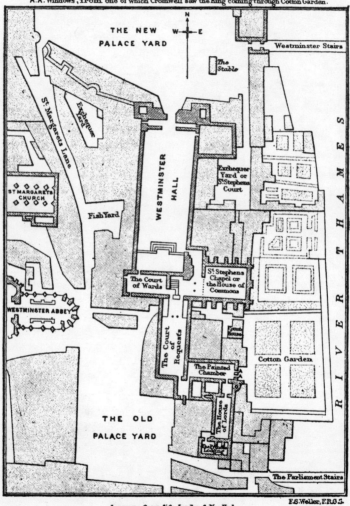

THE NEW PALACE YARD

N W E

Westminster Stairs

The Stable

Exchequer Yard

St Margarets Lane

St MARGARETS CHURCH

Fish Yard

WESTMINSTER HALL

Exchequer Yard or St Stephens Court

WESTMINSTER ABBEY

The Court of Wards

St Stephens Chapel or the House of Commons

The Court of Requests

The Painted Chamber

Cotton Garden

RIVER THAMES

THE OLD PALACE YARD

The House of Lords

The Parliament Stairs

Longmans, Green & Co, London & New York.

F.S. Weller, F.R.G.S.

Hacker, who were appointed to secure his person, and behind them, again, were drawn up a large number of soldiers under Colonel Axtell, whose duty it was to keep back the crowd, which was freely admitted through the great entrance at the northern end of the Hall.   On either side of the Court, at the corners of the Hall, were two galleries, filled with ladies and other privileged persons.   It was doubtless in fear of danger from this quarter that Bradshaw provided himself with the shot-proof hat which is still preserved in the Ashmolean Museum at Oxford.

When the roll was called, sixty-eight of the judges answered to their names.   To that of Fairfax the only response was a cry from masked lady in the gallery—afterwards ascertained to be Lady Fairfax: " He has more wit than to be here." [1]   As soon as the call was over, the King, having been brought in by the guards, took his seat.   He gazed round at the soldiers, but, as might have been expected, showed no sign of respect to the Court. [2]

Lady Fairfax's cry.

Charl s brought in.

The charge was read by John Cook, who had been appointed solicitor of the Commonwealth for the purposes of this trial.   In the main it followed the lines of the Act on which it was based, alleging that Charles Stuart, King of England, having been 'trusted with a limited power to govern by and according to the laws of the land, and not otherwise, had attempted to erect an unlimited and tyrannical power to rule according to his will, and, in pursuance of this design, had levied war against the present Parliament, and the people therein represented.'   Then, after reciting instances in which Charles had appeared in arms during the first war, the charge proceeded to accuse him of being the author of the second war, and of the revolt of the fleet.   Since that time, it was alleged, he had issued commissions to the ' Prince and other rebels and foreigners, and ' also to 'Ormond, and to the Irish rebels and revolters associated with him.'   On these grounds, Cook impeached Charles Stuart ' as a tyrant, traitor, murderer, and a public and implacable enemy of the Commonwealth of England.' [3]

The charge read.

[1] *Clarendon,* xi. 235.   [2] *State Trials,* iv. 1,069.   [3] *Id.* iv. 1,070.

Those who promoted this charge threw their case away by forsaking the political ground on which they were strong for Weakness of the legal case against Charles. the legal ground on which they were weak. In Charles they had to do with the man who of all others was most capable of taking advantage of their error. Even whilst Cook was still speaking, Charles had attempted to interrupt him by touching the sleeve of his gown with a silver-headed cane. The head of the cane fell off, and Charles, accustomed, even at Carisbrooke and Hurst Castle, to be waited on by those who were ready to anticipate his slightest wish, looked round in vain for someone to pick it up. For a moment his loneliness was brought home to him, as it had never been before. Yet he quickly recovered himself, stooping to pick up what he had lost, and being able, on hearing himself styled a traitor, to burst into a laugh.[1]

When Cook had completed his task, Bradshaw called on the King to answer to the charge, 'in the behalf of the Commons Charles called on to answer. assembled in Parliament and the good people of England.' Once more Lady Fairfax's voice was raised. Another interruption from Lady Fairfax. "It is a lie," she said; "not half, nor a quarter of the people of England. Oliver Cromwell is a traitor." Axtell, losing his temper, ordered his men to fire into the gallery; but the men, better advised, disobeyed the order, and Lady Fairfax was induced to leave the Court.[2]

When the disturbance was at an end, Charles, as Cromwell Charles questions the authority of the Court. had foreseen, asked by what authority he had been brought to the bar. There were, he said, many unlawful authorities in the world, such as thieves and robbers. He refused to reply to the charge against him, till that preliminary question had been answered.

[1] "Also the head of his staff happened to fall off, at which he wondered; and seeing none to take it up, he stooped for it himself." *State Trials*, iv. 1,074. This seems more probable than that, as was said at the time, he regarded the fall of the head of the cane as ominous of his own impending fate.

[2] I take the full form as given by the Chief Justice at Axtell's trial (*idem*, v. 1,146). Axtell did not deny the statement that he ordered the men to fire, and the story may therefore be regarded as true, at least in its main points.

Bradshaw replied that the prisoner was where he was by the authority of the people of England, by whom he had been

A warm controversy. elected King. It was but to introduce one more controversial point into a controversy sufficiently heated before. Charles declared that he was king by inheritance, not by election. For him to answer, except to lawful authority, would be to betray his trust and the liberties

The King withdrawn. of the people. After this, Charles was removed to Cotton House, the soldiers, as he passed, shouting "Justice ! Justice !" at Axtell's bidding. From the lower end of the hall to which civilian spectators were admitted, counter cries were raised of "God save the King !"

Argumentatively, the victory lay with Charles; but it was hard for the Court to acknowledge the weakness of its reason-

Jan. 22. Another wrangle. ing, and, on the 22nd, he was brought back to the bar that he might once more hear from Bradshaw's lips a reassertion of that authority of the Court which he had defied two days before. Being perfectly devoid of fear, and careless whether he saved his life or lost it, Charles now spoke out yet more plainly than on the previous occasion. "It is not," he said, "my case alone ; it is the freedom and liberty of the people of England ; and do you pretend what you will, I stand more for their liberties ; for, if power without law may make laws, may alter the fundamental laws of the kingdom, I do not know what subject he is in England that can be sure of his life, or anything that he calls his own." [1] Charles's reasoning was not unanswerable ; but it could not be satisfactorily answered by those who were attempting to give a legal form to a revolutionary proceeding, and after a prolonged altercation Bradshaw had no choice but to order the removal of the prisoner.

What effect the King's language must have had upon persons untouched by party spirit may be judged from a

Effect of the King's language. letter addressed to Fairfax by Major White, who, in 1647, had been temporarily expelled from the army for avowing that there was at that time no power in England excepting that of the sword.[2] He now reverted to

[1] *State Trials*, iv. 1,082.   [2] See vol. iii. 362.

the same idea. "I do not understand," he wrote, "how it' (that is to say, the taking away of the King's life) "may be done by any legal authority, according to the kingly government : though it may be a just thing, yet I know not how it may justly be done. I never heard of any throne erected on earth either by God or men for the judging of a king, until the erecting of this late tribunal at Westminster. . . . If it be thoroughly examined, we may find that the King hath no other right to the military, regal, and legislative power than the sword did constitute and invest him with by Divine permission, the people submitting thereto for fear, and to avoid greater [1] mischief ; but now, the King and his party being conquered by the sword, I believe the sword may justly remove the power from him, and settle it in its original fountain next under God — the people ; but to judge or execute his person I do not understand any legal authority in being can justly do it. I doubt not but the sword may do it ; but how righteous judgment that may be, that God and future generations will judge. It is clear that the military power is exalted above the regal and legislative power, and is now come to the throne of God and under no other legal judgment until there be a legal authority erected as is offered in the *Agreement of the People*, to which it may submit ; and seeing God hath, in righteousness, for the sins of the people and their king, brought us into this unhappy condition, I therefore plead with your Excellency to use the sword with as much tenderness as may be to preserve the lives of men, and especially the life of the King."

Major White's argument.

"I am not against judging the person of the King," continued White ; "but I say it is by no legal authority but only what the sword exalteth. Although it be not an exact martial court, yet it is little different, and not a legitimate authority to the King. Yet it may as justly judge him as ever he judged the people, and may dethrone him and divest him of all power and authority in the English nation ; and I think it is necessary so far to proceed and to detain him a prisoner of war till he may be delivered with safety to yourself and the

[1] 'greatest' as printed.

nation. . . . I do not understand any essential good can accrue to the people by the taking away his life, for it is not so much the person that can hurt as the power that is made up in the kingly office by the corrupt constitution ; for if the person be taken away, presently another layeth claim to the kingly office, and, for anything I know, hath as much right to the dominion as his predecessor had, and will questionless have all the assistance that this person can procure for the attaining thereof, and will be able to do more mischief because he is at liberty, and this [1] under your power." [2]

To such reasoning, based on considerations of practical expediency, the Court was as impervious as it was to Charles's

The Court impervious to his objections. reasonings based on considerations of constitutional legality. It was only with the latter that it was officially called upon to deal, and it could not, even if it had wished to do so, now abandon the position that it had

Jan. 23. Another attempt to make Charles plead. legal authority over the King. On the 23rd another attempt was made to bring the King to plead, but there was nothing to be spoken on either side that had not been already said, and before Charles was, for the third time, removed, Bradshaw directed the clerk to

His default recorded. 'record his default.' The Court then adjourned to a private session in the Painted Chamber, announcing its intention to reassemble in Westminster Hall

Intention to sentence him as contumacious. on the following morning. From the language of Cook and Bradshaw there can be little doubt that the more active spirits amongst the judges had resolved to treat the King as contumacious, and to proceed without delay to pronounce judgment against him.

Jan. 24. Postponement of the public sittings. When, however, the clock struck ten on the morning of the 24th, the crowd which had gathered to witness the scene was informed that the Court was sitting in the Painted Chamber, and that there would be no public session on that day.

---

[1] *i.e.* this one.

[2] White to Fairfax, Jan. 22, *The Copies of several Letters,* E. 548, 6. The paragraph about danger from the Prince makes it likely that White was the author of the letter mentioned at p. 282, note 2.

What little is known of the internal proceedings of the Court points to dissensions between its members as being the

Dissensions among the members of the Court. cause of this unexpected decision. Some of those who had consented to sit as judges had done so with considerable qualms of conscience.[1] Others, like Nicholas Love,[2] may have persuaded themselves that the result of the trial would be a surrender on the part of the King, whilst there were others again who wished the proceedings to terminate in his mere deposition. Much, too, had occurred during the last few days to shake the resolutions of some of those who had been at first inclined to support a harsher sentence. Not only had the bearing of the King been dignified and his appeal to the law convincing, but there could be no shadow of doubt that the Court was thoroughly

A Presbyterian argument. unpopular. The Presbyterian clergy had preached heartily in the King's favour, and had drawn up an

Jan. 21. Hugh Peters's sermon. argumentative criticism of the claim of the Court to try him,[3] which was hardly counterbalanced by a fiery sermon preached on the previous Sunday by Hugh Peters from the text, " To bind their kings in chains and their nobles in fetters of iron."

Far more serious was the possibility that all this seething disquietude might find a leader in Fairfax, whose great popu-

Fairfax's position. larity in the army would make it difficult to persist in a design which he resolved actively to oppose.[4] Fairfax, however, had not sufficient decision of character to take a decided course of his own, and he remained now, according to his usual habit, as politically helpless as he was vigorous in the field.

---

[1] Downes may be taken as a specimen of this class. *State Trials*, v. 1,210.   [2] See p. 284.

[3] *An Apologetical Declaration*, E. 539, 9. This was published on the 24th.

[4] " Sunday was se'nnight," *i.e.* Jan. 21, " Cromwell put a guard upon Fairfax, accusing him of an intention to deliver the King." News from Rouen, $\frac{Jan. 31}{Feb. 10}$, *Carte MSS.* xxiii. fol. 395. If this had been true, something would have been heard of it from other quarters, but it is more than probable that Cromwell was at this time anxious about Fairfax.

The wave of feeling passing over England gave additional weight to the protests raised by a body of Scottish commis-
Protests of the Scottish Commis-sioners. sioners, who with Lothian at their head had recently arrived from Edinburgh. On three occasions—on the 6th, the 19th, and the 22nd—they denounced, in the name, first, of the Committee of Estates, and, secondly, of the Scottish Parliament, the proceedings taken against the King.[1] The alliance between Cromwell and Argyle had been too artificial to last long, and had now entirely broken down. When the new Scottish Parliament, summoned by Argyle, met on January 4, it declared strongly against the trial, partly, no doubt, through abiding affection towards the native King of Scotland ; partly also through the dread of the dangerous predominance of the Independent army.[2]

Even on the 23rd there were signs of an attempt on the part of those who directed the proceedings of the Court to
Jan. 23. Signs of division. conciliate opposition, as the crime charged against the King of being a tyrant, traitor, and murderer then dwindled, in the mouth of the clerk, to his having been guilty of 'divers high crimes and treasons.'[3] Judging from the course taken on the 24th, there is strong reason to believe that when, on the 23rd, the Court held a private sitting after the King had been removed for the third time, there was a revolt against the proposal to put him to death as contumacious.

However this may have been, when the judges again met on the morning of the 24th, not, as had been proclaimed on
Jan. 24. A meeting in the Painted Chamber. the preceding day, in Westminster Hall, but in the Painted Chamber, it was announced that the Court was about to take evidence for its own satisfaction, a course which cannot be regarded as anything else than a mere device for gaining time, whilst an effort was being made to heal the existing divisions. It is certain that the depositions, the reading of which occupied two days, served

---

[1] *A Letter from the Commissioners of Scotland*, E. 539, 11.
[2] *Acts of the Parl. of Scotl.*, vi. part ii. 140.
[3] *State Trials*, iv. 1,098.

no other purpose. They referred, for the most part, to the presence of the King at the head of his army on various

Jan. 24, 25.
Evidence
produced.

occasions, and they were followed by the reading of papers, the contents of which have not been handed down, but which were probably concerned with the messages sent by the King at various times to invite foreign armies into England.[1]

Such evidence could convince no one who was not convinced already, and the real interest of the two days lay in the

The evi-
dence
worthless.

arguments and solicitations of those who were most eager to obtain the King's conviction ; though assuredly neither they, nor the other members of the court based their convictions on the details now painfully recited in the Painted Chamber. The attendance was scanty, and though there were three roll-calls during the two days, Ireton's name does not appear on any one, whilst that of Cromwell, though only once lacking, appears on the list as eleventh on one occasion, and eighteenth on another. It is, therefore, probable that on both days he came into Court some time after the commencement of the proceedings.[2]

Ireton and Cromwell were no doubt busily employed in steeling the hearts of the weak. "The general," wrote an

Cromwell
and Ireton
busy.

observant spectator, "was baited with fresh dogs all Tuesday night,[3] to bring him into the Hall on the morrow to countenance the business ; but by no means would he consent."[4]

Cromwell fancied it possible to convince even the Scots. With them, we are told on what is perhaps sufficient

Cromwell
argues with
the Scots.

authority for the main drift of his reasoning,[5] he 'entered into a long discourse of the nature of the regal power according to the principles of Mariana and Buchanan.[6] He thought a breach of trust in the King ought to

---

[1] *State Trials,* iv. 1,099.   [2] *Ibid.* iv. 1,099, 1,100, 1,111.

[3] *i.e.* the night of the 23rd

[4] Lawrans to Nicholas, Jan. 26. *Clar. St. P.* ii. li.

[5] Burnet, *Hist. of his Own Time,* i. 42. Burnet was told this by Lieut.-Gen. Drummond, who was present.

[6] It is hardly likely that Cromwell quoted either, and least of all

be punished more than any crime whatsoever; he said, as to their covenant, they swore to the preservation of the King's person in defence of the true religion: if, then, it appeared that the settlement of the true religion was obstructed by the King, so that they could not come at it but by putting him out of the way, then their oath could not bind them to the preserving him any longer. He said, also, their covenant did bind them to bring all malignants, incendiaries, and enemies to the cause to condign punishment, and was not this to be exercised impartially? What were all those on whom public justice had been done, especially those who suffered for joining with Montrose, but small offenders acting by commission from the King, who was, therefore, the principal, and so the most guilty.'

Such were the arguments which it may be supposed that Cromwell also addressed with some alteration to his English colleagues. Not the technical breach of the law by appearing in arms at Edgehill or Naseby was the rock of offence with him, but the breach of trust and the calculated design to suppress what he held to be the true religion.

When the dreary reading of evidence came to an end on the 25th, it appeared that Cromwell had not argued in vain.[1]

Jan. 25.   It was resolved 'that the court will proceed to
A prelimi-   sentence against Charles Stuart, King of England;
nary resolu-   that the condemnation of the King shall be for
tion.
tyrant, traitor, and murderer; that the condemnation of the King shall be likewise for being a public enemy to the Commonwealth of England; that this condemnation shall extend to death.'[2] Those who passed this resolution, however, numbered only forty-six, and it was probably on this ground that the votes were declared to be merely preliminary and not bind-

Mariana. Burnet or Drummond probably meant that Cromwell's principles were those held by Mariana and Buchanan.

[1] It was said by some of the regicides when they were tried that threats were used. Mrs. Hutchinson, however, who hated Cromwell, declares that there was nothing of the kind (*Life of Col. Hutchinson*, ed. Firth, ii. 159). After the Restoration the regicides were, of course, interested in describing themselves as threatened, and persuasion from the mouth of the master of the army would sound very like a threat.

[2] *State Trials*, iv. 1,113.

ing on the Court. At the same time a committee was appointed to draw up a sentence on the King, with a blank for the manner of his death.

On the morning of the 26th, no less than sixty-two commissioners assembled in the Painted Chamber. The struggle

Jan. 26.
The sentence
accepted by
the Court.

between the resolute and irresolute was now approaching its termination. Those who had a definite aim before them carried the day, gaining their object on all points of importance. They now procured the assent of the whole Court to a sentence upon the King which had been drafted by the Committee appointed at the last sitting, according to which Charles 'as a tyrant, traitor, murderer, and public enemy to the good people of this nation, shall be put to death by the severing of his head from his body.'[1] The specific charge of high treason was not mentioned, probably to meet the scruples of those who urged that it could only be committed legally against the person of a king.

On a minor point the sterner members of the Court had to submit to a compromise. As late as the 24th they intended

Was the
King to be
sentenced
as contu-
macious?

that the King should not be heard again, and that the sentence should be pronounced on him as contumacious in his absence,—as appears from his removal on that day from Cotton House in the immediate neighbourhood of Westminster Hall to St. James's Palace,—and it is highly probable that they were still of the same mind on the 25th, and even on the morning of Friday, the 26th. On the last-named day, however, the idea of condemning him in his absence was definitely abandoned, as appears from a clause added to the sentence then adopted from the report of the Committee, to the effect 'that the King

The King
to be
brought to
hear his
sentence.

be brought to Westminster to-morrow to receive his sentence.' By far the most probable hypothesis is that this addition was called forth by the reluctance of some of the judges to proceed further without giving the King one more chance of pleading for his life. How strong was their unwillingness to proceed to extremities is manifested by their refusal to sign the death-warrant—in which

[1] *State Trials,* iv. 1,121.

the charge of high treason definitely reappears—though it had not only been drawn up on the evening of the 25th or the morning of the 26th, but had already been signed by some of their more resolute colleagues. There can be little doubt that those who had thus prepared and signed it expected that the King would be sentenced as contumacious on the 26th, and would be executed on the following day, the 27th.[1] At all

---

[1] The late Mr. Thoms, in a series of articles in *Notes and Queries* for July, 1872 (reprinted in pamphlet form in 1880 under the title of *The Death Warrant of Charles I.*), reproduced, as far as its reproduction is possible in type, the original warrant now in the library of the House of Lords. The following copy is therefore taken from Mr. Thoms's pamphlet.

The Death Warrant of Charles I.

At the high Coᵍt of Justice for the tryinge and iudginge of Charles
Steuart Kinge of England January xxix.ᵗʰ Anno Dñi 1648.

Whereas Charles Steuart Kinge of England is and standeth convicted attaynted and condemned of High Treason and other high Crymes, And sentence *vppon Saturday last* pronounced against him by this Coᵍt to be putt to death by the severinge of his head from his body Of wᶜʰ sentence execucõn yet remayneth to be done, These are therefore to will and require you to see the said sentence executed *In the* open Streete before Whitehall vppon the morrowe being the Thirtieth day of this instante moneth of January betweene the houres of Tenn in the morninge and *Five* in the afternoone of the same day wᵗʰ full effect And for soe doing this shall be yoʳ sufficient warrant And these are to require All Officers and Souldiers and other the good people of this Nation of England to be assistinge vnto *you in* this Service Given vnder oᵍ hands and Seales

To *Colonell Ffrancis Hacker, Colonell* Huncks
and Lievtenant Colonell Phayre and to every of
them.

				Valentine Wanton	L.S.
				Symon Mayne	L.S.
				Tho Horton	L.S.
				J. Jones	L.S.
Jo. Bradshawe	L.S.	Per. Pelham	L.S.	John Moore	L.S.
Tho. Grey	L.S.	Ri. Deane	L.S.	Gilbt. Millington	L.S.
O. Cromwell	L.S.	Robert Tichborne	L.S.	G. Fleetwood	L.S.
Edw. Whalley	L.S.	H. Edwardes	L.S.	J. Alured	L.S.
M. Liuesey	L.S.	Daniel Blagraue	L.S.	Robt. Lilburne	L.S.
John Okey	L.S.	Owen Rowe	L.S.	Will. Say	L.S.
J Dañers	L.S.	William Purefoy	L.S.	Anth. Stapley	L.S.
Jo. Bourchier	L.S.	Ad. Scrope	L.S.	Greg. Norton	L.S.
H. Ireton	L S.	James Temple	L.S.	Tho. Challoner	L.S.
Tho. Mauleuerer	L.S.	A. Garland	L.S.	Tho. Wogan	L.S.
Har. Waller	L.S.	Edm. Ludlowe	L.S.	John Venn	L.S.
John Blakiston	L.S.	Henry Marten	L.S.	*Gregory Clement*	L.S.
J. Hutchinson	L.S.	Vinct. Potter	L S.	Jo. Downes	L.S.
Willi. Goff	L.S.	Wm. Constable	L.S.	Tho. Wayte	L.S.
Tho. Pride	L.S.	Rich. Ingoldesby	L.S.	Tho. Scot	L.S.
Pe. Temple	L.S.	Willi. Cawley	L.S.	Jo. Carew	L.S.
T. Harrison	L.S.	Jo. Barkestead	L.S.	Miles Corbet	L.S.
J. Hewson	L.S.	Isaa. Ewer	L.S.		
Hen. Smyth	L.S.	John Dixwell	L.S.		

events it is capable of proof that those who signed on the 26th
were not more in number than twenty-eight, if indeed they

The words in italics have been written over erasures, except the
signature of Gregory Clement, which is merely erased.   The word
'thirtieth' is spread out so as to occupy a space large enough to contain
'twenty-sixth' or 'twenty-seventh.'

From the evidence of the erasures in the death warrant, Mr. Thoms
argued that it was originally drawn up not later than the 26th, the date
to which he assigned it.   In three articles in the *Athenæum* for Jan. and
Feb. 1881, Mr. Reginald Palgrave argued at length that the date assigned
to the warrant by Mr. Thoms was not early enough, and that it was
really drawn up on the afternoon of the 23rd or the morning of the 24th.
Whilst acknowledging the service rendered by him in pointing out the
signs of hesitation in the Court from the 23rd to the 26th, I find myself
unable to concur in his main proposition.

His belief is that there was a preliminary sentence given on the 23rd
and a warrant founded on it, but that they were held back in consequence
of the Scottish remonstrance on the 22nd.   That the Scottish remonstrance had some part in the delay is likely enough, but the attitude of
the Scots had been known since the 6th, and I cannot but think that
internal dissensions in the Court and the opposition of Fairfax had more
to do with the matter.   This is, however, a mere question of opinion,
and it is also unnecessary to dwell on Mr. Palgrave's mistake in speaking
of a Presbyterian party in the Court itself.

As Mr. Palgrave cannot produce any official evidence of a sentence
delivered on Jan. 23, he has recourse to two passages, one in Mrs.
Hutchinson's *Memoirs* and the other in those of Ludlow, to show that
the King was sentenced on the third day of the trial - the 23rd.   Mrs.
Hutchinson (ed. Firth, ii. 152) writes thus : ' The King refused to plead,
disowning the authority of the Court, and after three several days persist-
ing in contempt thereof was sentenced to suffer death.'   I can see nothing
in these words except a compressed statement that the King was heard on
three days and afterwards sentenced to death.   Mrs. Hutchinson wrote
long after the time from general recollection, and if she had had a curious
piece of secret history to reveal she would surely have been more explicit.
Ludlow is still less to the point.   He, too, mentions the three days, and
then (ed. 1751, i. 241) says that 'the Court adjourned into the Painted
Chamber ; and, upon serious consideration, declared the King to be a
tyrant, traitor, murderer, and a public enemy to the Commonwealth.'
Ludlow, who is never particular about dates, did not, I presume, think it
necessary to specify that the serious consideration occupied two days
whilst witnesses were examined for form's sake.

On the other hand, there is the strongest *primâ facie* evidence that

were so many.[1] No doubt only a radical misunderstanding of Charles's character could lead to the supposition that he might be induced by the terror of death to descend from the high position which he had taken up on the 23rd; but there were men sitting in that Court ready to resort to any subterfuges in the vain hope of delaying the fatal day a little longer.

Accordingly the death warrant was set aside for the time. On Saturday, the 27th, Charles was once more brought to the

Jan. 27.
The King again at the bar.

bar of the Court, sixty-seven commissioners being present. As he entered the hall, cries for 'justice and execution' were loudly raised. Stopping an attempt made by Charles to speak, Bradshaw opened the

the date selected by Mr. Thoms—the 26th—was the one which it was intended to bear, though it may have been actually written out on the evening of the 25th. The death warrant in its unaltered parts refers to a sentence pronounced against Charles to be executed by beheading for treason 'upon the morrow.' The 27th was a Saturday, and as Puritans would not, as Mr. Palgrave argues, have imagined it possible to fix the execution for a Sunday, the ostensible date of the warrant cannot be later than Friday, the 26th, the day on which the Court would have sentenced Charles *in contumaciam*, if that course had been adopted. On the other hand, we have no positive evidence of any weight to induce us to accept an earlier date for the warrant.

Mr. Palgrave's negative evidence appears to me equally unsatisfactory. As the warrant directed in unaltered words that the execution should take place on the following day, he argues that it could not have been drawn up on the 26th, because the 27th was fully occupied with the sitting of the Court in which Charles was actually sentenced. This argument would be deserving of consideration if it could be shown that those who drew up the death warrant expected things to take the turn they did. It vanishes if we accept what appears to me the very probable hypothesis, that those who prepared the warrant and dated it on the 26th, expected the Court to sentence the King as contumacious, and without hearing him again to have him executed on the 27th. I cannot see that there is any knot to be unravelled which makes it worth while to have recourse to what is in itself a very improbable explanation without a scrap of direct evidence in its favour.

[1] Garland, whose name stands twenty-ninth, stated (*State Trials*, v. 1,215), when tried in 1660, "I do confess this; I sat and on the day of sentence signed the warrant for execution." This is, to my mind, a plain statement that he signed it on the 27th.

proceedings with a narrative showing the past forbearance
of the Court. Charles, he said, had been called to answer
Bradshaw's speech. in the name of the people of England. At this
point he was interrupted by a cry of 'Not half the
people!' from a lady present.[1] As soon as order was restored Bradshaw went on to say that, upon the contumacy
of the prisoner and the notoriety of the fact, the Court had
agreed upon a sentence, but that, as the prisoner had expressed a wish to be heard, it was ready to listen to him
provided that he did not question its jurisdiction Charles
replied by protesting that he had taken his course through
regard for the liberties of his subjects and not at all for his
Charles appeals to Parliament. own interests, and ended by asking to be heard
before the Lords and Commons in the Painted
Chamber. In other words, he wished to appeal
from the Court to a political assembly.

To consider this point the Court adjourned for half an
hour, the more readily, it was afterwards alleged, because one
of their number, John Downes, was about in spite of Cromwell's anger to rise and startle the audience by pleading
publicly that the King's request might be granted.[2] On its
The King's request rejected. return the Court declared against Charles's request,
and, after two more attempts made by the King to
reopen the question, Bradshaw made a long speech,
Bradshaw cites pre-cedents. in which, after quoting the precedents of the depositions of Edward II., Richard II., and Mary,
Queen of Scots, and arguing that Charles had planned the
destruction of the realm, he called on the clerk to read the
formal sentence. In vain Charles pleaded for permission to
The sen-tence read. answer Bradshaw's imputations. He was told that
it was too late, and the formal sentence upon him of
being beheaded as a traitor was then read.

After this Bradshaw called on the members of the Court
to testify their approval by standing up. Not a member

---

[1] *A Continuation of the Narrative*, E. 540, 14.

[2] *State Trials*, v. 1,210–13. All stories told against Cromwell at the
trial of the regicides must, of course, be received with suspicion.

remained seated. The work of the day was at an end. In
vain the King called out to be heard. Bradshaw at once

The Court approves.

Charles removed.

interrupted him on the ground that the sentence
had been already given. In broken words Charles
uttered his protest whilst he was being dragged
away. "I am not suffered to speak," were his last
words ; "expect what justice other people will have." [1] Cries
of " Justice, justice ! " were again raised as he was for the last
time led away.

[1] *A Continuation of the Narrative,* E. 540, 14; *State Trials,* iv.
1,116.

CHAPTER LXXI.

THE LAST DAYS OF CHARLES I.

As soon as the fatal sentence had been pronounced, Charles was led back to Cotton House, and then, after a short delay,

Jan. 27. Charles removed to Whitehall.

Jan. 28. Juxon reads prayers.

Charles taken to St. James's.

removed to Whitehall, where he was allowed to spend the night. On Sunday, the 28th, he listened with reverent devotion to the prayers of the Church read to him by Bishop Juxon, who had been allowed to visit him now that he was lying under sentence of death.[1] At five o'clock in the afternoon he was conducted back to St. James's,[2] perhaps in order that the preparations for his execution might not reach his ears.

Words very different from those consolations which Juxon addressed to the King resounded on that Sunday morning in the Chapel of Whitehall, where Hugh Peters preached

Hugh Peters preaches at Whitehall.

before the members of the High Court of Justice in justification of those who were seeking the King's death.[3] There was need of all his rude eloquence if those judges who had not yet given their signatures to the death warrant were to be steeled to the work before them. The protests against any attempt to act on that sentence were

---

[1] In his letter of the 26th Lawrans states that Juxon was allowed to see the King on the 25th. This is, I believe, a mistake. See *C.J.* vi. 123, and Leicester's diary in *Blencowe*, 57.

[2] *The Moderate*, E. 540, 20.

[3] Extracts from his sermons were given at his trial (*State Trials*, v. 1,131-34), but there is some difficulty in assigning any one of them either to this sermon or to the one delivered on the previous Sunday.

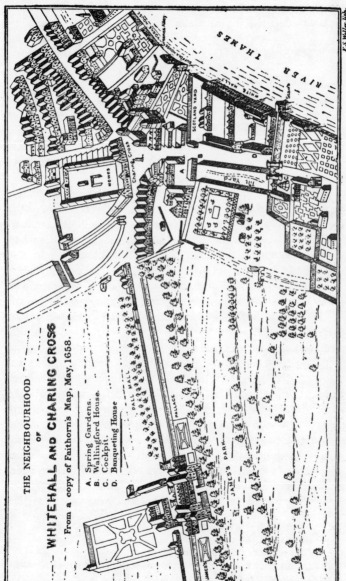

THE NEIGHBOURHOOD
OF
WHITEHALL AND CHARING CROSS

From a copy of Faithorn's Map, May, 1658.

A. Spring Gardens.
B. Wallingford House.
C. Cockpit.
D. Banqueting House

Longmans, Green & Co. London & New York.

many and loud. On the 29th the members of the Assembly
of Divines joined in supplicating for the King's life,[1] and on
Jan. 29.
Efforts to
save the
King's life. the same day two Dutch ambassadors, who had
been specially despatched from the Netherlands
for the purpose, made a similar request to the
House of Commons.[2] It was also reported that Fairfax had
urged the Council of Officers in the same direction,[3] whilst it
was no secret that the Prince of Wales had sent a blank sheet
of paper, signed and sealed by himself, on which the Parliament might inscribe any terms they pleased. That the vast
majority of the English people would have accepted this offer
gladly was beyond all reasonable doubt.[4]

It was but a small knot of men—a bare majority, if they
were even that, amongst the sitting members of the High
A resolute
minority. Court of Justice itself—who had fixedly determined
that there should be no relenting ; but they had
Cromwell amongst them, and Cromwell's will, when once his
mind had been made up, was absolutely inflexible. They
had, moreover, behind them the greater part of the rank and
file of the army, to whom the shortest issue seemed the best.

The first difficulty encountered by those who were bent on
carrying out the sentence of the Court was that of obtaining
Jan. 27.
Difficulty of
obtaining
signatures
to the death
warrant, signatures to the death warrant in sufficient numbers
to give even an appearance of unanimity amongst
the judges. On Saturday, the 27th, a few more
signatures had been added to those obtained on the
26th, but on the morning of Monday, the 29th, not only were
many still wanting, but there was reason to believe that some
of the judges who had already signed would refuse to repeat
their signatures if called on to do so. Yet it was impossible to
make use of the warrant in its existing condition. It had been,
as there is little doubt, dated on the 26th, and it presupposed
a sentence passed on that day, whereas it was notorious that

[1] Evidence of Corbet at Harvey's trial, *State Trials*, v. 1,197.

[2] *C.J.* vi. 125.

[3] *The Kingdom's Faithful Scout*, E. 541, 5.

[4] A facsimile of this sheet of paper forms the frontispiece of Ellis's
Original Letters, ser. I. vol. iii.

no sentence had been passed till the 27th.   Under these circumstances the natural course of proceeding would have been
which bore   to re-copy the warrant with altered dates and to
an incor-   have it signed afresh.   What was actually done was
rect date.   to erase the existing date, and to make such other
alterations as were requisite to bring the whole document into
conformity with actual facts.   Of the names of the three officers
finally charged with the execution of the sentence, Hacker,
Huncks, and Phayre, that of Huncks alone was unaltered.
The names over which those of Hacker and Phayre were
written are now illegible, but they can hardly fail to have been
those of men who shrank from carrying out the grim duty
assigned to them.[1]

Having by this extraordinary means secured the retention
of the signatures already given, the managers of the business,
How more   whoever they were, applied themselves energetically
signatures   to increase the number.   The testimony of those
were ob-   regicides who pleaded after the Restoration that
tained.
they had acted under compulsion must, indeed, be received
with the utmost caution ; but there is no reason to doubt that
considerable pressure was put upon those judges who having
agreed to the sentence now showed a disinclination to sign the
warrant.   In all the stories by the regicides on their defence
Cromwell takes a prominent place, and it is easy to understand
how meanly he must have thought of men who, after joining
in passing the sentence, declined to sign the warrant.   When
those members of the Court who were also members of Parliament took their places in the House, Cromwell is reported
to have called on them to sign without further delay.   "Those
that are gone in," he said, "shall set their hands.   I will have
their hands now."[2]

Later in the day, when the warrant lay for signature on
a table in the Painted Chamber, the scene grew animated.
It is said that Cromwell, whose pent-up feelings sometimes
manifested themselves in horseplay, drew an inky pen across

[1] The evidence for all this is given in Thoms's *Death Warrant of
Charles I.*, the warrant itself being in the library of the House of Lords.

[2] *State Trials*, v. 1,219.

Marten's face, and that Marten inked Cromwell's face in
return.[1] According to another story, which was for a long time
accepted as true, Cromwell dragged Ingoldsby to the
table, and forced him to sign by grasping his hand
with a pen in it.[2] The firmness of Ingoldsby's signa·
ture, however, contradicts the latter part of the assertion,
though it is possible that some kind of compulsion was previously used to bring him to the point.

A scene in the Painted Chamber.

On the whole it will be safe to assume that great pressure
was put, sometimes in rough military fashion, on those who
hung back.   On the other hand, there was no evidence given by any of the regicides, when put upon
their trial, of any definite threats being used against
those who made difficulties about signing.   Downes, indeed,
who did not sign at all, described himself as having been
frightened into assenting to the judgment, but he had nothing
to say about any ill effects resulting to him on account of his
refusal to sign.[3]

Nature of the pressure employed.

In one way or another fifty-nine signatures were at last
obtained.   Nine out of the sixty-seven who had
given sentence did not sign ; but, on the other hand,
Ingoldsby, who signed the warrant, had been absent
when the sentence was passed.

Number of the signa- tures.

Meanwhile, Charles was awaiting his certain fate with quiet
dignity at St. James's.   Ever since the commencement of the
trial he had been annoyed by the presence of soldiers
drinking and smoking even in his bedroom.   Colonel
Tomlinson, who had a general superintendence over the
arrangements for his personal accommodation, was a man of
humanity and discretion, and did his best to check the insolence of the men ; but Hacker, who commanded the soldiers,
was less considerate.   Yet even Hacker was induced, a few
nights before the trial was ended, to leave the King's bedchamber free, and this particular form of insult was not repeated.[4]

Charles at St. James's.

[1] *State Trials,* v. 1,200.   [2] *Clarendon,* xvi. 225.
[3] *State Trials,* v. 1,212.
[4] Evidence at Hacker's trial, *ibid.* v. 1,176 ; *Herbert,* 123.

On the morning of the 29th Charles burnt his papers, including the keys of his ciphered correspondence.[1] His two

Jan. 29.
Charles
burns his
papers, and
is visited by
his children. youngest children were then admitted to see him for the last time. Elizabeth, who had just completed her thirteenth year, was a delicate child, and had taken her father's misfortunes so deeply to heart that during the first days of the trial she was reported to have died of sorrow. Her brother, the little Duke of Gloucester, was still in his tenth year.

Both the children burst into tears when they met their father's eye. Charles took them on his knees, telling his

His last
words to his
daughter, daughter not to sorrow overmuch as he was about to die a glorious death 'for the laws and liberties of this land and for maintaining the true Protestant religion.' He then recommended her to 'read Bishop Andrewes's Sermons, Hooker's Ecclesiastical Polity, and Bishop Laud's book against Fisher.' As for himself, he added, he had forgiven all his enemies, and hoped that God would also forgive them. He then charged his daughter to let her mother know 'that his thoughts had never strayed from her, and that his love should be the same to the last.' More followed of the outpourings of a father's heart, ending with an injunction to the girl to forgive those who were now bringing him to the scaffold, but never to trust them, 'as they had been most false to him.'

Charles had spoken to Elizabeth as to one come to years of discretion. He addressed his son in language suitable to

and to his
son. his younger age. " Sweetheart," he said, " now they will cut off thy father's head ; mark, child, what I say : they will cut off my head and perhaps make thee a king ; but, mark what I say : you must not be a king so long as your brothers Charles and James do live ; for they will cut off your brothers' heads when they can catch them, and cut off thy head too at the last, and therefore I charge you do not be made a king by them." " I will sooner be torn in pieces first ! " cried the gallant boy, gladdening his father's heart by his words. In the end Charles divided his jewels between the children,

[1] *The Moderate*, E. 540, 20.

retaining only the George cut in onyx and surrounded by diamonds. After many tears and embracings he dismissed them both, returning to prayer in the company of Juxon and Herbert.[1]

On the morning of the 30th, the day appointed for his execution, Charles rose early. Herbert told him that he had dreamt of Laud's coming into the room and kissing his old master's hand. Charles had no thoughts to waste upon dreams, and merely replied " It is re-markable." " Herbert," he continued, " this is my second marriage-day. I would be as trim to-day as may be ; for before night I hope to be espoused to my blessed Jesus." Then turning to things of earth—" Let me have," he said, " a shirt on more than ordinary, by reason the season is so sharp as probably may make me shake, which some observers may imagine proceeds from fear. I would have no such imputa-tion ; I fear not death. Death is not terrible to me : I bless my God I am prepared."

Jan 30. Charles's last morn-ing.

After a while Juxon arrived, and as soon as the gifts in-tended for the children had been set aside, Charles spent half an hour with him in private prayer. Then, in Herbert's presence, the Bishop read the morning service. By a re-markable coincidence the lesson for the day was the twenty-seventh chapter of Matthew, which contains the narrative of the Passion of the Lord. After the close of the service Charles continued in prayer and meditation till Hacker knocked at the door to summon him to Whitehall. Charles at once prepared to obey, and, accompanied by Tomlinson and Juxon, and closely followed by Herbert, walked across St. James's Park between a double row of soldiers. When he arrived at Whitehall, he was allowed to rest for some time. Having eaten a piece of bread and drunk a glass of wine, he betook himself to prayer for the remainder of his allotted time.[2]

He is con-ducted to Whitehall.

[1] The relations of this scene, two of them by the Princess Elizabeth herself, first appeared in an early edition of *Eikon Basilikè*, published in 1649, *i.e.* on or after March 25.

[2] Thus far I have followed Herbert, though with grave misgivings as to his accuracy of detail.

In the meanwhile strange preparations were being made on the scaffold which had been erected in front of the Banqueting House. Charles's refusal to plead before the Court had given rise to an idea that he might also refuse to submit voluntarily to the execution of the sentence which it had pronounced against him. Staples were therefore hammered into the floor of the scaffold to afford a purchase for ropes,[1] by aid of which, if any resistance were offered, the King could be forced down into the prone attitude in which victims were at that time beheaded. The delay in leading out the King was, however, too great to be accounted for by the time required for completing this arrangement, and it is not unlikely that the execution was deliberately postponed till the House had passed an Act forbidding the proclamation of any successor.[2] It was not till two o'clock that Charles was finally summoned to his earthly doom.[3]

Preparations on the scaffold.

The execution delayed.

When Charles stepped out upon the scaffold—probably from the central window of the Banqueting House [4]—the only friend who followed him was Juxon, Herbert having begged to be excused from witnessing the painful sight. No other persons were admitted to a place on the scaffold excepting Colonels Hacker and Tomlinson and the two masked figures of the executioner and his assistant. Below was a crowded mass of men and women who had come, for the most part, with sorrowing hearts, to witness Charles's last moments upon earth. To them he would gladly have confided that last appeal to his subjects which he had been forbidden to make when he was hurried away from the Court ; but the ranks of soldiers, horse and foot, drawn up immediately round the foot of the scaffold rendered all communication

Charles on the scaffold.

---

[1] *State Trials*, v. 1,127, 1,128.

[2] It was not passed till the beginning of the afternoon sitting. *C.J.* vi. 125.

[3] *Moderate Intelligencer*, E. 541–4.

[4] See Mr. Wyatt Papworth's argument in *Notes and Queries*, 3rd ser. iv. 195. This view is corroborated by Grignon's statement that Charles entered the scaffold 'par une des fenestres de la grande salle de Whitehall.' Grignon to Brienne, Feb. $\frac{1}{11}$, *R.O. Transcripts*.

impossible.   Charles therefore addressed himself to Juxon and Tomlinson, declaring that not he, but the Parliament, had ori-

His last
speech.   ginated the Civil War.   He then prayed that his enemies might be forgiven, and protested against the subjection of the country to the power of the sword.   Nothing, he said, would prosper till men gave their dues to God, to the King, and to the people.   For their duty to God, he recommended the convocation of a national synod freely chosen. For their duty to the King, it was not for him to speak. "For the people," he continued, "truly I desire their liberty and freedom as much as anybody whatsoever; but I must tell you that their liberty and freedom consists in having government, those laws by which their lives and their goods may be most their own.   It is not their having a share in the government ; that is nothing appertaining unto them.   A subject and a sovereign are clean different things ; and, therefore, until you do that—I mean that you put the people in that liberty— they will never enjoy themselves." [1]

After another protest against the rule of the sword, and a declaration made at Juxon's instance, that he died 'a Christian

A confession
of faith.   according to the profession of the Church of England,' Charles prepared for death.   With the assistance of

Charles
prepares
for death.   the executioner,[2] whose features as well as those of his assistant were effectually concealed by a mask, he confined his straggling locks within a white satin nightcap. He then exchanged with Juxon a few words of religious consolation, after which, placing in the Bishop's hands the George which he wore round his neck, he addressed to him the simple word 'Remember,' meaning, probably, to impress on him the importance of delivering the messages to the Prince and others with which he had already charged him.

Having bidden the executioner to refrain from striking till

[1] Fuller, in his *Church History*, xi. 41, says that this speech was not correctly taken.   It can hardly be more than verbally inaccurate, as neither Juxon nor Tomlinson ever hinted that any correction was needed.

[2] There has always been a doubt as to the name of the executioner, but the evidence at Hulet's trial (*State Trials*, v. 1,185) points to Brandon, the ordinary hangman.

he stretched out his hands as a sign that he was ready, Charles laid himself down, placing his neck on the low block provided.[1]

The execution. After a short delay, he made the signal agreed on. The axe fell, and the kingly head, with its crown of sorrows, dropped upon the scaffold. The executioner caught it up, and, holding it aloft, pronounced the accustomed formula, "Behold the head of a traitor!" A loud groan of horror and displeasure was the answer of the people to the announcement. They, at least, had no part in that day's deed. So hostile was their attitude, that orders were given to two troops of horse to patrol up and down the street in order to disperse the angry crowd.[2]

[1] 'S'est luy mesme depouillé et mis par terre.' Grignon to Brienne, Feb. $\frac{1}{11}$, *R.O. Transcripts*. A Spanish account of the execution, to which my attention has been drawn by Major Hume (*Add. MSS.* 28,470, fol. 162), says that there was placed in the middle of the scaffold 'un leño de pie y medio de largo y medio de alto.' The block was therefore eighteen inches long and six high. These two passages, and the evidence of a rough woodcut in a contemporary broadside, of which a copy may be seen in my *Students' History of England*, is all that I need add to the controversy on the subject of the high and low block carried on in the newspapers in the summer of 1890. The author of *The Bloody Court* agrees with Grignon. That pamphlet, however, which has recently been alleged by Mr. Thorpe, in a paper read before the Society of Antiquaries on Feb. 26, 1891, and also in a communication to *The Antiquary* for May 1891, to be a contemporary production of high value, was really, as has been shown by Mr. Firth (*Academy*, Sept. 19, 1891), compiled after the Restoration. The greater part of it is reprinted with slight alterations from Τὸ ξειφος [*sic*] των μαρτυρων, E. 637, 2, published July 10, 1651, and the rest from other pamphlets. Since his letter in the *Academy* was written, Mr. Firth has found a pamphlet in the Bodleian Library, "Hugh Peters' Figures, printed for George Horton, living in Fig Tree Court in Barbican, 1660," thus disposing of Mr. Thorpe's argument that no book could have been printed by Horton so late as in that year. Mr. Firth is inclined to attribute *The Bloody Court* to Gauden, and adds that if this be the case 'no statement contained in it can be received without independent confirmation.' Mr. Freeman suggested to me that the sentence for treason being, in the case of men, to be hanged, drawn, and quartered, a low block would be more convenient than a high one for beheading a corpse, and that the same block was likely to be used in the exceptional cases when beheading was substituted by the grace of the sovereign for the ordinary sentence.

[2] *State Trials*, v. 1,185.

The King's body was at once placed in a coffin, and covered with a velvet pall. For some days it lay in the chamber at Whitehall in which Charles had spent his last minutes before his summons to the scaffold.

The disposal of the King's body.

It was there carefully embalmed, and when that operation had been accomplished was removed to St. James's. A request that it might be buried in Henry the Seventh's Chapel having been refused, Juxon and Herbert were allowed to inter their dead master in St. George's Chapel at Windsor. The sad procession set out from St. James's on February 7.

Feb. 8.
The King's funeral.

On the 8th, the funeral at Windsor was attended by Richmond, Hertford, Southampton, Lindsey, and Juxon. As the coffin was brought to the chapel snow began to fall, and gave to the pall, as the little company loved to remember, 'the colour of innocency.' The White King, as men named him—calling to memory the white satin dress in which, unlike his predecessors, he had clothed himself at his coronation, and the omens of disaster which were believed to be connected with the name—was borne to the grave in silence. Juxon had prepared himself to read the burial service from the Book of Common Prayer, but Which-cott, the governor of the Castle, forbade him to use any other form but that of the Directory. The coffin was then lowered into the vault which had been opened to receive it—the same in which Henry VIII. and Jane Seymour had been buried more than a century before.[1]

Those who brought Charles to the scaffold strengthened the revulsion of feeling in his favour which had begun to set in ever since it had been clearly brought home to the nation that its choice lay between the rule of the King and the rule of the sword. It is indeed true that the feeling hostile to the army was not created by the execution of Charles, but its intensity was greatly strengthened by the horror caused by the spectacle of sufferings so meekly endured.

Charles's own patience, and the gentleness with which he met harshness and insult, together with his own personal dignity, won hearts which might otherwise have been steeled

[1] Herbert's *Memoirs*, 135–144.

against his pretensions. The often-quoted lines of Andrew Marvell set forth the impression which Charles's bearing on the scaffold produced on even hostile spectators :—

> He nothing common did or mean
> Upon that memorable scene,
>   But with his keener eye
>   The axe's edge did try ;
> Nor called the gods, with vulgar spite,
> To vindicate his helpless right ;
>   But bowed his comely head
>   Down, as upon a bed.

Marvell's verses embodied his own recollections of the external dignity of the man. A little book, which under the title of *Eikon Basiliké* was issued with calculated timeliness to the world on February 9,[1] the day after the King's funeral, purported to be the product of Charles's own pen, and aimed at being a spiritual revelation of the inmost thoughts of the justest of sovereigns and the most self-denying of martyrs. Its real author, Dr. John Gauden,[2] a nominally Presbyterian divine, caught with great felicity the higher motives which were never absent from Charles's mind, and gave to the narratives and meditations of which the book consisted enough of dramatic veracity to convince all who were prepared to believe it that they had before them the real thoughts of the man who had died because he refused to sacrifice law and religion to an intriguing Parliament and a ruffianly army. The demand for the book was well nigh unlimited. Edition after edition was exhausted almost as soon as it left the press. The greedily devoured volumes served to create an ideal image of Charles which went far to make the permanent overthrow of the monarchy impossible.

The ideal thus created had the stronger hold on men's minds because it faithfully reproduced at least one side of

Feb. 9. Eikon Basiliké.

[1] The copy in the Museum Library (E. 1,096), marked by Thomason ' The first impression,' is also noted by him as being issued on ' Feb. 9th.'

[2] Mr. Doble's letters in *The Academy* for May 12, 26, June 9, 30, 1883, have finally disposed of Charles's claim to the authorship of the book.

Charles's character. The other side—his persistent determination to ignore all opinions divergent from his own, and to
The two sides of Charles's character. treat all by whom they were entertained as knaves or
fools—had been abundantly illustrated in the course
of the various negotiations which had been carried
on from time to time in the course of the Civil War. It
His claim to the Negative Voice, finally led to a struggle for the possession of that
Negative Voice which, if only the King could suc-
ceed in retaining it, would enable him to frustrate
all new legislation even when supported by a determined
national resolve. On the one side was undoubtedly both law
and uncom-promising attitude. and tradition ; on the other side the necessity of
shaping legislation by the wishes of the nation,
and not by the wishes of a single man or of a single
class.

Fortunately or unfortunately, such abstract considerations
seldom admit of direct application to politics. It is at all
times hard to discover what the wishes of a nation really are,
and least of all can this be done amidst the fears and passions
of a revolutionary struggle. Only after long years does a
nation make clear its definite resolve, and for this reason wise
statesmen—whether monarchical or republican—watch the
currents of opinion, and submit to compromises which will
enable the national sentiment to make its way without a succession of violent shocks. Charles's fault lay not so much in
his claim to retain the Negative Voice as in his absolute disregard of the conditions of the time, and of the feelings and
opinions of every class of his subjects with which he happened
to disagree. Even if those who opposed Charles in the later
stages of his career failed to rally the majority of the people to
their side, they were undoubtedly acting in accordance with a
permanent national demand for that government of compromise
which slowly but irresistibly developed itself in the course of
the century.

Nor can it be doubted that, if Charles had, under any
conditions, been permitted to reseat himself on the throne, he
would quickly have provoked a new resistance. As long as
he remained a factor in English politics, government by com-

promise was impossible. His own conception of government was that of a wise prince constantly interfering to check the madness of the people. In the Isle of Wight he wrote down with approval the lines in which Claudian, the servile poet of the Court of Honorius, declared it to be an error to give the name of slavery to the service of the best of princes, and asserted that liberty never had a greater charm than under a pious king.[1] Even on the scaffold he reminded his subjects that a share in government was nothing appertaining to the people. It was the tragedy of Charles's life that he was entirely unable to satisfy the cravings of those who inarticulately hoped for the establishment of a monarchy which, while it kept up the old traditions of the country, and thus saved England from a blind plunge into an unknown future, would yet allow the people of the country to be to some extent masters of their own destiny.

Charles's conception of politics.

Yet if Charles persistently alienated this large and important section of his subjects, so also did his most determined opponents. The very merits of the Independents— their love of toleration and of legal and political reform, together with their advocacy of democratic change—raised opposition in a nation which was prepared for none of these things, and drove them step by step to rely on armed strength rather than upon the free play of constitutional action. But for this, it is probable that the Vote of No Addresses would have received a practically unanimous support in the Parliament and the nation, and that in the beginning of 1648 Charles would have been dethroned, and a new government of some kind or other established with good hope of success. As it was, in their despair of constitutional support, the Independents were led in spite of their better feelings to the employment of the army as an instrument of government.

The Independents driven to rely on the army.

The situation, complicated enough already, had been still further complicated by Charles's duplicity. Men who would

[1] " Fallitur egregio quisquis sub Principe credit
Servitium ; nunquam libertas gratior extat
Quam sub Rege pio."—*Herbert*, 45.

have been willing to come to terms with him, despaired of
any constitutional arrangement in which he was to be a factor ;
Charles's
duplicity. and men who had long been alienated from him
were irritated into active hostility. By these he was
regarded with increasing intensity as the one disturbing force
with which no understanding was possible and no settled order
consistent. To remove him out of the way appeared, even to
those who had no thought of punishing him for past offences,
to be the only possible road to peace for the troubled nation.
It seemed that so long as Charles lived deluded nations and
deluded parties would be stirred up, by promises never intended to be fulfilled, to fling themselves, as they had flung
themselves in the Second Civil War, against the new order of
things which was struggling to establish itself in England.

Of this latter class Cromwell made himself the mouthpiece.
Himself a man of compromises, he had been thrust, sorely
Cromwell
and Charles. against his will, into direct antagonism with the
uncompromising King. He had striven long to
mediate between the old order and the new, first by restoring
Charles as a constitutional King, and afterwards by substituting one of his children for him. Failing in this, and angered
by the persistence with which Charles stirred up Scottish
armies and Irish armies against England, Cromwell finally
associated himself with those who cried out most loudly for
the King's blood. No one knew better than Cromwell that it
was folly to cover the execution of the King with the semblance of constitutional propriety, and he may well have
thought that, though law and constitution had both broken down,
the first step to be taken towards their reconstruction was the
infliction of the penalty of death upon the man who had shown
himself so wanting in that elemental quality of veracity upon
which laws and constitutions are built up. All that is known
of Cromwell's conduct at the trial—his anger with Downes's
scruples and the pressure which he put upon those who were
unwilling to sign the death-warrant—point to his contempt for
the legal forms with which others were attempting to cover an
action essentially illegal.

Tradition has handed down an anecdote which points to

the same explanation of the workings of Cromwell's mind. "The night after King Charles was beheaded," it is said, "my

<small>Cruel necessity.</small> Lord Southampton and a friend of his got leave to sit up by the body in the Banqueting House at Whitehall.[1] As they were sitting very melancholy there, about two o'clock in the morning they heard the tread of somebody coming very slowly upstairs. By-and-by the door opened, and a man entered very much muffled up in his cloak, and his face quite hid in it. He approached the body, considered it very attentively for some time, and then shook his head, sighed out the words, 'Cruel necessity !' He then departed in the same slow and concealed manner as he had come. Lord Southampton used to say that he could not distinguish anything of his face ; but that by his voice and gait he took him to be Oliver Cromwell.' [2]

Whether the necessity really existed or was but the tyrant's plea is a question upon the answer to which men have long

<small>Was there a necessity?</small> differed, and will probably continue to differ. All can perceive that with Charles's death the main obstacle to the establishment of a constitutional system was removed. Personal rulers might indeed reappear, and Parliament had not yet so displayed its superiority as a governing power to make Englishmen anxious to dispense with monarchy in some form or other. The monarchy, as Charles understood it, had disappeared for ever. Insecurity of tenure would make it impossible for future rulers long to set public opinion at naught, as Charles had done. The scaffold at Whitehall accomplished that which neither the eloquence of Eliot and

---

[1] I gather from Herbert's narrative that the body was at once placed in the room in which Charles passed the last hours before he was conducted through the Hall. The substitution of the Hall for the room is, however, of little moment in deciding upon the general accuracy of this tradition.

[2] Spence's *Anecdotes*, 286. Spence heard the story from Pope, and there need have been only one intermediate narrator between Pope and Southampton. The story has the appearance of truth, especially as any-one inventing it at the end of the seventeenth or the beginning of the eighteenth century would have been likely to ascribe Cromwell's conduct to personal ambition, not to a sense of 'cruel necessity.'

Pym nor the Statutes and Ordinances of the Long Parliament
had been capable of effecting.

So far the work of Cromwell and his associates had been
purely negative. They had overthrown everything ; they had
constituted nothing. They fondly hoped that when the obstacle to peace had been removed they would be able securely
to walk in the ways of peace. It was not so to be. The sword
destroys but it can do no more, and it would be left for others
than the stern warriors who guarded the scaffold of the King
to build up slowly and painfully that edifice of constitutional
compromise for which Cromwell had cleared the ground.

INDEX.

Bideford, holds out for the Parliament, i. 139; surrenders, 207

Birch, John, Colonel, brings on the battle of Cheriton, i. 323; takes part in the surprisal of Hereford, iii. 21; joins in defeating Astley at Stow-on-the-Wold, 79

Birmingham, sacked by Rupert, i. 107

Birr Castle, taken by Preston, i. 122

Bishop, Captain, declares against the man of blood, iv. 7

Bishop's lands, vested in trustees, iii. 145

Bishops, *see* Episcopacy

Blackheath, the Kentish insurgents appoint a rendezvous at, iv. 136; occupied by Fairfax, *ib.*; the Earl of Norwich at, 144

Blake, Robert, Colonel, defends a fort at Bristol, i. 357; takes part in the defence of Lyme, *ib.*; is governor of Taunton, ii. 94; prepares to resist a siege, 183; defence of Taunton by, 208; reduces Dunster Castle, iii. 92

Blasphemy and heresy, ordinance against, in committee, iii. 139; passes, iv. 122

Blechington House, taken by Cromwell, ii. 201

Blewbury, Cromwell and Waller advance to, ii. 53

Bloody Tenent of Persecution, The, publication of, i. 288

Blue Boar, the, a letter of the king's intercepted by Cromwell and Ireton at, iv. 29

Boarstall House, attacked by Fairfax, ii. 237; surrenders, iii. 109

Boconnock, occupied by the royalists, ii. 13

Bodmin, Hopton retreats to, iii. 66; occupied by Fairfax, 67

Bolingbroke, Earl of, 1624 (Oliver St. John), votes for Fairfax's commission, ii. 190

Bolton, stormed by Rupert, i. 366

Bolton Castle, reduction of, ii. 377

Boreman, Thomas, Captain, appointed one of those in charge of the Isle of Wight in Hammond's absence, iv. 255; declares himself powerless to resist the attempt to remove the king to Hurst Castle, 257; admits that there is a design to carry off the king, 258

Boroughs, Jeremiah, one of the five Dissenting Brethren, i. 261

Boston, retreat of Willoughby to, i. 191; meeting of parliamentary commanders at, 240

Boswell, Sir William, intercepted letter of, iv. 83

Boteler, William, his house plundered, i. 12

Bouillon, Duke of (Frédéric-Maurice de la Tour d'Auvergne), proposed as commander of a force to be sent to England, iii. 44

Bourchier, George, executed for a plot to betray Bristol to Rupert, i. 99

Bourton-on-the-Water, arrival of Charles at, i. 352

Bovey Tracey, Cromwell surprises Wentworth at, iii. 59

Bow (in Devonshire), Sir Hardress Waller at, iii. 59

Bow Bridge, occupied by Norwich's troops, iv. 144

Bowes, Lambert quarters soldiers at, iv. 165

Boynton, Matthew, carries over Scarborough to the king, iv. 173

Boys, John, Colonel, defends Donnington Castle, ii. 43; *see* Boys, Sir John

Boys, Sir John, refuses to surrender, ii. 54

Bradford, Sir T. Fairfax at, i. 87; lost by the Fairfaxes, 116

Bradock Down, Hopton's victory at, i. 86

Bradshaw, John, President of the High Court of Justice, iv. 294; wears a shotproof hat, 299; declares Charles to be an elected king, 301; orders the clerk to record the king's default, 303; his speech when the king is brought for the last time before the Court, 312; orders the sentence to be read, *ib.*; refuses to allow the king to speak after sentence, 313

Braintree, mutiny of soldiers at, iii. 263; seizure of the county magazine at, iv. 148

Brent, Sir Nathaniel, chairman of the visitors of the University of Oxford, iii 313

Brentford, Rupert's attack on, i. 57; re-occupied by Essex, 59

Brentford, Earl of, 1644 (Patrick Ruthven), Charles thinks of removing from the command, ii. 11; superseded by Rupert, 56; his character as a commander, 63

Brentwood, junction of Norwich and Lucas at, iv. 148

Brereton, Sir William, successes of, in Cheshire, i. 88; takes part in the combat on Hopton Heath, 106; occupies Wem, 248; oppos d to Rupert in Cheshire, ii. 25; raises the sieges of Chester and Hawarden Castle, 214; the Self-denying Ordinance dispensed with in the case of, 254; joins in defeating Astley at Stow-on-the-Wold, iii. 80

Bribes, taken in the House of Commons, iv. 76

Bridge, William, one of the five Dissenting Brethren, i. 261

Bridgwater, abandoned to the royalists, i. 166; arrival of the Prince of Wales at, ii. 205; siege of, 273; taken by Fairfax, 274

Brill, garrisoned by the king, i. 66

Bristol, Rupert fails in an attempt to surprise, i. 99; secured by Waller. 104; surrenders to Rupert, 179; dispute about the governorship of, 196; Hopton

prince to France, 119; sent to remonstrate against the cession of the Channel Islands to France, 172; joins the royalists at Chelmsford, iv. 148; assured of quarter after the surrender of Colchester, 206; resolution of the Houses for the banishment of, 246

Capuchins, expelled from England, i. 102

Cardenas, Alonso de, attempts to p r-suade the English to relieve Dunkirk, iii. 170

Cardiff, Charles sets out from, ii. 290

Careston Castle, Montrose escapes to, ii. 220

Carew, Sir Alexander, attempts to betray Plymouth, i. 207; sentence and execution of, ii. 103

Carisbrooke Castle, Charles lodged in, iv. 19; Parliament orders the detension of Charles in, 50; plot for the king's escape from, 91; Charles unable to get through a window of, 94; Charles freed from confinement in, 214; Charles guarded by the local trained bands in, 257

Carlisle, besieged by David Leslie, ii. 62; surrender of, 263; projected seizure of, iv. 90; seized by the royalists, 123; Langdale driven into, 156; occupied by Hamilton, 165; surrendered by the Scots to Cromwell, 230

Carlisle, Countess of, said to have intrigued with the eleven members, iii. 322; is the medium of communication between the queen and the royalists, iv. 138; Lauderdale's correspondence with, 169

Carlow, surprised by Preston, iv. 104

Carnarvon, Earl of, 1628 (Robert Dormer), a moderate royalist, i. 6; his successes in Dorsetshire, 192; complains of Maurice's plunderings, 197; takes p rt in the siege of Gloucester, 205; killed at Newbury, 218

Carnwath, Earl of, 1639 (Robert Dalzell), seizes the king's bridle at Naseby, ii. 249

Carrickfergus, surprised by Monk, iv. 229

Case of the Army truly stated, The, presented to Fairfax, iii. 378

Cashel, refuses to admit Ormond, iii. 159; Inchiquin storms the Rock of, iv. 107

Cassilis, Earl of, 1615 (John Kennedy), bands raised by him dispersed, ii. 349

Castle Dinas, Hopton's rendezvous at, iii. 67

Castle Dor, surrender of Essex's infantry at, ii. 17

Castlehaven, Earl of, 1634 (James Touchet), defeats Vavasour in Munster, i. 221; successful campaign of, iii. 31

Catholics, the English, support the king, i. 35; measures taken by Parliament against, 76; excluded from toleration by the author of *Liberty of Conscience*, 291; Charles consents to

the repeal of the laws against, ii. 174; Charles offers freedom of conscience to, iii. 72; Fairfax and Cromwell offer toleration to, 316; agreement of the king and the army leaders to grant toleration to, 354; debate of toleration for, 376

Catholics, the French, the queen hopes to obtain help from, iii. 15

Cavalry tactics, Rupert's, adopted at Auldearn, ii. 226

Cavendish, Charles, tries to regain Gainsborough, i. 188; killed at Gainsborough, 190

Caversham, taken by Essex, i. 128; Charles lodged in Lord Craven's house at, iii. 308

Cawood Castle, taken by Hotham, i. 33

Cecil, Captain, dissents from the Army Remonstrance, iv. 245

Cessation, the Irish, i. 225

Chagford, Hopton's army, repulsed at, i. 86

Chalgrove Field, fight at, i. 151

Chaloner, Richard, collects money for a royalist plot, i. 144; gives the king's commission of array to Tompkins, 148; executed, 157

Chaloner, Thomas, absents himself from Lilburne's committee on the *Agreement of the People*, iv. 268

Channel Islands, the, alleged proposal to pledge, iii. 44; Jermyn proposes to cede, 172

Chard, junction of Hopton with Maurice and Hertford at, i. 166; halt of Charles at, ii. 32

Charles I. (King of England, Scotland, and Ireland), makes Rupert general of the horse, i. 2; attempts to restrain plundering, 13; sends Southampton and Culpepper to negotiate, *ib.*; sends Spencer and Falkland to negotiate, 16; increase of the army of, 18; leaves Nottingham, and issues a manifesto to his army, 23; occupies Shrewsbury and Chester, 25; refuses to receive a petition from Essex, 31; sells a peerage, 35; asks the Catholics to support him, *ib.*; marches from Shrewsbury, 37; sends for help to Denmark, 39; reaches Edgehill, 42; his conduct at Edgehill, 48; enters Oxford, 51; marches towards London, 54; orders an attack on Brentford, 57; checked at Turnham Green, 59; retires to Oatlands, 60; is charged with duplicity, 61; withdraws to Reading, *ib.*; rejects the terms of Parliament, and establishes himself at Oxford, 63; receives money and arms from Denmark, 64; issues a declaration against Parliament, 65; military position of, 66; strategy of, 67; congratulates Newcastle, 71; receives a petition from the City, 81; his answer read in the City, 82; receives the parliamentary peace proposals at Oxford, 89;

stir from Oxford till Rupert brings horses, 204; calls Fairfax the 'rebels' new brutish general,' 206; leaves Oxford, 208; assembles a council of war at Stow-on-the-Wold, 209; resolves to divide his army, 210; reaches Droitwich, *ib.*; orders Ormond to consent to the repeal of the penal laws, 211; moves forward towards the north, 213; marches towards Leicestershire, 230; takes Leicester, 233; weakness of his situation, 234; arrives at Daventry, and relieves Oxford, 235; despises the New Model Army, 236; finds fault with his council at Oxford for meddling with military affairs, 239; marches to Market Harborough, 241; hesitates about his course, 243; resolves to fight a battle, 244; rides off from Naseby, 249; reaches Hereford, 259; appeals to Ormond for Irish troops, *ib.*; instructs his son as to his conduct in the event of being himself captured, 261; receives at Raglan the news of Goring's defeat at Langport, 275; confers with Rupert at Blackrock, 276; learns that Bridgwater is lost, *ib.*; thinks of going into the north, 277; depressed by the lukewarmness of the gentry of South Wales, 284; sends for Ormond, 285; receives overtures from some Scottish lords, *ib.*; refuses even to appear to abandon episcopacy, 286; rejects Rupert's proposal that he shall make peace, 287; prepares for martyrdom, 288; sets out from Cardiff to join Montrose, 290; reaches Doncaster, but is obliged to turn back, *ib.*; hears of the battle of Kilsyth at Huntingdon, 291; declares his resolution to stand by the Church and the Crown, 301; forced to retire from Huntingdon, 302; passes through Oxford, 304; raises the siege of Hereford, 309, 310; fails to obtain recruits in Wales, 311; effect of the surrender of Bristol on, 317; commands Rupert to leave England, and orders the arrest of Legge, *ib.*; sets out from Raglan to join Montrose, 343; enters Chester, 344; watches the defeat of his followers from the walls of Chester, 345; intends to go to Newark, 347; orders Culpepper to send the Prince of Wales to France, 357; reaches Newark and sends for the Duke of York, 359; listens to various military schemes, 366; again marches to join Montrose, 367; his advance stopped, 369; returns to Newark, 372; sends Rupert before a council of war, 373; insolence of Rupert towards, *ib.*; postpones his departure from Newark, 375; goes to Oxford, 376; vexed at his followers' desire for peace, 377; deludes the Presbyterians and Independents, iii. 1; proposal that the Scottish army shall give shelter to, 2; negotiates secretly with the Independents, 16; urged by the royalists to make peace, *ib.*;

alleged plot to deliver up, *ib.*; proposes to come to Westminster to negotiate, 17; repeats his orders to the Prince of Wales to leave England, and directs the concentration of garrisons at Worcester, 18; wishes to come to terms with the Scots, *ib.*; joined by Rupert, 19; objects to employ Will Murray in Scotland, 20; retains his confidence in Montrose, *ib.*; invited to the Scottish camp, 21; repeats his request to be allowed to come to Westminster and offers further concessions, 22; refuses to establish Presbyterianism, 23; proposes to tolerate Presbyterianism, 24; contemptuous reply of the Houses to, *ib*; makes a formal overture to the Scots, 25; makes offers on religion to Parliament, 26; explains his position to the queen, 27; his relations with Glamorgan, 34; offers to allow the Catholics to build chapels, *ib.*; Glamorgan threatens to use force against, 38; attacked on account of Glamorgan's treaty, 42; proposed deposition of, *ib.*; demands an answer from Parliament, 43; disavows Glamorgan, 45; offers to abandon Ireland to Parliament, 46; tries to explain his share in Glamorgan's mission, 47; assures Glamorgan of his favour, 48; thinks of marching into Kent, and asks the queen to send an army to Hastings, 64; refuses to make religious concessions, 70; appeals to the Independents, 71; assures the queen of his dislike of the Presbyterians, 72; offers freedom of conscience to the Roman Catholics, *ib.*; distrusts Montreuil, 79; causes of his military failure, 80; again asks to return to Westminster, 83; sends a secret message to the Scots, and offers to surrender Newark, 86; exchanges engagements with Montreuil, 87; his vow to maintain the Church, 90; asks Montrose to join the Covenanters, *ib.*; resolves to take refuge in Lynn, 91; sends a message to Ireton, 95; asks Rainsborough to protect him, 96; takes leave of his council, 97; leaves Oxford, *ib.*; reaches Southwell, 102; his reception by the Scots, 103; removed to Newcastle, 104; asks to see Henderson and Loudoun, 106; writes to give assurance of his desire for peace, 107; offers to direct Glemham to surrender Oxford, *ib.*; sends Montreuil to ask help from France, 110; seeks the support of the Pope, and orders the prince to be removed from Jersey and Montrose to leave Scotland, *ib.*; his controversy with Henderson, 111; proposes a continuation of episcopacy in certain dioceses, 112; an intercepted letter reveals the complicity of the Scots in the escape of, 113; being pressed to sign the covenant, asks Parliament to hasten the sending of propositions, 114, 115; tells the queen

posal to the Houses, 24; his sincerity to
be tested, 26; his letter to the queen
intercepted at the Blue Boar, 29; is
hostile to the Four Propositions, 33;
appeals to Fairfax to secure him a personal treaty, *ib.*; thinks it easy to escape, 35; applies to the Scottish commissioners, 37; decides to accept the
Scottish terms, 38; agrees to the Engagement, and rejects the Four Bills,
41; his character compared with that of
Charles II., 42; his contradictory promises about toleration, 43; his prospect
of securing popular support, 45; fails to
effect his escape, 48; is secured by
Hammond, 49; is virtually a prisoner,
ib.; motion for the impeachment of, 50;
vote of no addresses to, 51, 53; reduction in the number of the attendants of,
59; urged by the Hamilton party to
make fresh concessions to the Presbyterians, 88; plot for the escape of, 91;
prevents Hammond from seizing his
papers, 92; failure of his attempt to
escape, 94; the Independents offer to
restore, 95; fresh appeal of the Independents to, 96; alleged offer of the
Independents to treat on the basis of
The Heads of the Proposals with, 124;
proposal of the Commons to treat with,
130; again prepares to escape, 131; his
plan discovered and frustrated, *ib.*; refuses to be bound by the manifesto of
the Scots, 172; removed to Newport,
214; stipulates that none of his concessions shall be valid until a complete
understanding is arrived at, *ib.*; urged
by Holles and Grimston not to waste
time, and by Vane to grant toleration,
217; answers a demand for the establishment of Presbyterianism, *ib.*; his
character as a controversialist, 218; defends episcopacy, 219; plans his escape,
220; offers to grant limited episcopacy,
222; continues anxious to escape, 223;
orders Ormond to disobey commands
not sent by the queen, 225; gives an
evasive answer to a demand that he
shall disavow Ormond, *ib.*; expected to
stir up another war, 226; petitions for
justice against, *ib.*; demand of the Army
Remonstrance for justice against, 235;
again prepares to escape, 242; rejects a
fresh overture from the army, 244;
pretends to satisfy Parliament about
Ormond, 247; left by the parliamentary
commissioners, *ib.*; his removal to Hurst
Castle ordered, 256; Cobbet and Merryman directed to remove, 257; is warned
of an intention to carry him off, *ib.*;
refuses to attempt to escape, 258; carried off from Newport, 259; his imprisonment at Hurst Castle, 260; his
final answer from Newport discussed in
the House of Commons, 265; his treatment at Hurst Castle, 278; fears assassination, 279; removed from Hurst

Castle, *ib.*; arrives at Windsor, 280;
rejects a final overture from the army,
286; first ordinance for the trial of, 288;
Act passed by the Commons for the
trial of, 290; question raised of merely
deposing, 296; brought to St. James's,
and to Cotton House, 297; brought
before the High Court of Justice, 299;
questions the authority of the court,
300; brought a second time before the
court, 301; brought a third time before
the court, 303; intention to sentence as
contumacious, *ib.*; the court hears evidence against, 305; the death warrant
of, 309, *n.*; brought to the bar to be
sentenced, 311; sentenced to death,
312; forcibly removed, 313; removed
to Whitehall, and afterwards to St.
James's, 314; takes leave of his two
youngest children, 319; conducted to
Whitehall, 320; steps upon the scaffold,
321; last speech of, 322; execution of,
323; funeral of, 324; cha acter given in
Eikon Basiliké to, 325; defects in the
character of, 326; story of Cromwell's
visit to the body of, 329

Charles, Prince of Wales, pleads for the
life of Colonel Feilding, i. 130; seizure
of the revenue of, 244; proposed marriage of, with a daughter of the Prince
of Orange, 328, 348; sent to Bristol, ii.
181; arrives at Bristol, 182; Goring refuses obedience to, 108; arrives at
Bridgwater and attempts to raise an
army, 205; receives instructions from
his father, 261; suggests proposals of
peace to Fairfax, 338; is ordered to go
to France, 357; ordered a second time
to go to France, iii. 18; proposed
declaration against, 43; proposal for
his marriage to the Great Mademoiselle,
44; with his army at Tavistock, 59;
falls back on Launceston, *ib.*; retreats
to Truro, 66; a plot to carry off, 67;
takes refuge in the Scilly Isles, *ib.*;
goes to Jersey, 110; his father directs
his removal from Jersey, 111; reported
intention of Digby to carry to Ireland,
113; attempt to remove from Jersey,
118; embarks for France, 119; proposal to place him in command of a new
army in England, 176; courts the Great
Mademoiselle, 238; first illegitimate son
of, *ib.*; invited to Scotland, 278, 302;
Argyle suggests that he should come to
Scotland, 359; attempt of Cromwell to
substitute for his father, iv. 56; revival
of the plan for placing on the throne, 85;
his journey to Calais decided on, 87; his
offer to come to Scotland carried by
Sir W. Fleming, 91; invited to Ireland,
109; is formally invited to Scotland,
123; impersonated at Sandwich, 133;
sets out for Holland, 154; the Scots
informed of the terms on which he
is willing to come to Scotland, 166;
arrives in Holland, 170; divisions in the

the plight of the army, 61 ; his qualities as a statesman, 79 ; prepares a parliamentary attack against Manchester, 82 ; brings a charge against Manchester, 82 ; counter-statement of Manchester against, 83 ; conference to consider the impeachment of, 86 ; criticises Manchester's charge against him, 88 ; proposes that officers shall waive their private interests, 90 ; his relations with Tate, 91 ; acts as teller for the appointment of Fairfax to the command of the New Model, 119 ; supports the advance of the Scots, 120 ; opposes the nomination of officers by the Houses, 128 ; good character of the soldiers of, 178 ; ordered to join Waller, *ib.* ; takes part in the surprise of Wiltshire horse near Devizes, 183 ; urges Lilburne to take the covenant, 195 ; his view on distinctions of rank, 196 ; his raid round Oxford, 200 ; joins Fairfax at Newbury, 206 ; ordered to join Fairfax in investing Oxford, 212 ; takes part in the siege of Oxford, 213 ; sent to secure the Isle of Ely, 231 ; the City requests that he may command the forces of the Eastern Association, 236 ; the officers ask for his appointment as lieutenant-general, 237 ; puts the Isle of Ely in a state of defence, and gathers volunteers in the Eastern Association, 238 ; appointed lieutenant-general by the Commons, *ib.* ; is received enthusiastically by the army, 242 ; advises the drawing back of the army at Naseby, 245 ; his successful charge, 248 ; attacks the king's infantry, 249 ; pleads for liberty of conscience, 252 ; his lieutenant-generalship confirmed by the Lords, 254 ; pursues the royalists at Langport, 272 ; sent against the clubmen, 305 ; captures Hambledon Hill, 306 ; his despatch after the surrender of Bristol, 319 ; his despatch mutilated, 320 ; is cool towards Baxter, 328 ; moderating influence of, 330 ; supports Lilburne's claims, 331 ; compared with Montrose, 351 ; takes Devizes, 359 ; marches into Hampshire, 360 ; takes Winchester Castle, 362 ; sends plunderers to the governor of Oxford, *ib.* ; storms Basing House, 363 ; advises the establishment of a garrison at Newbury, 365 ; rejoins Fairfax at Crediton, 366 ; a barony asked for, iii 12 ; surprises Lord Wentworth, 59 ; addresses the Devonshire recruits, 62 ; growing importance of, 81 ; sees to the observance of the conditions of Exeter, 92 ; receives the thanks of the House, 95 ; reproves Ireton, 96 ; marries his daughter to Ireton, 109 ; objects to the introduction of the ballot into the House of Commons, 146 ; an estate voted to, 147 ; excluded from the new army by a vote of the Commons, 220 ; comments on the temper of the Presbyterians, *ib.* ; complains of

having to serve a Parliament, 221 ; but declares that the army will obey it, 222 ; offers to serve in Germany, *ib.* ; resolves to remain in England, 223 ; dissatisfied with the petition of the soldiers, 226 ; talk of arresting, 228 ; passes through a period of hesitation, and absents himself from the House, 241 ; sent as a commissioner to quiet the army, 245 ; intentions of, 246 ; is satisfied with the *Declaration of the Army,* 248 ; does not suggest that the army should resist disbandment, 249 ; reads the report of the military commissioners, 257 ; again declares that the army will disband, 258 ; his reasons for abandoning his obedience to Parliament, 264 ; his relations with the Agitators, 266 ; authorises Joyce to go to Holmby, *ib.* ; escapes to Newmarket, 279 ; his part in the *Solemn Engagement of the Army,* 281 ; discussion of the evidence on the charge of hypocrisy against, 282, *n.* 1 ; visits Charles at Childerley, 285 ; is the chief author of the letter from the officers to the City, 287 ; evidence on the charge of hypocrisy against, 289 ; directs Whalley not to allow the removal of the king's chaplains, 306 ; has an interview with the king, 308 ; desires an understanding with the king, 310 ; tells Bellièvre that no one rises so high as he who knows not whither he is going, 316 ; assures Bellièvre that he is ready to tolerate even the Roman Catholics, *ib.* ; impresses Berkeley with a conviction of his honesty, 318 ; is favourably impressed with Charles, 319 ; wishes the terms offered to be as conciliatory as possible, *ib.* ; opinion of an Agitator on the character of, 320 ; opinion of a Presbyterian on, *ib.* ; argues against a proposal that the army shall march to London, 326 ; his attitude in the strife between Parliament and army, 328 ; Charles appeals to the supposed cupidity of, 341 ; rides through the City at the head of the cavalry, 345 ; supports the Agitators' petition for a purge of the House, 350 ; menaces the House with military intervention, 351 ; obtains an ordinance annulling the votes carried in the absence of the speakers, 352 ; distrusted by Charles, 353 ; tells Charles that the Newcastle propositions are only revived to satisfy the Scots, 355 ; gives assurances to the king, 358 ; makes large offers to the Scots, 360 ; is suspected of too great a compliance with the king, 361 ; takes part in the expulsion of Major White from the army, 362 ; asserts that he does not wish to cast down Presbytery, 363 ; tries to win over Lilburne, *ib.* ; moves for a committee to search for precedents in Lilburne's case, 364 ; attacked by Rainsborough and the London newspapers, 365 ; opposes

Gangræna, enumeration of heresies in, iv. 81

Gascoigne, Sir Bernard (Bernardo Guasconi), condemned to be shot, iv. 202; reprieved, 204

Gauden, John, Dr., author of *Eikon Basiliké*, iv. 323

Gayer, Sir John, active as lord mayor in resisting the army, iii. 292; impeached, 369

Gell, Sir John, surrender of Lichfield to, i. 98; takes part in the combat on Hopton Heath, 106; fails to co-operate with Cromwell, 142; joins Cromwell at Nottingham, 159; his men undisciplined, *ib.*; joins Leven, ii. 263

General Assemb'y of the Church of Scotland, *see* Scotland, the General Assembly of the Church of

General Assembly of the Irish Confederate Catholics, *see* Confederate Catholics, General Assembly of

Gerard, Lord, 1645 (Charles Gerard), collects troops in Shropshire, ii. 312; supports Rupert's insubordination, 374; *see* Gerard, Sir Charles

Gerard, Sir Charles, commands the royalists in South Wales, ii. 32; accompanies Rupert to Oxford, 56; defeats Laugharne, 217; dismissed and raised to the peerage, 289; *see* Gerard, Lord

Gerard, Sir George, acts as parliamentary agent at Paris, iii. 43

Gerard, Sir Gilbert, urges the Commons to levy taxes, i. 91; promises to assist Lady Verney, iv. 74

Gibbons, Major, sent to relieve Dover, iv. 137; falsely reported to have raised the siege of Dover Castle, 146; employed to suppress a disturbance at Horsham, 157

Glamorgan, Earl of, 1644 (Edward Somerset), character and aims of, ii. 158; commissioned to bring Irish soldiers to England, 159; great promises made to, 160; sent to Ireland, 164; instructions of, 166; receives from Charles an engagement to confirm his actions, 167; explains the meaning of the engagement, 168; receives a commission to levy troops, *ib.*; receives a commission to treat with the confederates, 175; assures Charles that he will bring him 6,000 Irish, 176; is wrecked on the coast of Lancashire, *ib.*; sets out for Dublin, 260; is delayed on his way, 285; arrives in Dublin, iii. 30; sets out for Kilkenny, 32; signs a secret treaty, 33; defeasance of, 35; distrusted by Scarampi, 36; is promised an army for England, 37; agrees with the Supreme Council to compel Charles to assent to its terms, 38; expects to gain the support of Rinuccini, 39; is won over by Rinuccini, 40; makes a second secret treaty, *ib.* arrest of, 41; his treaty

denounced before the Irish Council, *ib.*; his treaty known to the English Parliament, 42; disavowed by Charles, 45; assured of Charles's favour, 48; is liberated and goe to Kilkenny, 49; urges Ormond to satisfy Rinuccini, 51; submits to Rinuccini, 52; prepares to go to the Continent, and enters into a third treaty, 53; prepares to relieve Chester, *ib.*; learns that Charles has disavowed him, 54; gives up hope of conducting an Irish army to England, 56; letters from, intercepted at Padstow, 69; proposed by Rinuccini as lord-lieutenant, 160

Glamorganshire, conditions imposed on Charles by the gentry of, ii. 284; unpopularity of Gerard in, 289

Glasgow, Montrose at, ii. 348; a Parliament summoned to meet at, 349; Sir James Turner quarters soldiers on the householders of, iv. 155

Glastonbury, skirmish at, i. 166

Glemham, Sir Thomas, surrenders Carlisle, ii. 263; appointed governor of Oxford, 317; sets at liberty plunderers sent to him by Cromwell, 362; tells the king that his enemies will quarrel, 377; bids farewell to the king, iii. 97; ordered to surrender Oxford, 108; proposed seizure of Lynn by, 176; joins Langdale in Scotland, iv. 91

Gloucester, Stamford retreats to, i. 76; holds out for Parliament, 86; the Welsh insist on besieging, 195; condition of the garrison of, 198; summoned by the king, 199; beginning of the siege of, *ib.*; relief of, 206; Backhouse pretends willingness to betray, 260; failure of an attempt to supply, 320; receives supply, 344; Cromwell reviews his forces at, iv. 124

Gloucester, Henry, Duke of (1644), proposal to crown, ii. 189, iii. 43; alleged intention of the Independents to crown, 130; increase of the household of, iv. 101; project of placing him on the throne revived, 168; takes leave of his father, 317; *see* Henry, son of Charles I.

Gloucestershire, royalist successes in, i. 86; Waller's successes in, 104

Glyn, John, objects to the peace propositions of the Lords, i. 188; imprisoned and expelled from the House of Commons, iii. 357; *see* Eleven Members, the

Godolphin, Sidney, death of i. 86

Goffe, William, Major afterwards Colonel, proposes a prayer-meeting, iii. 385; declares that Heaven is against Charles, iv. 5; takes part in a prayer-meeting at Windsor, 119, is a witness of the execution of Lucas and Lisle, 203; sits as one of the king's judges, 293

disinclined to come to terms with the Scots, 12 ; asks the continental Catholics for help, 13 ; is on bad terms with Rinuccini, 14 ; sends Sir Kenelm Digby to Rome, *ib.* ; hopes that Mazarin will lend her troops, 15 ; approves reluctantly of a negotiation with the Scots, 19 ; urges the French court to assist Charles, 43 ; expects help from the French clergy, 44 ; talks of marrying her son to the daughter of the Duke of Orleans, *ib.* ; her negotiation with the Scots, and her scheme of a French invasion discovered by an intercepted letter, 63 ; favours an alliance with the Scots, 70 ; urges the prince to come to France, 118 ; has instructions prepared for Bellièvre, 128 ; urges Charles to accept Presbyterianism without the covenant, 135 ; again urges compliance with the Scottish terms, 142 ; threatens to retire into a nunnery, 167 ; urges Charles to abandon the bishops and hold to the militia, 169 ; assures Charles that Mazarin will help him, 171 ; derides Charles for talking of abdicating, 182 ; fresh Presbyterian proposals sent to, 214 ; teaches the Prince of Wales to make love to the Great Mademoiselle, 238 ; mission of Dunfermline to, 278 ; tries to pawn her jewels, iv. 87 ; sends Father Leyburn to Ireland, 104 ; Irish commissioners sent to, 109 ; makes arrangements for a rising in England, 138 ; raises money for Ormond, 163 ; parties at the court of, 164 ; sends Fleming to Scotland with a small supply of arms and money, 166 ; her hopes of aid from France cut short by the Fronde, 223 ; negotiates with the Duke of Lorraine for troops and with Venice for money, and offers Irish soldiers to Mazarin, 224 ; hopes for assistance from Ireland, *ib.* ; asks leave to visit her husband, 289

Henrietta, Princess, birth of, ii. 7 ; is to remain under Lady Dalkeith's charge, iii. 91 ; carried off to France, 184

Henry, son of Charles I., kept as a hostage, i. 52 ; *see* Gloucester, Duke of

Herbert, George, parody on his *Sacrifice*, iii. 309

Herbert of Cherbury, Lord, 1629 (Edward Herbert), surrenders Montgomery Castle, ii. 93

Herbert of Raglan, Lord (Edward Somerset), raises a Welsh army, i. 76 ; defeated by Waller at Highnam, 86 ; lends immense sums to Charles, ii. 158 ; created Earl of Glamorgan by warrant, *ib.* ; *see* Glamorgan, Earl of

Herbert, Sir Edward, refuses the attorney-generalship, ii. 311

Herbert, Thomas, accompanies Charles to Hurst Castle, iv. 259 ; remains in attendance on Charles after his sentence, 320 ; **accompanies Charles to Whitehall,** *ib.* ;

asks to be excused from appearing on the scaffold, 321

Hereford, occupied by the Parliamentarians, i. 32 ; evacuated by Stamford, 76 ; taken by Waller, 130 ; abandoned by Waller, 139 ; arrival of Charles at, ii. 259 : besieged by Leven, 284 ; progress of the siege of, 308 ; Charles raises the siege of, 310 ; surprised by Birch and Morgan, iii. 21

Herefordshire, rising of countrymen in, ii. 185 ; royalists defeated in, 259 ; desertion of royalist levies in, 275 ; plundered by the Scots, 309

Heresies, enumerated in *Gangræna*, iv. 81

Herle, Charles, signs a declaration in favour of toleration, i. 368

Herne, Mr., brings the king's answer from Oxford, i. 83

Hertford, Marquis of, 1640 (William Seymour), holds out for the king at Sherborne, i. 19 ; abandons Sherborne and goes into Wales, 32 ; joins the king at Oxford with Welsh levies, 86 ; sets out from Oxford and occupies Salisbury, 140 ; joins Hopton at Chard, 166 ; advances with him towards Bath, 169 ; moves off towards Salisbury, 173 ; his dispute with Waller, 196 ; accompanies the king to Oxford, *ib.* ; takes part in the Treaty of Uxbridge, ii. 121 ; attends a council at Hampton Court, 371 ; attends the king's funeral, iv. 324

Hertfordshire, petitions for peace, i. 82 ; outrages by soldiers in, ii. 194

Hewson, John, Colonel, directs Whalley to resist the removal of the king's chaplains, iii. 306 ; sent to enforce the payment of money in London, iv. 24 ; one of the king's judges, 293

High Court of Justice, the first and second reading of the ordinance for the erection of, iv. 289 ; act passed by the Commons only for the erection of, 290 ; meets in the Painted Chamber, 293 ; its preliminary sittings, 295, 297 ; sits in Westminster Hall, *ib.* ; the king brought in and charged before, 299 ; its authority questioned by Charles, 300 ; the king a second time before, 301 ; the king a third time before, 303 ; dissensions amongst the members of, 304 ; rejects a proposal to put the king to death as contumacious, and hears evidence in the Painted Chamber, 305 ; passes preliminary sentence, 307 ; the king for the fourth time before, 311 ; sentences the king to death, 312

Highnam, Waller's victory at, i. 104

Hillesden House, taken by Cromwell, i. 311

Hodder Bridge, Cromwell holds a council of war at, iv. 184

Holborn, Major-General, sent to relieve Taunton, ii. 94 ; relieves Taunton, 98 ; retreats from Taunton, 183

The Declaration of the Army ascribed to, 295 ; tells Charles that the army intends to mediate between him and Parliament, 307 ; entrusted with the preparation of the terms to be offered to the king, 319, 326 ; his constitutional scheme submitted to the Council of the Army, 329 ; asks Charles not to be troubled about the revival of the Newcastle propositions, 355 ; talks of purging the House, 358 ; suspected of too great compliance with the king, 361 ; opposes Marten's motion for a vote of No Addresses, 360 ; persists in treating with the king, 369 ; explains his conduct in negotiating with the king, 382 ; attacks Wildman for talking of natural rights, 385 ; declares against manhood suffrage, and argues that no one ought to have a vote who has not a fixed interest in the kingdom, 388 ; replies to Sexby, 389 ; takes offence and leaves the Council of the Army, iv. 8 ; wishes to fight both king and Parliament, 26 ; urges Hammond to keep the king from escaping, 27 ; said to have accompanied Cromwell to the Blue Boar, 29 ; declares against the king in the House of Commons, 50 ; accepts the surrender of Canterbury, 146 ; appointed to witness the execution of Lucas and Lisle, 203 ; advises the postponement of the application of force to the Houses, 213 ; urges the purging of the House of Commons and offers to resign his commission, 215 ; retires to Windsor, 216 ; prepares a demand for justice on the king, 227 ; draws up *The Remonstrance of the Army*, 233 ; urges Fairfax to allow the army to consider his draft, 236 ; is in communication with Lilburne, 238 ; agrees to an addition to *The Remonstrance of the Army*, 239, 240 ; has no hope that Charles will accept the new overtures from the army, 242 ; joins in a letter to urge Hammond not to allow the king to escape, 243 ; disagreement with Lilburne, 261 ; believed by Lilburne to have promised that the decision of a proposed committee on a new *Agreement of the People* shall be final, 262 ; thinks that the magistrate ought to punish offences against the first table, 277 ; his views on a dissolution, 269 ; proposes that the king shall be tried and imprisoned, 281 ; advocates the fixing of an early date for the dissolution, 291 ; sits as one of the king's judges, 293 ; urges the condemnation of the king, 306

Irish army, an, intended for service in England, the queen proposes to employ, i. 72 ; Charles sanctions the transportation of, 125 ; Taaffe is to lead a detachment of, 249 ; Byron urges the sending of, 295 ; English feeling against the employment of, 296 ; Antrim asks for the despatch of, 332 ; Charles's anxiety

to employ, 346 ; to be commanded by Glamorgan, ii. 159 ; committee in France for providing money for, 170 ; Byron anxious for the landing of, 186 ; Charles presses Ormond to send, 259 ; preparations for the sending of, 260 ; effect on Englishmen of the attempt to bring over, 261 ; Charles despairs of the arrival of, 285 ; proposal regarding the sending of, iii. 50 ; Glamorgan offers to expedite the sending of, 51, 53 ; to be sent to the relief of Chester, 56 ; countermanded, 57 ; reported coming of, 113 ; fresh suggestion for bringing over, iv. 83

Irish soldiers in England, drowned by Swanley, i. 337 ; ordinance directing the killing of, ii. 94 ; spared at Liverpool, *ib.* ; put to death at Shrewsbury, 179

Irish women, taken at Nantwich, but sent home by Fairfax, i. 296 ; ill-treated at Lyme, 357 ; killed after Naseby, ii. 252 ; killed after Philiphaugh, 355 ; alleged fecundity of, iii. 38

Ironside, name of, first given by Rupert to Cromwell, ii. 1

Ironsides, name of, first given to Cromwell's soldiers, iv. 179

Isle of Wight, the, Hammond governor of, iv. 13 ; arrival of Berkeley and Ashburnham in, 18 ; arrival of Charles in, *ib.* ; removal of Hammond from, 256 ; removal of Charles from, 259

Islip, Essex fails to take, i. 150 ; Essex establishes himself at, 351 ; Cromwell defeats Northampton at, ii. 201

JACKSON, Thomas, Colonel, mutiny against, iii. 263

James I., King of Great Britain, his saying ' No Bishop, No King,' iii. 173 ; revival of the story of his having been poisoned, iv. 61

James, son of Charles I., *see* York, Duke of

Jenkins, David, Judge, imprisoned for asserting that the rule of the law is inseparable from the rule of the king, iii. 309 ; denounces parliamentary ordinances. iv. 68 ; bill of attainder against, *ib.* ; resolution of the Houses that he shall be excepted from pardon, 246

Jermyn, Henry, placed in command of the queen's army, i. 163 ; raised to the peerage, 166 ; *see* Jermyn, Lord

Jermyn, Lord, 1643 (Henry Jermyn), advocates a policy of foreign alliances, i. 196 ; employed to urge Mazarin to help Charles, ii. 38 ; intercepted letter from, iii. 63 ; urges the prince to come to France, 118 ; Charles's opinion of, 167 ; proposes to cede the Channel Islands to France, 172 ; takes part in arranging a royalist insurrection, iv. 138 ; treats Hyde with rudeness, 170 ; *see* Jermyn, Henry

at Marston Moor, i. 376 ; his conduct at Marston Moor, 378 ; destroys the Whitecoats, 381 ; attaches himself to Cromwell, ii. 1 ; besieges Carlisle, 62 ; sent against Rupert, 185 ; takes Carlisle, and occupies it with a Scottish garrison, 263 ; advances southwards to join Leven, 276 ; sent in pursuit of Charles, 290 ; marches towards Scotland, 309 ; enters Scotland, 353 ; marches after Montrose, 354 ; defeats Montrose at Philiphaugh, 355 ; allows prisoners to be killed at Linlithgow, 356 ; sends Middleton after Montrose, 368 ; remains in the Lothians, 369 ; in command of the Scottish army round Newark, iii. 103 ; is probably attached to Callander's party, 141 ; refuses a dukedom as the price of supporting Charles, 187 ; placed in command of a new army in Scotland, 251 ; captures Huntly's strongholds, *ib.* ; overruns Huntly's country, 299 ; drives Alaster Macdonald out of Kintyre, 300 ; refuses a command in Hamilton's army, iv. 132 ; does not venture to resist Hamilton, 155 ; supports the Whiggamore Raid, 228

Leslie, Ludowick, governor of Berwick, iv. 230

Leslie, Robin, sent to England to prepare the way for Lanark and Loudoun, iii. 359

L'Estrange, Roger, sentenced to death and reprieved, ii. 113

Levellers, the, origin of the name, iii. 380 ; Cromwell's hostility to, *ib.* : admitted to the discussion in the army council on *The Case of the Army*, 382 ; talk of carrying the king to Ely, iv. 2 ; object to the constitutional scheme of the committee of the army council, 9 ; distrust Cromwell, 47 ; hold a meeting at East Smithfield, 54 ; petition of the, 213 ; hold conference with the Independents of the army, 238 ; addition to the Army Remonstrance proposed by a committee of, 239 ; attempt of the army leaders to come to an understanding with, 260 ; admitted into a committee formed to consider a new *Agreement of the People*, 262 ; their opinions on a dissolution, 268

Leven, Earl of, 1641 (Alexander Leslie), visits Ireland, i. 115 ; appointed to command the Scottish army in England, 232 ; refuses to consent to the deposition of the king, 368 ; flight of, 380 , asks for a settlement of church government and peace, ii. 3 ; besieges Newcastle, 4 ; sends David Leslie against Rupert, 185 ; ordered to send Baillie and Hurry against Montrose, 204 ; ordered by the Committee of Both Kingdoms to march against the king, 211 ; insists upon marching through Westmoreland, 214 ; wishes to protect Scotland, *ib.* ; effect of the battle of Auldearn on, 227 ;

marches to Mansfield, 256 ; invited to besiege Hereford, 263 ; waits for money at Alcester, *ib.* : besieges Hereford, 284 ; refuses to allow Fleming to visit the Scottish camp, 285 ; is not to be gained by the king, 285 ; complains that the pay for his army is kept back, 308 ; abandons the siege of Hereford, 310 ; proposal to recall to Scotland, 340 ; urged by Digby to join the king, 343 ; quartered on the Tees, 369 ; invited to besiege Newark, iii. 2 ; refuses to negotiate with the king, 3 ; invests Newark, 11 ; withdraws to Newcastle, 103 ; secures Edinburgh Castle for the Whiggamores, iv. 228

Leyburn, Father, sent by the queen to Ireland under the name of Winter Grant, iv. 104

Liberty of conscience, offered by Charles to Vane, i. 274 ; not yet a prob'em for practical statesmen, 276 ; anonymous tract on, 290 ; Cromwell pleads for, ii. 252, 319 ; accepted by the Dissenting Brethren, iii. 10 ; London petitions against, 11

Liberty of Prophesying, The, publication of, iii. 311

Licensing of the press, ordinance for, i. 147

Lichfield, besieged by Lord Brooke, 97 ; surrenders to Gell, 98 ; recovered by Rupert, 108

Lichfield, Earl of, 1645 (Bernard Stuart), killed, ii. 345 ; *see* Stuart, Lord Bernard

Liége, forces for Charles's service from, ii. 159

Lilburne, Henry, Colonel, is the probable writer of a letter which warns Charles that his murder is being planned, iv. 15 ; his defection and death, 179

Lilburne, John, captured at Brentford, and sentenced to death as a traitor, i. 73 ; threatened to be hanged for taking Tickhill Castle, ii. 22 ; character of, 110 ; his letter to Prynne, *ib.* ; importance of his views, 112 ; excluded from the New Model Army, 195 ; arrested and liberated by the Committee of Examinations, 330 ; prints his reasons for toleration, and is again arrested and liberated, 331 ; his claims on Parliament, *ib.* ; brings charges against Holles and the Lenthalls, 332 ; taken into custody, *ib.* ; his views on the authority of the House of Commons, 333 ; his constitutional position, 334 ; liberation of, *ib.* ; committed to Newgate by the Lords, iii. 125 ; sentenced to fine and imprisonment by the Lords, *ib.* ; his influence with the army, 235 ; holds that Parliament has no legal existence, 362 ; is visited by Cromwell, and offers to leave England if the Commons will adopt his view on the Lords' jurisdiction, 363 ; denounces Cromwell, 364 ; liberation and re-arrest of, iv. 54 ; holds that toleration should be unlimited, 81 ;

set at liberty in order that he may attack Cromwell, 175 ; attacks Huntington, 176 ; makes overtures to Cromwell, *ib.* ; writes part of the petition of the London Levellers, 213 ; in communication with Ireton, 238 ; objects to the king's execution without security against the army, *ib.* ; fails to agree with Ireton, 261 ; proposes to Harrison the appointment of a committee to draw up a new *Agreement of the People,* 262 ; believes Ireton to have promised that the decision of the committee shall be final, *ib.* ; forms a committee, 267 ; disappointed that the draft of his committee is discussed in the Council of Officers, 277 ; withdraws from the discussion, 295

Lilburne, Robert, Colonel, takes part in the officers' petition on service in Ireland iii. 224 ; summoned by the House of Commons, 228 ; prevents Kempson from taking his men to Ireland, 235 ; mutiny in the regiment of, iv. 23

Lilburnian party, the petition presented by, iii. 254 ; second and third petitions of, 257 ; fourth petition of, 275 ; *see* Levellers, the

Limerick, Ormond's herald attacked at, iii. 157

Lincoln, Earl of, 1619 (Theophilus Clinton), impeached, iii. 357

Lincoln, the Hothams offer to betray, i. 141 ; the queen expects to gain, 160 ; failure of a plot for the betrayal of, 163 ; abandoned by Willoughby, 191 ; taken by Manchester, 242 ; given up to the royalists, 318 ; stormed by Manchester, 345 ; Manchester establishes himself at, ii. 22

Lincolnshire, added to the Eastern Association, i. 239 ; pacified by Manchester, 245 ; defeat of royalist insurgents in, iv. 145

Lindsay, Earl of, *see* Crawford and Lindsay, Earl of

Lindsey, first Earl of, 1626 (Robert Bertie), commander-in-chief of the king's army, i. 3 ; refuses to act as general at Edgehill, 43 ; death of, 49

Lindsey, second Earl of, 1642 (Montague Bertie), sent to negotiate with Rainsborough, iii. 96 ; urges Charles to escape from Newport, iv. 258 ; attends the king's funeral, 324

Lingen, Sir Henry, said to have risen in Herefordshire, iv. 192 ; routed in Montgomeryshire, 194 ; resolution of the Houses for the banishment of, 246

Linlithgow, prisoners killed at, ii. 356

Linton Lord (John Stewart), sent to join Montrose, and recalled, ii. 354

Liskeard, arrival of Charles at, ii 10

Lisle, John, in the chair of a committee of privileges, ii. 89 ; makes his report, 118

Lisle, Sir George, takes part in the battle

of Cheriton, i. 322 ; joins the royalists in Essex, iv. 148 ; condemned to be shot, 202 ; execution of, 203

Lisle Viscount (Philip Sidney), heads an expedition in Ireland, ii. 116 ; allied with Parsons, 122 ; appointed parliamentary lord-lieutenant of Ireland, iii. 232 ; recall of, *ib.* ; Monk serves under, iv. 108

Liverpool, taken by Rupert, i. 367 ; taken by Meldrum, ii. 62, 93

Livesey, Sir Michael, ordered to suppress Holland's rising, iv. 157 ; pursues Holland, 160

Lobsters, the Hazlerigg's cavalry nicknamed, i. 170 ; defeated on Roundway Down, 173

Local feeling, strength of, i. 68 ; the Cornish, 70 ; parliamentary armies divided by, 134 ; its effect on the king's army after the victory of Roundway Down, 194 ; danger of relying on, 340 ; weakens the king's army after the taking of Leicester, ii. 235

London, City of, provides money for the parliamentary army, i. 28 ; offers the service of its trained bands, 38 ; hopefulness of the royalists in, *ib.* ; earthworks raised round, 52 ; asked by Parliament for support, 55 ; Pym's application to, 56 ; sends its trained bands to Turnham Green, 58 ; protests against an accommodation, 63 ; raises a loan, 65 ; royalists in, 74 ; peace riots in, *ib.* ; raises a fresh loan, 96 ; orders given for the fortification of, 98 ; royalist party in, 144 ; discovery of Waller's plot in, 146 ; authorised to command its own forces, 178 ; sends troops into Kent, 180 ; asks that Waller may command a new army, *ib.* ; intrusted with the guard of the Tower, 181 ; anti-royalist feeling in, *ib.* ; is irritated by the intention of the Houses to negotiate after Roundway Down, 185 ; petitions against peace propositions, *ib.* ; a forced loan of fifty subsidies imposed on, 202 ; preparations for the relief of Gloucester in, 203 ; review of the trained bands in, 237 ; finds money for the Scots, 238 ; asks for the recall of its trained bands, 251 ; Brooke's plot for winning for the king, 269 ; dinner given to the Houses by, 273 ; offers men and money to Essex, 340 ; offers five regiments after Essex's surrender, ii. 37 ; petition of the clergy of, against toleration, 75 ; petition for the execution of Laud and Wren in, 102 ; asked for a loan to pay the first expenses of the New Model Army, 187 ; entertains the two Houses at a banquet, 256 ; entry of the prisoners from Naseby into, *ib.* ; religion of the citizens of, iii 8 ; petitions against toleration, 28 ; supports the terms offered to the king by the Scots, 76 ; proposal to put the suburban militia under the authorities of, *ib.* ; its petition on excommunication, 78 ; military importance of, 81 ; is reconciled with the House of Commons, 84 ; election of elders in, 126 ; asks for the disbandment of the army, 183 ; distrusts Charles, 215 ; petitions for the disbandment of the army, 221 ; asks for a new militia committee of its own choosing, 250 ; urged by Massey to rise against the army, 278 ; asks that the army may be disbanded, and that the City may be permitted to raise cavalry, 286 ; letter of twelve officers to, 287 ; want of martial enthusiasm in, 291 ; temporises with the army, 292 ; sends a deputation to the army, 293 ; men under arms in, 302 ; signature of *The Solemn Engagement of the City* in, 335 ; prepares to resist the army, 338 ; Massey named commander of the forces of, 339 ; danger of anarchy in, 343 ; yields to Fairfax, 344 ; passage of the army through, 345 ; difficulty of raising the assessment for the army, in, 362 ; the election of Lord Mayor Warner secured by military intervention in, 370 ; Hewson ordered to enforce payment of the assessments in, iv. 24 ; riot on Christmas Day in, 46 ; opinion favourable to Charles in, 94 ; riot in, 97 ; attack on Westminster made by a mob from, *ib.* ; riot suppressed by soldiers in, 98 ; removal of posts and chains from the streets of, *ib.* ; conciliated by Cromwell and Vane, 115 ; posts and chains restored to, *ib.* ; Cromwell anxious to spare, 121 ; offered permission to nominate its own militia committee and the lieutenant of the Tower, 125 ; hesitation, in, 126 ; receives coolly the news of the victory at St. Fagans, 127 ; distrusts Charles, 129 ; welcomes the concessions made by Parliament, 130 ; presses for a personal treaty with the king, 143 ; Norwich hopes to be admitted into, 145 ; apprehension lest Holland shall receive aid from, 161 ; prisoners rescued in the streets of, 162 ; listing of forces by Skippon in, 172 ; effect of the prince's seizure of merchantmen upon, 173 ; talk of raising an army for the Prince of Wales in, 196; is more conciliatory towards the army, 212 ; army enters London, 264 ; seizure by Fairfax of money in, 274

London, Committee of the Militia of the City of, placed in command of forces raised for the defence of the City, i. 179 ; demands that the suburban militia shall be subjected to, iii. 76 ; a new one authorised by ordinance, and chosen by the City, 250 ; newly constituted by the Presbyterians, *ib.* ; committee of safety appointed to confer with, 291 ; orders the trained bands to resist the army, 292 ; restoration of the old, 335 ; restoration of the new, 336, 337 ; repeal of ordinance restoring the new, 352 ; again proposed to be nominated by the City, iv. 125 ;

passing of an ordinance nominating according to the choice of the City, 129

London, Common Council of the City of, petitions for the return of the king, i. 78 ; sends agents to Oxford, 81 ; Charles's answer to, *ib.* ; rejects Charles's terms, 83 ; asks for the formation of an association, 99 ; orders the destruction of Cheapside Cross, 132 ; petitions for the rejection of the peace propositions, 185 ; makes suggestions as to the management of the war, ii. 236 ; transmits to Parliament petitions against liberty of conscience, iii. 11 ; draws up a temporising answer to the letter of the twelve officers, 292 ; objects to a new war, 298 ; urges the House of Commons to give way to the army, 304 ; petitions for the restoration of the new militia committee, 336 ; announces to Fairfax its readiness to yield, 344 ; offers to live and die with Parliament, and asks for the resumption of negotiations with the king, iv. 130 ; asks that the king may be brought to London, 158

London, Common Hall of the City of, Charles's answer to the peace proposals read to, i. 82 ; Brooke's plot described to, 273

London, Trained Bands of, appear on Turnham Green, i. 58 ; their march to Gloucester, 202; their conduct at Newbury, 214 ; welcomed on their return, 237 ; dislike of permanent service amongst, 243 ; offer to retake Reading, *ib.* ; recover Newport Pagnell, 244 ; mutiny of, 250 ; their recall demanded, 251 ; desert Waller, 340 ; are unfit for permanent service, iii. 5 ; Waller complains of the desertion of, 6 ; hang back when summoned to resist the army, iii. 292

Lords, House of, the peace party in, i. 53 ; prepares propositions for peace, 75 ; completes the propositions, 78 ; votes for a cessation of arms, 90 ; alienated from the king, 99 ; continued hopes of the peace party in, 145 ; refuses to reopen negotiations, 165 ; prepares peace propositions, 183 ; persists in supporting the propositions, 184 ; threatened by a mob, 185 ; deserted by seven peers, 199 ; amends the covenant, 234 ; takes the covenant, 244 ; proposal to proceed with the queen's impeachment in, 270 ; its attitude towards the scheme of the Commons for the Committee of Both Kingdoms, 305 ; its attitude towards a proposed Dutch mediation, 329 ; proposes to open a negotiation, 341 ; in conflict with the Commons, 342 ; attempts to reverse a decision of the Committee of Both Kingdoms, 355 ; asks the Assembly to settle church government, ii. 75 ; supports Manchester against Cromwell, 83 ; inclined to peace, 99 ; Laud at the

of his readiness to push on, 29;
ordered to join Waller, 31; movements
of, 35; hesitates to fight, 36; urged
to advance, 39; refuses to advance
into the West, 40; is joined by
Waller, 43; joined by Essex, 44;
false attack by, 47; inactivity of, 49;
his attack on Shaw House repulsed,
51; blamed for permitting the king's
escape, 52; holds back from pursuing
the king, 53; is eager for peace, 54;
advances slowly in pursuit, *ib.*; declares it to be useless to defeat the
king, 59; is ordered to conform to
the advice of the council of war, 60;
a typical Presbyterian, 66; defends
himself against Cromwell's charge,
83; makes a counter-charge against
Cromwell, 84; his accusation criticised
by Cromwel, 88; the Commons make
a show of reviving Cromwell's charge
against, 116; officers' petition for the
continuance in command of, 118; report of Lisle's committee in favour of
investigating the charges relating to,
ib.; resigns his command, 190; takes
part in proposing to send terms to the
king, iii. 213; takes refuge with the army,
339, 344; returns to the chair of the House
of Lords, 345; opposes the ordinance for
the king's trial, iv. 289
Manhood suffrage, discussion in the
Council of the Army on, iii. 388
Mansfield, arrival of the Scottish army at,
ii. 256
Mardyk, gained by France, iii. 169
Marlborough, stormed and plundered by
the royalists, i. 66
Marshall, Stephen, accompanies the
English commissioners to Scotland, i.
228; preaches at Pym's funeral, 255;
signs a declaration in favour of toleration, 268
Marston Moor, the parliamentary army
marches from York to, i. 372; movements of the army at, 373; arrival of the
royalists at, 377; battle of, *ib.*
Marten, Henry, blames the inactivity of
Essex, i. 72; takes part in stripping the
queen's chapel, 102; speaks against the
continuance of the treaty of Oxford,
109; quarrels with Northumberland, 131;
wishes Parliament to declare itself sovereign, 133; expelled the House, and imprisoned, 202; re-elected, iii. 77; wishes
Charles to be prepared for heaven,
216; jests about the king's evil, 242. is
chairman of a committee on Lilburne's
imprisonment, 363; is a leader of the
republican fraction of the Independents,
366; moves a vote of no addresses, *ib.*;
talks of killing Cromwell, 372; asks
for toleration for Catholics, 377; talks
of impeaching Cromwell, iv. 21; again
suspects Cromwell, 57; holds that
toleration should be unlimited. 81; offers
to support the Scots, 86; proposes to

dethrone the king, 94; talks of restoring
Charles, if it is necessary to have a king,
96; takes part in Lilburne's committee
on *The Agreement of the People*, 267;
seizes horses in Berkshire, and goes into
the North, 268; returns to Westminster
after Pride's Purge, 272; sits as one of
the king's judges, 293; declares the
authority by which the High Court of
Justice sits, 247; story of his inking
Cromwell's face, 316
Martial law, the Lords refuse to renew
the ordinance for, ii. 105; re-establish-
ment of, *ib.*
Marvell, Andrew, his idea that Cromwell
brought about the king's flight from
Hampton Court examined, iv. 17, *n.*;
his lines on Charles's execution, 325
Massey, Edward, Colonel, governor of
Gloucester, i. 198; probable treachery
of, *ib.*; gains successes round Gloucester, 345; takes Malmesbury, 349;
takes Tewkesbury, 353; urges the
Herefordshire countrymen to take part
with Parliament, ii. 185; storms Eve-
sham, 229; his force inadequate to secure
Taunton, 262; surprises Goring, 270;
disbandment of the troops of, iii. 147;
appointed to command under Skippon
in Ireland, 232; sent as commissioner to
Saffron Walden, 233; urges the City to
rise against the army, 278; suggested
for the command of the London forces,
338; placed on the Committee of Safety,
339; named commander of the forces of
the City, *ib.*; escapes to Holland, 349;
returns to England, iv. 196; proposal to
place the London forces under, *ib.*;
arrested, 275; escapes, *ib.*
Mauchlin, Middleton suppresses resistance
to Hamilton's levies at, iv. 156
Maurice, Prince, checks Waller, i. 104;
accompanies Hertford, 140; is joined by
Hopton at Chard, 166; leaves Hopton
after the battle of Lansdown, 173; takes
part in the battle of Roundway Down,
ib.; his successes in Dorsetshire, 192;
opposes the civilians at court, 196; misconduct of, *ib.*; occupies Dartmouth,
238; named captain general in Scotland, 299; besieges Lyme, 343; raises
the siege of Lyme, 357; mismanage-
ment of, ii. 43; his part in the second
battle of Newbury, 48; his name on the
parliamentary list of proscription, 85;
sent into Cheshire, 184; enters Oxford
with Rupert, 206; brings a reinforce-
ment to the king, 357; joins Rupert in a
petition to the king, 375; leaves Oxford,
iii. 109
Maynard, John, joins the peace party, i.
53, 80; wishes to negotiate before disbandment, 92; consulted by Loudoun
on a proposed impeachment of Cromwell, ii. 87
Maynard, Lord, 1639 (William Maynard)
impeached, iii. 357

Monro, Sir George, expected to join Hamilton's army, iv. 165; brings reinforcements to Hamilton, 181; directed to remain in the rear of Hamilton's army, *ib.*; joined by fugitives from Preston, 188; refuses to march southwards, 189; retreats to Scotland, 227; protects the Committee of Estates at Stirling, 228; maltreatment of the soldiers of, 229

Montague, Lord, offers money to the Irish Catholics, ii. 171

Montague, Walter, imprisoned, i. 272

Montgomery Castle, reduced by Middleton, ii. 93

Montgomery, Lord (Hugh Montgomery), joins in an overture to the king, ii. 285

Montgomery, Robert, Colonel, bargains for Scottish prisoners, iv. 231

Montreuil, Jean de, sent to England as agent to the Scottish Government, ii. 339; receives a suggestion that Charles should take refuge in the Scottish army, iii. 2; receives from the Scottish commissioners the terms on which they will make peace, 4; urges the king to come to terms with the Scots, 19; resolves to go to Charles, 22; arrives in Oxford, and urges Charles to accept the Scottish terms, 23; warns Charles against playing with the Scots, 27; gains possession of a letter from the queen, 70; tries to extract the lowest terms from the Scottish commissioners, 72; obtains a modification of the Scottish terms, 74; receives from Moray their final terms, 75; takes them to Oxford, 76; finds Charles unwilling to concede Presbyterianism, 79; presses the Scots for a reply to Charles's message, 87; exchanges engagements with the king, *ib.*; goes to the Scottish army, 88; dissatisfied with his reception, 89; assures Charles of the good disposition of the Scots, 96; obtains verbal assurances from the Scots, 100; receives Charles at Southwell, 102; sent to France by Charles, 110; returns to Newcastle, 132; sent back to France, 134; returns to Newcastle, and urges Charles to yield to the Scots, 166

Montrose, Earl of, 1626 (James Graham), proposes to attack Argyle, i. 126; his plan for a rising in Scotland and an Irish invasion, 175; has a conference with Huntly, 177; urges Charles to allow him to begin war in Scotland, 225; urges Charles to action in Scotland, 297; urges Charles to send him to Scotland, 298; named lieutenant-general to Prince Maurice, 299; disappointed of troops from Ireland, 335; named the king's lieutenant-general and invades Scotland, 336; created a Marquis, *ib.*; *see* Montrose, Marquis of

Montrose, Marquis of, 1644 (James Graham), political ideas of, ii. 132; asks

Rupert for help and sends spies to Scotland, 134; makes his way to Perthshire, *ib.*; summons Alaster Macdonald to Athol, 138; saves him from destruction, *ib.*; is accepted as a leader by the Athol clans, 139; marches on Perth, *ib.*; character of his army, 140; defeats Elcho at Tippermuir, *ib.*; a price set on the head of, 143; eager to obtain the help of the Gordons, *ib.*; summons Aberdeen, 145; defeats the Covenanters at the battle of Aberdeen, 147; permits a massacre at Aberdeen, 148; plot for the murder of, 149; marches up and down the Highlands, *ib.*; defends Fyvie Castle, 150; joined by the Macdonalds, 151; ravages Argyle, 152; manœuvres to cut off the Campbells, 153; defeats the Campbells at Inverlochy, 154; offers to come to England with his army, 155; hears from Charles of his intention to join him, 203; joined by Lord Gordon and Lord Lewis Gordon, 215; plunders the lands of the Covenanters, 216; excommunicated and declared a traitor, *ib.*; manœuvres against Baillie, 217; his army melts away, 218; takes Dundee, 219; escapes from Baillie, *ib.*; outmanœuvres Baillie, 220; marches against Hurry, 222; defeats Hurry at Auldearn, 225; versatility of, 227; condition of his force after Auldearn, 278; deserted by the Gordons, 279; offers battle to Baillie at Keith, 280; defeats Baillie at Alford, 283; Charles attempts to join, 290; a new army raised to oppose, 291; obtains Highland reinforcements, 292; manœuvres round Perth, *ib.*; joined by Aboyne at Dunkeld, 294; reaches Kilsyth, *ib.*; wins a victory at Kilsyth, 298; his difficulties after Kilsyth, 347; goes through Glasgow to Bothwell, 348; deserted by the Highlanders, 349; compared with Cromwell, 351; character of the followers of, *ib.*; welcomed by the border Lords, 353; his movements in the south of Scotland, 354; defeated at Philiphaugh, 355; his movements after his defeat, 367; again deserted by the Gordons, 368; marches towards Glasgow, *ib.*; Charles continues to express confidence in, iii. 20; Charles's strong expressions of affection for, 23, 25; hangs about the Highlands, 90; asked by Charles to join the Covenanters, *ib.*; ordered to leave Scotland, 111; ordered publicly to disband his men and privately to keep them together, 132; escapes from Scotland, 143; proposal that he shall again take the field, 171; Lauderdale's opinion of, iv. 196; *see* Montrose, Earl of

Moray, Sir Robert, appointed to carry the Scottish terms to the queen, iii. 4; his negotiations with the queen, 12; returns to England, 19; declares the terms of the Scots, 73; gives Montreuil their final terms, 75

iv. 63 ; appointing Reynolds vice-chancellor of the University of Oxford, 65 ; against stage plays revived, 68 ; strengthened against stage plays, 69 ; declaring Poyer a traitor, 84 ; against blasphemy and heresy, 122 ; nominating a new militia committee, 129 ; indemnifying those who seized the Essex committee, 147 ; establishing the Presbyterian system, 216 ; the first for the king's trial, 288 ; the second for the king's trial read twice in the Commons, 289 ; passed by the Commons alone with the name of an act of Parliament, 290

Ordination, debate in the Commons on a form of, ii. 29

Orkney, proposed cession of, i. 140

Ormond, Earl of, 1632 (James Butler), defeats the Irish at Kilrush, i. 114 ; conciliatory tendencies of, 116 ; created a marquis, 117 ; *see* Ormond, Marquis of

Ormond, **Marquis of,** 1642 (James Butler), appointed a commissioner to confer with the confederate Catholics, i. 120 ; induces the English officers to expect redress of their grievances from the king, 121 ; defeats Preston at Ross, 122 ; answers the confederate Catholics' demand for a free Parliament, 220 ; negotiates and fights at the same time, 221 ; resumes negotiations, 224 ; agrees to the cessation, 225 ; appointed lord-lieutenant of Ireland, 248 ; receives instructions to outwit the Scots, *ib.* ; entrusted with the Irish negotiation, 347 ; rejects the command of the Irish army, ii. 161 ; has little hope of succeeding in his negotiation with the confederates, 162 ; offers to resign, 164 ; is ordered to procure peace by the repeal of the penal laws, 211 ; the confederate Catholics re-open negotiations with, iii. 30 ; keeps secret Charles's offer to repeal the penal laws, 32 ; negotiation continued with, 36 ; receives a copy of Glamorgan's treaty, 41 ; replies to Glamorgan's request that he should satisfy Rinuccini, 51 ; signs a treaty with the Supreme Council, 55 ; is asked by Charles to seize a post in Lancashire, 144 ; is urged by the Supreme Council to publish the peace, 153 ; is ordered by the king not to proceed with the treaty, *ib.* ; is ordered to obey the queen and prince, and to proceed with the treaty, 154 ; proclaims the peace in Dublin, 155 ; fails in an attempt to support the Supreme Council, 159 ; resolves to give over Dublin to the English Parliament, 160 ; sends commissioners to propose terms of surrender, 161 ; his terms only partly accepted by Parliament. 164 ; refuses to surrender Dublin, 187 ; again urged by Charles to come to terms with the Irish, *ib.* ; surrenders the lord-lieutenancy to Parliament, iii. 2 ; attends a council at

Hampton Court, 371 ; his proceedings in Ireland before his surrender of the sword, iv. 102 ; sends Colonel Barry to bring over Inchiquin to the royalists, 110 ; resolution of the queen to send back, as lord-lieutenant, 163 ; detained in France, *ib.* ; sent to Ireland, 224 ; ordered to obey no orders except those of the queen, 225 ; Charles evades a request to disavow, *ib.* ; prepares to combine with Rupert, 243 ; Charles persists in refusing to disavow, 247 ; *see* Ormond, Earl of

Osborne, Richard, joins in a plot for the king's escape from Carisbrooke, iv. 92

Owen, Sir John, rising of, iv. 145 ; resolution of the Houses for the banishment of, 246 ; Cromwell indignant at the order for the removal to London of, 251

Oxford clergy, the, propound a scheme of toleration, ii. 125

Oxford, occupied successively by Byron, Goodwin, and Say, i. 28, 29 ; entry of the king into, 51 ; the king establishes his head-quarters at, 63 ; agents of the City of London received by Charles at, 81 ; weakness of Charles's position at, 131 ; Essex advances towards, 150 ; Rupert sallies from, *ib.* ; state of opinion at, during the siege of Gloucester, 200 ; Charles returns from Gloucester to, 201 ; Charles returns from Newbury to, 219 ; arrival of arms at, 320 ; want of provisions at, 353 ; return of the king to, ii. 56 ; the king's triumphal entry into, 62 ; parliamentary commissioners received by the king at, 85 ; poverty at, 114 ; weakness of, 180 ; effect of Cromwell's raid on, 204 ; Charles marches out of, 208 ; Fairfax ordered to besiege, 211 ; first siege of, 213 ; is short of provisions, 231 ; relieved by Charles, 235 ; Fairfax ordered to quit the siege of, 236 ; an attack on the Eastern Association advocated by the king's council at, 239 ; return of Charles to, 304 ; Charles again returns to, 377 ; strong desire for peace amongst the royalists at, *ib.* ; pressure put on the king by the peace party at, iii. 16 ; Rupert joins the king at, 19 ; Charles leaves for the last time, 97 ; summoned by Fairfax, 108 ; surrenders, 109 ; attempt to remove artillery from, 264 ; proceedings of Joyce at, 314 ; the royalists propose to seize, iv. 91 ; plot to seize, 174

Oxford, the royalist Parliament at, *see* Parliament, the Oxford

Oxford, the University of, sends money and plate to the king, i. 28 ; seizure of plate in the colleges of, 29 ; ordinance for the visitation of, iii. 313 ; abortive visitation of, 314 ; ordinance giving fresh powers to the Visitors of, iv. 63 ; resistance to the visitation of, 64 ; enforcement of the visitation of, 66 ; expulsion of members of, *ib.*

Putney, head-quarters of the army removed to, iii 354

Putney Projects, publication of, iv. 47

Pye, Sir Robert, objects to swear to the treaty with the Scots, i. 234

Pym, John, opposes the expulsion of Culpepper, i. 14 ; proposes an association, 39 ; explains to the City the intention of the Houses in negotiating with the king, 56 ; his policy as leader of the war party, 61 ; proposes to levy taxes, 64 ; claims for Parliament power to act unconditionally, 74 ; strength of his position as leader of the war party, 80 ; fails to induce the Commons to make a league with Scotland, 82 ; urges an immediate disbandment, 91 ; said to be supported by mean and beggarly fellows, 101 ; proposes an excise, *ib* ; asks that committees may be sent to Holland and Scotland, 132 ; opens a secret negotiation with the queen, 133 ; his report on Waller's plot, 149 ; remonstrates with Essex, 156 ; advises the rejection of Essex's proposal to reopen negotiations with the king, 165 ; is on good terms with Argyle, 175 ; mediates between Essex and Waller, 182 ; sent to draw over Essex to the war party, 183 ; outcry of a mob of women against, 186 ; supports the covenant on the ground of political necessity, 233 ; appointed master of the ordnance, 255 ; death and funeral of, *ib.* ; his character and work, 256

QUEEN's regiment, the, behaves badly at Cheriton, i. 326

RADCOT, surrender of, iii. 109

Raglan Castle, Charles negotiates with the Welsh at, ii. 275 ; Charles sets out from, 343 ; holds out for the king, 376 ; surrender of, iii. 139

Rainsborough, Thomas, Colonel, attacks Woodstock, iii. 96 : quells a mutiny at Abingdon, 264 ; takes offence at Charles's language, 342 ; talks of forcing *The Heads of the Proposals* on Parliament, 348 ; attacks Cromwell, 365 ; is a leader of the republican fraction of the Independents, 366 ; selected as vice-admiral by the Commons, 370 ; declares for manhood suffrage, 388 ; argues that the poor are oppressed for want of a vote, 389 ; asks that the question of manhood suffrage may be referred to the whole army, 390 ; declares for a vote of No Addresses, iv. 9 ; talks of impeaching Cromwell, 21 : presents the *Agreement of the People* to Fairfax, 22 ; comes to terms with Cromwell, 44 ; the Commons vote for his appointment as vice-admiral, *ib.* ; expelled from the fleet, 135 ; appointed to witness the execution of Lucas and Lisle, 203 ; murdered, 232

Ramsay, Sir James, guards Kingston Bridge, i. 59

Reade, John, Colonel, tortured, i. 112 ; es apes to Oxford, 269

Reading, garrisoned by the king, i. 63 ; besieged by Essex, 128 ; surrenders, 129 ; reached by Essex after the first battle of Newbury, 219 ; occupied by Astley, 238 ; offer of the City trained bands to retake, 243 ; occupied by Essex and Waller, 346 ; occupied by Browne, ii. 7 ; junction of Manchester and Essex at, 44 ; Fairfax's head-quarters removed to, 308

Recruiters, the, election of, iii. 77

Reformadoes, the, make a demonstration against the House of Commons, iii. 276 ; beset the House of Commons, 285 ; demands of the army for the disbandment of, 305, 323 ; ordinance for the removal of, 324 ; remain in the City, 325 ; talk of plundering the City, 343

Reformation, the English, two elements in, iii. 200

Reigate, Holland's raid upon, iv. 160

Remonstrance of the Army, The, Ireton's draft of, iv. 233 ; addition to, 240 ; accepted by the Council of Officers and presented to the House of Commons, 245 ; the Commons adjourn the debate on, 263

Rents, fall of, iii. 196

Republican party, the, Marten and Rainsborough the leaders of, iii. 366

Respryn Bridge, seized by Grenvile, ii. 13

Revenue, the, estimate of, iii. 194

Reynolds, Edward, Dr., appointed vicechancellor of the University of Oxford, iv. 65

Reynolds, Robert, sent to Dublin by the English House of Commons, i. 119 ; leaves Dublin, 121

Rich, Nathaniel, Colonel, asks Manchester if the army is to winter at Newbury, ii. 40 ; takes part in the discussion on the officers' petition on service in Ireland, iii. 224 ; argues that manhood suffrage will lead to tyranny, iii. 389 ; occupies the Mews, iv. 54 ; secures Southwark against the Kentish insurgents, 134 ; relieves Dover Castle, 146 ; blockades the castles in the Downs, *ib.* ; defeats a force landed from the prince's fleet, 195 ; dissents from the Army Remonstrance, 245

Richelieu, Cardinal, death of, i. 72

Richmond (1641) and Lennox, Duke of, 1624 (James Stuart), proposal to send, with proposals of peace to Westminster, ii. 86 : sent back to Oxford, 99 ; shows Charles Rupert's letter urging him to make peace, 287 ; does not accompany Charles when he leaves Oxford, 304 ; allowed to visit the king, iii. 301 ; visits the king at Hatfield, 306 ; attends a council at Hampton Court, 371 ; waits on Charles before his removal from New-

castle, 44; invited to move southwards, 82; Cromwell supports the advance of, 120; marches by way of Westmoreland, 214; left unpaid and unsupplied, 228; moves southwards, 254; marches towards Hereford, 263; besieges Hereford, 284; dissatisfaction of the English Parliament with, 285; overtures to the king from lords in, *ib.*; plunders Herefordshire, 309; abandons the siege of Hereford, 310; quartered on the Tees, 369; invited to besiege Newark, iii. 2; suggestion that Charles shall take refuge in, *ib.*; complaints in the House of Commons of, 3; besieges Newark, 11; the king proposes to go to, 19; negotiation for the neutrality of, 45; Charles offers to go to, 86; Charles takes refuge in, 102; treatment of Charles after his arrival in, 103; surrender of Newark to, *ib.*; retreats to Newcastle, 104; proposal to withdraw, 137; money voted for the payment of, 138; makes itself unpopular in the North, 175; arrangements for the departure of, 180; offers made to Charles by the officers of, 186; leaves Newcastle, and recrosses the Tweed, 188

Scottish army in Ulster, distress of, **i.** 333

Scottish army under the Duke of Hamilton, the, appointment of commanders for, iv. 132; delay in raising men for, *ib*; suppression of resistance to the levies for, 155; discussion on the movements of, 156; deficiencies of, 165; reduces Appleby Castle, and advances to Kendal, 166; advances to Hornby, 182; dispersion of, 185; abandons Langdale at Preston, 186; retreats after the battle of Preston, 188, 189; capitulation of the infantry of, 190; capitulation of the cavalry of, 192; treatment of the prisoners of, 193, 231

Scottish commissioners in England, the, Charles rejects an offer to mediate by, i. 125; arrival of, in 1643, 234; to be sent to treat on matters arising out of the league between the kingdoms, 304; obtain the withdrawal of a suggestion that the king may be dethroned, 328; discover Cromwell's proposal to make war on the Scots, ii. 84; take part in a conference on impeaching Cromwell, 87; are principally concerned in the Treaty of Uxbridge, 121; reveal their policy to Sabran, 122; complain of Leven's treatment and of the plan of campaign of the Committee of Both Kingdoms, 228; ask for the reopening of negotiations with the king, 335; ask the English Parliament for aid against Montrose, 340; agree to submit terms of peace to the queen, *ib.*; ask that the Scottish army may be paid, iii. 2; notify to Montreuil the terms on which they

will make peace, 3; request that their terms may be sent to the queen, 4; their negotiation with Will Murray, 45; refuse to set down their terms in writing, 73; modify their conditions, 74; consult on the reception of the king, 89; urge the Houses to come to terms with the king, 93; the Commons order the burning of the papers of, *ib.*; protest that they knew nothing of Charles's coming, 103; their complicity in Charles's escape revealed by an intercepted letter, 113; deny their complicity, 114; hope that Charles will accept the Newcastle propositions, 131; urge Charles to accept them, 133; on hearing of Charles's refusal, offer to withdraw their army, 137; reject the terms brought from the king by Will Murray, 168; mission of a fresh body of, to treat in London, 251; accept Charles's answer to the propositions, 253; treat with the English Presbyterians for a Scottish intervention, 265; remonstrate on an insult to Lauderdale, 355; join in the presentation of the Hampton Court propositions, 357; receive instruction from the Committee of Estates, 360; reinforced by the arrival of Lanark and Loudoun, 373; visit Charles at Hampton Court and urge him to escape, iv. 1; request that the king may be removed to London, 10; condemn Charles's overture to Parliament, 26; propose to Charles to escape to Berwick, 35; try to come to an understanding with Charles, 37; protest against the treatment of Charles, and visit him at Carisbrooke, 38; engagement signed by Charles with, 39; accept the engagement, 41; return to Edinburgh, 56; prepare for a rising in England, 86; stir up the Scots against the English Parliament, 87; protest against the king's trial, 304

Scrope, Adrian, Colonel, captures the Earl of Holland, iv. 161

Scudamore, Sir Barnabas, defends Hereford, ii. 308

Seaforth, Earl of, 1633 (George Mackenzie), refuses to receive Alaster Macdonald, ii. 137; attempts to cut off Montrose, 153; dispersal of the army of, 215; submits to Montrose, 216; goes over to the Covenanters, 222; said to be ready to join the king, iii. 132

Sectaries, the, character of, i. 312

Sedgemoor, Goring musters his troops on, ii. 228

Selby, retreat of Lord Fairfax to, **i.** 71; captured by the Fairfaxes, 337

Selden, John, advocates peace, **i.** 80; complains of the ambition of the clergy, ii. 29; is the probable author of the questions put to the Assembly, 95; advocates toleration for Catholics, iii. 377; **moves the omission of a clause from the**

THE END.

**PHOENIX
PRESS**

GENERAL EDITORS:
SIMON SCHAMA AND ANTONIA FRASER

Phoenix Press publishes and re-publishes hundreds of the very best new and out of print books about the past. For a free colour catalogue listing more than 500 titles please

telephone: +44 (0) 1903 828 500
fax: +44 (0) 1903 828 802
e-mail: mailorder@lbsltd.co.uk
or visit our website at www.phoenixpress.co.uk

The following books might be of interest to you:

History of the Great Civil War
Volume I – 1642–1644
S.R. GARDINER

The first volume in S.R. Gardiner's epic four-volume history of the English Civil War traces events from the beginning of the conflict to the battle of Marston Moor which was to prove the turning point for the Parliamentarian cause.

Paperback
UK £9.99   416pp   1 84212 639 3
USA $16.95
CAN $25.95

History of the Great Civil War
Volume II – 1644–1645
S.R. GARDINER

The second volume takes the story up to 1645, a year which saw the demise of royalist hopes.

Paperback
UK £9.99   416pp   1 84212 640 7
USA $16.95
CAN $25.95

History of the Great Civil War
Volume III – *1645–1647*
S.R. GARDINER

Volume three describes the victories of the New Model Army in the campaigns of 1645 and 1646 and the extraordinary political and religious upheavals of 1647.

Paperback
UK £9.99   416pp   1 84212 641 5
USA $16.95
CAN $25.95

History of the Great Civil War
Volume IV – *1647–1649*
S.R. GARDINER

The fourth and final volume covers Charles' escape from his confinement at Hampton Court to the tragic climax of his execution in 1649.

Paperback
UK £9.99   416pp   1 84212 642 3
USA $16.95
CAN $25.95

Commonwealth to Protectorate
AUSTIN WOOLRYCH

The Barebones Parliament and Cromwell's response. 'It will be essential reading for all students of the period' Christopher Hill, '. . . a work to savour' T.C. Barnard, *History*

Paperback
UK £14.99   464pp   1 84212 201 0
USA $21.95
CAN $31.95